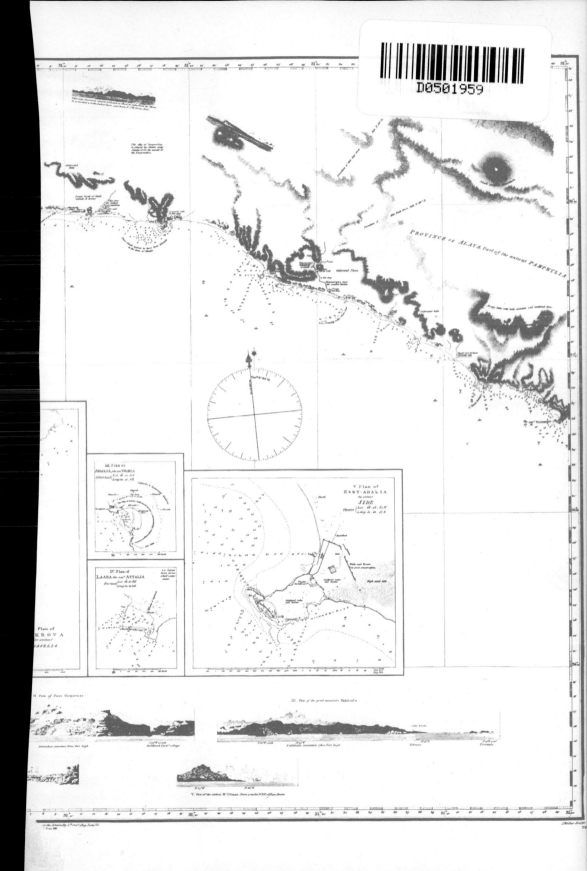

Beaufort *of* *the* Admiralty

1st Amended,

154

Beaufort *of* *the* Admiralty

The Life of
Sir Francis Beaufort
1774-1857

ALFRED FRIENDLY

Random House  New York

First American Edition

Copyright © 1977 by Alfred Friendly

All rights reserved under International and
Pan-American Copyright Conventions.
Published in the United States by
Random House, Inc., New York.
Originally published in Great Britain by
Hutchinson & Co. (Publishers) Ltd.,
London, England.

Library of Congress Cataloging in
Publication Data

Friendly, Alfred.
Beaufort of the Admiralty.

1. Beaufort, Francis, Sir, 1774–1857.
2. Surveyors, Marine—Great Britain—
Biography.
3. Admirals—Great Britain—Biography.
I. Title.
VK597.G72F74   1977   526.9'9'0924   [B]
ISBN 0-394-41760-7   77-6022

Manufactured in the United States of America

For Jean

Contents

LIST OF ILLUSTRATIONS 9

ACKNOWLEDGEMENTS 11

INTRODUCTION 13

1. An Irish Childhood (1774–1789) 17
2. *Vansittart*: 'Guinea Pig' (1789) 26
3. *Latona*: Young Gentleman (1790) 38
4. *Aquilon*: 'Rum, Sodomy and the Lash' (1791–1792) 47
5. *Aquilon*: 'The Glorious First of June' (1793–1794) 57
6. *Phaeton*: Cornwallis's Retreat (1795–1799) 68
7. Of Mind and Body (1789–1800) 83
8. *Phaeton*: Vain Toil (1799–1800) 93
9. *San Josef*: 'Glory' (1800–1801) 102
10. Ireland (1801–1805) 109
11. Charlotte (1802–1807) 123
12. *Woolwich*: 'A Bad Beginning . . .' (1805–1806) 129
13. Wind Scale (1806) 142
14. *Woolwich*: The Good Shepherd (1806–1807) 148
15. *Woolwich*: 'Interest' (1807–1809) 162
16. *Blossom* (1809–1810) 169
17. Post-Captain (1810) 177
18. *Frederickssteen*: *Terra Incognita* (1811) 182
19. *Frederickssteen*: A Matter of Mercy (1811) 193
20. *Frederickssteen*: Survey to Syria (1812) 202
21. Author and Chartmaker (1812–1817) 218
22. Interim (1815–1829) 225
23. Recognition (1815–1829) 234
24. Hydrographer: The Right Man 245
25. Hydrographer: The Admiralty Chart 255

26. Private Life 267
27. Hydrographer: 'In Addition to Other Duties . . .' 276
28. The Scientists' Middleman 285
29. 'This Sacred Cause' (1847–1855) 301
30. 'Yellow Admiral' 323

NOTES 335
BIBLIOGRAPHY 347
INDEX 353

List *of* Illustrations

Between pages 128 and 129

Daniel Augustus Beaufort
Mary Waller Beaufort
Francis Beaufort, a Daguerrotype of 1848
Lestock Wilson
Alicia Wilson Beaufort as a young girl
Richard Lovell Edgeworth, 1785
Francis Beaufort, a crayon sketch of 1838
Francis Beaufort, from the Stephen Pearce painting of 1851

Between pages 288 and 289

The Arctic Council. The full Stephen Pearce painting of 1851
Beaufort's sketches: The coast of Asia Minor, Kingstown Harbour,
    Co. Dublin, Lichfield Cathedral and Drumglass Colliery
A chart prepared by Beaufort for the Society for the Diffusion of
    Useful Knowledge

Maps

Pages 188–9 The South Coast of Turkey, the area of Beaufort's great
    surveys

Pages 304–5 The Arctic, showing the area of the search for Franklin

Endpaper

Beaufort's chart of Karamania

Acknowledgements

For their unfailing kindness and devotion of more time and effort than I had any right to demand, I am deeply grateful to the curators, librarians and archivists of more than a dozen repositories of manuscript material and reference collections, in particular those of the Henry E. Huntington Library, San Marino, California, and the Hydrographic Department of the Royal Navy, Taunton, Somerset. Together they hold, in some tens of thousands of items, the overwhelming portion of the original papers of Sir Francis Beaufort. Other institutions whose staff have been of great assistance are the British Library, the Institute of Navigation, London Library, National Library of Ireland, National Maritime Museum, National Portrait Gallery, Public Record Office, Public Record Office of Belfast, Royal Astronomical Society, Royal Geographical Society, Royal Society and Scott Polar Research Institute.

My thanks go also to Angela, Lady Walker, and Rear-Admiral M. J. Ross, RN (Ret.) for permission to use manuscript material in their possession, and particularly to Christina Colvin for letting me examine and quote from the extensive Edgeworth–Beaufort papers held by her family.

Detailing the specifics of the generosity of the many other individuals who helped me in the preparation of this book is impossible; if they recall half as vividly as I the assistance they gave me, they will know the depth of my debt to them. They include Professors Henry Barcroft and George E. Bean, Francis Beaufort, Francis Beaufort-Palmer, Marylin Butler, Commander Michael Craig Waller, RN (Ret.), Patrick Craig Waller, Margaret Deacon, Captain Henry Denham, RN (Ret.), Canon C. C. Ellison, Elsbeth Evans, Frank George, Sybille and Denys Haynes, Clive A. Holland, A. G. E. Jones, Dr Naomi M. Kanof,

Christine Kelly, Professor Roy Macleod, Douglas Matthews, Russell Moseley, Brian Portway, Jean Preston, Chaim Raphael, M. W. Richey, Rear-Admiral G. S. Ritchie, RN (Ret.), Virginia Rust, David Stanbury and Anne Woodruffe.

For help in research I must thank Frank Pichini, Jonathan Harsch and particularly Roy Laishley, who worked closely with me from the inception of this book to its conclusion. Jane Russell, who cheerfully if endlessly typed and re-typed the MS drafts during the same period, must be aware of my gratitude to her. I am deeply thankful, as well, to the painstaking care, counsel and friendship of my editor at Hutchinson's, Anthony Whittome.

My greatest debt, by a very large factor, is to Lieutenant-Commander Andrew David, RN, of the Hydrographic Department, who patiently devoted himself to opening the Department's enormous archives to me, who laboured both as ferret and the most expert of counsellors and, by his reading of the MS, saved me from a mountain of mistakes. For those errors both of fact and judgement that remain in the text, however, I must claim the role of sole inventor.

It is customary, if not indeed obligatory, in an acknowledgement such as this to refer to one's wife, 'without whose patience, forbearance and long-suffering, etc. etc.' In this case, such a tribute would be inexact. If anything, my wife took even more pleasure than I in working on this book and helping with most of the research that went into it; my debt to her is for her unflagging and contagious enthusiasm.

A.F.

London, January 1977

Introduction

... though most unworthy to be compared with the
brilliant services of my active and fortunate brother
officers, yet I shall have done something before I die
of utility to my profession and of credit to my
country.

BEAUFORT'S JOURNAL, spring 1812

To yachtsmen 'Beaufort' signifies the international scale of wind force;
to cryptographers the name identifies a famous variation of a famous
cipher. Yet valid and useful as these inventions are, neither represent
the true stature of the man whose name they bear. The surveyors and
charters of the world's oceans know more truly the value of his
achievements. Greatest of British hydrographers, Francis Beaufort was
the organizer, standard-setter and driving force of an institution that
lifted the shroud of ignorance and uncertainty – more deadly to the
mariner, once the curse of scurvy was ended, than any danger except
the weather – from the coasts and anchorages of the Seven Seas. If he
was not the father of modern hydrography he was, along with the
American Matthew Fontaine Maury, the worthiest son.

At fifty-five, an age when his present-day successors are obliged to
quit the post, Beaufort became the Hydrographer of the Admiralty
and so remained for a quarter of a century, longer than anyone before
or since. He converted what was little more than a lacklustre chart
depot in 1829 into the world's finest maritime surveying and chart-
making institution. It was he who made the Admiralty Chart the
model of excellence, accuracy and completeness. As Americans could
once say, in choosing a simile for integrity, 'sound as a dollar', so the
British coined an equivalent phrase in the nineteenth century, 'safe as
an Admiralty Chart'. Beaufort's work was its mint.

Shipwrecked and in danger of death at fifteen because of the lack of
an accurate chart – and as a result of trying to produce one – Beaufort
was obsessed for the rest of his long life with the compelling importance,

as one of his companions put it, of 'fixing the bounds of the oceans – thus far shalt thou go and no further'. As a 'Guinea Pig' on an East Indiaman, as midshipman, lieutenant, commander and captain in His Majesty's Navy, he embraced surveying as an addiction. The few spare moments that were vouchsafed a wartime officer on or near shore in the days of full-rigged ships Beaufort spent on sounding and taking bearings, making astronomical observations to determine latitude and longitude, sketching the shoreline and reducing the sum of his observations to a new chart.

When at last he was officially assigned, as a captain, to do what he had before been volunteering, his survey of the coast of southern Turkey, hitherto totally uncharted, was at once acknowledged as the finest work of that kind ever submitted to the Admiralty. Beaufort was quoted as the principal authority for the surveys of almost the whole of the southern coast of Turkey until 1972; in 1976 his chart is still given authority for its eastern stretch and almost all of his plans of the minor ports and anchorages along that coast are still published by the Hydrographic Office. During his tenure as Hydrographer the Office produced a total of nearly 1500 new Admiralty Charts, and Beaufort himself spent several days on each to refine it to his standards of perfection. Now, 125 to 150 years later, copper plates of some eighty of those charts – corrected, to be sure, by new data tapped into the metal – remain in the racks for current use.

Almost as important as the surveys he made and directed, although much less well known, was his liaison role between the scientists of his time and the British government. The former had recourse to him to forward their projects because the latter trusted his recommendations. It was Beaufort who politicked and wheedled for funds for most of the great seaborne scientific expeditions of the second quarter of the nineteenth century, who augmented the surveying roles of each of his ships with scientific assignments, equipment and investigators. It was he who made possible Darwin's sailing with Fitzroy on board the *Beagle*, who saw to the support of the Greenwich and Cape Town observatories, who obtained funds and assigned some of his own staff so that the great work on tides of John Lubbock and William Whewell could be undertaken, who connived with the Cambridge scientists to mount James Clark Ross's monumentally important magnetic observation voyage to Antarctica. Although indifferently or at least meagrely educated – his schooling ended at fourteen – Beaufort made himself

into a scientist, not as a creative theorist, experimenter or basic investigator but – to use a word of his times – as a savant who understood, counselled, appreciated and enormously aided the professionals.

Somehow, Beaufort found time to educate himself into the learned
man he became while he was still a junior officer on frigates warring
against France and Napoleon in the Channel and the Mediterranean. A
veteran of a dozen Naval encounters, he ended his fighting days with
the capture of a Spanish warship in which he accumulated nineteen
wounds in a matter of minutes. His personal surveying was ended
with a shot that should have killed him on a far-off beach in the
Levant.

The happy chance that his letters and journals covering almost
the entirety of the great struggle with France have been preserved
has provided an unsurpassed personal history of Naval life and warfare
in those crucial days. They also offer, in a chronicle of frustration and
injustice, a textbook case of one of the Navy's most besetting evils,
the system of 'interest', i.e. patronage or 'pull'. Those who, like
Beaufort, had none – neither petticoat nor political – were denied the
fruits of their labours and talents while promotion and choice assignments went to the well-born and the well-connected.

Honours, accordingly, came to Beaufort only late in life: his admiral's flag, knighthood, an honorary DCL from Oxford, membership
in a dozen learned and professional societies in the United States,
France and Italy as well as in Britain.

Beaufort overcame the bitterness bred of maltreatment by his em-
ployers in the first half of his life to become – by universal account of
his associates – the kindliest and most agreeable of men. He emerges
from his private papers and the official records as an engagingly
human person: mostly wise but occasionally foolish, furiously patriotic
but resentful of real or fancied abuses from his country, usually
magnanimous but now and again self-pitying, generous with his own
money and time and effort but quarrelsome about pay and emoluments,
dedicated to his office but often despising his superiors.

Above all, he emerges as a master of his craft, architect and builder
of the most expert institution of its kind. Commander L. S. Dawson,
a hydrographic surveyor himself, writing the first history of the
Hydrographic Office, looked back over 135 years of its work and
concluded that 'The master mind of Beaufort . . . did more for the
advancement of maritime geography than was effected by all the

surveyors of European countries united.' Admiral G. S. Ritchie, himself Hydrographer from 1966 to 1971, declared that Beaufort's tenure marked the high noon of the institution's history.

The fruits of his work, in the lines and figures drawn from the surveys he made and directed, in the standards of cartographic excellence he established, in the oceanographic knowledge he fostered, remain for our use today in the atlases of every library, on the charts of every navigator.

I

An Irish Childhood
(1774-1789)

At the age of five he had manifested the most decided
preference for the sea, had even refused to learn Latin
or any of the rudiments of a learned profession &
uniformly persisted in choosing a Naval life for his
department . . . he was instinctively impelled to make
such a choice: for it was formed and disclosed long
before he had ever seen salt water or could have conceived the nature of a ship.

(LOUISA?) BEAUFORT, 1801[1]

Ever since the Massacre of St Bartholomew the de Beauforts had been
what Francis later described as a 'strictly nomadic family'. For the
earlier generations, change of scene had been largely a matter of
necessity. A certain François, who split from his titled Catholic
ancestors and founded a Huguenot branch, found himself obliged to
flee Meaux, in Brie, and settle in Sedan during the terrible days of
1572.[2] With the revocation of the Edict of Nantes, his grandson,
another François, left France forever to find haven and advancement
in Protestant lands beyond the Rhine. He became Court Chancellor
of Lippe-Detmold and, by the decree of Emperor Joseph I, a Noble
of the Holy Roman Empire. The honour, it would appear from the
elaborate document conferring the title in 1710, derived less from
any notable accomplishments than from recognition of his noble
inheritance from his French forebears. The citation bestowed the
rank on all François' legitimate children and their heirs of either
sex 'to be held and borne perpetually'. A splendid crest was authorized,
featuring a virago, or Amazon, rising above a turreted fortress; the

legends played on the family name: *La Vertu est un Beau Fort* and *Turris Fortis Deus Meus*.

François' son, Daniel Cornelis, born in Wessel in 1700, took service in the Prussian Army, but then relinquished a military career to study at Utrecht for the Calvinist ministry. Soon afterwards, and apparently as poor as the proverbial church mouse, he migrated to England when he was twenty-eight. He served as minister to several Huguenot chapels for three years, then took Anglican orders. In 1738 he took a wife, also of French Huguenot descent, and, apparently having made some influential friends, went to Ireland as chaplain to Lord Harrington. Four years later he became rector of Navan, a pleasant town twenty-eight miles north-west of Dublin, in County Meath. By then a British citizen, he dropped the 'de' but kept the crest. After eighteen years he relinquished the living to his only child, Daniel Augustus, born in 1739.

An equally valuable endowment from him and his wife was a set of longevity genes. Daniel Cornelis and his wife lived to be eighty-eight, their son eighty-two. His five children who survived childhood (born of a wife who died at ninety-four) were similarly hugely long-lived.

Francis, the second of Daniel Augustus' sons, is the subject of this narrative, but so close was he to his father and so large a part did the father play in the son's life that Daniel's character and history deserve more than passing attention.

He was tiny – in middle age he weighed less than 140 pounds – but he was bigger than life.[3] 'DAB', or 'Beau', made up for his jockey size with endless ebullience and activity. He was architect, topographer, geographer, tireless traveller and diarist, gentleman farmer and *bonvivant* as well as cleric, which last occupation seemed to occupy only the lesser part of his interest. His early education was at school in Navan, whence he went to Trinity College, Dublin, for his BA in 1757 and his MA two years later. An honorary LLD in 1789 gave him the 'Dr' which thereafter was firmly fixed to his name.

He took Holy Orders when he was twenty-three; at twenty-six, thanks to Daniel Cornelis, he became rector of Navan and so remained until 1818. In 1789 John Foster, Speaker of the Irish House of Commons and Chancellor of the Irish Exchequer, also presented him with the vicarage of Collon, twelve miles away in County Louth, and leased him a farm. There was a glebe for the church at Navan but no glebe house, but there was a vicarage in Collon, a well-built three-storey Queen Anne structure with a garden. He promptly moved there, thinking himself now 'easy and happy for life'. Later he added a neighbouring sinecure parish of Athlumney to his clerical domain.

He served his parishes in the manner of the times and seemed to have created in Navan more of a religious life than in most similar parishes, but on moving to Collon left its affairs largely to a curate, which was again in harmony with the practices of that age; his absence was probably not too severely felt, for the spiritual temperature of the eighteenth century was tepid. Even so, he seems somewhat to have overstepped the lenient practices of his times. He saw no objection to absenting himself entirely from Ireland, once for five years in South Wales and Cheltenham, later for five separate stays of as much as a year at a time in London. The Bishop of Meath and Speaker Foster were far from pleased.

Canon C. C. Ellison, a successor of Dr Beaufort in the church at Navan and his sympathetic biographer, writes that he was a 'cut above the average eighteenth-century parson', which is not saying much. But the once-renowned novelist Maria Edgeworth, a long and close friend of the Beaufort family, described him as 'an excellent clergyman' and Ellison agrees that after making allowances for the spirit and customs of his time 'he was a much more truly pious and conscientious cleric than most'.

Of more interest to him, it is clear, were his scientific, architectural, landscaping and farming pursuits, for all of which the cloth provided leisure and respectability. His interests in astronomy, mapping and design profoundly influenced the intellectual life of his children.

One thing that 'DAB' was not was a competent man of business. Easy-going or indifferent, he neglected his own affairs to the point of being in debt for most of his life, unable to collect his rates and tithes. He was no peculator but he was not above using as security for his own borrowing church funds and properties in estates of which, as a parson, he was a frequent executor. A stay in Mountrath with his father and the five-year absence in Wales and Cheltenham was in good part to live more cheaply, while his rents accumulated in Ireland, and to dodge his creditors the while. Throughout much of their adult life, his two sons were kept in financial straits, skimping and borrowing to pay their father's mounting debts; in his old age their resources were at an end and their father escaped a debtors' prison only by dying a few weeks before the bailiffs came for him. Those harrowing times left an unhappy mark on Francis, rendering him unpleasantly quarrelsome and insistent about what he felt was due to him from the Navy (although he was generous with his own funds). Yet despite his money troubles 'DAB' made for himself a buoyant and happy life, because an immensely busy and varied one – a circumstance that had an equally deep influence on Francis' character and a much more benign one.

Whether at Trinity or from later study, Dr Beaufort made himself into an accomplished topographer, expert at surveying and location by celestial observation. His great achievement in that role was the first good map of Ireland ever made, geographically exact and beautifully executed, to replace existing ones which were incomplete or inaccurate. A massive sheet, it was published in London in 1792, accompanied by a handsome quarto *Memoir . . . of Ireland illustrating the topography of that Kingdom and containing a short Account of its present state civil and ecclesiastical*. Besides the expected geographical features of rivers and towns, mountains and bays, it listed every religious establishment from bishops' seats to curates' lodges – Church of Ireland ones, that is: a stranger would never discover from map or *Memoir* that there was one Roman Catholic in all of Erin. The work, dedicated to George III and boasting an impressive list of noble and important patrons, met with considerable success: in eighteen months 2000 copies were sold and it went into a second edition. From then on until the last days of his life, Daniel Augustus talked about putting out a revised edition, but in constant wrestling with his major sin of procrastination he always lost.

The second string in his versatile bow was his taste and talent as architect and designer. His papers and elegant drawings show that he had a greater or lesser hand in the building or remodelling of no less than seventeen churches and great houses in Ireland.

Vastly less productive were his efforts over a period of many years to wrest a fortune for himself, his relations and a number of patrons, all of whom had claims on a rich estate, perhaps worth as much as half a million pounds. It had belonged to Thomas Newport, Fifth Earl of Bradford, who died insane in 1762. 'DAB' undertook to represent the claimants but received for himself little more than lawsuits, frustration, time-wasting and alienation of his in-laws. Much of his time during his several stays in London was devoted to 'the Newport affair'. Lawyers, the Crown and some of the claimants did well out of it: some of Dr Beaufort's expenses were paid and permitted him to live well enough in London but otherwise his reward for years of toil fell miserably below his expectations.

His outstandingly wise decision was his choice of a wife, Mary Waller, co-heiress of a well-off county family in nearby Allenstown, County Meath. Both partners were twenty-eight when they married. Mary's surviving letters and the references to her in letters by adoring children and friends show her to have been a remarkably fine woman, exceptionally intelligent and cultivated, with fluent French and Italian and a graceful literary style. She became a paragon of a parson's wife. One senses that she supplied the ballast to 'DAB's' ship, otherwise all sail.

Children came apace, seven in fourteen years, all before the move to Collon. The first, a daughter, born in 1767, died at birth or soon after. The second, born two years later, was Frances Anne (Fanny), who grew to be an engaging personage in her own right. Sent to school at Portarlington, not far from Dublin, she learned substantially better than schoolgirl French and quickly displayed a remarkable talent for drawing and painting, the study of which she continued under a good instructor in London. It was she who designed the handsome vignette for her father's map.[4] A sheaf of several score of her water-colours of flowers, now preserved in the Huntingdon Library, San Marino, California, are surpassingly beautiful and professionally exact. She was an early illustrator of one of Maria Edgeworth's educational books; we will hear much more of her as fourth wife of Maria's father, to whom 'DAB' was first to give the lasting soubriquet, 'The Ingenious Mr Edgeworth'. For fifty-seven years, until her death at ninety-four, she was the matriarch, as steady as she was tactful, of his huge family.

William Lewis, the elder son, was born in 1771 to a life of quiet desperation. He wanted to be a diplomat but 'sacrificed himself' to his father's wishes by taking the cloth, and then convinced himself he was fit for no other profession. Married to the daughter of the Bishop of Cork and Ross, he doubtless owed what little advancement he obtained to his father-in-law's influence. He became a rector and prebendary in County Cork and ultimately Commissary for the Bishop. He had been well-educated: Francis was to rely on him heavily for Latin and Greek history and nomenclature when he wrote his book on the classical treasures he rediscovered on the south coast of Asia Minor. William was also something of a surveyor and amateur geologist, pursuits he dabbled in as an escape from the dullness of his clerical life. He fathered ten children in dreary succession, embarrassed by his own fecundity and kept poverty-stricken by it. Of the hundreds of Francis' surviving letters to his siblings, those to William show a special rapport and tenderness. It was to his brother that he confided most readily, and to him that his sympathy poured out, in clear realization of how drab and melancholy William's life had been made by his father's self-gratifying decision.

After Francis, born 27 May 1774, came three more daughters, one who died in her teens, then Henrietta (Harriet) in 1778 and Louisa Catherine in 1781. Both remained unmarried throughout their long lives. They kept house on occasion for their parents, for their mother's aged relatives and for Francis during his widowerhood. Harriet wrote two books for children, both anonymously. Louisa wrote engaging travel journals, a book on entomology and an essay on proto-historic Irish art and architecture, read to the Royal Irish Academy. She ultimately became a member of that august institution.

The familial feeling among the Beauforts was exceedingly deep, perhaps even more so than in most families of the time, when the closeness of ties among parents and children was far greater than now. Like others of the age, and especially those in rural surroundings, the Beaufort household was largely dependent on its own resources for intellectual stimulus, for fun and games, for discipline, standards of value and virtue, and probably for no small part of the children's education.

Francis saw his father as the epitome of wisdom and parental perfection; his letters to him for several years after he went to sea are almost embarrassing by today's taste in their idolatry and in their appeals for counsel and decision about even the smallest matters that one would have thought a battle-scarred, hard-drinking Navy officer would have made for himself. Years later, even when he was middle-aged and after he had been long harassed by the old man's debts and general fecklessness and was conscious of the decision that wasted William's life, Francis's adoration of 'DAB' burned almost as brightly as ever. He conceded only that 'his talents were not perhaps of the very highest order'. But otherwise, in a rapturous panegyric written in his journal on his father's death, Francis still extolled him as a prince among men.

Francis was only two when the family left their small but happily located house, 'Flower Hill', with its view from a rise above Navan down to the junction of the Blackwater and the Boyne, to find cheaper living in Mountrath, Wales and England. By the time they returned to Collon, Francis was almost ready to go to sea. But in whatever homes they had, one may picture a tightly knit family life. There would have been reading, probably often aloud, much letter writing, and surely parentally guided studies: drawing, French (Francis had a good working knowledge by the time he went to sea and must have received some of it, formally or otherwise, from Mary and 'DAB') and, for the boys, mathematics.

Yet we know very few specifics about Francis as a youngster, not even what he looked like. It is certain from many references that he was of small stature, not as short as his father perhaps, but notably short nevertheless. From the portraits of him when he was beyond middle age we can guess at some of his childhood features: blue eyes, a high forehead, a roundish face but with a good-sized nose and a firm set to his jaw. He was a handsome man in later life and we may assume that he was a good-looking boy once a miraculous red-hot needle cured a crop of warts on his chin.

On occasion his father would call him 'a giddy whelp', which could mean anything or nothing, but most probably was only an affectionate term for an active child. We can be sure he was at least normally active. He once recalled to his brother that ever since he had first received 'the manly weapon of a penny knife' he had never been without 'a cut or bruise, a broken head or what was worse a bleeding heart'. Those afflictions continued in over-full measure the rest of his life.

An entry in Dr Beaufort's diary says that as a baby or very small child Francis' health was deemed to be 'delicate', the doctor recommending sea-water baths. But he grew sturdy enough to survive a case of smallpox without any ill effects (or pockmarks) and, according to a little anecdote book about him compiled many years later by his own adoring daughters, he had two fights on his first day of school, and never another.

At fourteen, when he first met Alicia Wilson, the girl whom he married more than twenty years later, she reported him as 'a remarkably clever, well-informed & well-behaved boy, although from bashfulness somewhat brusque in manner'. Her account of how she tried to please him suggests, at least on her part, love at first sight.

During the five years of bailiff-dodging exile from Ireland the father entered his two sons in a Cheltenham grammar school, but they were immediately expelled, the master saying that they spoke with such an atrocious Hibernian accent that they would spoil the pronunciation of the boys at his school. 'What an impertinence!' 'DAB' snorted in his diary. The boys then received some private tutoring but all that is certain is that fairly soon after 1784 Francis was sent to Master David Bates' Military and Marine Academy in Dublin. What he was taught there besides mathematics and possibly some elementary seamanship, can only be guessed at; there or elsewhere it is known that he took lessons in drawing and penmanship, and he may have had some instruction in French besides that from his parents and tutors.

From his time with Master Bates a hard-cover school notebook of about fifty pages has survived. Very neatly scripted almost in copper-plate with a fine pen, it consists of a series of theorems in plane geometry, calling for some use of trigonometry and logarithms.

The turn of mind towards astronomy came early, no doubt at his father's initiative. A small sheet, labelled by the proud parent, 'Observation of Francis Beaufort', is among his papers. Written in a child's hand, it reads:

On the 12th of Decr. 1788 at a little after 11 o'clock I saw a circle around the moon at the distance of about 8' or 9' the breadth of it was a semi [diameter] of the moon it consisted of three shades the internal one that next the ☽ was a lightish purple next that a light red, and next a greenish yellow . . .*

He was fourteen at the time.

Within a few months his celestial observations were trained to be rather more sophisticated. In 1788 his father sent him to his friend Dr Henry Ussher, Professor of Astronomy at Trinity College, Dublin, for five months' study at the College's newly founded Dunsink Observatory in Dublin. As his later career testified, Francis profited greatly. He was enormously proud of himself for the honour of having been educated in the heavenly mysteries by the famous man and terribly anxious to prove himself worthy.

*In quotations that appear hereafter I have reproduced as far as possible Beaufort's spelling and aberrant capitalizations but for the most part have modernized his punctuation – or the lack of it – for easier comprehension.

Armed with his new learning and loaded down with observational instruments, he was dispatched by his father to take readings of latitude and longitude of Athlone for 'DAB's' new map. The pleased but modest father noted in the accompanying *Memoir* that the location was determined by 'a pupil of Dr Ussher's', making the young topographer swell with pride.

The passage at the head of this chapter was written a dozen years later, when Francis was twenty-six, and so cannot be taken as a set of conclusions only about his boyhood. Moreover, it was written by a young sister, and so is perhaps more an illustration of a loving family feeling than an objective verdict by a dispassionate judge. Yet some of it and its continuation below must have been drawn from childhood impressions.

He is the soul of honour, high spirited, brave, open and generous; he is moderate and affectionate to a degree almost romantic; he is fond of knowledge, & regrets the obstinacy with which in early youth he regarded the more elegant acquirements. Were I writing for the public eye, I should blush at having so panegyrised my brother, but I write for no eye but mine own. . . . He united the proudest self-consistence of a closetted Domini with the frankness of a British sailor.

Dr Beaufort moved his family to London in 1789 to put his map into publication and to pursue the hapless 'Newport affair'. Young Francis was prepared to the greatest extent possible, or affordable, for his career at sea; there remained only to find him a place. The hard choice was between the Navy and the merchant service. In the end, through mutual acquaintances, Dr Beaufort was able to interest a veteran East India Company captain in his son and to arrange, for the payment of a hundred guineas, for the lad to be taken aboard the *Vansittart* for a long trading and surveying voyage to the East Indies and China. The father accompanied the boy, two months short of his fifteenth birthday, to Gravesend and bade him his tearful farewells on 20 March 1789. From the Downs, three days later, Francis sent his first letter home to his mother. He was vilely seasick.

2

Vansittart:
'Guinea Pig'
(1789)

On the whole I think being at sea when [I am] not sick
in such a fine large ship and having pleasant Gentⁿ. on
Board is one of the most delightful places in the world.

BEAUFORT to his father[1]

The seasickness was vanquished in a week (the conquest of syntax
took some years more) and exhilaration replaced it. Francis' obsession
with the sea, his determination to make it his career, conceived when
he was still a small child, had not been mistaken. From the beginning,
the joy and the thrill almost banished the homesickness to be expected
in a lad not yet fifteen and never before out of sight of the family to
which he was so intensely attached. (He confessed to only a touch of it:
in an outburst of love and affection at the end of his first letter at
sea, he declared, 'Tho' I am a sailor I can't help shedding some
tears.')

His enthusiasm, indeed, led to exaggeration. A ship making two
inches of water an hour when she was only four days clear of the
Thames, and two months later making from six to nine,[2] was somewhat
less than a 'fine' one; nor, by East India Company standards, was she
particularly large.

By the time of Beaufort's voyage in the *Vansittart* the East India
Company had only recently lost its plenipotentiary dominion over
India and was beginning to recover from the financial disasters of some
fifteen years before by a new emphasis on its profitable China trade.
During the decade of peace before the French conflict, service in 'The
Honourable Company' was arguably as attractive to a young man
opting for a career at sea as the Royal Navy itself. It certainly offered

a better prospect of monetary reward and of travel to distant shores and exotic scenes. The boy Francis could be grateful to his father for the hundred guineas that had placed him so well.

Above all, he was lucky in his captain, Lestock Wilson, a veteran of six previous trips to and long sojourns in the Far East, a captain since 1786 and before that many years a chief mate on East India Company ships. An excellent commander, he was in addition an able and dedicated marine surveyor and as such was repeatedly employed by the Company to discover and chart new routes in the Far East.[3] He was born about 1752, the child of a 'Mayfair marriage', i.e. clandestine or at least hurried.*

Young Lestock went to sea at twelve and from that hard life and those difficult beginnings ultimately made his way to a substantial fortune and considerable position in business affairs in London. His success as a captain and later in commercial dealings suggests that he was a man of strong character, courage and ability. At Madras, during one of his voyages, he met and married Bonne Boileau, daughter of an important East India merchant family, with distinguished Huguenot ancestors. By the time he set sail in the *Vansittart* on what was to be her last voyage, he was supporting his growing family in increasing comfort. Among his children was a girl of seven, Alicia, who, as Captain Wilson could not have suspected at the time, was twenty-five years later to marry the exuberant young 'Guinea Pig' (the generic nickname for lads enrolled for the standard hundred-guinea payment to the captain) he had just taken aboard.[4]

A cordial relationship developed swiftly between protector and protégé: within a month or two of Francis' signing-on Wilson wrote to Dr Beaufort that the lad was well and was 'a very fine boy'. Years later, congratulating Francis on his promotion to the rank of commander in the Royal Navy, Wilson told him that he rejoiced in it almost as if it had been conferred on his own son, and added: 'Your very early attainments with a Mind so happily constructed, left me but little to perform in your instructions and afforded a very sanguinary Hope respecting you.' Wilson was glad to have him aboard, not merely for the hundred-guinea fee but because Wilson's ancillary duty on the trip was to survey the Straits of Gaspar and Bangka off the east coast

*So called from a marriage mill run for several years in Curzon Street by a scallywag cleric who advertised complete ceremonies for one guinea, no questions asked and without publication of banns.

of Sumatra, to find better routes for the increasingly important China trade and particularly to fix precisely the location of a shoal in the Straits on which a valuable East Indiaman had been lost.[5] A youngster taught surveying and celestial observation by Ireland's most distinguished geographer and polished by the famous astronomer, Dr Ussher, would have been welcomed on any Quarter Deck. Francis earned his salt: he was kept busy making sightings and taking bearings throughout the voyage and apparently did the lion's share of them.

The *Vansittart* was made ready for her voyage to China at Deptford, the huge East India Company docks downriver from London. The cargo was exceptionally rich, being listed at a value of £90 655 and including, among the merchandise for China, a dozen or more chests of 'treasure', presumably specie, to be handed over, with dispatches Wilson was charged with carrying, to the 'Secret Committee in Canton'. The ship sailed down the Thames on 26 March 1789 for the long voyage down the west coast of Africa, around the Cape of Good Hope and on to the Indies and China.

At a wage of £1 3s. a month, Francis was entered on the rolls as 'Captain's Servant'. He was of course no such thing, nor had the term carried the implication of menial for many decades.[6] In 1789 'Captain's Servant' meant nothing so lowly (or romantic) as cabin boy, but quite the opposite: a young gentleman, a protégé of the captain, heading up the career ladder of the Quarter Deck, in effect an apprentice to the genteel role of officer, selected by the captain, who pocketed his wage if he saw fit or doled out all or part of it, as a father would bestow an allowance on a child.

From the start, Francis was teacher's pet. He had obviously inherited his father's charm and good manners. The ship's officers liked and coddled him. Captain Wilson at once rescued him from the berth first given him, 'a nasty dank hole [at] the upper end of the Gun Deck' with no space to get at his chest, and put him into the Great Cabin, aft on the Gun Deck.

Conditions aboard an English ship in the late eighteenth century would be considered insufferable today: the monstrous crowding, the utter absence of privacy, the lack of space and quiet for study or reading, the brutality below decks, the monotony, the impossibility of escaping from the searing heat of the tropics and the minimal protection from the raw cold in stormy weather, the lack of ventilation

and the bare pretence of lighting, the inescapable, continuous, pestilen-
tial stench of the bilges which John Masefield declared was 'unlike
any other smell in the world'.[7]* Indeed, in the Royal Navy of the
period 'life was unpleasant almost beyond our wildest imaginings'.

In its physical circumstances it could not have been much better on
the Honourable Company's ships. In his letters home, however, Francis
voiced no complaint. Probably it did not occur to him that he had
anything to complain about.

The conditions he found on the *Vansittart* seemed to him wonderful. In the first of the many 'journalizing' letters he sent over the years
to his family he described the delights. He wrote that Captain Wilson
was a great tease, terrifying the Channel pilot by telling him he would
not be put ashore but carried instead to China unless some inward-
bound vessel was encountered (providentially, an American brig
bound up-Channel came along).

Wilson also set a fine table where Francis frequently dined with him
and the other officers. Two weeks out, at any rate, the dinner menu was
'roast and boiled Mutton, Soup, A Goose, two fowl, some duck,
Curry with Rice and an apple Pie afterwards with Potatoes, Carrots –
so you see we don't live very badly'.

If the midshipmen were a sorry lot – 'I never saw a greater set of
Bl[k].guards in my life . . . and indeed I would [not] for anything mess
with them for they do nothing but quarrel the whole time' – the other
'Guinea Pig' aboard, one Andrew Hardy, was likeable from the start.
'That Hardy is [the] most troublesome Brat that ever was,' Francis
wrote in obvious affection.†

Even the storms – the *Vansittart* encountered some severe ones –
were a source of amusement: '. . . at dinner, there was all the Plates
and Dishes flying about . . . but one of the large Potatoes jumped out
and hit the Captain right in the eye.'

Wilson's fatherly consideration of his charge continued. He did not

---

*Years later, aboard a warship cruising in the Channel Islands, where roses abounded,
Francis wrote to his mother for her 'recipe for making the stuff she puts in pots con-
sisting of roseleaves and spice etc. I want something much to destroy the constant smell
of the bilge water with which we are blessed here.' It would have been about as effective
as a garden hose applied to Vesuvius.

†Like Beaufort, Hardy was an Irish lad of Huguenot descent and, as his fellow
'Guinea Pig' did, soon transferred to the Navy. During the Naval mutinies of 1797 in
the Nore he was a midshipman on the *Nassau* and appears to have initiated action that
induced the sailors to abandon their rebellion.[8]

allow Francis to stand watch until the Equator was crossed and then only half a regular spell. But the boy's training in celestial navigation was not allowed to grow stale. 'This day the Captain, Mr Carruthers [chief mate] and myself made near a hundred observations of [the sun and the moon*]. Tell Dr Ussher that.' When the head of the mizzen mast was sprung a new top mast was got up, 'which was a fine job for me, who was in the Top all the Day'.

Above all were the wonders of the sea life itself – the sightings of the Canaries and Cape Verde Islands gleaming under the hot tropical sun, the bustle of taking bearings on them; the flying fish, sharks, albacores and bonitos; the miraculous feat of a quartermaster falling from the main yard arm and saving himself by catching a line far below; the chance encounters with passing ships – a thousand new sights and happenings to put a lad's eyes to goggling and set his fancies on fire.

The Line was crossed with due ceremony on 23 April 'and their [sic] came aboard Mr and Mrs Neptune up the Bows, with the Barber and his Assistant etc and they shaved etc. 48 of the People. I bought myself off.'

Bad storms were encountered on rounding the Cape, and heavy damage was inflicted on masts and spars. The buffeting sprung the seams so seriously that within a week the ship was making six to nine inches of water an hour, with the pumps working constantly. And as the salt water rose in the well the fresh water – or what had been fresh three months before – fell in the casks, diminishing to danger point. Wilson had not touched at the Cape to replenish his supplies and by July, with the *Vansittart* off the Java coast making soundings in the Straits of Sunda, the captain concluded he ought to go no further without refilling the water barrels. Moreover, ten men were down with scurvy. The ship's people had long since been living on the standard sea diet of the times, weevily biscuits and salt meat.

In accordance with Company regulations Wilson put the question to his officers whether to keep to his original orders or to proceed to Batavia (present-day Jakarta). He received their unanimous written assent to the change, inscribed in the ship's log. But on the way trouble still pursued. A day before making port, in the outer approaches, 'the

---

*Showing off his professional competence to his learned father Francis used the conventional astronomer's symbols for the heavenly bodies in his letters. Here the symbols were ○ and ☽, respectively.

Ship Struck on a Knowle & Hung forwards'. The guns were moved aft, the boats put out and after five hours of struggling the ship was hauled free, apparently undamaged. The cause of the accident was a buoy that had sunk and was left on the shallow bottom.[9]

'No one helped us out,' complained Francis in a letter home. 'At last came the Harbourmaster (a Dutchman all over) . . . who stood with his hands behind his back, and all the assistance he gave us, saying Ya! Mynheer and Nouy Mynheer to everything we asked him.'

To add insult to indifference, when the *Vansittart* finally made her way into the harbour next day and saluted with eleven guns, the Dutch commodore answered with only seven, 'which put Cap'. Wilson into a great passion and he swears that in going away he will not salute them at all (but I told him that in a Dutch place he must expect Dutch manners)'. Wilson's reaction to that worldly-wise counsel from a fifteen-year-old is not recorded.

Francis found Batavia 'horrid . . . I have never heard of such a nasty disagreeable place in my life', unhealthy, with constant fogs. Even the pineapples, melons and oranges are 'not half so good as in England and have no flavour. . . . N.B. You need never wish for turtle, it is very bad; mock turtle is much better in my opinion.' The young traveller reserved his deepest scorn, however, for the observatory in Batavia, built by a certain 'M. de More':*

. . . such an Observatory I never saw. There is but one room in the house calculated to observe in, which is at the top of the house, near one hundred feet from the ground, [affording only the most awkward viewing and so built that] if you just stamp in any one part of the house it shakes the Observation room. Indeed we find that a person walking about on the stairs or in any . . . room of the house shakes the Horizon and makes the objects turn about in the Equatorial Telescopes like anything. . . . In short I never saw or heard of such a place in my life. Pray read all that to Dr. Ussher, I'm sure it will divert him greatly. And also tell him that all those inconveniences does not hinder us to observe.

The boy was obviously pleased with himself. Wilson had obtained permission to use the observatory, however inadequate it was, and for three weeks he and Francis repaired to it each day, laden with sextants, chronometers, artificial horizons and 'the Equatorial', starting

*Johan Mauritz Mohr, a Dutch cleric and astronomer, erected an observatory at Batavia in the latter part of the eighteenth century. His not very accurate determination of the town's geographical coordinates was accepted for many years.

at 6 a.m. and finishing at sunset, with time out only for meals. To his father, proficient map-maker and astronomer that he was, Francis described in vast detail the multitude of observations he was called upon to make and the foibles of the instruments he used. In the end, he proudly reported, the captain left to him the task of working out all Wilson's own observations, 'which I assure you is no trifle'.

The arduous daily observations were no idle contrivances of the captain to kill time while his ship was watering: before Beaufort's own great achievement, beginning forty years later, the absence of reliable charts for the multitude of routes spanning the globe from Australia to Greenland that British merchant ships and men-of-war were obliged to navigate constituted a most dangerous hazard. During the Napoleonic Wars British losses by shipwreck, caused by bad charts as well as by bad storms, were eight times greater than those inflicted by enemy action.[10] As noted above, one of Wilson's tasks was to survey Gaspar Strait between the islands off the Sumatra coast, the shortest passage for a ship coming from the Cape and bound for China. The exact location of Batavia, as a measuring point, was important.

The chart information about Batavia, headquarters of the Dutch East India Company's operations for 170 years, was itself an example of the lack of precision navigators had to contend with. Its latitude was listed in the navigation tables as 6° 10′ S., the authority being the same M. de Mohr whose observatory Francis so deplored. The error was about three miles. The fifteen-year-old Francis tackled the problem: 'I make the Lat. from 6° 8′ to 6° 8′ 40″ S . . . I'm so conceited as to think that my Lat is much nearer to the mark [than Mohr's] because I have got so many [observations] and none of them disagree more than 20″ from each other.' He was indeed nearer the mark, only a mile or so off the exact figure, 6° 7′ 40″. He set out to determine Batavia's longitude as well, confident that for that too he was bound to obtain a more accurate reading than Mohr. Francis said he proposed to work out his calculations during the long hours at sea on the next leg of the voyage. If he did, they saw not the light of day but the bottom of the ocean.*

*In his long, fourteen-page letter from Batavia, as in many other letters during his first few years at sea, Francis dutifully tried – doubtless on his father's orders – to write as much as he could in French. Occasionally he managed the first page of a four-page letter. Here, he did only the first and last paragraph in French, apologizing for the short-fall because 'en verité je ne puis pas parler assez fluently pour vous donner une description d'un place étrangère . . .'

The *Vansittart* departed from Batavia on 6 August, heading for disaster. Returning to his original orders, Wilson ran lines of soundings in the Gaspar Straits for three weeks, his boats ahead casting the lead, the ship following cautiously. On 24 August, in the captain's words, she was 'making one last traverse across the Channel' – the eleventh – to determine the best entrance to the passage when shoal water was seen ahead. The cutter was sent out to investigate, returned and was making her report when the ship herself ran on a shoal. The *Vansittart* had accomplished her principal surveying mission, but only by a catastrophe: she had fallen upon the very shallows she had set out to chart.[11]

The bower anchor was lowered at once 'in swinging to which, she was bro'. up under the Mizzen Chains, by some Sharp Perpendicular Rocks. . . .' There followed some intricate and expert seamanship by which the ship was quickly freed and moved into deep water lying all about. But the death blow had been delivered. The *Vansittart* was discovered to be taking on four feet of water an hour. Heroic and ingenious measures were taken but the damage was not to be remedied. At daylight next day, when the full extent of the catastrophe was evident, it was agreed to attempt to keep the ship afloat if possible and to run for the nearest point of land of Sumatra.

The distance would have been about 80 to 100 miles and the run was impossible. By early evening there was five and a half feet of water in the hold; the ship was *in extremis*. An island was spotted from the masthead and the *Vansittart* headed for it, while all hands that could be spared from the pumps were set to hauling up fresh water and provisions from the forehold. The long boat was got out and small arms and ammunition were assembled. By nightfall the ship was settling fast and just before 9 p.m. she was run ashore on a sand bank within a rocky reef, about three-quarters of a mile from an island some seven miles off the south-eastern tip of Bangka. Next morning (the 26th) an officer went ashore in the jolly boat to search for water but returned unsuccessful after the most diligent efforts. The situation was desperate.

Before the holds were flooded completely, enough water casks were hoisted out to supply the ship's company for about twenty days on the most meagre rations. That, 'which with eight Casks of Porter was all the Liquids we cou'd get at except Spirits'.

Then as now, the decision to abandon ship was the most agonizing a captain could be called upon to take. For Wilson it meant losing the profits from the voyage and hazarding his future with the Honourable Company, which would not take kindly to losing cargo and coin chests if there was the slightest chance of staying on board while rescue was being sought. But the arguments against remaining were overwhelming and Wilson was careful to have them set down fully in the log against the day of the inevitable trial in the East India Company offices in London – if he was lucky enough ever to return.

First, there was no hope of retrieving more water casks; the efforts would have meant more consumption of water by those engaged in the task than the scanty allowance proposed for the crew's subsistence. Second,

From the known Piratical disposition of the Malays we cannot hope to remain in peaceful possession of the Ship, but must expect attacks from them against which altho we may be probably able to defend ourselves as long as the ship remains intire, yet if she parts assunder, breaks up or heels off which is very much to be apprehended from her Situation on a Lee Shore with the Swell setting right on it . . . we should derive no Benefit from our Guns and must Fall a Conquest to Numbers which the Fires on Shore and a Prow already Hovering about us as if to reconnoitre shew to be Considerable.

Third, being on an unknown and unfrequented Coast no Chance means of deliverance can Possibly arise.

The most promising quarter from which rescue could be sought was the Dutch settlements at Palembang, with the chance of encountering en route a ship bound for China in the Bangka Strait. But to send a boat there in that hope while the main body of crew stayed with the *Vansittart* and waited for succour would be to play a fool's game. The distance the little open craft would have to negotiate, the lateness of the season and the Malay pirates that could be expected on the way made any such venture almost impossible, and in any event not before water and provisions on the stranded hulk gave out. Meanwhile,

the People who remained by the Wreck must be left in Doubts and Suspense with all the Evils to be apprehended from a Want of unanimity & Obedience to Command, at the Same time with the Temptation of so great an Object before them [i.e. the specie] to Concert wild projects and Risque the Destruction of the Whole . . . Staying by the Ship will serve to Convince the Malays there is an Object to preserve which the quitting of her may probably delude them in & may induce them to be satisfied with what they can pick up on the Decks, while Treasure remains conceal'd from their search; whence if we shou'd be able to return at a future Day we may find untouch'd & be able to Save it for the Honble Company . . .

The decision for the whole ship's company to take to the boats was unanimous. Thirteen treasure chests that had been hoisted to the deck were thrown overboard in the hope of later retrieval, along with ammunition in excess of that needed for the boats. The guns on the Quarter Deck were spiked and, barely twenty-four hours after the ship struck the rocks, all hands, including a dozen on the sick list, took to the cutter, the long boat, the pinnace, the yawl, the jolly boat and the gig. One may guess that the two 'Guinea Pigs', to whom the captain stood *in loco parentis*, were with him and the chief mate in the cutter.

The little flotilla of open boats proposed to stand to the north through Gaspar Strait, hoping to round the top of Bangka and then to turn south into Bangka Strait towards Palembang. The start was anything but auspicious: the long boat, most heavily laden with fifty-nine men, more than half the entire complement, could not win her way clear of the reef against an onshore wind; when the cutter ran out a warp to her, 'Drunkenness prevented them making a proper use of it'. The boats were obliged to lie under the lee of the wreck until next morning by which time – after Divine Service was read to the company – another warp was run out to the long boat and she was hauled clear. A long night on the verge of a rocky reef had apparently done wonders to restore sobriety.

The half-dozen small craft, struggling against wind and rain, sailed well offshore to prevent sightings by Malays on the coast. In a little more than two days they rounded the north end of the big island and headed into Bangka Strait. Throughout, the gig, manned by the boatswain and four crew, had been a source of anxiety, drifting too far from the main body and having to be warned to stay close. At daylight on the 28th, after a night at anchor, she had disappeared altogether. A lookout was kept from the mast of the long boat but the situation was much too dangerous to pause for a search, for in the morning light one large prow had been sighted at anchor and five others soon began to manoeuvre as if to attack. Seeing the Englishmen armed and ready for the assault, however, they allowed them to pass unmolested.

The troubles were soon over. Two hours later, by 11 a.m., the leading boat beheld the sight which all had prayed for: in the distance, two ships at anchor in Booloo Bay. The captain warned the other boats not to increase their water rations on what might be a false hope and went on ahead to investigate. The cutter weathered a furious two-hour squall and by mid-afternoon came near enough to hoist her colours. The blessed answer was two English flags; the ships were also those of the Company, the *Nonsuch* and *General Elliott*, bound for China and 'by whom we were received with the greatest Hospitality'. By dusk all the weary company were taken aboard by their rescuers; the cutter, her crew refreshed, turned back to search for the gig. 'At 3 in the Morning she return'd without Success.' The five men aboard the gig were never seen again.

The *Nonsuch* and *Elliott* agreed at once to return to the wreck and arrived at what has come to be known as 'Vansittart's Island' within the week. By prodigious effort, thirty-three of the Company's chests and seven personal ones were hauled out of the flooded hulk and divers succeeded in bringing up three of the thirteen cast overboard. The men, exhausted, nevertheless tried to work on, 'but notwithstanding every effort were unable to recover any more, the water which was about 5 feet in the Gun Room by the Motion of the Wreck wash'd from Side to Side with great Violence' and the cargo and furnishings had been sloshed into an impenetrable barrier. The wreck and the ten chests of gold and silver coin in the sand and water below were abandoned.

The *Vansittart*'s company were now divided, some going in the long boat to Palembang, the rest sailing on to China on the two ships. With Captain Wilson, Francis went on board the *Nonsuch* and a month later arrived at Whampoa, in China.

News of the shipwreck arrived in England the following March, almost twelve months after the *Vansittart* had left the Thames. It was brought by Captain William Bligh on his return from the Far East in a Dutch ship after the famous mutiny on the *Bounty* and his incredible 3600-mile voyage in an open boat to Timor. In Collon 'DAB', reading the newspaper aloud to his ailing wife, saw Bligh's account in time and passed over it, aghast.[12] Happily, he did not have to endure the suspense for long: within a few days a letter arrived from Francis, written the night of his rescue. It is unfortunately not among his surviving papers.

Francis stayed in Canton for two months where, as if compulsively, he made astronomical observations and asked that that fact be reported to Dr Ussher. At last he was given passage with Wilson and others on the East Indiaman *Lascelles*, and travelled in comfort on the relatively uneventful seventeen-week voyage in the cuddy, the passenger cabin in the East India Company vessels. On 25 April 1790 he landed in Portland, thirteen months after the *Vansittart* set sail.

Captain Wilson wrote to Dr Beaufort that Francis was 'an excellent boy' and that throughout the voyage he had all the timekeepers aboard under his command. The young man had been in no doubt about priorities.

3

Latona:
Young Gentleman
(1790)

I flatter myself that the *Latona* will cut a dash among
this fleet, which but the other day consisted of 50 ships
of the line and 20 smaller ships, in all 70. What a
glorious sight to see them fire 21 guns which they did
yesterday being [the anniversary of] the King's
Accession ... Tell William that he might well call me a
handsome little fellow (which he does in his letter) if
he saw me in my full dress and sword, etc.

BEAUFORT to his father[1]

On 1 May 1790 Francis was reunited with his family, 'very much
grown', his father noted, 'in good spirits and health', despite having
lost all his possessions in the wreck and acquired a hernia, the first of
the gruesome number of ailments he was to suffer at sea and one that
was to plague him for years.*

The young man set out at once to find a new berth. Captain Wilson
offered to take him aboard his next command, which he expected in
the following year, but recommended that in the interim Francis
should cruise aboard a man-of-war. That was surely the advice a young
fire-eater wanted to hear, for in May 1790 there was the glorious
prospect of a naval war with the forces of His Catholic Majesty,
Charles IV of Spain.

The occasion was a short but furious dispute over a small British
settlement established at Nootka, on the west coast of Vancouver
Island. The controversy was settled before the matter came to blows,

---

*Hernia was among the most common of seamen's injuries, induced by constant strain
on the stomach muscles in the violent exertions demanded on a sailing ship: hauling at
ropes and sails and heaving intolerably heavy casks and barrels.[2]

but while it was raging Parliament ordered a number of warships to be put in commission and a large fleet to be assembled.

In that expanding situation it was no doubt easier than usual for a boy of Beaufort's experience to find himself a ship. Indispensable help came from James Stopford, second Earl of Courtown, and his wife, daughter of the Earl of Cardigan. He was of a County Wexford family many of whose members entered the Church, including one son who was Bishop of Ferns (Wexford), and who became the friend of Dr Beaufort. Lord Courtown was a Member of Parliament at various times from 1761 to 1793 and was Lord of the Bedchamber to the Prince of Wales from 1780 to 1784. In 1790, when Francis needed 'interest', Lord Courtown was Treasurer of the Royal Household, with a residence in London, and was thus in a position of considerable influence. At Dr Beaufort's request and on the appeal of other friends to Lady Courtown, who took a fancy to the young man, Lord Courtown secured an appointment for Francis aboard the frigate *Latona*, with Captain Albermarle Bertie newly in command.

Again Francis was lucky in his captain. Bertie, son of Lord Robert Bertie, had been a commissioned officer for more than twenty years. He had fought in the Battle of Ushant, was later captured by the French, soon released and promoted to captain in 1782.

Bertie, like Wilson, also quickly made a favourite of Francis and frequently invited him to dine with him and 'on the whole has been remarkably civil to me', as the boy wrote to his family. 'All the officers agree he is the mildest and quietest captain in the Service.' Francis was delighted with his favourite toast: 'To all our friends and damn the rest of our Relations!' Bertie, in turn, wrote enthusiastically of Francis to Dr Beaufort.

Bertie's new command was a Fifth Rate, with thirty-eight guns and 280 men.* She was fitting out at Long Reach, in the Thames, and under orders to join Howe's fleet at Spithead for Channel service.

Dealing with the King's shilling and not his own, Bertie could afford

---

*Ship ratings in the Royal Navy in the eighteenth and nineteenth centuries were determined by the number of carriage-guns carried (usually not including carronades). Ships-of-the-line ranged from First Rates with 100 or more guns down to Fourth Rates, with fifty. Frigates, classed as Fifth and Sixth Rates, were armed with a maximum of forty-four to a minimum of twenty. The *Latona*, with thirty-eight, was accordingly one of the larger frigates. In general, the frigates, faster sailers and more easily handled, served as the eyes and ears of the fleet, its messengers, patrollers, lookouts and raiders.

to be generous. He took Francis aboard as an able seaman, to obtain for him a £3 bounty to which volunteers of that rating were entitled. A week later, the bonus paid, young Beaufort was listed on the muster books as midshipman, officially a 'Young Gentleman'. Both appointments were entirely usual and entirely illegal. Official requirements for an able seaman were three years afloat and eighteen years of age. Service in the merchant navy could be counted, but Francis had served at best one year, part of that as a passenger, and was just sixteen. Similarly, two years' service at sea was required for a midshipman's rating. On paper, though, Francis met this last requirement. For a year before he sailed in the *Vansittart* he had been entered in the muster books of the ship-of-the-line *Colossus*, a vessel he never set foot on until he visited her years later. A phantom enrolment of that kind was the practice of the times. A captain, obliging a friend (and pocketing for himself the non-serving boy's pay), would put down the favoured lad's name on his muster books as volunteer or captain's servant so that when he actually went to sea he could have credited to him, against his appointment as an able seaman or midshipman, service afloat for as long as he had been on the books. That too was illegal but it was ignored or taken for granted. The *Colossus*'s captain solemnly signed and transmitted for Beaufort's files a formal declaration that he had served as midshipman on the warship from June 1787 until the end of May 1788.

The appointment of young gentlemen to any of their conventional beginning ratings, captain's servant, first-class volunteer, able seaman or midshipman, was exclusively the captain's prerogative. They were appointed and subsequently promoted through 'interest', an institution whose pervasive and malign workings were to figure so miserably in Beaufort's later career at sea.

With a few exceptions – there were some officers, and good ones, who worked their way up from the Lower Deck – a commission in the Royal Navy came after service as a midshipman. The midshipmen were 'young gentlemen, the heirs to all that this magic word implied'.[3] Given responsibility as well as schooling (formal under a schoolmaster for those under fifteen on ships-of-the-line; less formal, but rigorous, under the captains and lieutenants later) 'a sea-going midshipman might be described as a man and boy rolled into one; not by any means a bad combination'.[4]

No 'youngster' but an experienced hand at sea, as well educated as his peers and certainly proficient at celestial navigation, Beaufort could look forward confidently to becoming, in the prescribed two years, a master's mate, directly involved with the ship's handling and navigation and, four years after that, to being commissioned as lieutenant on passing an examination.

But meanwhile, captain's pet or not, life at sea for a young gentleman on a warship in the last decade of the eighteenth century was no frolic; in theory Francis should have been miserable.

One may turn to John Masefield's descriptive classic, *Sea Life in Nelson's Time*, for a picture of the midshipmen's life and lodgings. Their mess was in the after cockpit, generally below the waterline, in a dingy den barely illuminated by a lantern, its deckhead perhaps 5 feet 6 inches above the deck. The air was foul and the furniture consisted of the boys' chests and a table, provided not from any generosity of the Admiralty but because it was needed by the surgeon for operations after a battle. It was covered by a cloth or old hammock, which had to last a week and doubled in service as a dish-cloth and knife-and-fork cleaner. The mess boy, a dirty, greasy lad fit for nothing else, saw to the cooking and the cleaning, if any. Masefield continues:

The life in the midshipmen's berth . . . was rough and ready, and sufficiently brutal. There was a good deal of noisy horseplay, a good deal of vice and cruelty, and a little fun and sea philosophy, to allay its many miseries. A midshipman lived on 'monkey's allowance – more kicks than halfpence', and had to put up with bullying and injustice unless he was strong enough to hold his own. A weakling was robbed of his fair allowance of food, and imposed upon in other ways, as by tardy relief at night, after keeping his watch on deck, etc. A thin-skinned or sensitive boy was out of his element in such a place. There was no privacy aboard a man-of-war. A student or scholar had little opportunity for reading. Down in his berth, during the daytime, there was a continual Dover Court (all talkers and no hearers) so that study there was out of the question. A midshipman was continually fighting, quarrelling, or playing the fool. The berth was a sort of beargarden . . . which not even the captain would control or keep in order . . . The berth was almost the noisiest and most lawless place aboard.

Remarkably, and especially for one who was later to be harried by frequent visitations of what he called his 'blue devils' – spells of depression – Francis found no more to complain about than he had on the *Vansittart*. As for wretched accommodations in the mess, he could write cheerily that they were happy in contrast to those his parents had related to him when they had recently moved back to Collon from London and lived for a time without furniture or furnishings. The midshipman's pay was derisory, only a little more than £2 a month, and private means to supplement it – the requisite minima were variously estimated from £20 to £100 a year[5] – were indispensable to pay for the extras, the midshipman's mess bills, laundry (clothes were dirtied at a formidable rate) and generally to maintain gentlemanly claims.* Yet although Francis's allowance from his father was a mere £6 a quarter he chose to crow: 'I don't take *little* conceit to myself for being so prudent &tc. and taking care of my things, in so much that I pass for an expensive fellow, with a good fortune tied to my tail . . . and for another thing I take care never to go into debt, even a little.'

To be sure, the salt junk† that was the diet on the *Latona* 'is not so pleasant after living as well as I have done on board the *Vansittart*, and the *Lascelles*', but the boy made little of the deprivation.‡ Instead he wrote of the wonder (and doubtless pleasure) at the improvement of a midshipman's status on a Naval ship: 'I find myself quite a different thing to what the midshipmen of an Indiaman are. [There] a sailor thinks nothing of striking a midshipman but it is death to anyone who strikes me.'§

*On fitting himself out for his next ship a year later Francis rendered an account to his father of his expenditures. His stockings alone cost 18s. (with another 9d. for having them washed); his gloves 2s. 3d.; his cocked hat £1 6s.; his hairdresser 7s.; the shoemaker £2 17s.; a hair ribbon 1s.; the same for a shaving brush; and a staggering £10 17s. 6d. for the tailor's bill.

†The epithet is derived from the sailor's word for bits and ends of rope.

‡Even in later years, under much worse conditions, at sea during winter in the Channel with no fresh provisions for four months, Beaufort rarely mentioned terrible diet in his letters and then without ever complaining. How dreadful food could be on a warship is illustrated by a letter from an eight-year-old [!] midshipman to his mother in 1802: 'We live on beef which has been ten or eleven years in a cask, and on biscuits which makes your throat cold in eating it, owing to the maggots which are very cold when you eat them! Like calves foot jelly or blomange – being very fat indeed! . . . We drink water the colour of the bark of a pear tree with plenty of little maggots and weevils in it, and wine, which is exactly like bullock's blood and sawdust mixed together.' For other accounts of salt beef being used as material for whittling and of how to lure weevils out of a biscuit by placing a fresh fish on the bread bags, see, *inter alia*, *Snotty*, by Commander Geoffrey Penn, 1957, pp. 60–1, quoting reminiscences of Sir John Dalrymple Hay.

§He was not exaggerating. The social distinction between Quarter Deck and Lower Deck and the discipline deriving from it and maintaining it were beyond any that come readily to mind today. 'A midshipman had power to bully and maltreat all those beneath

Also, the young man was enjoying himself in an art new to him, that of a dandy. He fretted that a shoe clasp was broken so that 'my handsome buckles are of no use', and at his need for a sword-knot for his 'very handsome' weapon. Neither was the lace for his hat of the right sort, he wrote home, 'and no body wears them with lace round the crown except they have it laced round the edge, so I must take it off, I believe'. He told of plans for buying a couple of dark waistcoats and also 'some more Psalm-singing stockings [i.e. for Sunday best] for I [have] but 8 of white cotton – The midshipmen are a great deal smarter dressed than I imagined and still more so aboard the *Valiant*; the Prince* puts his Mid^n. under arrest for a fortnight if ever they come upon the Quarterdeck without their hair dressed and in full uniform.'

At his work Beaufort would have worn a short blue coat like the rounded jacket of a sailor. But for dress, his uniform would have been a tailcoat of good blue cloth, ornamented with small gold anchor buttons. Breeches and waistcoats were of thin jean or white nankeen, the hat three-cornered with a gold loop and a cockade. Regulations also demanded a stand-up wing collar, known as the 'weekly account' and called by midshipmen themselves 'the mark of the beast'.[7]

Proud of his ship and obviously pleased with himself, the new midshipman had only one basic complaint: no fighting for King, glory and prize money. For, as the British Fleet assembled for war, the King of Spain took a second look at the Nootka situation and prudently backed down.

The episode, known in history's footnotes as 'the Spanish Armament', cost the government £3 million but it was by no means wasted. On the contrary, its effect was to lift the Navy out of the neglect into which it had fallen after the disasters of the American War of Independence, ended seven years before. Sir Charles Middleton, the great Controller of the Navy (later Lord Barham), had been waiting for the opportunity and at last had the funds to bring about intense activity

---

him ... to resent his cruelty would be mutiny. A midshipman had but to complain to a lieutenant to get the man flogged at the gangway.... It was in his power to follow a man day after day, visiting him with every oppression that malice could suggest.'[6]

*William Henry, Duke of Clarence, third son of George III and to become King William IV, was a professional Naval officer. Promoted to captain in 1786, he commanded the *Valiant* in 1790.

in the shipyards. A 'Russian Armament' providentially following the Spanish one, Middleton was able by 1792 to put sixty of the nation's eighty-seven ships-of-the-line into fighting condition.[8] When, a year later, the great confrontation with France began, 'for once, the outbreak of war had found the British Fleet not only ready but waiting'.[9]

But for Francis, in whose collection of observational instruments there was no crystal ball, a sanguine future was no comfort for present disappointments. He heard the deplorable news of the Spanish capitulation early in August at Spithead and wrote to his father:

> Alas! Alas! my dearest Father, after all that has been done we are to have no war . . . so what is to be done, my dearest Father, go back to India Service? No, I should rather stay a little time in His Majesty's service. It is I hear an equal chance that Capt[n]. Bertie goes to the Mediterranean; if so I should like that station, tho' it is rather an expensive one . . .

Uneventfully, the *Latona* laboured at her duties for another four months, plying from Spithead, Torbay and Plymouth out to the Channel, keeping a wary eye on the French harbours for whatever unpredictable madness the mutinous revolutionary seamen might indulge in. There were rumours of war, this time with Russia, on which Francis eagerly pounced, only to revert, when each hope was dashed, to the more mundane problem of how fierce were the costs of getting his clothes laundered.

He was also learning, whether consciously or not, about the ugly realities of Naval life. The cruellest, to which he had his share of exposure, was impressment. In principle the requirement of a citizen to serve in the armed forces in defence of his country is still widely practised under the name of conscription or selective service. What was insufferable in eighteenth-century Britain was its manner of execution. Impressment was almost as monstrous as slavery and in many respects resembled it.

The most heart-breaking form of pressing was that done at sea. Naval ships needing men intercepted homeward-bound merchant convoys (outward-bound ships were protected by law against such molestation) and seized bodies as needed, in some cases almost the entire crew. They were hustled aboard the warships and kept at sea for many more brutal years.

Ashore, in more peaceful periods, the same goal was accomplished by the cajolery of recruiting officers, with lies about gold and glory or infusions of enough spirits down the victim's throat in an ale-house rendezvous (known as the 'Rondy') to make him insensible. But more usually, during the seemingly endless wars, it was done by brute force by the 'hot press'. Gangs of seamen, under the command of a lieutenant and with the help of a midshipman or two, prowled seafront towns (and often some inland ones) to search out 'volunteers'. Those captured were penned up until they could be dispatched to a tender – an ancient ship or hulk – and were there imprisoned below hatches in indescribably awful conditions until they were transferred to permanent – all too permanent – berths aboard warships.

The first task of the *Latona*, with Beaufort newly aboard, was to carry 200 pressed Londoners from the Downs to Portsmouth; there were other similar voyages during the few months he served in her.

In Portsmouth itself, Francis had a not-too-uncommon experience of the hazards of the impressment process. At sixteen the young man could keep his courage and a cool head:

I was sent ashore in the evening and I pressed about 10 men and such work as that was. But in the boat bringing them aboard the *Carysfort* [presumably the tender] I was near to having a mutiny in the boat, and indeed had I not reached the ship [in] time enough I should certainly have been chucked overboard. However, I had pistols in one hand and a drawn sword in the other, and if they had, it would have cost them a life or two for it. All the crew of the *Carysfort* being turned over to other ships and there not being more than 5 hands in the Ship they would not take care of them.

Sagely, Francis made a deal, swapping his unruly catch for a like number of more peaceable new conscripts on the *Carysfort*, and brought them back to the *Latona* 'where I got aboard at ½ past 2 in the morning'.

Other aspects of Francis' life as a midshipman also required fortitude although, to be sure, of a different kind. The following episode was recounted by the famous mathematician, Augustus De Morgan, about a year after Beaufort's death, a good sixty years after the event itself:[10]

We were talking of a midshipman's appetite, as a thing which bears a high character for energy and punctuality, and Captain Beaufort said it had never been fully tried how many dinners a midshipman could eat in one day.

'I,' said he, 'got as far as three. I had eaten my dinner at the midshipman's table, and a very good one, as I always did. After it, the captain's steward came up, and said –

' "The captain's compliments, and desires the favour of your company to dinner."

' "But I've dined," said I.

' "For mercy's sake, don't say that, sir," said he, "for I shall be in a scrape if you do: I ought to have asked you this morning, but I forgot."

'So I thought I must go; and two hours afterwards I did go, and I dined, and I think I made my usual good dinner. Just as we rose from table, a signal was made by the admiral to send an officer on board, and as it was my turn, I had to go off in the boat. When I got on board the admiral's ship, the admiral said to me:

' "Ah! Mr Beaufort, I believe?"

' "Yes, sir," said I.

' "Well, Mr Beaufort," said he, "the papers you are to take back will not be ready this half-hour; but I am just sitting down to dinner, and shall be glad of your company."

'Now, as to a midshipman refusing to dine with the admiral, there are not the words for it in the naval dictionary. So I sat down to my third dinner, and I am sure I did very well; and I got back to my own ship just in time for tea.'

By mid-November 1790 it was learned that the *Latona* was to be paid off and removed from active service. Francis canvassed energetically for a new berth, writing to his father at every turn for advice and even permission. Again, thanks to Lord and Lady Courtown, a good offer was forthcoming: their second son, Captain the Hon. Robert Stopford, had a new command, the four-year-old fast frigate *Aquilon*, and, influenced by a good recommendation of Francis from Captain Bertie, said that 'he would be proud of the honour of my company in about two months' time to the Mediterranean'.

4

Aquilon:
'Rum, Sodomy and the Lash'
(1791-1792)

Oh, my dearest Mother, what an awful thing it was.
T'was the first thing of the kind that ever I saw, and I
assure you I was greatly affected by it, the tears (tho' I
have been a sailor so long) running as fast from my
eyes as they did from the poor fellows' whose lot it
was to shoot their comrade. Oh! dear Mot^r., the
dreadful moment has been present to my eyes almost
ever since when he dropped the signal from his hand
to send him to eternity which was succeeded by four
balls through the heart.

BEAUFORT to his mother[1]

It was not until 10 June 1791, after four months of delays, that the
Aquilon finished fitting out at Portsmouth and the new midshipman
came aboard. The beginning was less than auspicious. Early the next
month Francis was sculling about in the harbour in a small boat and,
on returning to his ship, attempted to fasten his cockleshell to one of
the scuttle-rings.

In foolish eagerness I stepped upon the gunwale, the boat of course upset,
and I fell into the water, and not knowing how to swim, all my efforts to lay
hold either of the boat or of the floating sculls were useless. The transaction
had not been observed by the sentinel at the gangway, and therefore it
was not till the tide had drifted me some distance astern of the ship
that a man in the foretop saw me splashing in the water and gave the
alarm.

That recollection was set down only in 1825, some thirty-four years
later, in Beaufort's letter to the renowned William Hyde Wollaston,
one of the most gifted natural scientists of the early nineteenth century.

Beaufort had told him the story and Wollaston, fascinated by its apparent validation of the folklore of a drowning man's total recall, demanded that he put it on paper. Beaufort obliged; his letter to Wollaston was published in 1847 in the autobiography of Sir John Barrow, for forty years Second Secretary to the Admiralty. The document was widely discussed by savants during the nineteenth century.[2] The letter continues:

The first lieutenant* instantly and gallantly jumped overboard, the carpenter followed his example, and the gunner hastened into a boat and pulled after them.

With the violent but vain attempts to make myself heard I had swallowed much water; I was soon exhausted by my struggles, and before any relief reached me sank below the surface – all hope had fled – all exertions ceased – and I *felt* that I was drowning.

So far these facts were either partially remembered after my recovery or supplied by those who had latterly witnessed the scene; for during an interval of such agitation a drowning person is too much occupied in catching at every passing straw, or too much absorbed by alternate hope and despair, to mark the succession of events very accurately. Not so however with the facts which immediately ensued; my mind had then undergone the sudden revolution which appeared to you so remarkable – and all the circumstances of which are now as vividly fresh in my memory as if they had occurred but yesterday.

From the moment that all exertion had ceased . . . a calm feeling of the most perfect tranquillity superseded the previous tumultous sensations – it might be called apathy, certainly not resignation, for drowning no longer appeared to be an evil – I no longer thought of being rescued, nor was I in any bodily pain. On the contrary, my sensations were now of a rather pleasurable ease, partaking of that dull but contented sort of feeling which precedes the sleep produced by fatigue. Though the senses were thus deadened, not so the mind; its activity seemed to be invigorated in a ratio which defies all description. . . . The course of those thoughts I can even now in a great measure retrace. . . . Every past incident of my life seemed to glance across my recollection in retrograde succession; not, however, in mere outline, as here stated, but the picture filled up with every minute and collateral feature; in short, the whole period of my existence seemed to be placed before me in a kind of panoramic view, and each act of it seemed to be accompanied by a consciousness of right or wrong, or by some reflection on

*He was Robert Dudley Oliver, an officer whose brave and brilliant Navy career brought him to the rank of Admiral of the Red in 1841.

its cause or its consequences; indeed many trifling events which had been long forgotten then crowded into my imagination, and with the character of recent familiarity. . . .*

One circumstance was highly remarkable; that the innumerable ideas which flashed into my mind were all retrospective . . . I had been religiously brought up . . . yet at that inexplicable moment, when I had a full conviction that I had already crossed the threshold, not a single thought wandered into the future – I was wrapt up entirely in the past.

The length of time that was occupied by this deluge of ideas, or rather the shortness of time into which they were condensed, I cannot now state with precision, yet certainly two minutes could not have elapsed from the moment of my suffocation to that of my being hauled up.

The strength of the flood-tide made it expedient to pull the boat at once to another ship, where I underwent the usual vulgar process of emptying the water by letting my head hang downwards, then bleeding, chafing, and even administering gin; but my submersion had been really so brief, that, according to the account of the lookers on, I was very quickly restored to animation.

My feelings while life was returning were the reverse in every point of those which have been described above. . . . Again, instead of being absolutely free from all bodily pain, as in my drowning state, I was tortured by pain all over me; and though I have been since wounded in several places, and have often submitted to severe surgical discipline, yet my sufferings were at that time far greater; at least, in general distress. On one occasion I was shot in the lungs, and after lying on the deck at night for some hours bleeding from other wounds I at length fainted. Now as I felt sure that the wound in the lungs was mortal, it will appear obvious that the overwhelming sensation which accompanies fainting must have produced a perfect conviction that I was then in the act of dying. Yet nothing in the least resembling the operations of my mind when drowning took place; and when I began to recover, I returned to a clear conception of my real state.

If these *involuntary experiments* on the operation of death afford any satisfaction or interest to you, they will not have been suffered quite in vain by

Yours very truly
F. Beaufort

Thus by the age of seventeen, Beaufort had experienced two hair's-breadth escapes from death at sea, the first being his shipwreck. Before he finished his career aboard frigates twenty years later he suffered

*The phenomenon of 'panoramic memory' on the point of death, often encompassing a person's entire past, is now credited as a psychological reality. See *The Experience of Dying*, by Dr Russell Noyes, in *Psychiatry, 35*, no.2, May 1972.

two further and even narrower brushes, each time horribly wounded by point-blank gunfire. In addition he wounded himself severely in the thigh with broken glass, to the point where he was confined for a long period to his bunk; he suffered a 'flux' and a relapse in an epidemic that bore off two of his shipmates; a massive concussion from a capstan bar loosed in a gale; a blow across the face from an oar; interminable colds; coughs of three months' duration which aggravated his hernia; and a rare and virtually intractable skin disease prolonged over years. The temptation accordingly is to think of Beaufort as a born loser or, at a minimum, accident-prone. More probably, except for the last-mentioned illness, his experiences were fairly typical of those of his seafaring contemporaries.

Beaufort tended to minimize and in some cases completely withhold from his parents news of his accidents and the severity of his sickness. He mentioned them briefly or only in enciphered passages in his letters for his elder brother, William. Their cipher, apparently worked out by the boys in their schooldays, was ludicrously simple (Beaufort was singularly naive as a youthful cryptographer). It was a juvenile concoction of Greek letters, astronomical symbols and invented squiggles used in one-for-one substitution for the letters of the alphabet (technically, a Caesar substitution by symbols). Anyone who has ever amused himself with cryptogram puzzles could solve it in a matter of minutes and a professional cryptanalyst might almost read it off. A typical example of his cipher, set down on 21 April 1793 in a page of the journal he kept at sea, is reproduced opposite for anyone who wishes to try his hand at cryptanalysis. The clear text is given in Chapter 5, page 61.

Francis must have had a poor opinion of his father's intelligence, or else assumed that he had little curiosity, if he fancied that that learned gentleman would not decipher his communications. He wrote to Dr Beaufort begging him 'never take it ill my writing things [to] William in a concealed hand or manner, for let me assure you 'tis only little jokes or trifles between us – and in general they serve to let one another see that we have not entirely forgot the hand'.

The explanation was disingenuous: besides relating the true state of his health and enlisting William's help in getting his repeatedly break-ing truss repaired, Francis used the cipher to order through his brother odd bits of finery and haberdashery which he must have assumed his *for the same precaution there as at the Gates of the City, the road for Carriages encompassing the foot walk which are allowed only to drive one way — but we were not at Cadis in the right time of the Year, for in the Summer months the first people walk and drive there*

father would not approve of; to inquire into his brother's sex life ('Have you got foul of any of the lasses of Collon yet?'), and, both in letters and in his journal, to report on the price, appearance, availability and incidence of disease of the prostitutes at various Mediterranean harbours, e.g. 'The whores here [Leghorn] are very nasty but you are secure from pox or theft as they are licensed.' On one occasion he wrote to William an entire four-page folio letter in cipher, one half laying bare his doubts about his father's religious tenets and the other half ordering clothes and supplies.

Francis also confided in cipher to his brother that he was miserable aboard the *Aquilon*. The problem was her captain, Stopford. A very few years later Beaufort developed a close intimacy with 'Bob' Stopford, reporting in his letters and journal kindness and flattering offers from him. Still later, in Beaufort's most dismal days of denied promotion, Stopford wrote in outrage at the injustice being done his one-time midshipman and even took the matter up directly with Admiral Nelson. The friendship lasted to the end of Stopford's life more than a half-century later. But in the beginning matters were much less agreeable. 'I am and shall be unhappy on board th[is] ship', he cryptographed to his brother, and noted that his erstwhile rescuer from drowning, First Lieutenant Robert Oliver, had been transferred to another ship where he was happy 'which between you and I he could never be on board this ship (nor anybody else)'. Francis commented on Stopford's arrogance and his imperious manner to local dignitaries and, again in cipher, wrote that the second lieutenant had left the ship ostensibly because of an injury, 'but really he was tired of the disagreeable and ungentlemanlike behaviour of our captain (and not to him alone)'.

Very little has been published about Stopford as a person. His Naval feats, however, fill columns in the standard biographical dictionaries. He was one of the most spectacularly active and successful commanders of his age. Before he died in 1847 at the age of seventy-nine Stopford had become Admiral of the Red, Rear-Admiral of the United Kingdom, GCB and CCMG. He also received glowing honours from the Sultan of Turkey and three European monarchs, when, as commander-in-chief of the fleet given the task of suppressing the martial exuberance of Mohammed Ali, Pasha of Egypt, against his overlord, the Sultan, Stopford averted a European crisis in 1840. He harried the French and their allies from Copenhagen to Java, from the West Indies to Acre. The tally of the enemy ships he captured or destroyed is voluminous; the evidence of his tactical brillance and shrewd judgement is impressive. After a few years under his command Beaufort was to accuse him (privately) of timidity by denying permission for proposed cutting-out operations on a couple of occasions in the *Phaeton*, his next ship after the *Aquilon*, but Stopford's record of hammer-blow victories over the decades makes the charge hard to credit. As a newly-commissioned lieutenant, Beaufort simply may have been over-eager whenever any French vessel was in sight.

It is conceivable that the behaviour of Stopford of which Beaufort complained during the first two years on the *Aquilon* was caused by a specially difficult problem confronting the captain – that of discipline. Early in September 1791, only three months after being fitted out, the frigate paid off her crew and took a new one aboard with the intention, as Beaufort wrote, 'to give those men an opportunity of leaving the ship who were pressed or who have repented of entering – also we have a very miserable ship's company. To get a better . . . the Captain means to take none but men of 5 feet 10 inches and complete seamen. . . .' Yet the change seems to have been disastrous, exactly contrary to what was intended, in terms of discipline as measured – and no other measure is available – by the number of floggings handed out. The logs of other ships under Stopford's

command and of the *Aquilon* itself in earlier and later periods show
that the captain was no compulsive flogger. Yet in the two years from
October 1791 to October 1793 he ordered the lash brought down on
the backs of 106 men. The ship's company was about 200. Allowing
for a few men flogged more than once, it would seem that within
twenty-four months at least half of the crew were seized to a grating
at the gangway to receive the boatswain's cat-o'-nine-tails. In all, the
lash came down more than 1400 times in two years. Most of the
punishments were for twelve lashes, the maximum authorized by
regulations for one offence; there were a few of only six, eleven of
twenty-four (one on Christmas Day), and four of thirty-six lashes,
these last for desertion, mutinous behaviour, theft and drunkenness.[3]

This did not constitute a record, but was not far from one. Nelson,
in time of peace, inflicted forty-eight floggings on a crew of 190 in one
year; the captain of one ship-of-the-line ordered 117 in six months. But
one researcher has calculated that the annual average was about
twenty-five for large ships and sixteen for frigates, even during the
War of American Independence when the ships were full of pressed
men, the sweeping of slums and jails.[4]

The largest category of crime for which Stopford ordered flogging
was neglect, the second was drunkenness.

With her new, drunken and disobedient crew aboard, the *Aquilon*
was ordered in the early autumn of 1791 to Gibraltar whence she
shuttled endlessly to Genoa, Leghorn, Naples, Palermo, Toulon, the
North African coast and Tangier, carrying messages, making surveys
and generally keeping an eye on French activities, increasingly worri-
some as the Revolution ran through its first violent phase.

If life on board for Francis was ridden with sickness, mishaps and
an unloved commander, the visits ashore to new scenes were unmixed
delights. The young man's description in his letters home and his
private journal are almost parodies of the typical accounts of British
tourists of the time: Palermo was dirty and the inns terrible; the castle
in Naples was built by a tax on prostitutes and called 'de Novo' because
that is the term given to anything that is indecent; the Sicilian blood
oranges are produced by grafting the citrus branches on a pomegranate
tree; there are beggars in Pisa, but the finest shops in the world are at
Leghorn and 'there is a proverb here that you might as well strike the
Grand Duke as a Jew'. There are also three English hotels where,
heaven be praised, 'you are served exactly in the English style'.

A Venetian frigate, although one of a species of 'the most dirty ill-managed, lubbery ships for men of war that ever I saw', beats the *Aquilon* 'most shamefully' into the Bay of Palermo; the houses in Tangier are like dog kennels and the residents the greatest cheats and villains in the world; Spanish troops are ugly, dirty and slovenly 'and, by much, worse looking than any troops I have seen aloft'. A Turk, escaped from the galleys, climbs aboard the *Aquilon* and clings passionately to the ensign staff, convinced it is his succour. Some of the officers visit Toulon and are forced by the populace to wear red cockades in their hats; Francis will not go ashore in uniform lest such shame befall it, and makes his visit in mufti instead. Twenty pages of his journal are devoted to the wonders of Pompeii and Herculaneum, to Ischia and Pozzuoli and other classical sites around Naples and to the noxious sulphur fumes at the Grotto del Cane. There, to sniff the terrible exhalations at the fissure, covered with a locked building, Francis put his nose at the threshold of a door, 'which gave me a shock that I did not recover for the rest of the evening. It struck me exactly in the same manner as by holding your nose too close to a lighted match, only much stronger. This vapour will put a flambeau out, nor can you fire a pistol off it. . . .'

There was horror, too. At Gibraltar Beaufort watched (and described in the passage that heads this chapter) the execution of a British soldier. Along with another 'promising young man', the soldier had attempted to desert the garrison from the highest point of the Rock by lowering himself with signal ropes. His accomplice's foot slipped and he was dashed to pieces on the stones below while the instigator himself became hopelessly stuck at the end of his rope. He screamed for help and an engineer sent down to rescue him slipped and was killed, leaving a widow and five orphans. Captured at last, the deserter was court-martialled and ordered to be shot. 'Four men took it by lot, of his own regiment, and when he looked not quite dead, one of the Reserves stepped up by order and blew his brains out.' He was the first man who had suffered the penalty in the last three years, and probably he might have escaped but for the fact that the Governor was so exasperated at repeated desertion 'that he resolved to reprieve no more'.

Death came in other ways, one of which was the flux – dysentery or acute diarrhoea from the fevers and infections that were so chronic aboard ships. One of its victims on the *Aquilon* was Francis' fellow-midshipman, the Hon. George Byng, son of Lord Torrington, grandson of the ill-fated Vice-Admiral John Byng, who had been executed in 1757 for 'error of judgement'.* The young man was 'of a horrid bad disposition and temper, which grew upon him every day', Francis wrote to his family, 'but I really lament the case of his noble father, to lose an amiable wife, an only son (for the rest are already dead). . . . It is a pity that the same family should send their only two male children into the Navy, as it were to retrieve the honour of their family . . . and for both of them to turn out so much the reverse.'

In the journal that he kept intermittently for twenty years Beaufort noted that Byng might have been saved except for the 'obstinacy and selfishness' of the ship's surgeon who did not have him moved soon enough to the hospital in Gibraltar.

Francis took to cipher for a final word: 'One great blemish in his character was that of frigging everybody who asked him.'

The observation is of more interest than its mere shock value. Homosexuality was obviously rife in the Navy – Churchill's scathing characterization of Navy life as 'rum, sodomy and the lash' was not an empty *bon mot* – yet there has been until recently remarkably little published discussion of it by Naval historians. Professor Lewis gives the subject only a footnote in his otherwise extensive study, *A Social History of the Navy*. The court-martial proceedings, he notes, show a considerable crop of homosexual offences on the Lower Decks. The practice was probably inevitable, given men crowded together and for years totally deprived of normal sexual opportunities. But, says Lewis, 'the memoir-writers hardly ever mention the subject' perhaps because by the time most of them set down their reminiscences for publication Victorian prudery was in the ascendant – and 'about officers, they are even more reticent: indeed, all but mute'.

Thus Beaufort's notation is a rarity. Its bald, almost matter-of-fact tone suggests that sodomy was not particularly remarkable even on the Quarter Deck; his censure seems to run not so much against the act by Byng *per se* but against his lack of discrimination.

Young Beaufort found other things to occupy himself with besides death and tourism. The limitations of the miserable midshipmen's berth notwithstanding, he had begun to read extensively, begging

---

*Historians now tend to agree Byng was politically murdered by a court martial for what amounted to public relations purposes. The Seven Years War, begun shockingly for Britain, needed a victim, in Voltaire's famous phrase, *'pour encourager les autres'*.

from his father books on philosophy, science, astronomy and religion; he was studying Italian; he observed the daily movements of sunspots.

Less than six months after coming aboard he was made a 'Dickey' i.e. acting; master's mate (his period of service at sea being still short of that required for permanent posting) and at the same time became caterer to his berth, in which role, '*je me flatte*', he would see to it that he and his messmates 'live a little more *like* gentlemen than we did. . . . I am neither the oldest nor the senior in the Berth, but I had the suffrages of almost all my shipmates, for I am the *honestest*, and as good a one as any of them'.

And, as always, the compulsion to make surveys and charts was not to be resisted. With the help of the ship's master, he made a survey of 'Port Especcia' (La Spezia) and in November 1792, 'recovered from the flux', he occupied himself 'in the hours not dedicated to writ^g. read^g. draw^g. &x' to devising a plan (which he illustrated with a neat small sketch in a letter to his father) of surveying a large part of Gibraltar Bay 'which, tho' laid down pretty exactly already, will serve to keep my hand in, and will give both you and me great satisfaction'. His notion was to plane two planks straight and square, about seven feet long, on which he would cut grooves with a fine saw to mark off exact distances of six feet. He would place the first nick of one against the second of the other, and continuing the process, thus make an exactly measured base line, and do triangulations from staffs placed along it at known intervals.

The process would have served, although placing seven-foot planks one after another in a straight line down the beach would surely have been more awkward than using a chain. Here, as with almost all the mechanical inventions Beaufort conceived of in the next several years – none progressing beyond the embryo stage – the need was perceived, the principle of the method was correct, but the device proposed was awesomely clumsy.

It is probable, though, that Beaufort never got around to carrying out his plan. There were other more interesting things to do: by mid-December, French aggression in Europe had mounted ominously. Early in the new year Francis joyfully noted in his journal, 'We begin now to be entertained daily with hopes of a French war.'

5

Aquilon:
'The Glorious First of June'
(1793-1794)

We dismasted completely 9 sail of the line! 1 of which
sank – and six of which we took!! We also disabled
completely two ships of 120 guns each. They ran
away . . . no person of consequence killed except
Captain Montagu. Two Admirals have their legs shot
off.

BEAUFORT to his mother[1]

For almost three years after 1789 the French Revolution appeared to
Britain as an affair not requiring direct or massive intervention. As
late as February 1792 William Pitt the Younger could hold out to the
Commons the prospect of fifteen years of peace, of permanent prosperity and of an end to 'the season of our severe trial'.[2] In fact, of
course, the nation stood on the threshold of a desperate struggle for
its survival.

For twenty years there was to be a mortal duel between the most
formidable land power and the mightiest sea power the world had
ever known. In the end it was the Royal Navy that proved itself, in
Lidell Hart's words, 'the deadliest weapon which any nation has
wielded throughout history'.[3]

If, when war came, the Royal Navy was not able at once to step
into its role as saviour of the country it was in a position to do so
within a year. At the outset, though, the Navy was by no means ready.
Before 1792, the year before hostilities began, it had in commission
at home only twelve ships-of-the-line and in the Mediterranean
not even one. Its first obligations, moreover, were necessarily defensive,
to protect the seaborne trade without which Britain would perish and

to safeguard the empire's numerous outposts, many of them frighteningly vulnerable. In menacing opposition stood some 250 French warships, including eighty-two of-the-line, of which three-quarters were ready for sea or in a serviceable state.

Fortunately, England was given breathing space, and the mobilization of the Royal Navy went forward energetically. By the end of 1793, eighty-five ships-of-the-line had been brought into commission. The regenerated Fleet's first priority was to escort homeward- and outward-bound merchant convoys and particularly to patrol the coasts of France, to attack its shipping and to protect the Irish Sea and other critical areas. Ships were sent in substantial numbers to reinforce the inadequate or at best minimal forces far from home, as in the Caribbean and the Mediterranean where a large portion of the French Navy was based at Toulon.

It was to the Mediterranean command, soon to be led by Admiral Hood in the *Victory*, that the *Aquilon* with her eager dickey-mate Beaufort was attached. Action came with gratifying speed. By mid-February 1793, but still without news that war had been declared, the cruisers at Gibraltar heard that all French ports had been embargoed and that British ships there had been held captive. Accordingly, the squadron went to sea with orders to seize what French ships and cargoes they could. In less than a week, Beaufort joyfully reported, the *Aquilon* took her first prize, the brig *Antoine*, laden with lemons and sulphur. No great glory but at least a start.

By 5 March, however, Rear-Admiral Goodall, commanding the Naval forces at Gibraltar, began to worry about the orders he had given in the absence of firm news of a declaration of war. He had nightmares of his being engaged in what was nothing less than piracy, with the prospect of financial ruin if he were obliged to recompense the French from his own purse for each vessel his warships seized, for the Admiralty would surely not itself make restitution. Goodall put the matter to the officers under his command, implying that he would rescind the seizure orders unless his ships agreed to share the risk. When the question was put to the *Aquilon* a good bit about the character already formed in one nineteen-year old midshipman was revealed. Beaufort wrote in his journal:

> The Captain [Stopford] said for his part he agreed to it – as he thought it was but fair. All the Gunroom [i.e. the lieutenants and junior officers]

scouted it, the ship's Company grumbled (indeed I think it would have been much better had he left them out of the question); the petty officers said nothing 'till the Captain asked had we no opinion. Nobody answering I stepped forward and in spite of example gave my determined consent. The Boatswain . . . also gave his, and our example was immediately followed by the other two mates and the rest of the Warrant Officers. The midshipmen also gave theirs. We then explained the matter to the men, gave them our reasons and at last they also agreed. The Gunroom, seeing they stood solus, gave their consent more from that reason, as they said, than from any wish to promote the business. So the Captain and 1st and 2nd Lieutenants signed for all hands.

Beaufort guessed that the alternative would have been an order to the *Aquilon* to return to harbour, 'there to lay', which for him would have been intolerable. Moreover, he guessed that the suspense would be brief. He was right; next day official word came that the war was on.

Meanwhile, all ships in the squadron had agreed to share prize money to prevent unfairness to those on what Beaufort described as 'bad cruising ground' where there was little prospect of captures, or on convoy escort or courier duty. The deal was a fortunate one for the *Aquilon*: in and out of Gibraltar, cruising as far north as Cape Finisterre and as far east as Leghorn until early autumn, she never made another capture. Strange sails on the horizon, chased and overhauled, proved always to be Spanish, Portuguese or those of other neutrals.

Again weighed from Gibraltar Bay and stood to sea [Beaufort noted in his journal on 19 March]. Spoke several ships but alas! all were Friends. Really I believe we have had the luck of speaking to every Dane and Swede that has come past the Gut and they have a great trade up here. I am well convinced that several of them have French cargoes if examined.

Disappointments trod on each other's heels: the *Aquilon* 'vainly chaced' what was probably a Guernsey privateer, fleeing in fear of having her men pressed. Under French colours Stopford spoke to a Spanish brig 'who showed the most extravagant symptoms of joy on finding out what we really were'. At one point Admiral Hood had word of a superior enemy fleet and ordered a general chase, but thereupon instructed the *Aquilon* and two other ships to sail on a different mission in the opposite direction. Beaufort mourned:

What a change there was through the whole ship! from the greatest mirth and spirits which animated everybody in her, that they really could hardly contain themselves; a general gloom and discontent prevailed. In the place of studding sails actually flying up, the tacks would hardly come on board; everything seemed stiff and unwieldy and even ropes and sails seemed to partake of our universal illhumour.

As it happened, Hood was responding to a false alarm and the *Aquilon* was cheated of nothing but the joy of anticipation. The three detached ships bore down on Genoa half a day too late to catch an incoming French convoy of twenty merchantmen escorted by a forty-gun frigate and a smaller ship of twenty guns which, tucked into the neutral harbour, could safely thumb their noses at the British cruisers. Coming on them a few hours earlier, Beaufort fumed, the little British flotilla would have taken half of the vessels in the French convoy as prizes.

Others of Goodall's squadron had better luck. By summer Beaufort could at least share in the prize money, to the extent of about £300. Now a man of property, he executed his first will in favour of his father, and wrote to that adored figure: 'But oh my dear Father, there is little occasion, I hope, to say that if you want it now or ever that every farthing of it is heartily at your disposal.'

It was as much work running down allies and neutrals as foes. Cruising between Cape Spartel and Cape Finisterre in June, Francis attempted to report to his father (in French: with lapses back into his mother tongue when the technical terms grew too difficult to translate) what his routine was like. His father might suppose, he wrote, that nothing stops him from giving an hour or so to writing a letter and that he was often idle. Not so.

My duties as Master's Mate are, first to take the watch every eight hours for four hours, and if all hands are called while I am below, I have to come up with them, and that happens often, for example if the Captain wants to give chase to some vessel, or more sail is required; if he wants to take in sail, if he wants to punish someone, and a hundred other things, they must be done swiftly, as required on a warship, and all hands have to be at their stations. Moreover, every third day it is my turn to be Mate of the Day, which is to say, I am obliged to see that all water, provisions, wine and everything else in the hold is properly distributed to the men and well stowed, to attend the different decks, to see that there is no noise or confusion, no dirt, and that all is swept at the right time. It is also necessary to write the journal for the day and give it to the master, and many other things – so you see that each third day I have not one moment to myself. . . .

But there was time for a bit of sightseeing: the view of the cathedral and fortifications of Malaga, seen from the sea, a closer look, on land, at the 'beautifully designed' cathedral and city of Cadiz where (prudishly in cipher, even in his journal) the young sailor noted: 'There are no females there but whores which indeed are in great abundance in this place but $\frac{9}{10}$ of them have the pox. It is very common to take them into a gateway where they'll frig you for a rial.'

The *Aquilon*'s loss by half a day of prize money and glory at Genoa came in the course of a royal but unwarlike assignment to sail to Leghorn to convoy George III's sixth son, Prince Augustus Frederick, back to England. Twenty years old at the time, educated at the University of Göttingen and a Germanophile, he was liberal in his politics and distrusted by his father's court. Worse, while in Rome he 'became intimate' with Lady Augusta Murray, daughter of the Earl of Dunmore, and in April 1793 entered into a marriage ceremony with her. His royal father was furiously opposed to the marriage with 'Goosey' (who, according to one historian,[4] 'was over thirty and not virginal') and it may have been his orders, or possibly the young man's ill-health, that led to his return.* Augustus Frederick was a lifelong friend of Stopford, which may explain why the *Aquilon* was chosen to convey him home.

His Royal Highness was embarked at Leghorn on 2 August 'with some difficulty', Stopford noted in his journal,[5] which suggested that Augustus may have been loath to leave his Augusta. He was landed at Spithead on 7 September, having proved himself, according to Beaufort, a very pleasing young man well liked by everyone on the ship – though the captain was possibly irritated on occasion. In later years, as recorded in a notebook of their father's yarns kept by his adoring children, Beaufort related how Stopford hated smoking, had forbidden it aboard and found his prohibition not merely flouted by the royal passenger but mocked: the Prince would sidle up to Stopford unawares and blow smoke in his face, to the delight of all hands. After five weeks of glorious leave in London with his father and brother while the *Aquilon* received a much-needed refit, Beaufort found his ship once again Prince Augustus Frederick's sea-going carriage, this time

---

*The lady followed, and a second wedding ceremony was performed in England in December 1793. A month later a son was born and in 1801 a daughter. George III declared the marriage void in 1794 but Augustus defied him for seven years until he capitulated and later married someone else.

taking him back to Leghorn. Schooled to abhor everything undisciplined, convinced warships were for fighting and lusting for glorious encounters, Francis viewed the voyage sourly.

I carried all his baggage, servants, etc. etc. on shore in the boats and never did I do anything with greater pleasure except the landing of himself, for although he had not lost any of that affability which made him beloved, yet all of the spirit, discipline, activity etc. which is so very necessary to the existence of men of war and of which I can with confidence say much prevailed in the *Aquilon*, was entirely destroyed by the attention and *fuss* with regard to him and the impertinence of his numerous German sycophants and servants.

The voyage, otherwise uneventful, gave Francis at least one bad moment. On 31 January 1794, in a gale with heavy seas off the Spanish coast, he was coming up a ladder when the ship lurched and a capstan bar, a ten- to twelve-foot ashen staff four or five inches in diameter, was flung from its racks. Falling almost six feet, it hit Beaufort directly on his head and 'blood gushed plentifully'. He was helped to his berth where he became unconscious. The ship's surgeon found it 'next to impossible' that his skull was not fractured. The episode was, he wrote to his father, 'the 4th escape from death I have had on this ship'.

The *Aquilon* was back at Spithead by early April, joining the Channel Fleet under the command of Lord Howe. She was about to be caught up in the kind of action the young fire-eater dreamed about but had not expected so soon. In common with a large body of critics in the Fleet and an even noisier one in the press Beaufort had begun to believe that the fire had gone out of Lord Howe's belly.

After outstanding performances at sea in the Seven Years War and as commander of the American station in the first two years of the War of American Independence, and after a five-year stint as First Lord of the Admiralty during Pitt's first administration, Admiral Earl Richard Howe* was called back to raise his flag at the outbreak of hostilities with the French. He was by then almost sixty-eight years old. Although he was personally adored by the men of the Fleet and dubbed by them 'Black Dick', from his swarthy complexion and saturnine expression, the soubriquet soon gave way to a less affectionate one, 'Lord Torbay',

---

*His brother, General William Howe, commanded the land forces during the same period. Both Howes sympathized with the Colonists' cause.

because for months on end he kept his ships-of-the-line in the sheltered anchorage of Torbay eastward of Plymouth. Instead of maintaining a close blockade of the French Fleet, Howe saw as his priority the preservation of his own ships in good condition, rather than staying at sea in the Channel's wintry storms. For that policy and for failure to bring the enemy fleet to action he was being bitterly criticized in the press.*

Beaufort joined the clamour: 'what can be the reason of Lord Howe's inactivity in Torbay?' he wrote as early as October 1793. 'How very imprudent it is of the Admiralty to permit such a valuable fleet to lie here at this time of the year', he wrote two months later from Plymouth, complaining that the *Aquilon* had been without orders for a fortnight. When in November in the Bay of Biscay Howe failed to bring a French fleet into battle (for which, however, he was completely exculpated, at least in James's description of the affair),[6] Francis fumed: 'Everybody seems, and I fear justly, enraged at Howe. It seems he certainly might have caught some of them when he *threw out the signal to give up the chase.*'

In April new orders choked off further grousing. Late in the month, the Fleet moved up channel to St Helen's Road, the anchorage at the Isle of Wight, to prepare to escort an East India convoy of more than a hundred merchantmen out of the channel. The *Aquilon* was assigned to be the repeating frigate (relaying signals from the commander) of the Rear Division, and Beaufort was chosen as signal midshipman.

'I shall not be very glad of that as it will be very troublesome,' Francis lied transparently to his family in a piece of teenage self-importance, 'but to tell the truth should be, out of pride, much sorrier to see anybody else appointed to it.' Troublesome it was, indeed – for more than a month, without respite, he was on deck at his chests of signal flags from 4 a.m. until 8 p.m. with ten minutes off for breakfast and thirty for dinner – but superbly rewarding, for the climax was the battle of the 'Glorious First of June', the encounter ending on 1 June 1794 that brought Britain its first great victory of the war, thrilling a success-starved nation and grievously disabling the French Fleet. In

*Such Naval historians as Mahan and Marcus have been equally condemnatory although Sir John Barrow, in his idolatrous biography, *The Life of Richard Earl Howe*, KG, takes a contrary view. The number of Howe's ships was limited, with few reserves. His policy was at least arguable.

his old age Beaufort was for many years the last surviving officer of the action.

The four-day engagement has been chronicled so often and in such detail that only a brief summary and *Aquilon*'s part in it need be given here.[7]

In the winter of 1793–4 a vast grain convoy, its cargo indispensable for staving off a prospective famine in France, assembled in Hampton Roads, at the mouth of Chesapeake Bay, and was shortly joined by French merchantmen from the West Indies. Rear-Admiral Van Stabel with two ships-of-the-line and three smaller vessels sailed unseen and unmolested from Brest, reached the Chesapeake safely and on 11 April began to shepherd his charges home. Inexplicably, the Admiralty, which should have had intelligence of the French movements, made no attempt to intercept the convoy at Chesapeake Bay. Meanwhile, Rear-Admiral Neilly, like Van Stabel a brave and able officer, similarly sailed without hindrance out of Brest with five ships-of-the-line on 1 April to rendezvous with the returning grain convoy at a point 30 miles west of Belle Ile.

On 2 May Howe took his fleet of twenty-one ships-of-the-line, fifteen frigates and other smaller craft and the huge British convoy to sea from St Helen's Road with the dual objective of escorting the merchantmen as far south as the latitude of northern Spain and subsequently intercepting the French convoy. His frigates reconnoitred Brest early in the month and found the enemy's main battle fleet still at anchor. Howe cruised back and forth in the Bay of Biscay and again examined Brest on 19 May, this time discovering an empty harbour. Three days earlier the great French Fleet of twenty-five ships-of-the-line, one of 120 guns and three of 110, had sailed out undetected to rendezvous with Neilly and meet the grain convoy from America. The Fleet was under the command of Rear-Admiral Louis-Thomas Villaret-Joyeuse whose mission was to avoid battle with the British Fleet if possible but at all costs to get the grain convoy home safely. Failure, Robespierre had made clear to him, would cost him his head.[8]

Howe, driving his ships westward in the hope of making an interception, had his first word of the French whereabouts very early on 21 May, thanks in good part to the *Aquilon*. With other frigates, she had come upon and recaptured elements of an English convoy of cargo ships from Lisbon, seized two days before by Villaret-Joyeuse and now under French prize crews. Those on the brig *Tiber*, out of Yarmouth, which the *Aquilon* boarded, were apparently no great seamen. 'There was only one Englishman left aboard her, the mate', Beaufort noted, 'who from stupidity or fear could give us but little intelligence. There was six men and a quartermaster of the *Patriot* [one of Villaret-Joyeuse's vessels] all of whom except the quartermaster were laying seasick on deck when we boarded her.'[9] The non-seasick petty officer revealed that he had been with the French Fleet only the day before and that it was heading westward. Howe gave orders for pursuit and, unable to spare crews to man the prizes, ordered them burnt. Beaufort and one of the frigate's lieutenants carried out the order on one of them 'with a great deal of glee by setting fire to her'.

Early on the 25th, eager to be the first to report the enemy, Francis spotted a French man-of-war from the masthead but made no signal, thinking it superfluous because Howe's own command ship, the *Queen Charlotte*, was two miles closer to her. Unaccountably, however, the *Queen Charlotte* did not see the Frenchman until much later. Belatedly, the *Thunderer* gave chase but Howe soon called her off, obtaining compliance only after repeated signals. Beaufort wrote: 'I secretly applauded the [*Thunderer*'s captain's] perseverance and cursed old Howe in my Heart. But no doubt the old Boy was right, in not letting his attention be drawn from the Fleet, or the grand convoy, the main chance.' He went on to conclude on the basis of the information from the recaptured Lisbon ships about the relatively small amount of canvas carried by the French, that 'I fear we have overshot the mark, as we have been carrying a press of sail all the time'. He was right: Howe had sailed about 100 miles west of the French rendezvous point before he realized his mistake and turned back.

It was not until 28 May that Howe finally made contact and the first shots were fired. Francis crowed with pride at the *Aquilon*'s showing: from a beginning sternmost and leewardmost of the fleet at 1.45 p.m., she was ahead and windward of all by 6 p.m. 'Never did a ship display her superiority of sailing so satisfactorily as did the *Aquilon* that evening.'

Beaufort's journal of the events from 22 May to 1 June covers twenty-three closely written pages of careful tactical detail. It ends, abruptly, at 3.45 a.m. on the climactic day itself.

His judgement of the poor performance of the leading ship-of-the-line, the *Caesar*, agrees with that of such historians of the battle as James and Mahan. His guess on the eve before the final engagement as to Villaret-Joyeuse's strategy was equally correct: 'In my opinion their object is to draw us off from the Track of their Convoy, even at the hazard of an action which tho' I think by no means they wish for, yet, I believe, their orders are to risque it rather than the loss of their convoy.'

By brilliant manoeuvres and battle tactics Howe made up in some part for his gross strategic mistakes. His manoeuvres to gain the weather gauge from an initial position to leeward, the superior seamanship of his men-of-war and particularly their superior gunnery combined to win an overwhelming tactical victory, its dimensions suggested by Beaufort's paean, written to his mother as the triumphant Fleet returned to Portsmouth, quoted at the head of this chapter. But it was a 'glorious' victory more in a psychological sense than in a substantive one: yes, the enemy had been overwhelmed, six ships captured and one sunk, but nineteen returned to French havens, including four that had been dismasted but were succoured by Villaret-Joyeuse. Howe failed to pursue when he could have and should have. A squadron that he had detached a few days before the battle should have been able to cut off the crippled French ships but did not. Most important of all, the crucial grain convoy with Van Stabel's escort reached France without ever having been sighted by a British vessel. 'Strategically', Marcus concludes, 'the French fleet achieved its object . . . Great Britain's opportunity of dealing the young Republic a mortal blow had been lost.'

The *Aquilon* did not fire a shot in anger. During the days before the battle, the frigates' roles were as scouts and messengers; during the engagements themselves, the *Aquilon* for the Rear and two other frigates for the Van and Centre sailed parallel to, but on the unengaged side of, the line of battle, repeating signals from their respective command ships to the others in their divisions. Their task was indispensable inasmuch as in the hurly-burly the distance between the ships and especially the impenetrable clouds of smoke once the firing began made direct viewing of the signal flags by ships engaged in the battle chancy or impossible. Under unwritten rules of Naval warfare, frigates were not to be fired upon by enemy ships-of-the-line unless they had the temerity to initiate hostilities themselves.*

The *Aquilon* nevertheless distinguished herself in the engagement. She was first to spot the enemy on 31 May after sight of the French had been lost during thirty-six hours of heavy fog. Towards the end of the battle itself, she deftly bore down on the *Marlborough* (seventy-four guns), dismasted and surrounded by enemy ships, and took her in tow, saving her from further punishment a few minutes before all firing ceased.

Battered but triumphant, Howe's Fleet made its way back to Portsmouth by 13 June, there to be received with enormous celebration and rejoicing. Towards the end of the month George III, the Queen, Prince Ernest and three of the monarch's swell of six daughters arrived for five days of ceremonial jubilation and the passing around of honours. On the afternoon of the 28th 'the Royals' (Beaufort's term) were entertained at dinner by Stopford on board the *Aquilon*. It is not entirely clear why a mere frigate was chosen for the distinction but Stopford had close connections at court; his father had just retired from the post of Treasurer to the Royal Household. The guests were sailed about outside the harbour and down towards Cowes. But at 5.30 p.m., working back to Portsmouth, the *Aquilon* ran aground, the master apparently having taken aboard a liquid cargo as well as a royal one. The ship stuck fast for two hideously embarrassing hours and freed herself only with the loss of her stream anchor, the kedge and parts of two hawsers. Their Majesties had to be rowed ashore to Portsmouth in the frigate's boats. Before the ordeal was over and the ship was able to take the royal party aboard next day to sail to Southampton, all the capstan bars were broken in an attempt to hoist anchor and the cable had to be cut.[11] All in all, it had not been Captain the Honourable Robert Stopford's finest hour.

---

*The exception in the Battle of the First of June was the frigate *Phaeton*, to which Beaufort was soon to transfer. Passing under the stern and then to the port side of a dismasted French seventy-four, the *Phaeton* was cannonaded for ten minutes and returned the fire, suffering two men killed and five wounded. The French action was considered to have been 'rascally'.[10]

6

Phaeton:
Cornwallis's Retreat
(1795-1799)

... the battle of the 17 of June 1795 ... was more
characteristic of the true high-toned valour of true
fortitude than any of the combats that have ever
graced the annals of the British Navy.

BEAUFORT to Sir Thomas Byam Martin[1]

His Majesty could not have been too put out. In the promotions and
new assignments that followed the Glorious First of June, Stopford
was given command of a larger frigate, moving from the thirty-two-
gun *Aquilon* to the thirty-eight-gun *Phaeton*. Beaufort, temporarily
somewhat more reconciled to serving with Stopford but less well
disposed to his fellow officers on the *Aquilon*, went with him.

The ship spent the summer of 1794 cruising off Dover, watching the
Scheldt and harassing enemy coastal shipping. By autumn she had
rejoined Howe's Fleet in the role of a 'Channel Groper', acting as
lookout, reporting strange sails and occasionally giving chase, weather-
ing storms, frequently putting into port for refit of sails and spars lost
to the gales, only to set out again on the same tasks until well into the
spring of 1795.[2]

On 28 May, with all hands fingering pockets full of the final prize
money paid from the Glorious First of June of the year before,
the *Phaeton* set sail with a small squadron under the command of
Vice-Admiral Cornwallis, out for mischief off Ushant and further
south.

Sir William Cornwallis, younger brother of General Lord Charles
Cornwallis whose surrender at Yorktown ended the hostilities of the
American War of Independence, had behind him a distinguished

career, commanding ships at the battles of Grenada, St Kitts and Dominica, at the relief of Gibraltar and in India. His cruise off Ushant was luckily timed: with his hundred-gun flagship, the *Royal Sovereign*, four of seventy-four guns, the *Phaeton*, another frigate and a brig, he intercepted a smaller French squadron, under Rear-Admiral Jean-Gaspar Vence, off the Penmarcks. It consisted of three seventy-four-gun ships and six or seven frigates, escorting a large convoy.

The *Phaeton*, in the lead, sighted a frigate, gave chase and soon came on the highly vulnerable convoy. Along with one ship-of-the-line and the brig, the *Phaeton* was able to close sufficiently to open fire. But the rest of Cornwallis's squadron was too far in the rear to come up soon enough to engage. The French turned tail and ran for the shelter of Belle Ile.[3]

Fired a great deal at them [Beaufort wrote home]. If supported, would have cut some of them off. They ran away and got into Belisle where 8 sail more were laying. Stood off from the Island. Saw at the other side two frigates with a Dutchman in Tow. Chased them again. They let go their Prize. Got up close under the Quarter of one of them, just on the point of taking her, all life, spirits, joy. Lo! we bore round up, and left her – the infamous dog of a Pilot said there was danger [of shoaling] – and went away. However, at parting we made a hole in his stern you might have driven a Coach and Six into. Took 8 Prizes that evening. Next morning we were ordered in under some forts [on Belle Ile] to cut out a man-of-war brig. Fell almost calm, very lucky we were not sunk. Got two guns dismounted. 1 man killed and six wounded. The ships were never intended to go against Stone Walls.

Stood off, took two more Prizes . . .

Cornwallis turned back toward the mouth of the Channel and on 1 June dispatched the brig to take his prizes, laden with wine and brandy, back to England. He then turned again toward France, no doubt hoping to find M. Vence and his convoy once again at sea. Meanwhile, however, the French Naval command at Brest, mistakenly thinking Cornwallis was still blockading Vence at Belle Ile, dispatched to the rescue a force of nine ships-of-the-line (one of them the formidable 120-gun *Montagne*, flagship at the Glorious First of June and now renamed the *Peuple*), the two fifty-gun *rasés* (ships-of-the-line lightened by the removal of their upper works), seven frigates and four corvettes, under command of Villaret-Joyeuse. On the 15th he fell in with Vence's squadron, which had left Belle Ile when Cornwallis departed, and was resuming its way to Lorient.

It was this combined fleet and not the smaller squadron that Cornwallis was to encounter the next day. The tables were now drastically turned: Cornwallis's five ships-of-the-line and two frigates were heading merrily toward the enemy's twelve of-the-line, eleven frigates and several smaller warships. Again the *Phaeton* was in the lead. Stopford was either careless or too sanguine: he signalled to Cornwallis of his sighting a superior force but did not haul his wind and return to the squadron. The Admiral must have concluded that the signal related to the number of enemy sail and not their strength, and so continued to advance much closer than he would have done had he known the facts.

By 11 a.m. the superiority of the French force was evident and so was Cornwallis's grave predicament. The squadron hauled its wind and sought to get away, but two of the ships-of-the-line were heavy sailers and the wind favoured the French. Cornwallis had two options, each grim: either to abandon the two slowest ships of his squadron to the enemy or, fearfully outnumbered, to try to protect them during the retreat and thus risk the loss of the whole squadron. He chose the second.

The chase continued through the day and the following night. By 9 a.m. the next day the French had caught up and opened fire on the *Mars*, the rearmost British ship. Cornwallis and his other good sailer hung back, putting the two slower craft and his fifth ship-of-the-line ahead and to the side, and took the brunt of the battle which continued throughout the afternoon. Suddenly, about 7 p.m., the French shortened sail and discontinued the pursuit, tacking and standing back toward the French coast.

This otherwise inexplicable withdrawal was the consequence of a *ruse de guerre*, one of the most successful of the war and one which Beaufort, signal midshipman on the *Phaeton*,[4] had the pleasure of executing.

In the morning, in desperate straits, Cornwallis had ordered the fast-sailing *Phaeton* to move out ahead of his slowly retreating squadron. At a distance of some miles, but still in sight of the now battling squadrons, the *Phaeton* began making signals, reporting the sighting of strange sails and later giving the well-known signal for sighting a fleet, by letting fly the topgallant sheets and firing two guns in quick succession. At 3 p.m., by then very far ahead, the *Phaeton* made the private (i.e. code) signal to the supposed fleet and then the tabular signal, which it was known the French were well acquainted with, telling Cornwallis that the fleet were ships-of-the-line and friends, i.e. British.

By marvellous coincidence an hour or so later there actually appeared on the horizon several sail from the quarter towards which the *Phaeton* had supposedly been signalling. Villaret-Joyeuse saw them, assumed they were the Channel Fleet, and turned tail.[5]

The *Phaeton* added to the ruse a piece of embroidery which Beaufort described in a jubilant report to his mother:

> ... Fought them nearly all that day. The *Phaeton* was sent ahead to pretend she saw a Fleet, which dexterous manoeuvre was I am sure a great reason for the French, the dastardly rascals, taking their a—s in their hand – for at 7 we returned to the Fleet, passed under the Stern of the *R*[l]. *Sovereign*, gave her 3 most hearty cheers. The French, who had kept up a tremendous fire all day, tho' at a very *awful* distance, seeing us in good spirits and supposing that we really saw a squadron, and some of them having been very roughly handled actually (oh! monstrous Cowardice, Sheer Cowardice) tacked and left us. I could hardly believe they meant it; I was sure it was only a manoeuvre but [God's] troth it was in good earnest – and we saw no more of them. *Mars*, the sternmost ship who rec[d]. most of the fire, had only 12 men wounded!!!
>
> Just before they came to action I was sent on board the Admiral to answer a Signal [and presumably to carry back to Stopford the plan of the ruse]. The men out of the Lower deck Ports sent their Comp[ts]. by our Boats Crew to the *Phaeton*, to say that they were resolved to sink before they'd strike. Dear Fellows!

The affair was properly lauded at the time but when medals came to be awarded in 1848, fifty-three years later, for 'boat actions' in the war, none was authorized for the engagement that had passed into Naval history as 'Cornwallis's Retreat'. Angry at the oversight, Beaufort protested to the awarding commission. Comparing the other famous battles of the Napoleonic Wars with the 'high-toned valour' of that of 17 June 1795 (as in the passage at the head of this chapter) he argued:

> ... not one of those justly celebrated conflicts surpassed that of Admiral Cornwallis either in the skill of his manoeuvres, or in his bold defiance with his seven sail of the twenty-eight by which he was surrounded, or in the

dignity with which he drew off his little but compact squadron under their three topsails, or in his stern determination to go down with flag and colours flying, or, above all, in the moral impression it made on the hearts of both foes and friends.

For my own part, of all the various services with which I had the good fortune to be connected during that triumphant war, I look back with by far the most exultation to the honour of having shared in the glory of the 17 of June.

By the end of 1795, after other failures, the French faced up to their inadequacy and abandoned further efforts to contest the supremacy of the sea. France held its numerically formidable warships in port, retaining their potential threat, and sent out only small squadrons to menace British colonies and destroy commerce. These, however, made of the Atlantic coast and the Mediterranean a cockpit of fierce individual engagements, continuing over the years. In particular, French privateers and *chasse marées* inflicted dreadful damage on British shipping.

The Royal Navy's tasks, accordingly, were to blockade the French ports, principally Brest, against the ever-present threat of large French units putting to sea, to destroy the smaller French raiders along the coast and sometimes far out, and to strangle as best it could the seaborne trade of France itself. In this last duty, British warships seized the vessels of all nations, whether French, allied or neutral, carrying cargo to the enemy. Whatever the law of the sea, possession was nine-tenths of it and Britain was the possessor.

The *Phaeton* was in the thick of that continuing mêlée along the Atlantic coast. From June 1795 until June 1799 she made fifteen cruises of from one to three months, from the north tip of Ireland to the south coast of Portugal, putting back usually into Spithead or Plymouth for provisioning, repair, re-coppering and replacement of the sails, masts and spars that Captain Stopford prodigally sacrificed, not as a drunken sailor but as a determined one, in pursuit of the enemy.

In the process, Stopford made a name for himself. Not counting French coastal vessels taken by the frigate's boats or the several sizable craft driven ashore and wrecked by his pursuit, the *Phaeton* took almost thirty prizes during the period. They included some small fishing and coastal vessels, a number of neutrals, a splendid tally of privateers, those stinging wasps that preyed so fiercely on British merchantmen and coasters, and a thoroughly satisfactory bag of warships.

Even a partial list is impressive: *L'Echoue* of twenty guns, driven ashore and wrecked on Ile de Ré; *La Bonne Citoyenne*, corvette of twenty guns; *L'Hirondelle* (twenty); the *Daphne* (twenty), an English ship taken by the French and recaptured by the *Phaeton* with the help of another frigate; the frigate *La Flore* (thirty-six); lesser privateers such as *L'Actif* (eighteen) – Beaufort's first if brief command, as prize-master; *La Petite Chérie* (four); *La Chasseur* (six), *L'Indian* (sixteen), *L'Aventure*, *La Légère*, *Le Mercure* and *La Résolue* (all eighteen), *La Découverte* and *L'Hasard* (both fourteen), *Le Lévrier* (sixteen) and *La Résource* (ten).[6]

There were, of course, no great deeds of derring-do associated with the capture of the privateers and smaller warships. The problem was to spot them, to be indefatigable in the chase and to overhaul them. Once near, the *Phaeton's* thirty-eight guns needed only to be cleared for action and the lighter-armed enemy vessel would surrender without contesting the question of which was the stronger. Even *La Bonne Cityoenne* staged only a formal minuet, satisfying naval protocol if not honour by firing her lee broadside into the water before striking her colours.

It was a different matter with some other warships.

We have had 2 adventures and one prize, a Guineaman laden with Elephants teeth recaptured [Beaufort wrote to his brother on 2 April 1798 in a typical account]. The two adventures were a chace after a French Frigate [*La Charente*, of thirty-six guns] into Bordeaux whom we got up to and exchanged broadsides, but, the *Canada* getting on shore, we were obliged to leave off chace to assist her and so lost [the French ship]. We have a number of shot about our hull & sails but nobody hurt; and a chace of a French corvette [*L'Echoue*] which we began at about a distance of 12 miles & were obliged to leave off at the distance of a pistol shot! having run her 120 miles & though 10 minutes more would have put us alongside her yet we could not outface the pilot refusing to run one inch further. However, we wrecked the poor wretch, for we fired a couple of broadsides into him [*sic*] at parting by way of Goodbye.

An average of almost one dozen prizes a year for four years should have cheered the most morose disposition but it failed to elicit rejoicing from Beaufort, at least in his correspondence. On occasion, he conceded in letters home that the *Phaeton* was the envy of the Fleet, but more usually he reported the steady flow of conquests to his family in matter-of-fact, almost indifferent tones, ordinarily without detail. More often, and in those cases with much more intense emotion, he wailed of failure and bad luck.

Late in 1798, when if French ships had had scalps the *Phaeton* would have sunk under their burden, and only one month after she had captured *La Flore* and returned to Cawsand Bay, Beaufort moaned:

How long Fortune will toss us to and fro and from post by post at the caprice of storms or, what is just about as capricious, the *gré* of Admirals and commodores I know not; this I know, that it is truly a melancholy state. Whilst other ships are *Drooping* beneath the weight of laurels, for I swear they are golden laurels, whilst others, and some our old consorts, have been so gallantly employed in perhaps the salvation of my country and my friends, here are we reduced to a tender, a guard ship, a mere utensil for courts martial.

Not only was Stopford sitting on a court martial but, worse, was enamoured of a young lady of the place and seemed in no hurry for new orders.

Part of Beaufort's distress was natural. He was a young man in a hurry who had entered the Navy at a relatively advanced age and had not been promoted to lieutenant until, after the requisite but inter-minable six years as a midshipman, he had achieved the antique age of twenty-two. He had seen how officers' sons, entering the service at eleven, and so many others coming at thirteen, had achieved that critical advancement so much earlier (Stopford, for instance, became a commander at twenty-two). He pined for dramatic battles that brought promotion in their wake. Further, his appetite for action was insatiable. He wanted prize money, of course – his father's perennial money troubles perhaps made him more anxious than most for the security to be felt from a few pounds in Consols – but mostly he wanted 'glory'. That was to be had, not from accepting the surrender of a privateer or brig or from driving a corvette on shore, but from besting some-thing of one's own size, which is to say a frigate. Such a victory would surely result in the promotion of his dearest friend on the *Phaeton*, the first lieutenant, James Hillyar (later to be singled out for commend-ation by Nelson, knighted and given flag rank), 'and thereby let me jump into his shoes, the only chance I am afraid there is of getting one step higher on the ladder I have been this long time a-climbing. . . .

The long and short of it is I want to get hold of a frigate of equal force, or perform some *valorous* deed or other.'

Becoming the *Phaeton*'s first lieutenant, he wrote to his father, would be a great step and 'would place me in a situation when I should never despair . . . but what am I haranguing about; I *am* happy for I *am* resigned. . . .'

Patently, he was *not* happy nor resigned and elsewhere said so – in cipher to his brother and often enough openly. There were other roots of Beaufort's malaise, deeper than the predictable ones of an impatient young officer. One was a chronic tendency to fits of depression. As a young man and indeed throughout his life, Beaufort's disposition was far from a merry one. To be sure, he experienced ebullient moments, but they were not long-lasting. He could be witty when he chose and amusingly self-deprecatory. But as his letters and journal entries demonstrate, he was usually deadly serious and too often disconsolate, especially as he grew older. He tended to harp on real or fancied injustices, and to remain unsatisfied with his own talents and accomplishments. On occasion his father was taken in by his son's stout assertions of being in good spirits – 'you have got the happy knack of seeing things *du bon côté*', Daniel Augustus once wrote to him – but the evidence indicates entirely the contrary.

Beaufort's fits of melancholy do not, however, seem to have been pathological and are certainly not indicative of a manic-depressive psychosis, for there is no evidence of the periodicity of rising swells of mad exuberance followed by the troughs of dejection or suicidal urges that characterize that shattering disease. More likely, they were the product of an introverted, insecure and highly sensitive personality. With pre-Freudian simplicity, Francis referred to his fits of depression as visitations of his 'blue devils' or, when he tried to exorcize them by self-mockery, his 'azure enemies'.

A second factor in his miseries was a ghastly and prolonged skin disease (described in the following chapter). Although apparently not diminishing his physical activity it severely depressed his spirits, despite his occasional declarations to his parents that it did not.

Above all, Beaufort bore disappointment hard. What propelled him to emotional heights – or rather depths – were the big fish that got away.

On 22 July 1795, cruising with the *Valiant* (seventy-four guns) and the frigate *Pallas*, the *Phaeton* was tricked famously by a French squadron of one fifty-gun ship and three frigates escorting a convoy. The British were inshore of them when they were sighted off Quiberon Bay. The French warships hove to, as if in no fear; the *Phaeton* thus presumed them Dutch and shortened sail while the merchantmen in the strange fleet sailed to leeward, towards shore. Suddenly the French bore up with every sail and the British gave chase.

How clever, how cunning! have those fellows always shewn themselves [Beaufort raged in his journal]. Always do they outwit us. . . . Had they continued their course or shewed the least inclination to be off, we being to leeward of them [thus between them and the shore] would almost certainly have cut them off. This they knew and got us to windward of them in that masterly means. I cannot find much to fault, am only grieved that we are so often duped by them. Their cowardice makes them fruitful in expedients, while English bravery make our commanders too dull in perceiving it . . .

The duped *Phaeton* came up fast, went after one of the frigates and drew close enough to fire a couple of broadsides into her as she pressed closer to shore in four fathoms of water.

Stood off and joined the *Pallas* and asked of their French pilot whether anything could be done. He said no – but was there any occasion to ask such a question? Surely what was to be done was evident to a child of 4 years old and I shall ever regret our not doing it. At quarters my Lieut[t]. [Hillyar, presumably] and me settled the plan, and much surprised indeed was I we did not do it. Surely with the wind offshore [apparently it had turned around by evening] in regular sounding we might have anchored within pistol shot of her when she would have instantly struck, and there being no forts there, we might in half an hour with an end of strong cable from our ship have had her off.

The failure was doubly bitter when the *Phaeton* learned much later that the Frenchman was the *Experiment*, captured from the British in the American war, employed latterly as the 'most villainous raider' off the African coast and now running for home laden with booty. 'How delightful it would have been', wrote Beaufort, still smarting, a week later, 'to have swaggered in with the 50 and three frigates – to have received the cheers of every ship *en passant*.'

Late in 1796, Stopford turned down another Hillyar–Beaufort plan after their ship had chased an enemy frigate for two days and exchanged shots only to see her take refuge under a French fort at the end of the Brest peninsula. Francis wrote to his father:

Hillyar and I volunteered to go cut her out at night, under circumstances which could not properly have failed. At first he [Stopford] assented but when the time came and that fortune had thrown in the way such means as our most sanguine wishes could hardly have hoped for, he changed his mind. He would not let others reap the glory and hence which he let slip. Am I doomed to stay forever with such a man? Is my fate to be tied to his?

The upbraiding was unfair in view of Stopford's achievements and, as nearly as one can judge from the *Phaeton*'s log, his behaviour. It is clear that by the time he was moved upward to command a ship-of-the-line in the summer of 1799 he had become a very different man from the days of the *Aquilon*. He ordered floggings rarely – an average of two a year – and relatively mild ones for attempted desertion. He was sedulous in his care of his men: except as a result of enemy action, only four died in five years. He must have cheered the hearts and stomachs of his crew, though not those of the port provisioners, by his repeated condemnations and heaving overboard of suspect provisions (the rancid butter he gave to the carpenter for tallow).

Best proof of the *esprit* on the *Phaeton* was the fact that it was almost untouched by the mutinies of 1797. These rebellions, when the Lower Decks took command of large numbers of ships in the Channel and Nore Fleets and for weeks refused to put to sea or indeed to obey any official orders, can be seen now for what they were, strikes for economic objectives, orderly, with a minimum of violence and provoked by the terrible conditions of life and pay – although at the time (not unlike thousands of labour disputes ever since) they were deemed to be the work of subversives and revolutionaries for treasonable purposes. Whereas on many ships ugly confrontations took place over several weeks from April to June and the mutineers took command of the ships at Spithead and the Nore, the *Phaeton* seems to have been worked normally while at sea during that period and her men went through nothing much more than the outward forms of mutiny when in port. They 'did not behave ill toward the officers', Stopford noted in his journal; in an Admiralty list of officers put ashore by the mutineers there is a note that the gunner was the only one expelled from the *Phaeton*. Beaufort's letters mention his eagerness to learn from officers of other ships what really went on.

Stopford's exploits steadily put money into Beaufort's pocket, enough to let him gratify his taste for Naval haberdashery, to augment his ever-increasing library, to buy the expensive navigational instruments he doted on and to let him live it up on his occasional leaves in London. By 1799 he was earnestly offering his brother his fortune of £400 invested 'in the stocks' and asking him and his father what they thought about Consols and whether Irish securities were sound investments.

However displeased Beaufort was with Stopford from time to time, the captain obviously esteemed his subordinate, moving him up the ladder to second lieutenant on the *Phaeton* when the chance came. Indeed, he had wanted to promote Beaufort to lieutenant eight months before his required six years were up, but could not, and he gave Francis an easy time when the examinations fell due.

According to Beaufort's account of the occasion years later reported by his children, 'Papa was in a fright – as he was always very bashful and had moreover a very modest opinion of himself'. The candidates preceding Beaufort in the examination sessions, lasting three hours, emerged with reports of a gruelling time. When Francis' turn came he produced for inspection his log book, similar to those kept by the captain and master, which midshipmen were required to maintain as part of their training. It was tidily written, as might be expected from such a punctilious young man, and illustrated with small deft sketches. The examiners, three captains, saw one of casks disposed in the hold, were charmed by it and fell to discussing how they themselves stowed provisions, to the point of eventually asking only a couple of questions and thereupon deciding, 'Oh! this is a nice fellow – he may certainly pass.'

The story has the ring of truth. The sketch, very professional, is in one of Beaufort's log books now in the archives of the Meteorological Office. One of the examiners was Stopford himself, the second was Beaufort's former captain, Bertie. Both certainly knew enough about the candidate at first hand to dispense with formal questions and the third captain would surely have taken their word. The promotion came on 10 May 1796, by which time Beaufort had served on His Majesty's ships for six years and three months, including eleven months of 'paper' enrolment on the *Colossus*. He was two weeks short of his twenty-second birthday.

His superiors could have been in no doubt of the new lieutenant's abilities at his prescribed duties but what they may not have known was the astuteness of his judgement in tactical and strategic matters,

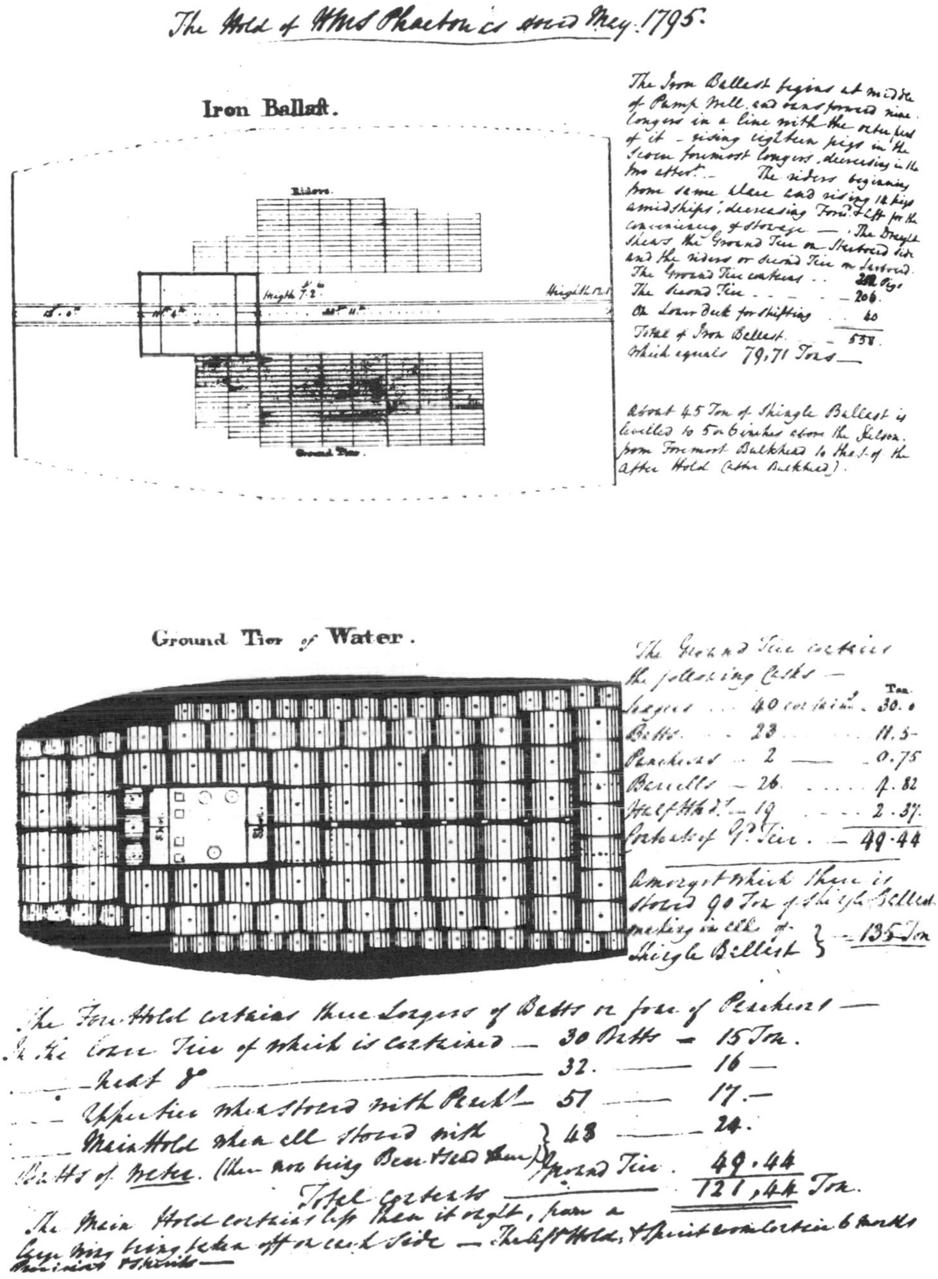

The Hold of HMS Phaeton as stored May 1795
Iron Ballast.
Riders.
Ground Tier.
Ground Tier of Water.
Total of Iron Ballast
Which equals 79,71 Tons
Total contents
121,44 Tons

Sketch by Beaufort, as a midshipman, of stowage in *Phaeton*'s hold, 1795 (Crown copyright and reproduced by permission of the Meteorological Office).

some examples of which have already been cited. There were others.

Beaufort recognized and railed against the failure of Alexander Hood, Lord Bridport, Howe's successor in command of the Channel Fleet, to stand in close to Ushant when an easterly wind blew. That, and his decision to keep the main Fleet anchorage at Spithead far to the east of Brest, had their most disgraceful results when a huge troop-carrying French fleet set sail in December 1796 unseen by any British units powerful enough to hinder it or give battle. The enemy objective was in Bantry Bay, at the south-west corner of Ireland, and an invasion which conceivably could have captured the entire country or at a minimum great quantities of stores, including a year's provisions for the Navy, collected in Cork. In the preceding years unrest in Ireland (which two years later led to the rising of 1798) had grown ominously; the French had every reason to expect a sympathetic reception.

Principally because of the weather and contrary winds and secondarily because of a variety of other French incompetencies and misfortunes, none of British making, the landings could not be effected. But Bridport did not set sail after the would-be invaders until eighteen days after they had left Brest and almost a week after they had abandoned their project and left Bantry Bay. Their ships had been anchored there, unmolested except by the weather, for two weeks.

At the beginning of the episode the *Phaeton* was attached to a squadron commanded by Sir Edward Pellew, whose mission was to reconnoitre periodically into Brest. The *Phaeton* was in company with him on a reconnaissance on 12 December and saw enough before the squadron was driven off to deduce next moves, especially since it was common knowledge (except, apparently, to the Admiralty and Bridport, living ashore almost a hundred miles from Portsmouth) that an Irish invasion was being prepared. Beaufort wrote to his father three days before the French sortie that a large fleet was being made ready for sea and could easily slip out unbeknown, given the British dispositions, by sailing southward through the Passage du Raz. That was precisely what it did (although some ships were frustrated by bad weather and sailed directly westward). If they were to come out with fifteen ships-of-the-line, Beaufort calculated (it turned out to be seventeen), and if the voyage was to be a short one, they could cram 1000 troops into each ship and some more into accompanying frigates, making a total force of about 20 000 soldiers plus 4000 marines.

Beaufort's reckoning could scarcely have been more exact: the French landing force was between 20 000 and 25 000 men.

Pellew spotted the sortie on 16 December and immediately tried to get word to Rear-Admiral Colpoys, with nine ships-of-the-line standing some forty-five miles west of Ushant. His own force was in no position to prevent a French sortie especially if it began with a southward exit through the Passage du Raz. 'Upon my word', Beaufort exploded in a journal entry of 18 December, 'Adm¹. Colpoys' conduct is very odd in staying so far off the land.' Such compliments as he had to give he bestowed correctly on the French.

The best example of Beaufort's potentialities as an intelligence officer, had that species then been invented, was his reading of the notorious escape of the French Fleet from Brest in April 1799.

The Admiralty had ample warning that the French were fitting out but Bridport, whose devotion to his stay-at-home policy was reinforced by its lack of success, was slow to put to sea and, when he did sail, it was with inadequate strength. When his frigates found eighteen ships-of-the-line ready for sea in Brest he called urgently for reinforcements and placed such units as he had twelve miles off Ushant. It was a favourable location – for the French. For, close surveillance removed, the fleet under Admiral Bruix sailed out on a dark and foggy night, once again southward through the Passage du Raz. Bridport's vessels were so ineptly placed that a French lugger, carrying false dispatches indicating another invasion of Ireland, 'had to cruise for several days before she discovered a frigate obliging enough to capture her'. 'It was, perhaps, Bridport's crowning exhibition of incompetence,' Marcus observes.[7]

In accordance with standing orders, which may partially exculpate Bridport but hardly the Admiralty, Bridport sailed at once for Ireland. Bruix sailed for Cadiz.

The *Phaeton* joined Bridport's forces at the northern tip of Ireland. Here is Beaufort, in a letter to his father written while uncertainty prevailed:

... And the picking up the dispatches coming in a french boat to Ireland indicating this part of the coast for their intended descent, appears to me to be a piece of artifice, which is confirmed by the sailors in that boat all *swearing* that there was not a soldier in the fleet – however this *might* be all a deep laid *double* plot ... but I really begin to hope [*sic*] from several circumstances that they are bound to the Southward, to defeat St Vincent who is probably weak, to relieve and join the Spanish fleet and proceed with them in the Mediterranean, to decide the fate of Malta, Naples, perhaps Minorca, to hem L^d. Nelson up in a purse, likewise Commod^e. Troubridge and to annihilate the Russian and Turkish Navy there and lastly to rescue and deliver the miserable remains of the army of the East. There is a plan for them of the utmost importance, exactly suitable to the genius of the French, and on my conscience I believe perfectly feasible and practicable and the counterfeit dispatches would contain this idea more than any other.

What Beaufort could not explain is why Bruix did not do just that, but then neither have subsequent historians. Every act that Beaufort postulated for the French was indeed 'feasible and practicable': St Vincent's forces *were* weak; Marcus concludes that on passing into the Mediterranean, as he did, Bruix could have gone eastward 'to attack and defeat in detail the scattered divisions lying at Port Mahon, Naples, Sicily, Malta and Acre', exactly as Beaufort forecast that he would. He threw away his chance. Beaufort, hypothesizing from the premise that the enemy was intelligent and capable, listed everything the French could and should have done.

7

Of Mind and Body
(1789-1800)

... the irregular division of harbour and sea ... the
regular interruption of any employment from my
watch at sea ... added to my unsteadiness, my want of
method and a constant thirst after knowledge, [force]
me to bury the subject of my study, to fly from
Philosophy to Morality, from them to History, from
politics to professional studies etc. etc. Instead of
sticking to one subject ... and making myself master
of it, away I fly to some other quite opposite which I
forget with as much ease as I read it with avidity. ...

BEAUFORT to his father[1]

Lord Elgin, who came to know Beaufort when the *Phaeton* ferried him
from England to Constantinople in 1799 (Chapter 8), wrote a 'To
Whom It May Concern' testimonial on his behalf saying that he had
never seen a gentleman 'who had read more, or to better purpose'.
This was more than a conventional piece of generosity. Despite the
fitful, disjointed life of an officer on a hard-fighting warship, the
roistering company in cockpit and gunroom, the cramped quarters, the
miserable light below and (until he was a lieutenant) the lack of
privacy, Beaufort somehow managed to read enormously and to
supplement amazingly an education that had been more technical than
liberal and, even so, had been cut short at fourteen.

His first worry on going aboard the *Vansittart* was where he could
shelter his books. From that time on for a decade his letters were full of
reports of books he wanted to buy but could not afford, of those he did
buy, and mostly of requests to his father to buy him more. Initially he
wanted technical works on navigation and astronomy but at eighteen

he was appealing for 'a general treatise on all the parts of philosophy' and another on the different sciences. He recited his longing for a munificent present from his dearest father:

My dear Sextant and my books, etc. for want of which food I am almost starving, for you know . . . philosophy ought to be my principal and substantial food, and poetry and travels etc. etc. should be my banqueting stuff – not forgetting the *Unicum Necessarium* (Divinity) without which the above mentioned food I could as well do as without some moisture or drink with our common victuals.

He claimed he read the theological books constantly, as well as Nicholson's *Journal* (a learned scientific periodical) and Vine's *Astronomy*. At the end of 1793, the learned young midshipman gave his father the catalogue of his library aboard the *Aquilon*: as might be expected, there was a store of nautical, astronomical and mathematical works plus of course his father's elegant Irish geography, the Bible and a ten-volume duodecimo set of Shakespeare. More remarkable, and evidence that there was more than filial piety or attempts at ingratiation in his requests for religious treatises, was the disproportionate number of theological books in the collection: Bishop John Conybeare's *A Defence of Revealed Religion*; some works by the cleric and teacher William Gilpin, probably his *Lectures on the Church Catechism*,* a translation of Grotius' famous *The Truth of the Christian Religion*, and two other unidentified volumes on morals and theology. All were intellectual fodder, intended as rational, would-be 'scientific' demonstrations. Books this eager student was soon to add to his library, such as William Paley's renowned *Evidences of Christianity*, his *Moral Philosophy* ('which has given me more pleasure than I can describe'), Thomas Gisbourne's attacks on Paley, *The Principles of Moral Philosophy*, William Wilberforce's *Practical Christianity* and Joseph Addison's posthumously published *Evidences of the Christian Religion*, were of the same kind, addressing themselves to reason not faith, based on purported proof not mysticism.

The study of religion appealed to Beaufort as a young man as much for its intellectual nourishment as for its sustenance of some deep inner spiritual need. This is not to say that he was not devout or convinced: his assertions about the protection that he believed Divine Providence

*Beaufort listed only the authors but for the most part the titles can be confidently deduced.

had always given him and his gratitude for it are obviously sincere and without reserve.

He had, however, little use for pious piffle. Among the books his father sent him was a volume originally published in 1678, with a sententious title page reading 'A Scriptural Catechism or THE DUTY OF MAN, laid down in the express words of A SCRIPTURE, chiefly intended for the benefit of the Younger Sort'. It 'is a very *good* book', Francis wrote to his father, apparently not wishing to chide him too much for an idiotic choice, 'but it is better calculated for a fine old Quartermaster to whom I have lent it.'

One exception to his usual intellectual approach was his passion for a book of prayers and devotions by Bishop Thomas Wilson, entitled *Sacra Privata*. He made it his *vade mecum* and read a passage from it on the night of his peaceful death some sixty-five years after he had first come upon it.[2] Very popular in its day, or rather century – it was first published in 1786 and seems still to have been standard religious fare well into the twentieth century – it strikes today's reader as a tedious and disorganized stream of dogmatic instructions written by someone certain of his knowledge of God's will, down to the minutiae. Why Beaufort should have cleaved to a book almost devoid of intellectual or philosophical content is hard to explain. Possibly its unequivocal certainties appealed to him, or perhaps it was simply an effective soporific.

What bothered him in his religious concerns were irrationalities, inconsistencies and uncertainties. As his later works attest, he was a precisionist, unhappy with fuzziness in any form, intent on reducing his conceptions into neat black-and-white divisions. On occasion, the Bible gave him a bad time.

Why, since Christianity embraced the Old as well as the New Testament, were the Mosaic injunctions against eating the blood of animals or mixing wool with linen in the same cloth no longer insisted upon? He found his father's explanations on the existence of devils unsatisfactory. And should the Apocrypha be read? 'I wish for some clear perspic⁵. commentary on the Bible which . . . will give a plain explanation of those passages whose meaning or whose consistency do not readily [illeg.] to me.' And how was it that while the Israelites were forbidden to have close contacts with the surrounding heathen they 'and David who almost always acted righteously' took the principal officers of their armies, their servants, and even their wives from the idolaters?

How to explain the smallness of Solomon's temple if it took 153 000 artificers seven years to build it? Why did Jesus forbid those he cured to tell of his good works? Why was he called the Son of Man?

Further, even as the grandson, son and brother of Anglican ministers, brought up in a household where religion in all its High Church form and observances was as unquestioned and automatic as breakfast, he nevertheless developed, temporarily, some doubts on an even deeper level. They were set forth in a long letter to William, entirely in cipher, in which he said he entertained

several unhappy or rather happy doubts respecting the religious tenets of my forefathers. The fact is that besides many points which I cannot explain . . . I despise and abhor almost all our form of prayer as being hardly anything else than a parcel of superstitious mummery and nonsense. . . . Is it not a reflection upon the wisdom and justice of the Almighty praying for a third person? Will not that person's merits or demerits entirely be the guide of God's rewards or punishments?

One instance: every Sunday in every church litany you pray for the P. of Wales and at that instant perhaps he may be committing a sin you have just prayed against with Mrs Fitz. – or some other nasty whore!!!*

I just say one thing more. Can an all-wise God like all the flattering adulating titles we give him in our prayers which would better suit the style of the cringing petition of an abject wretch to a mortal king who was to be won by servile flattery or insinuating expressions – [illeg.] ridiculous!! But those are not my doubts; I must explain in person.

Beaufort hazarded the same objections to his father, although in less robust terms. But two years before, he had been frank enough to reveal how deep his doubts were. He had a long and well lubricated dispute aboard ship with a Marine lieutenant who was a Voltairist, and thought he had come out on top when luckily a beat to quarters ended the argument.

But oh, my dear Father, though I appeared so stout and collected there, I am truly sorry to own that I am not really so in my own mind. For very little reflection has suggested so many difficulties, contradictions & even absurdities in the order and manner that things have been handed down to us that I am often almost distracted, and nothing can put me to rights but a very long

*Beaufort was unduly censorious. Although neither he nor most of Britain knew it at the time, 'Prinny' was canonically if illegally married to the widowed Mrs Fitzherbert.

and very serious conversation with you in which I intend to open my whole soul to you. I look forward to it with the greatest expectation and hope, for certain I am most of my doubts etc. can be solved and I'm sure no body can do it more effectually and satis[factorily] than my good Father. . . . All hands are again called, Adieu. Don't be in the least alarmed at what I have said.

Whether through reassurances from his father, from more reading, from simply growing out of the stage of schoolboy argumentation, or from a strong stock of ingrained conservatism, at least in his rejection of Voltairism, Beaufort eventually reconciled his doubts about the established church – or simply set them aside. As noted, he came to read Addison's religious essays with joy, found Wilberforce splendid (after an initial episode of dislike) and read Paley twice over to be able to write his father an eight-folio-page letter giving his objections to Gisbourne's attack on Paley's relatively laxer and more rationalist position. All this in the midst of the *Phaeton*'s hottest and most fruitful encounters with the French Navy.

By middle age Beaufort developed religious attitudes that would strike one today as almost offensively pious and formalistic; he became a devotee of William James Early Bennett, one of the most emphatic Tractarians of his age, those extremists of the High Church, and himself sired another Tractarian, albeit less famous.

Beaufort's study of his *Unicum Necessarium* was intense but not exclusive. His letters show him to have been reading Pope, Dryden, Gibbons, Smollett, Malsherbes, Montesquieu, Mme de Staël, the 'infamous' Voltaire, Diderot and d'Alembert, histories of France and Spain and a book entitled *Pursuit of Literature* which his mother urged on him. Its Latin, Greek and Italian notes, despite a dictionary of the first language which he obtained, were 'a most provoking circumstance to an ignoramus like me'. He read Adam Smith's *Wealth of Nations*, Defoe's history of the Scottish and English union, a history of Egypt, a history of modern Europe and one on German Illuminatism which seems to have cured any notions he might have been toying with about becoming a Freemason. He was able to detect that W. Rupell's *Modern Europe* was in part a word-for-word but unacknowledged translation from a French work and in part lifted from the writings of Lord Lyttelton.

A great deal of his reading was in French – he fussed at a bookseller for sending him an English translation of a book on the Jacobins instead of the French original – and he kept a French grammar and dictionary on his shelf. He assured his mother, who spoke Italian easily, that he was working hard on that language too.

By 1806 an inventory of his possessions sent to the first ship he commanded included 'exactly 202 books', a truly formidable sea-going library.

Predictably, he read whatever he could on the political and philosophical background of the French Revolution and seems to have had a certain sympathy for its early principles, a position perfectly compatible with patriotism in a period of vigorous defence of those principles by Charles James Fox and his followers in and out of Parliament. But he must have found William Godwin, whose *Political Justice* he seems to have read, much too radical, terming him 'that execrable scribbler'.

The elder Pitt's *Memoirs* troubled his faith in the Establishment and its works:

What a complicated scene of corruption and intrigue does it expose to the view, what a contemptible idea does it give me of (*all the* I was going to say) the parliaments of those days, nor bye the bye do I see much reason from comparing causes and effects to suppose that the present parliaments possess much more integrity and virtue. Truly the Constitution cannot exist without reform, a reform which must almost comprehend a revolution, and I must confess that I am at present so disgusted with the baseness, meanness, servility, corruption, in short every species of wickedness and treason in every department of the state, even with the dreadful example in other countries before our eyes that the idea of a revolution in England might be considered.

That was Francis' sole known outburst of youthful radicalism. He was no barn-burner.

Also to be expected was his absorption with the turbulent Irish scene of the late 1790s: Ireland was, after all, still home and the home of his family. Through a recent marriage, his eldest sister, Frances Anne ('Fanny'), was in the midst of the maelstrom. She and her husband, Richard Lovell Edgeworth, were forced to flee from their home in County Longford in the Rebellion of September 1798.*

*Unfashionably sensitive to the injustices and deprivations of the Catholic peasantry and as much a partisan to their cause as an Anglo-Irish landowner could be, Edgeworth encountered difficulties largely from the Protestant squirearchy. The rebels, marching through Edgeworthstown, left his house untouched.

Initially Beaufort thought union with Britain was a deplorable idea but later he came to endorse it completely.

As noted above, whether in religion or literature, Beaufort wanted all his i's dotted and t's crossed, as if obsessed with a terror of ambiguity. For example, in one huge letter – another eight folio pages – to his father from aboard the *Phaeton* he inveighed against variant and inconsistent spellings in the book he was reading, almost in the tone of someone personally injured. Not even Dr Johnson, whose *Dictionary* Beaufort acquired, was consistent: why accept the u in 'interiour' and reject it in 'exterior' both words being derived from the same French source? Why keep it in 'honour', why reject it from 'terror'? And why, according to the taste of different authors he had read, did he 'alledge' here and 'allege' there, or 'expense' and 'expence', 'centre' and 'center', 'enquire' and 'inquire'? The eager young orthographer said he was sure that clearing the language of useless and unimportant letters was desirable, yet he was 'aware of opening the door to innovation and revolution'. Conservatism and rationality warred within him.

Accordingly, would 'my beloved father . . . give me your reasons for any decision with which you may favour me, as it certainly is not enough to know what is right, but why it is so. "Be ready (as I think St Paul says) to give the reason of the faith that is in you." '

It is tempting to believe that Beaufort was not all that serious about the gravity of correct spelling. Yet the rest of young Francis' correspondence is so abject in declarations of his own lack of wisdom, so intense in its faith in his father's omniscience, that the document has to be taken at face value. In some ways the lad from Collon was terribly solemn and naive.

The youth who filled every dispatch to his father with appeals for parental guidance nevertheless soon grew more mature and assured, despite his protestations to the contrary. To be second in command of a fighting frigate and to command a prize ship on his own on occasion were steadying responsibilities. Beaufort was slowly becoming his own man. Tears that once flowed at the sight of an execution were replaced by clenched teeth:

I had yesterday the melancholy satisfaction of seeing four men launched into eternity at the same moment, for the most bloody and horrid conspiracy yet heard on board any of the ships [he wrote when he was dispatched to be an official witness of executions for mutiny on another ship to Plymouth harbour]. Exclaim not, my dear father, my tender mother, at my saying satisfaction. I am not unfeeling, I was truly affected, but examples are necessary; were it not for the most severe ones no one could depend upon a night's safety. . . . The toast amongst these fellows is, a dark night, a sharp knife and a bloody blanket.

But no amount of maturing and habituation to a rough life can build an armour against illness. Beaufort had his fair share of onslaughts, the more or less common lot of anyone in His Majesty's wartime Naval service. But a far greater and more agonizing ailment he had to endure for almost all his sea-going years was a surpassingly miserable skin disease. For the solace medicine could not give he was obliged to turn to his inner resources, which were fortunately strong, and to his religious faith.

He mentioned the trouble as early as the summer of 1794 but it probably did not become acute until eighteen months later: 'This *Cutaneous* disorder of mine gains ground every day on me. My hands are now almost all one scab, constantly splitting and cracking with the cold. My arms, my legs and feet are nearly as bad, but there are none on my body except for a few on my *bum.*' Two weeks later he told his father of 'spots so thick they frequently run into one continuous scab' on all his extremities. 'It peels off in large Flakes like Whitebran and is always succeeded by similar substance.'

He applied for help to the Surgeon of the Fleet, the eminent Thomas Trotter, and was so horrified with the diagnosis that his only recourse was to denounce the diagnostician:

To the most inexcusable obstinacy [he] adds, I am well convinced, a vast degree of ignorance (notwithstanding his situation, or his catchpenny publications).* He attributes it to the remains of a *venereal* complaint, not-withstanding my positive assurances that I never had any connection from whence such a disorder could possibly arise, and the as positive assurances from our [i.e. the *Phaeton's*] surgeon to the same effect, who has intimately known me these four years. And he recommends me to go through an immediate course of Mercury which [I] positively will *NOT.*

Francis went on to try an ocean of various ointments, warm and cold baths, tar, 'spirituous exhalations' and some sort of a 'cleansing' procedure in London, all to no avail. On the contrary:

---

*Trotter was a prolific author – of essays, verse and plays as well as of treatises on shipboard medicine.

I am really much worse – both in quantity and quality of the disease [he wrote in June 1797]. There are few parts of me where it is not spreading and spreading. . . . The quality is much more inveterate, my arms and rump crack and fly in all parts and are so sore that I cannot lay with any ease at night nor can I bend or straighten the former above a certain angle without the most acute pain. And another bad symptom: underneath those scales or scabs which used formerly to be almost dry there is now a sensible quantity of thick glutinous matter.

The ship's surgeon was as perplexed as the patient and the latter could only turn to Providence: '. . . by the grace of God my dependence on him daily increases. He sent it to me, and he will take it away, in due time. Very probably it will prove of infinite service to me. The more I reflect the more I am assured that God will never forsake those who sincerely depend on Him.'

But for comfort, the Bible proved counter-productive. A private physician ashore to whom Beaufort paid his 'golden guinea' pronounced the affliction to be 'Lepra Greca of the Ancients', something that Beaufort had suspected, having turned to Leviticus 13 and found that all his symptoms, except only the hair turning white, exactly conformed to the scriptural description of leprosy.

His anguish, physical and psychological, was intense. A glandular swelling appeared on his neck; an alarming pain in his breast yielded to a blister but the neck lump, which had subsided, thereupon began to enlarge again. He came to a new diagnosis, almost as terrifying as leprosy: all his disorders over the previous five years, he concluded, could be nothing else than scrofula, the 'King's Evil'.

To exorcize despair he turned to praise of God, gratitude for His blessings and trust in Providence:

How good is God! before he sends us afflictions and chastisement, to give us strength of mind enough, or more properly speaking resignation, to face them. . . . May he support me under this. What can be more afflicting than to look forward to a continuation tainted with the evil, to have it in my lot to stop the pure blood which has 'till now run in our veins. Pray for me, my good father, for a continuation and increase of the above blessings (if aught of others' prayers can avail) as I do for you and my beloved mother every day most fervently.

There were occasional remissions in the virulence of the disease over the next two years but no disappearance. Beaufort mentions his 'scaly hide' and 'scabby complaint' regularly until the end of 1799.

The ailment can be recognized without question as *porphyria cutanea tarda* (or symptomatic porphyria), not identified until this century. It is unrelenting, known to be worsened by alcohol and exposure to the sun and manifests itself by eruptions on the exposed parts of the body; it flares on slight trauma, as over the knuckles, knees and elbows, but can appear quite diffusely. It is probably the result of a metabolic malfunction and in some cases is caused by alcoholic disturbance of the liver.*

Beaufort's symptoms were precisely those of the disease and the hazards of his routine its predictable exacerbations. Life on board ship even for an officer was a constant succession of bangs and bumps; undrinkable water was dispensed with in favour of wine or heavily doctored with rum. And, in any event, Beaufort was no teetotaller: he once described what must have been a not too uncommon revelry at which he and a group of seventeen other young officers and guests on the *Phaeton* drank thirty-nine bottles of 'port, etc.'

Porphyria cutanea tarda remains one of the few diseases for which, even in the late twentieth century, not merely the treatment of choice but the *only* treatment is the removal of substantial quantities of blood.[3] Beaufort was to be cured by a phlebotomy, but the hard way.

---

*Not to be confused with *acute intermittent porphyria*, a rare, hereditary disease, also metabolic, which has been adduced (although not proved – there is still dispute on the matter) as the cause of George III's mental derangement.

8

Phaeton:
Vain Toil
(1799-1800)

I can assure you of my inclination to be useful to
[Beaufort]. At present he cannot be better off than 1st
Lieut of so fine a frigate – it shall be my business to
put her in the way of meeting an Enemy when his
promotion will of course follow.

HORATIO, LORD NELSON[1]

Stopford's captures had not gone unnoticed nor had his well-placed
connections diminished. In the summer of 1799 he was rewarded with
the command of a ship-of-the-line, the *Excellent* (seventy-four guns),
and he promptly invited Beaufort to go with him, as second lieutenant.
So friendly and gracious was the offer, Beaufort wrote home, that he
quite lost his resolve to cut ties with a man for whom at the moment
he did not care, and accepted on the spot. Almost at once, however,
he believed he had made a serious mistake: fortified by the advice of
Hillyar and others, he became convinced that it was far better to
become first lieutenant on a frigate – Hillyar was transferring to the
Excellent with Stopford, thus opening the way for Beaufort's promotion on the *Phaeton* – than second lieutenant even on one of the
workhorses of the Fleet.

He wormed his way out neatly, if disingenuously. He buttonholed
Stopford a few hours later to explain that he had made his decision
for reasons of friendship and loyalty; he therefore asked his captain to
put aside those considerations and to say, objectively, what he would
recommend as the best course. Apparently flattered, Stopford told
Beaufort to stay on the *Phaeton* where he would replace Hillyar.

Enormously pleased with himself for his diplomacy, Beaufort boasted to his father that he had handled the matter *'so cleverly* that I shall gain my point without affronting him, for by my *Generalship* I made him advise me of the plan which I was trying to effect'.

It is debatable how sound his judgement was. Within the year Hillyar was given his own command and, had Beaufort gone into the *Excellent*, he would have succeeded to Hillyar's berth and shared in Stopford's triumphs. One consideration possibly contributing to his decision was his own doubts about himself and about his readiness for more responsibility. Stopford had hinted to him the prospect of becoming first lieutenant on the *Excellent*

if I had a mind or preferred it . . . which I at once declined, giving him candidly my reason . . . for not liking a situation which I thought I could not execute with honour to myself or advantage to my ship or the service. The same reasons, though in a much less degree, make me anxious as to the figure I shall cut in my present situation, for knowing, dear Father, that every day increases my doubts whether I shall ever make what *I call* a great officer. To be anything inferior to that, to drawl through my navy career in a middling way as a goodnatured ass, is an ideal which wounds me to the quick. And sooner than acquire and preserve that character in my possession I would a thousand times rather drive one of your honour's carts . . . I have been unfortunate in serving my apprenticeship and the time so lost is never to be regained.

The passage is probably more faithful a reflection of Beaufort's character at that time than were either his adolescent boasts or his frequent apologies to his father for being too 'frivolous'. He was instead, painfully serious and self-critical, and in no way confident of his abilities. He was a worrier, gnawing at his psychic fingernails, forever feeling the need to prove himself but usually frightened at how the test would turn out.

Under another fine captain, James Nicoll Morris (who was to distinguish himself at Trafalgar and elsewhere and to become a vice-admiral), the *Phaeton* received orders to leave the Channel and sail to the Mediterranean. Beaufort professed himself delighted at the new venue, the only place left in the world, he declared, where there was still a chance of service – 'But alas! we are going with an intolerable *cargo*, L^d. and Lady Elgin, to Constantinople.'

For the moment, the *Phaeton* was once again a glorified ferry boat, a sea-going carriage for the Seventh Earl. Already seasoned as am-

bassador to Vienna and Brussels, Elgin had asked for the appointment
to the Sublime Porte, one reason being his supposition that a long sea
voyage would improve his health. He was newly married (for con-
venience – he was in debt) to Mary Nisbett, a gossipy, silly but
affectionate woman, already two months pregnant by the time the
Phaeton sailed from Portsmouth on 9 September 1799, and doomed to
seasickness. Inspired by his architect, Elgin was fired with the idea of
enhancing the décor of his English house with representations of Greek
sculpture, but was still thinking modestly in terms of plaster repro-
ductions;[2] hauling back what was left of the Parthenon sculptures was
a notion that came later.

A middling-sized frigate was anything but commodious: the *Phaeton*
had to pack in Elgin's considerable retinue like sardines. Here is the
list, with Beaufort's comments:

Elgin, 'rather heavy but is apparently a sensible man, most unfashionably attached to his wife'; the Countess herself, a 'goodnatured, unaffected affable little woman by no means handsome nor
resembling an ambassadress'; J. P. Morrier, Elgin's secretary, 'whom
I like least of the bunch'; William Richard Hamilton, a friend 'without
even an ostensible employment';* Hector McLean, Elgin's physician,
'a knowing Scotchman though well behaved enough'; the Rev. P.
Hunt, 'his chaplain, a pretty little prig of a parson; he gave us Divine
Service last Sunday and a long sermon on the meaning of *Noah's ark* –
I . . . wish my poor William had half the smiles and compliments with
which he makes his bow to his master and mistress'; J. D. Carlyle,
'a celebrated professor of Arabic in the University of Cambridge who
is sent to Turkey for the purpose of exploring the Turkish and archaic
manuscripts which it is supposed the present moment of good humour
of the Porte will permit'; a courier; three maids 'I suppose intentionally
ugly for fear Selim [Sultan Selim III] should fancy any of them'; and
'5 stewards out of livery and 7 in, comprise the remainder of our
troublesome cargo, at least the living part.'

---

*He was, in fact, Elgin's secretary and considerably more of a person than Beaufort's
flip comment would indicate. Sent by Elgin to Cairo in 1801, when the French were
evacuating Egypt, he took heroic and quick-witted action to secure the famous Rosetta
Stone for the British Museum after it had been put on board a French transport. As
Under-Secretary of the Foreign Office, 1809–22, he was an influential benefactor of
British explorers and antiquarian investigators in the Mediterranean. In 1830 he was a
founder of the Royal Geographical Society and, next only to John Barrow, the most
valuable moulder of its forms and activities.

At first Beaufort took a poor view of the entire operation:

I think in my last [he wrote after a week at sea], I . . . expressed my indignation about our passengers seeming to compare His M. ship to a stage coach in which they had nothing to do but take their place and be set down in safety at the place of destination. They carry on the joke and require easy stages, baiting places and halfway houses – because Lady Elgin s[. . .] a little when the ship begins to kick, forsooth she must have a day or two at Lisbon to recruit. Gibraltar and Naples being already chalked out, and as I suppose her ladyship or lord will be mighty sick *whenever abreast* of any port, *there seems* a pretty prospect I think in the term of the voyage.

But the trip could not have been too grim. In the 'To Whom It May Concern' letter mentioned above, his Lordship was gracious:

The interest you take in Mr Beaufort makes me think you will receive with pleasure the favourable testimony I am enabled to bear him. We have now been two months ship mates – and I have therefore confidence in saying I seldom have met with a better bred Gentleman, one who possesses more information, or who had read more, or to better purpose. As First Lieutenant of this ship he is called upon to do a great deal of Duty: and the reliance placed in him by Captain Morris, & the ship's company justifies the character he bears of an excellent seaman. I have enjoyed a great deal of his society during our voyage & have found him a great resource.[3]

Beaufort also met Nelson at Palermo, where the admiral's dalliance with Lady Hamilton was by then the talk of the Western world, and presented letters of recommendation that he had shrewdly promoted before he left England. If the Hero of the Nile did not name Beaufort his flag-captain on the spot, he at least found time to write a pleasant reply, quoted at the head of this chapter, to one of those who wrote to him on Beaufort's behalf.*

*The recipient, Richard Bulkeley, forwarded the letter to Richard Lovell Edgeworth, who had recently married Francis' older sister, Frances. She in turn sent it to her father, saying, '. . . . though short it is I think a very good letter and very characteristick and promises I think or hope some promotion to poor Frank while on the Mediterranean station if fortune favours him at all. It is wonderfully well and distinctly written for a man who has lately lost both his right hand and right eye.'[4] Edgeworth's daughter Maria, the novelist, wrote to her aunt that the letter was 'written very nicely in his left hand, and with the same noble simplicity which you must have admired in his public letters.'[5]

After Palermo, the *Phaeton* sailed eastward to Turkey's Aegean coast, where Elgin went ashore at the site of Ilium and at Alexandria Troas. Beaufort accompanied the Earl's party on the latter excursion and was enchanted. Here, beyond doubt, was the birthplace of the enthusiasm that he carried to his great survey of southern Turkey and its classical sites a dozen years later. From Constantinople he wrote to his younger sister Louisa:

> ... multitudes of broken columns of the most magnificent size, sarcophagi, bits of marble inscriptions, a theatre of 120 yards in diameter, a place whose antiquity outstrips history but the massiveness of whose walls equally defies time, a port and remains of a pier ... were the principal features in a scene which might well engage the attention & curiosity of the first of our cognoscenti, & which even in my insensible breast raised sensations I cannot describe.

Blocked at the entrance to the Bosporus for two days by contrary winds, the *Phaeton* was warped against its strong currents up to the Golden Horn, her track passing under the windows of the Topkapi Seraglio. That piece of seamanship, hauling the vessel by hawsers carried ahead and attached to anchors or fixed points on shore, which the Grand Seigneur had never beheld before, pleased him mightily, Beaufort reported. He ordered a present to the ship's company of twenty-five sheep one day, followed by forty the next, and then, daily for more than two weeks, a 'superfluity of beef & mutton & soft bread'. The English were welcomed everywhere in the Seraglio but in the harem itself.

With the ceremonies over, the 'troublesome cargo' safely disembarked (but with '4 Marble Stones in Cases' taken aboard – Elgin had begun collecting already),[6] and with Captain Morris £100 out of pocket from the Admiralty's reimbursement to him for his feeding of the lordly party,[7] the *Phaeton* left the Dardanelles early in December and resumed courier and patrol service in the Mediterranean.

The hard work began again in March 1800. After a year of French military disasters, the British and Austrians thought they had the opportunity to drive out of Italy the army that had once performed such prodigies under Bonaparte but which was now reduced to a supply-starved remnant of 25 000 men. Once they were expelled, the allies proposed to advance along the Riviera to Nice and ultimately invade Toulon. The odds looked favourable: 125 000 troops under Austrian command and subsidized by the British were poised against the French; the fleet of Lord Keith (to which the *Phaeton* was attached) would cut off reinforcements and supplies by sea.

As the campaign began, the *Phaeton* was harassing French strong-points and shipping along the coast from Genoa to Antibes. The tempo increased in April, with the *Phaeton* working in close cooperation with the Austrians as the French fell back from Savonna to Genoa, which was thereupon besieged. Between 22 April and 14 June the *Phaeton* performed every chore from joining in the blockades of Genoa and Toulon, sending boats ashore to destroy French artillery, ferrying and supplying the Austrian troops, supporting them with her guns close inshore as they engaged those elements of the French that had not been bottled up in Genoa and were retreating to the River Var. Beaufort was in one or another of the *Phaeton*'s boats, coasting close inshore or on ferrying or courier service, from early until late almost every day. It was a busy time.[8]

The *Phaeton* was engaged in a dozen actions, taking prizes – for the most part small ones – left and right from Genoa to Cannes. On 4 May the Austrian commander, General Melas, expressed his indebtedness for the *Phaeton*'s supporting fire and the good management of Captain Morris. Three days later he reported Morris' biggest coup: the seizure of twenty grain vessels and a depot of arms.[9] The services of the *Phaeton* were again particularly commended by another Austrian general, Baron d'Ott, who succeeded Melas in command.[10] Years later, Vice-Admiral Sir Thomas Briggs, captain of a frigate during the action round Genoa, recalled to Beaufort that at that time *Phaeton* was 'the then pride of the ocean'.[11]

The famine-stricken defenders of Genoa capitulated on 5 June but the Anglo-Austrian allies had reckoned without Napoleon. Leaving the débâcle he had presided over in Egypt and Syria, he had made his way back to France the previous October (probably sailing within a few miles of the *Phaeton* when she was carrying Elgin to Constantinople),[12] raised new armies and on 1 June entered Milan with the powerful force he had brought across the St Bernard Pass. Two weeks later, at Marengo, the game was over. Genoa was retaken by the French and the Austrians abandoned all of northern Italy. Keith and his ships sailed westward, their hard work overturned.

After a summer during which the frigate was reduced to helping maintain a desultory blockade off the Italian and French Rivieras, harassing shipping from there to Gibraltar, taking an odd prize or two and keeping occasional watch on Cadiz, she was ordered to join what should have been a more substantial enterprise.

During a summer that has been characterized as marking 'perhaps the lowest ebb of British military strategy in the war',[13] the British dispatched a large troop-carrying convoy to the Mediterranean without, however, any clear idea where to launch the amphibious attack of which it was capable. For months, the transports wandered fruitlessly east and west, from Gibraltar to Leghorn and back, via Malta and Minorca. At last, a decision was made to attack Cadiz and capture the large squadron of Spanish ships in its harbour. Under the command of Lord Keith and General Sir Ralph Abercromby, twenty-two ships-of-the-line, twenty-seven frigates, ten sloops and eighty transports carrying 21 000 troops assembled off Cadiz in early October.

The *Phaeton* had been on the spot, blockading Cadiz with a squadron under Admiral Sir Richard Bickerton, since August. Cadiz was reported to be in the grip of yellow fever, which was confirmed when the *Phaeton* received a letter on 1 October 'dipped in vinegar'* from a Spanish cutter's boat, flying a flag of truce.[14] Nevertheless, the main fleet proceeded from Gibraltar and on 4 October called on the city to surrender. The next day the Spanish governor, Don Thomas de Morla, sent the following letter to the British commander:[15]

The affliction which carried off in this city and its environs thousands of victims . . . being calculated to excite compassion, it is with surprise I see the squadron, under the command of your Excellency, come to augment the consternation of the inhabitants. I have too exalted an opinion of the humanity of the English people, and of yours in particular, to think that you will wish to render our condition more deplorable. However, if . . . you are inclined to draw down upon yourself the execration of all nations, to cover yourself with disgrace in the eyes of the whole universe, by oppressing the unfortunate and attacking those who are supposed to be incapable of defence, I declare to you that the garrison under my orders, accustomed to behold death with serene countenance, and to brave dangers much greater than all the perils of war, know how to make resistance, which shall not terminate

*At the time, vinegar was the standard disinfectant at sea; it has, in fact, only a limited antiseptic effect. Beaufort speaks in 1794 of hoping a 'disorder' on the *Phaeton* had been checked after the ship was 'fumigated with Powder Devils [a priming made of damped and bruised gunpowder] and washed . . . in hot vinegar; we keep these vinegar lamps burning. . . .'

but with their entire destruction. I hope that the answer of your Excellency will inform me whether I am to speak the language of consolation to the unfortunate inhabitants, or whether I am to rouse them to indignation and revenge.

May God preserve your Excellency!
T. de Morla

Oct. 5, 1800

The earlier historians, Brenton and James, assumed that it was this appeal, so deftly drafted to touch the conscience of a race professing the principles of Christ and cricket, that led the British to turn about and set sail back to Gibraltar.[16] As it happened, however, the appeal was rejected and arrangements were put in the hands of Captain Morris and Captain (later Admiral) Alexander Cochrane to effect a landing north of Rota just outside the Bay of Cadiz. Beaufort's journal gives a sour report of what soon became a fiasco. The commanders, as he saw it, thought the plague was to their advantage, and envisioned 'an easy conquest of the first Spanish arsenal, whose defenders, never very resolute, now had their numbers thinned and their minds enervated by the disease.' They ordered *Phaeton* to make soundings and explorations of the best landing spot, with Beaufort and the frigate's master doing the work.

Beaufort himself, meanwhile, was exploding with frustration, realizing that although the army had been assembled for seventeen days at Gibraltar, no plans for landing had been made. Moreover, there were no signs of any Spanish deployments to defend the shore.

Finally, two days later, a landing plan was agreed on – Beaufort thought it the clumsiest one possible – and the first forces were assembled on the night of 7 October for landing at daylight. Thereupon it began to rain heavily, then rain squalls increased in intensity and the whole enterprise was cancelled. Beaufort vented his rage in his journal:[17]

Thus ended this important expedition [which] as far as depended on orders from home seemed well planned, but all that was left to the assessments of the great men here was . . . disgraceful.

. . . waiting three weeks at Gibraltar and having rendezvoused there must have shewn the merest blockhead in Europe their intentions. At length they came out – *without a pilot or a guide from Gibraltar*, without a plan of attack or even the place of disembarkation agreed on. They arrived and three days elapsed in reconnoitring and resolution and countermanding, etc., and the fourth away we went with as little appearance of reason as any of their other proceedings.

That neither admiral nor general were sincere or hearty in the business was evident.

Beaufort was convinced that the commanders simply used the threat of infection to the invading forces as an excuse for their 'want of vigour, decision, foresight and ability', and that the ostensible reason for the cancellation 'can never account or atone for wasting the best equipped army of 21 000 men bearing musquets that England almost ever dispatched'.

9
San Josef: 'Glory' (1800-1801)

. . . nearly suffocated with blood internally, and 5 times fainting from loss of blood externally, in this situation laying upon the hard and wet deck, exposed to accidents in the dark from the zeal and eagerness of my own people, from the fire of the Fangarolle forts, and from a repetition of the goodnatured blunderbuss which had before selected me . . . you will confess I had but little prospect of ever hugging you again. . . .

BEAUFORT to Fanny Edgeworth[1]

On 28 October 1800, aboard the *Phaeton,* Beaufort penned an almost illegible scrawl to his father:

I have never dissembled or deceived my dearest parents in anything respecting my health, I therefore expect implicit belief. A Spanish King's polacre of 14 guns from 24 pounds to 4 lay in a tempting situation altho under Fangarolle [Fuengirola] castle near Melino. Your son had the honour of leading the boats upon the night of the 27th to the attack, but suffice it at present to say that after a short conflict my brave fellows carried her. I saw us complete masters of the deck and then I sank wounded in more places than one but none are now *dangerous.* – The Captain's behaviour to me on this occasion is beyond everything I could have expected. He has written in the most handsome manner to Lord Keith and spoken to him too and is now writing L^d. Spencer [First Lord of the Admiralty]. Some time ago I happened to tell him that I was related to Lady Spencer. He asked me if I had any objection to his mentioning that in his letter. I said no and he has done it. Was that wrong? The particulars of this business you may expect in my next. Till then be assured I am fast recovering – God bless you all

F. Beaufort

He was telling considerably less than the truth. The 'more places than one' where he was wounded in fact totalled nineteen: three sabre cuts and sixteen slugs from a blunderbuss fired point-blank at him. He was not recovering and he knew it; he was near death. That in such a situation he could worry at a possible social *faux pas* leaves one gasping.

On 27 October the *Phaeton* had chased a Spanish polacre (a three-masted Mediterranean brig) to an anchorage under the five protective guns of the fortress of Fuengirola, where the frigate dared not follow. She was a valuable prospective prize, with two long English iron 24-pounders in the bow and in the stern, all of 'beautiful Spanish brass', two 18-pounders, four long 12-pounders and six swivel 4-pounders.[2]

Beaufort had probably persuaded Morris to give him approval for a venture of the sort that Stopford had refused. His journal entry, obviously written several days or weeks later, begins the story. At 1 a.m. on the 28th

I went away with the Pinnace, two 5-oared cutters and the launch with carronade. . . .

At 3 o/c arrived in shore in smooth water, where I intended laying by a few minutes, to rest the peoples' arms after so fatiguing a pull. . . . But the alarm being given on the beach, and fires, musquets etc. communicating our station to the ship, I had no time to hesitate but pushed on directly.

We soon discovered her and, what was not expected, another vessel at anchor close to her bows [It was a French privateer brig that had slipped in unseen earlier in the night]. Had the launch been in company we might have divided to the attack, but with three boats I preferred making sure of our original object.

When with[in] about two cutter lengths she fired a few shots but without other effect than as a signal for us to rush on & giving inspiring cheer, I soon found myself under the S[tarboard] M[ain] chains. She was soon carried as the officers and sailors had deserted the deck and nobody remained upon it but the marines, who indeed defended it bravely.

Ten days after what he called '*ma petite affaire* at Fangarolle', and lying in a hospital bed, Beaufort described the next events in a long letter to his brother. If the thirty-four seamen aboard the Spaniard had fled below, there were still twenty marines to be dealt with by a boarding party whose numbers could have been little, if any larger. A seaman was shot and killed as the boats came alongside. At the same time a midshipman, Charles Augustus Hamilton, who was to become

Beaufort's lifelong friend, was wounded in the thigh and a lieutenant of marines, Duncan Campbell, was wounded slightly.

The construction of the polacre, with the hull projecting outwards at deck level, made her difficult to board. In the ascent the attackers were deprived of the use of their swords, hung by cord loops to their wrist to free their hands for climbing.

Beaufort was first aboard, taking two sabre cuts in the head and one in the shin as he mounted. The weapon was razor-sharp but the initial cut was somewhat minimized by a silk pocket handkerchief Beaufort had folded inside his hat. Once he was on deck, however, a blunderbuss was fired at him point-blank. He was luckily turned sideways to the blast and took most of its slugs in his left arm and a few in the chest, but had those latter 'met with less resistance from my clothes, great parts of which was carried in, or altered their direction but very little, [they] would have been fatal'.

The shock staggered and wheeled me round but instantly recovering I returned to the charge, the exertion however of giving another blow quite exhausted me, and gratified with seeing the deck in our possession, I had just time to totter round, against the Caboose [cookhouse] and fainted. When I recovered I could hardly breathe and the blood in my throat collecting fast and wanting strength to spit it up I fainted 4 times more when, having spit up a good deal of blood and lost a vast deal at my wounds, I breathed a little easier, but continued some hours laying on deck quite exhausted and in great pain till we joined the *Phaeton*.

After a short but furious fight on deck, and under the fire from the fort's guns above and musketry shots from the French brig nearby, the ship was carried.

At the moment I had got possession I received my last wound, and had only time [before fainting] to order the cables to be cut which I had forbid till she was fairly carried, and to desire Lieut Huish to carry on the war. Her sails were immed^y. loosed and she was soon out of reach of the Fort who however continued firing.

The prize was not able to rejoin the *Phaeton* until 8 a.m. because, in early light, the frigate had spotted another small Spanish polacre and sailed off to capture her. Once reunited, the prisoners were transferred, the wounded seen to and the body of the dead seaman committed to the deep: then the *Phaeton* made for Gibraltar where Beaufort was transferred to the hospital. The prize carried two names, the *San Josef* alias

L'Aglia. She was under the command of a French ensign; her losses were thirteen men wounded, six of them gravely.

Writing to his commander-in-chief, Lord Keith, Captain Norris said he was convinced that 'more determined Bravery could not have been displayed than has been shown by Lieutenants Beaufort and Huish, Lieutenant Duncan Campbell of the Marines, Messrs Hamilton and Stanton, Midshipmen, and Mr Deagon the Gunner and the Boats Crews'. It was incumbent on him, he added, to express his hope that 'Mr Beaufort's Conduct and wounds will entitle him to the protection [*sic*] given in the present War to Officers of distinguished Merit'.

Back aboard the *Phaeton*, Beaufort was bled forty ounces – two pints – in the succeeding forty-eight hours, fainting in the process but aware from the faces of his ministrants – as they later confessed – that they had little hope of his recovery. On 2 November, he wrote to his father in a bad scrawl that he was no worse but, inconsistently and probably more honestly, he added that his sending his family his ardent love 'is probably one of the last actions of my life'.

But recovery took place nonetheless. The most dangerous of the slugs, one that penetrated his left breast and into his lungs, he wrote to his brother some days later,

has not yet been nor will now be discovered. Yet as no inflammatory symptoms have as yet taken place, as the expectoration of clotted blood has these several days totally ceased, and as the oppressive pain or difficulty of inspiring daily abates, I may safely conclude that nothing of consequence has suffered from his unwelcome visit there, and most probably when he finds how much his mischievous intentions are disappointed, when he gets accustomed to his confinement and when I begin to leave mine, he will form a little bed or cyst for himself and quietly remain entombed there for the remainder of his days, or rather of mine. . . .

The slug did indeed remain forever embedded, causing Beaufort chest pains intermittently throughout his life. Other wounds in the side seem to have healed swiftly but those in his arm, 'into one of which I could just cram my inkbottle', took more time, as did one in his left hand which rendered three fingers 'cold and senseless' for a considerable period. A year later, in his memorial for a pension, he claimed the loss of use of his left arm, but as in most such petitions, the disability was probably overstated. Nevertheless, it was at least three years before he could begin to make effective use of his arm.

Recounting the episode, the historian James allowed himself some indignation about the sequel:[3]

Being a fine sailing little vessel, the *San-Josef* was immediately commissioned as a British sloop of war under the name of *Calpe*, the ancient name of Gibraltar. It would have gratified us to be able to state, that the officer, who as conductor of the enterprise had so gallantly and effectively co-operated, as well as so seriously suffered, in capturing the vessel, an officer 'in whom,' says Captain Morris, 'I have found a most capable and zealous assistant,' had been appointed to command her. But Vice-Admiral Lord Keith . . . chose to appoint to the *Calpe* an officer who, whatever may have been his merit in other respects, was both junior to Lieutenant Beaufort, and an utter stranger to the transaction at Fuengirola.*

But Beaufort was scarcely in a position to command his life, much less a warship. Nine months were to pass before he was sufficiently recovered to board a ship for home. But, as was the customary sequel to captures of the sort Beaufort made, he was promptly promoted commander and, on paper, given the sloop *Ferret*, on 13 November. The *Ferret* was a fire-ship and Beaufort's appointment to her was purely nominal. He never set foot on her.

We can only guess how much blood Beaufort lost in the darkness on the *San Josef*'s decks to be reckoned as addition to the two pints he was bled over the next two days, and we can only wonder how anyone with his wounds, suffering the inevitable shock from them, and so leeched, could have survived. But the total blood lost was obviously sufficient, if not over-abundant, to cure his six years of *porphyria cutanea tarda*. In a letter to his father ten months later, Beaufort thanked God that his '*untoward*' disease was entirely gone. He never wrote of it again. It is almost certain that he was forbidden liquor for some months, and he notes that for four weeks after the affray he was denied 'inflammatory food' including wine and meat. A few years later he speaks of being able to tolerate butter again, which suggests that for a long time he ate no fats. However accidentally – horribly accidentally – it came about, his treatment was appropriate for the symptomatic porphyria brought about by a liver malfunction which he had so long endured.

*The man appointed was the Hon. G. H. L. Dundas, a member of the prominent Scottish family of that name allied politically to Pitt. Its most prominent figure, Viscount Melville, was Treasurer of the Navy at the time, and soon to become First Lord.

In a few weeks he was well enough to worry about his future: a ship that should have brought him new orders had been captured by the French and he admitted that 'I am a *little* curious; you see, my dear father, that notwithstanding the *awakening* blow I have not yet abandoned all worldly and ambitious hopes.'

A passing British ship transferred him from Gibraltar to the English Naval Hospital at Almade, near Lisbon, where it was believed the good climate would hasten his recovery. The voyage, however, was injurious: the largest hole in his arm deepened to the size of an oyster before he got to his hospital bed on Christmas Day. Thereafter, however, improvement followed and within weeks he was hiking, riding, shooting and taking sizable excursions, including one to 'a house kept by an Englishwoman – an old faggot who has given a lucky young Dutchman a moiety of her bed & profits for the same reason that Kate the 2nd preferred that nation for her household officers!'

The convalescent also found time to fall in love, but not very seriously. He wrote briefly and without much detail to his brother William saying that the young lady, whom he did not identify, had an 'inexhaustible flow of spirits' and 'a confounded deal of wit' and would inherit £6000 or £7000 from a seventy-seven-year-old aunt. The maiden professed her love but Beaufort was 'dubious of the sincerity of my Dulcinia [*sic*]' since he claimed never to have discovered anything in himself to attract a female of wit and beauty. He confessed that his attachment was not so deep but that he could shake it off if necessary. This he seems to have done without much pain; we never hear of his 'Dulcinia' again.

Fears about his professional prospects deepened in letter after letter. By February he was told he should stay in Portugal a year or more and, if he were to enjoy a healthy remainder of his life, to give up the Navy, 'without promotion, without pension, on my half-pay'. To his father he confessed that he had very serious apprehensions about being able to serve again.

Concluding by midsummer 1801 that he had exhausted whatever benefit the climate might offer, he embarked on the frigate *Anson* to return to England. Worry, daydreaming and reminiscences combined to give him a troubled passage. He arrived in London on 1 September 1801 to unburden himself to his father with a letter written during the voyage:

Shall I be employed? Or shall I be consigned to oblivion? If the former –
When? – *Where?* How? . . . All depends upon others, the [Admiralty
medical] faculty, the admiralty, and Bonaparte being the quorum who must
decide upon my fate. This much I know that as any of these opinions yet
uppermost in my mind, or succeed each other which they do very rapidly,
that they affect me very differently according to the mood I happen to be in –
the flood or ebb of my spirits, or the degree of, or absense of, this pain in my
breast. . . . After dwelling for instance upon the heroick actions of some
tragedy character, changing . . . from a Gustavus to Coriolanus, from a wolf
to a Hawk, you cannot conceive how my little body swells with ambition.
I shut my book, slouch my hat and strutting about the quarter deck, in
imagination take perhaps the combined fleet with a single ship, or 'plucking
bright honour etc.', march in company with the doughty lord of Hawksbury
to the gates of Paris. On the contrary, if something more serious or moral
happens to have been my morning's food, such as the emptiness of ambition,
the worthlessness of the praise of the mob, or should any subject recall my
attention to my infirmities, the blessings of health, or the delights of content
and a country life, I pitch the service to the devil, and build some nice little
whitewashed cot, covered with woodbines and jipamines, and bargaining
for [constant?] spring, think myself the happiest of mortals cultivating my
cabbages on my half-pay! . . .

I have heard or read very cogent arguments against this castle-building.
But though probably *not one* of all my airy projects ever succeeded or came
to pass, *yet*, as I never found any ill consequences from allowing a warm
imagination to transport me for a short time into the regions of fancy from
some unpleasant scene where I was kicking my heels, I cannot pay them
sufficient deference to abandon a companion who so often soothed the bed
of pain and sickness, whose conversation has rendered me insensible to the
rain or storm, and who without a murmur accommodates herself to every
humour. . . .

Sept. 1st. London, I have just alighted in this gay town, and of course as
yet know nothing of my destiny. . . .

10

Ireland
(1801-1805)

> . . . 32 and no employment, no wife, no shilling and
> no hope.
>
> BEAUFORT to his brother[1]

Beaufort learned his destiny soon enough: to be cast ashore on a barren beach for more than four fruitless years. It was a time when his melancholy began an unhappy flowering in its least attractive forms: self-pity and recurrent bitterness. His failure to have been rewarded as he thought he should for the capture of the *San Josef* intensified a seething conviction that he was forever the victim of injustice. The sour taste was often in his mouth to the end of his life. Now and then it was washed out by his achievements and appropriate honours, but it always recurred.

As soon as he arrived in London in September 1801, he presented himself to Lord St Vincent, appointed First Lord of the Admiralty by the Addington government seven months earlier. He asked for a ship, which was his due as a new commander, and he wanted also to be 'posted,' i.e. promoted formally to the rank of captain, which was not his due inasmuch as he had only just been raised from lieutenant to commander. He was 'affably received', but however much the great man 'lamented' Beaufort's situation and agreed that no candidate had greater claims, a host of others had equal ones and − the crux of the matter − had been waiting vainly for vacancies much longer. They would have to be taken care of first; there was no telling when Beaufort's turn might come.

Although John Jervis, the hero of Cape St Vincent, was deeply involved in party politics,[2] there is no reason to question the justice or disinterestedness of his reply. Negotiations leading to the Peace of Amiens had begun as early as the preceding March and St Vincent certainly knew of them. The prospects, accordingly, were for fewer British warships in commission. If personal animosity against Beaufort was to be a factor later, as he insisted, it was almost certainly not the case then. For all his mean-spiritedness and foolish intrigues, St Vincent was the staunchest opponent of 'interest' and the sturdiest partisan of merit to have held the office of First Lord up to that time.

St Vincent advised Beaufort to apply for a pension. That was a world away from Beaufort's wishes but for the moment there appeared to be little else to hope for. He therefore made his application and was 'examined touching the state of my Carcase at Surgeon's Hall where I was bravely framed and fingered in my buff'.

Next day, he drew up his memorial to the King, describing his successful capture of a fourteen-gun ship of His Catholic Majesty and his nineteen wounds 'such that after a tedious and painful confinement of 8 months, he finds himself nearly deprived of the use' of his arm.

If there was a certain inconsistency in asking for the command of a warship one day and pleading the next for compensation for a disabled arm, the sufficient answer is that Nelson could command a fleet minus an arm – and an eye.

Beaufort was ultimately awarded his pension, of £45 12s. 6d. a year, in addition to half-pay. In later years, if not then, he was embittered at the niggardly amount but deeply disappointed as he was, he did not consider himself unjustly dealt with at the time in his failure to win a new command. In London two months later, after the preliminary agreements to the Peace of Amiens had been made public, he wrote to his brother, 'I candidly confess that I have no claims for another ship. . . . Employment if even possible to procure I would not accept in peace – at any rate yet.'

Before returning to Ireland, there to enter into a bucolic life for a time or forever, Beaufort had a second meeting with St Vincent, by no means as agreeable as the first. He discovered that the First Lord had recommended a rejection of his pension on the grounds that he had already received a promotion for his wounds. Yet it had been St Vincent who initially had advised Beaufort to seek the pension; the latter at once assumed that he had been treated with gross duplicity. However, the report of the surgeons had never reached St Vincent;

Beaufort discovered the office where it had gone astray and informed the First Lord. Ultimately, the grant was approved but ill-will had been generated and Beaufort realized it. He wrote to his father, 'Great men do not like either to confess to any irregularity at their boards or recast their opinions.'

The seeds were sown for a bitter harvest: Beaufort was later to repeat that St Vincent was the only enemy that he was conscious of ever having made, and that his prospects were hopeless as long as the old man held office. All too soon his initial recognition that St Vincent had not been unfair in denying him a command were forgotten, to be replaced by a burning insistence that he had been cruelly discriminated against.

Despite his declaration of unwillingness to serve in the Navy in peacetime, Beaufort was obviously distressed at leaving it. His letters to his brother, to whom he was more frank than to his parents, were melancholy. And, as always, his too voluble protestations that he was content and resigned were the surest proof that he was not.

By February 1802 he was reunited with his family in Collon. He had written ahead to ask his father to equip him with a good horse and servant, whom he had found he could not happily do without, for 'I am grown bachelorish'.

He did not remain long, returning to London by 1 May 1802, once again to press for appointment and promotion. No evidence survives to explain this renewed campaign which would seem to have been forlorn from the outset, the Peace of Amiens having been signed on 25 March and the prospect being a reduction in the active Fleet. It is probable that Beaufort had been pressed by family and friends who, at a distance, fancied that he could enlist effective 'interest' for himself.

One can only speculate about what occurred from Beaufort's later comments, reported above, of the enmity that St Vincent had conceived towards him. He probably importuned the noble Earl too hard and too often. St Vincent, Leslie Gardiner has written, was, despite his previous heroic acts and his battle against 'interest', an evil-tempered, mean-spirited and conceited man who pursued pointless vendettas with his juniors with the single-mindedness he once showed in hunting down the enemy at sea.[3]*

*Professor Lewis recounts (*A Social History of the Navy*, pp. 56–8) a monstrous piece of St Vincent's vindictiveness toward an over-eager applicant.

Once again, Beaufort insisted that he was not 'bluedevilled and dejected' by his failure. He wrote that 'all my airy castles of *bloody victories* would bow their heads to the more placid and tranquil picture of spending the *remainder* of my life in the bosom *of my family*! At this my mother and you will shake your heads and smile at the resolves of one who so often mounts a fresh hobby horse. Be it so.'

Dr and Mrs Beaufort might well have shaken their heads for their son was writing nonsense. His problem was not one of forever going off on a new course, however much he prattled of repeated decisions to do just that; it was, instead, a problem of being unable to be inconstant. He had lost his heart to the Navy.

Back in Collon by midsummer, Beaufort set out to find and buy a farm, meeting frustration on every attempt. He dabbled with the idea of becoming a surveyor but concluded that the expectable monetary return would be too meagre. One fruitless month followed another, the routine broken only in March 1803 when he and his sister Louisa accompanied their mother on a trip across the Irish Sea to Shrewsbury to consult Robert Warren Darwin, third son of Erasmus and father of Charles, who had set up a large medical practice there. For years Mrs Beaufort had suffered ill-health and had been particularly afflicted with a severe skin disease on her legs. Dr Darwin professed himself less concerned with Mrs Beaufort's legs than about her general health. Whatever his and her worries were about her ailments, they were not to carry the good woman off until she was ninety-four.

As early as April 1802, with news of worsening relations with France and a British government decision to order more ships into commission and make extensive Naval preparations, Beaufort at once notified the Admiralty that he was again ready for service.[4] There seems to have been no reply. A year later, in May 1803, the one-sided Peace of Amiens that Britain had foolishly accepted came to an end and hostilities were resumed. So also and at once were Beaufort's assaults on St Vincent. He seems to have been helped by a member of a prominent political family in the neighbourhood and by Lord Longford, a long-time friend and neighbour of Dr Beaufort. The details are unknown, only the result: a flat negative, along with a suggestion that he become an officer of the Sea Fencibles, a body of men raised for a limited period of service, junior to marines and senior to yeomen and volunteer militia.

Beaufort declared that he was astonished at St Vincent's implacability.

To serve in every sense of the word is my anxious wish and desire, and should I be appointed to the command of a bumboat or a cockleshell I will surely accept the appointment with as much zeal and alacrity as if it were to the *Endymion* or *Royal George* – but I would not *ask* for . . . an employment which at once defeats the leading objects (I confess) of my professional exertions – Avarice – Ambition. In a troopship, or even a convoy armed vessel, perseverance, cash, good luck may probably stumble one in the way of enterprize, may afford one a chance, but a captain of Sea Fencibles, unless he is accommodated with a command at his own door, can have no other avocation than to dream of battles, or to demolish the fortifications of Dunkirk in concert with a Corporal Trim and a Widow Wadman.*

This is Beaufort at his worst, sententiously proclaiming his patriotism and selflessness in the one breath and in the next his personal interest.

But in a period otherwise disappointing and bootless, Beaufort acquired one new friend who was to affect his life profoundly. This was his until then unknown brother-in-law, Richard Lovell Edgeworth, one of the most remarkable and fascinating men on the Irish scene. Despite the publication of his autobiography and a biography, and extensive and sensitive treatment of his life in a study by his once famous novelist daughter,[5] posterity has yet to grant that difficult but admirable polymath the recognition he deserves. Only one of his claims to eminence was that he was the educator, collaborator and inspiring influence of his daughter Maria Edgeworth, who was among the most renowned and admired best-selling women authors in the early nineteenth century. In his own right, Edgeworth was a savant, inventor, engineer, mechanical innovator, enlightened landowner, liberal politician, radical educationalist and champion of civil rights, a true son of the Age of Reason.

Occasional correspondence between him and Dr Beaufort had ripened into fast friendship by about 1796. Though their homes in Collon, County Lough, and Edgeworthstown, County Longford, were forty-five miles apart as the crow flies and much more over the wretched roads of the time, the two men corresponded continually and visited each other frequently.

Late in 1797 Edgeworth was widowed for the third time. Within

*Two characters in Sterne's *Tristram Shandy*.

two months he asked Dr Beaufort for the hand of his eldest child, Frances Anne (Fanny). She had met Edgeworth through his sister, Mrs Margaret Ruxton, who lived at Black Castle, near Navan, and with whom she had formed a close friendship. It was at Mrs Ruxton's suggestion that Frances was called on to do some illustrations for a new edition of Maria Edgeworth's famous book of children's stories, *Parent's Assistant*. Frances was twenty-eight, Edgeworth fifty-three, the father of sixteen children of whom fourteen were still living.

At first, and understandably, Maria was deeply opposed to the prospect of her father bringing into the household where she had been his almost inseparable confidante, secretary and collaborator, an intelligent woman a year younger than herself to be her stepmother. Soon, getting to know Frances better, she became reconciled and ultimately well content. The relationship grew almost at once into a deep and happy friendship.

Beaufort first visited Edgeworthstown when he returned to Ireland after his initial attempt in London to obtain a new command had failed. For someone who had been at sea almost uninterruptedly for a dozen years it was a new world of culture and intellectual stimulus. The house was a literary centre, visited by publishers and other friends and admirers of Maria and her father. Edgeworth himself was also in regular contact with distinguished figures throughout England and Ireland, politicians, scientists and in particular his old associates in the famous Lunar Society of Birmingham, a group of savants, industrialists and engineers whose common passion was what today would be termed technology. They included such men as Erasmus Darwin, the industrialists Matthew Boulton, Dr William Small and Josiah Wedgwood, the engineer James Watt and the industrial chemist James Keir.

The efforts of Beaufort to buy a farm or to rejoin the Navy having continued in vain for more than eighteen weary months, it was probably with gratitude and relief that he embraced an offer from Edgeworth to join him in a new and intriguing project: the construction of a telegraph – which is to say a semaphore system – across the breadth of Ireland, from Dublin to Galway. Its purpose was military, to alert the capital in the event of French forces landing on the west coast.

Edgeworth's interest in signal communications had been born years before. In 1766, as a young man of twenty-two escaping as best he could from an unloved wife and a boring household near London, he fell into the company of a fashionable, fast-living, hard-gambling set of gay blades in the capital, among them a prematurely ageing rake named Sir Francis Delaval. One one occasion in their midst one of the companions, Lord March, related how he had set up a fast relay of horses to bring him word by nine that evening of the outcome of a famous two-horse match to be run at Newmarket. He believed he would be first to know the winner and said he would 'manage my bets accordingly',[6] a phrase that raises considerable doubts about the noble lord's probity. Edgeworth promptly bet him £500 that he could obtain the same information by five o'clock. Delaval, ignorant of how it would be done but trusting his younger friend, put down a further £500 on Edgeworth's side. Once alone, Edgeworth explained to Delavel what he proposed to do: set up a series of towers or pillars on high ground, flying windmill sails or pointers, along the approximately fifty-five to sixty-mile stretch from Newmarket to London. Pre-arrangements for the position of the sails would indicate which horse had won.

Certain of success – he later constructed some of the apparatus around London to prove that the system worked – he and Delaval offered to double their bets. The other side agreed. But, always an honourable man even in scapegrace company, Edgeworth informed March and his friends that he was not depending on horses to carry the news but on other, presumably mechanical, contrivances. 'My opponents thanked me for my candour, reconsidered the matter and declined to bet,' Edgeworth recounted; 'my friends blamed me extremely for giving up such an advantageous speculation.'

What Edgeworth had done was to invent the world's first semaphore system depending on movable indicators, almost three decades before the man who is credited with having done so. But his mechanical passions were episodic as well as multitudinous. His interest in telegraphic signals lapsed until 1794 when news came to Britain of the semaphore developed in France by Citizen Claude Chappe. Nettled at credit going to another man for what he had devised twenty-eight years before,* Edgeworth returned to his former creation, refined it, set up

*Edgeworth in fact accused Chappe of plagiarizing his invention. On 27 November 1796 he wrote to Dr Beaufort: '. . . two years ago when my Tellograph was first shown at Collon somebody there described it in such a manner as to instruct the French how to emulate it, which they have since done, and since my Tellograph was shown to the Duke of York, his . . . Chaplain has put up the second hand French Tellograph to disguise his imitation of mine, but that shan't pass.'[7] Chappe's instrument, however, was a rather different device although its principle was identical with that conceived by Edgeworth.

two effective demonstrations in Ireland and succeeded, with a third, in sending signals across the Irish Sea to the coast of England. In the summer of 1795 he read to the Royal Irish Academy a long, flowery and elaborate paper, entitled 'An ESSAY on the ART of CONVEYING SECRET and SWIFT INTELLIGENCE' in which he sought to establish his claim of priority and described in detail the new semaphore machine he proposed to erect.

From early 1795 until late 1796 Edgeworth busied himself attempting to persuade the Dublin government of the need to set up a chain of his semaphores across the island. By September 1796 rumours of a French invasion of Ireland were rife and, in fact, a massive one was vainly attempted in Bantry Bay in December. But after initial encouragement, Edgeworth was flatly rebuffed. He was furious and let it be known that he was going to leave Ireland since he did not see how it could be defended.

But the Irish Rebellion of 1798, the actual landing of 1200 French troops in Ireland in August of that year, another attempted foray a few weeks later in which Wolfe Tone was captured, and Emmet's rising in Dublin in 1803, combined to change the government's mind and to accept a renewed proposal of Edgeworth. At once Edgeworthstown went into a flurry of activity. Edgeworth's yeomanry and some tenants were formed into a corps to build thirty stations on a line Dublin–Athlone–Galway and to man and operate them. Beaufort was enlisted as Edgeworth's first lieutenant and 'Everyone at Edgeworthstown who could read and write was set to work that October making two full copies of the code.'[8]

Unfortunately, the 'Tellograph'* Edgeworth had dreamed up was a pure monstrosity. To be sure, all such communication devices of that time were awful to a greater or lesser degree, but Edgeworth's may have had pride of place. The simplicity of a binary cipher – a concept at least as old as the Greeks, who signalled by alternately displaying and obscuring a torch – had been forgotten and was not to be recovered until the 1830s with Baron Schilling's right- and left-turning needle telegraph, and Steinheil's and Morse's dots and dashes.

Even Chappe's device, an upright pole crossed with a T-beam with

---

*Edgeworth explained to the Irish Academy that he coined the word because '*telegraph* is a proper name for a machine which describes at a distance. *Telelograph*, or contractedly Tellograph, is a proper name for a machine that describes *words* at a distance.' And that, indeed, was the trouble with it.

wig-wag members at both ends, was more capacious and flexible than Edgeworth's. The Admiralty's machine, clattering signals from White-hall to the Channel ports from 1795 to 1816 on huge shutter boards carrying six panels that could be flipped in combinations from black to white, was easier to read. But the flaw in all of them was that although they could indicate individual numbers or letters, they were meant to be read in groups of numbers, each group being a code-word. Thus they compelled the use of a code-book for every signal, 'as though soldiers or sailors under fire, or in peril from ship-wreck or other disasters, would be in a position to pull out pencil and paper and telegraphic dictionary, and calmly go through the process of coding and decoding'.[9] Spelling out words (even code-words) by letters permits a single garble, or even more, to be recognized without having it destroy the entire message. That is, in context, d-i-s-c-e-e-n-e-d can easily be discerned, but a single mistaken digit—say 7321 for 7325 in Edgeworth's code – would be the difference between 'All is quiet' and 'The French have landed at . . .'[10]

Edgeworth's code-book, as described to the Irish Academy, was a behemoth almost four feet high and two feet wide, of forty-nine pages each folded in the middle, and divided into seven parts, each of seven pages, separated by thin strips of mahogany. Each page contained forty-nine words. The repeating factor of seven was conditioned by the signalling device itself, four isosceles triangles mounted on pillars fifteen to twenty feet high, revolving like the hand of a clock so that the apex or pointer could describe a full circle. Edgeworth concluded that eight separate positions of the pointer could be distinguished with a good glass at twenty miles: upright, 45°, 90° and so on at 45° intervals, thus able to represent numbers from 0 to 7. The triangle on the viewer's right would give a number in thousands, the next in hundreds, the next in tens and the last in units. The various positions admitted of enough thousands of combinations to accommodate even the abstruse words Edgeworth chose to put in his code as, for example, the place names on the first page, ranging from such likely spots as Armagh and Athlone to Abydos, Acadia, Aleppo, Acapulco, Agin-court, Angola, Antioch, Aix-la-Chapelle and Abyssinia. It can only be deduced that Edgeworth foresaw a far-flung Napoleonic campaign with classical overtones. It is also difficult to envisage just what military circumstances might arise that would necessitate the signal transmission of such words as ablative, absolution, ace, abacus, acantha, achromatic, adder's tongue, adoscalation [*sic*] and adracanth. There was even a code group for a *grande finale*, 'Articles of capitulation agreed to', although one is left to guess whose capitulation Edgeworth expected.

By 1803 he had simplified his equipment considerably, reducing the code-book to portable proportions and the signal towers from four to one, having realized that one pointer put through four positions successively would do the work of four with one-fourth the manpower and equipment although at the cost of four times the transmission time. What he apparently did not take into account was Irish weather. The days in Ireland when visibility is possible from Dublin to Galway for each fifteen- to twenty-mile interval at about the same hour in the day are not, to understate the matter, terribly frequent.

Edgeworth's contrivance probably originated from his first experiments in London three decades before using windmill sails spread in different positions. As so often happens in the world of science and technology, an initial notion on theory or practice tends to quarantine the mind, shutting out thoughts of a different approach.

By late November Beaufort was in Edgeworthstown, eagerly at work supervising carpenters building the first fifteen towers and drilling and disciplining the yeomanry who were to man them. Before Christmas he set out to wrangle with the Dublin officials on budgets and a host of legal matters on leases and finances,[11] and thereafter set out on the work of constructing the stations. It was gruelling work in the Irish winter; for the most part Beaufort was distressed. When at one point it appeared that the incredibly duplicitous and niggling Dublin authorities were intent on diddling him out of the pay he was to receive (as if employed as a captain of the Sea Fencibles) he wrote to his father that remuneration was only a secondary object: '. . . at all counts I shall have the satisfaction of having *bestowed* six months' labours of mind and body – six months' privation of your society – six months' anxiety, six colds, six thoracic pains, six diarrhoeas – and six months' pay.'

Beaufort had seen from the outset that semi-illiterate peasantry were not going to be ideal telegraphers; his worries mounted as time went on. In March, by which time the chain from Athlone to Dublin had been completed, he noted that a test transmission had been made in eleven or twelve minutes, but this was probably between himself and Edgeworth or Edgeworth's son, Henry, who had been enlisted in the project. The men's practice was still insufficient and Beaufort hoped

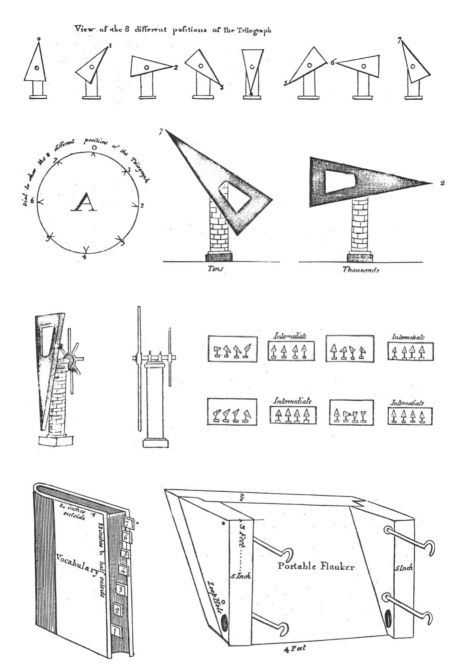

Richard Lovell Edgeworth's sketches for his 'Tellograph'; by permission of the National Library of Ireland.

that with training the speed could be increased. But, he fretted, there was the 'casual smoke of Dublin – and the storm which always blows on the top of Caston Tower'. All that, he told his father, 'is between you and I – for he is a dirty bird who ——— his own nest'. Matters grew no better as the line was extended west of Athlone to Galway in April, via a station 'called by the soft and harmonious name of Knockaghlaghtagh'.

Even in June, when the weather should not have been such a problem, garbles were the rule. Work sheets, now in the National Library of Ireland, show that during a twenty-day period when Henry was to be absent, he had set his men in Dublin a daily exercise of sending half a dozen groups, each of from four to six digits, across the island and having them repeated on the return transmission. Half of the days weather blocked the operation entirely; for the rest, scarcely a dozen groups were accurately returned.

The gala opening of the 'tellograph' in early July in the presence of the Lord Lieutenant of Ireland was a fiasco, the messages to and from Dublin both slow and wrong. Beaufort, still engrossed in his work, was sure that with time the system would improve and that there would be general rejoicing. But by late July he must have known the enterprise was a catastrophe. Reporting to Edgeworth on a test transmission which was a disaster, Beaufort exploded: 'Good Heavens, what does all this mean? Is it that after eight months' practice not one word out of the whole should come right? . . . I am almost out of my senses. Between today's failure, the inattention of all my stations and the attempt to twist a job out of you, I think there is cause enough.'[12]

The last item in Beaufort's cry of despair referred to the news that the authorities were moving to take the telegraph operation away from Edgeworth. Dublin did in fact oust Edgeworth a few weeks later and turned the telegraph over to the Army. Another officer was named to take over Beaufort's job. Beaufort gathered up Edgeworth's men at the various stations and led them back to their home.

The telegraph was apparently never put to useful service and after a time was abandoned. Since Napoleon never attempted another landing it was no great loss – except to Edgeworth's pride and purse: he had himself defrayed half the cost, putting out between £500 and £800, and for years afterwards was dunned by the government in Dublin for various expenses.

St Vincent, Beaufort's implacable enemy, had left office with the return of Pitt in May 1804. Beaufort could assume that he once again had a chance, this time with the new First Lord of the Admiralty, Henry Dundas, Viscount Melville. He assumed further that his way had been paved by a recommendation to Melville from Lord Hardwicke, the Lord Lieutenant of Ireland during the time the telegraph project was authorized and constructed. He had begun his campaign from Ireland in the spring of 1804 and probably felt by late autumn it was time to pursue it in person.

The result was shattering. He discovered on being received by Melville that Hardwicke had merely forwarded a letter from some other person asking that Melville give Beaufort an audience. Melville then fetched out Beaufort's dossier, 'diverted himself by reading half a dozen pages', and demanded to know if he had renewed his offer of services. Beaufort replied that he had not done so since the date he received an order from the Admiralty, apparently some time before, to place himself under the services of Admiral James Hawkins Whitshed, Naval adviser to the Lord Lieutenant of Ireland and head of the Sea Fencibles. He went on to say he had written to Whitshed but left Ireland before receiving a reply.

Melville, an arrogant man who had been Solicitor-General and Lord Advocate of Scotland, was in his element. 'Are you not then in a disagreeable situation – You have applied for orders and you avoided receiving them,' he said.

'He had me there,' Beaufort wrote to his family, 'and Mr Garrow* could not have run me harder in a cross-examination.'

Melville dismissed Beaufort curtly, telling him no promotion was in store for him and instructing him to go to the secretariat of the Admiralty and renew his offer of service.

Beaufort was first drowned in gloom and then enraged.

My wrongs shall furnish me with . . . a tongue, my services, my incontrovertible claims, and my professional but injured character shall – not *plead* for me – but compel attention. Attonement [*sic*] and justice are perhaps too much to expect from one whose only measure of merits is influence, and whose right hand perhaps never signed a commission 'till he had value received in his left.

*A famous barrister of the day.

The reference was to Melville who, six weeks after Beaufort had first seen him, had been plunged into the deepest political trouble. A Royal Commission had investigated his tenure of the Navy Treasurer's office some years earlier and had been disrespectfully treated by him. In revenge the Commission exposed certain malpractices of ten years before. The Whigs were gleeful: by striking at Melville they could hit Pitt.[13] The proceedings in the House of Commons were doubtless something of an antidote for the 'blue devils'. A vote of censure was carried and Melville resigned.

I can't describe the joy manifested in everybody's countenance at the decision against Lord M. [Beaufort wrote, sanctimoniously adding what was not true:] I pity him from the bottom of my heart, though I feel for the situation of a man who has enjoyed the highest offices, and the highest confidence for 30 years, and who is now precipitated into irretrievable disgrace. . . . [Beaufort continued, now in a more credible vein] I cannot but rejoice at the glorious practical proof our legislators have given of the excellence of our constitution – nor can I be sorry for a man in a personal view of the case who has treated me with duplicity and contempt.

Beaufort was not one to see an inconsistency when he himself committed it.

In two weeks Pitt, who survived the crisis, named as Melville's successor Sir Charles Middleton, by now Lord Barham, the greatest Naval administrator since Pepys. Beaufort wrote to him twice, and stayed in London, waiting. At last he sent a brusque reply: 'Your services are noted and placed against your name which was already entered on my list, but the number of Candidates out of employ puts it out of my power to make any promises whatsoever.'

II

Charlotte
(1802-1807)

For if thou dar'st not hope, thou dost not love.

BEAUFORT to his brother[1]

Before he left Ireland for his melancholy ordeal in London Edgeworthstown had become a magnet to capture not only Beaufort's mind but also his heart. He fell profoundly in love, apparently at first sight, with Edgeworth's nineteen-year-old daughter, Charlotte. His passion was as consuming as only a first love can be.

By the testimony of all who knew her and of two family sketches, Charlotte was a great beauty. The Edgeworths' Swiss publisher, Marc-Auguste Pictet, who visited them in 1801, described her as *'jolie, fraiche comme la rose'*, and her eyes full of intelligence.[2] Dr Beaufort, who was to involve himself in his son's cause, felt her 'charming' and 'deserving' not only for her beauty but for 'her manner, temper and talents'. Her father and her siblings adored her. Beaufort's sister Fanny, newly become Charlotte's stepmother, especially befriended her and the affection was fully returned. Fanny wrote[3] to one of her sisters: 'Charlotte looks like a May Bush, so sweet, so white, so neat & rather like the branch of sweet Lily of the Valley I have at this moment in my breast.'

Such of Charlotte's letters as have come down to us, written when she was twenty-one to members of her family and to Dr Beaufort (by then her 'dear Grand papa') and two of his daughters (a trifle older than she whom she teasingly addressed as 'Honor'd and most respected Aunts'), show her as gay, charming, out-going and unaffected.[4] The letters were written in 1802 when she, Maria, Fanny and Richard Lovell Edgeworth made a triumphant visit to Paris (during the Peace of Amiens) where Maria and her father were warmly received and the entire party fêted by a number of admirers. Charlotte was enchanted by the experience and to judge from Maria's and her father's letters, was herself enchanting. Her letters are largely 'journalizing' ones, but reveal the writer as without guile, full of affection and with a heart soon made glad.

Beaufort met Charlotte on his first visit to his sister Fanny at Edgeworthstown on 17 March 1802, a date which he was long to remember. He had been mildly smitten before but this was different. By August he wrote to William of his fear (unfounded, it would seem) that someone was trying 'to ruin my fondest hopes'. Two months later, again to William, he related that he was 'decided and resolved' about his 'beloved . . . as if we had been brought up with our tongues in the same noggin'.

Beaufort was an inhibited suitor. By October, when Charlotte was about to depart for Paris, he wrote to William: 'I did not let an atom of my overflowing heart reach her ears.' Three months later, with Charlotte still in Paris, he assured William (this time in cipher) that he felt confident of her health and heart, that she would not hurt the one or lose the other abroad.

We will never know for sure the state of Charlotte's heart, but the state of her health was becoming ominously clear, especially to her family, although Beaufort refused to see it. Charlotte was the daughter of Edgeworth's third wife, Elizabeth Sneyd, who died at the age of forty-four of tuberculosis, a disease that was fatal to a dozen other members of the Sneyd family. From Paris, Edgeworth wrote[5] to Charlotte Sneyd, sister of his second and third wives, that the 'Sneyd part of all my children is the best in every circumstance but two – strength of lungs and self-confidence'. In his, Fanny's and Maria's other letters during their journey there is a reflection of tension and worry in their repeated assurances to those at home that Charlotte's health remained unimpaired by the rigours of the trip and the cold of the Paris winter.

For some reasons that are now hard to fathom and which he himself confessed might appear quixotic, and probably also because he had no secure employment or prospects of it and was thus in no position to ask for Charlotte's hand, Beaufort never made a direct profession of love to her. For three years he also kept his feelings secret from all but his brother William and her brother Sneyd[6] (who had become his close friend and confidant). Neither did he knew how Charlotte regarded him although at one point he declared, surely not believing it, that he expected nothing to come of his love. Nevertheless, on the second anniversary of his first meeting with her, he assured William – with an awesomely mixed metaphor – that 'the seeds had been planted' which would either 'waft me on the wings of love and harmony through life' or would produce 'the black and gathering storm which will yet rive & tear my firm soul'. But in any event, he had 'nailed my compass and resolved to steer a certain course despite wind and weather'.

Charlotte must have known Beaufort's feelings toward her. He himself thought she was favourably inclined toward him for 'knowing as she has for some time past of my attachment . . . she would have at once answered them had she opposite feelings'. When Beaufort returned to London, probably in November or December of 1804, once again to seek a Naval appointment, Charlotte wrote him a letter which leaves little doubt that she knew his intentions:

My dear Francis
    Though I should have regretted exceedingly not seeing you before you left Ireland and though there were many things I wished to say to you, yet I found it impossible to utter even kindness to you last night – but it as has often been with me when the last moment arrives in which I could express what I wish – all recollection seems to foresake me & every idea seems for a time suspended.
    But I cannot let you depart perhaps to enter on a life of [illeg.] and danger thus. As I feel a sister's affection for you why may I not express a sister's feelings. Why may I not assure you I have and always shall set a high value on your friendship & why may I not thank you for the uniform & steady friendship I have experienced from you. . . .
    I am sorry you are going away but as my regard for you is sincere, I consider much more what may be for your advantage. I hope you may be placed in a situation where your talents and your merits may be rendered conspicuous & I truly hope you may return in Safety, to enjoy ease & happiness. I am much better this morning – and I shall ever be your sincere and

Affectionate friend
Charlotte

Written today, the letter could hardly be interpreted as anything other than a classic 'Dear John' message: the maiden lets the suitor down, gently but firmly, by announcing that she regards him as a brother and not a lover. Yet, considering the locutions of the early nineteenth century, one comes to the opposite assumption. 'Sister' was probably the strongest term a young lady of Charlotte's station could modestly use to indicate her affections to someone who had not explicitly asked her and her father for her hand in marriage.

Six months later, by which time Beaufort had finally been given a command, he felt himself in a position to take that formal step and ask Edgeworth for permission to declare his hopes to her. Edgeworth had been in England and Beaufort met him at Oxford for 'a great deal of conversation respecting his lovely daughter'. Edgeworth's response was to persuade the would-be suitor not to write his proposal to Charlotte. Beaufort acquiesced. He wrote to his father, for the first time intimating to him his attachment to Charlotte: 'I threw my die which was an excellent one, but I believe I threw it in an incautious manner & now I must abide by the cast.'

The reason Edgeworth gave in dissuading Beaufort from proposing was that the act might disturb Charlotte's 'health and tranquillity'. What Edgeworth surely had in mind was the true state of her health which made marriage out of the question for her.

Dr Beaufort suggested that he might talk to Maria to discover her half-sister's state of mind but later, reconsidering Francis' agonized letter, he decided to reconnoitre directly. It is clear from his subsequent action, as from his son's letters, that neither of them suspected what we must assume was Edgeworth's real reason for deterring the young man from proposing.

Dr Beaufort, eager to have Charlotte as his daughter-in-law, deduced that she might be lost to his son 'through ignorance of your attachment', and asked Francis if he should approach her to explore her sentiments. He did not await permission, however, but acted on his impulse. The response he elicited was of a piece with Charlotte's letter six months before: she told Dr Beaufort that she really did not know his son – a patent piece of dissimulation – and that she hoped he would feel as uncommitted as she did.

Dr Beaufort had had doubts ever since he first heard of what he considered the 'hopeless passion' of his son and advised him to abandon it and search elsewhere for a wife. Francis had already rejected the thought emphatically but declined to argue the point: 'If I was to swear by the whole firmament of stars that I could never change you would only smile at the hyperbolic effusions of a lover.'

With the outcome of his unproclaimed suit still in doubt, Beaufort suddenly was restored to active duty and ordered to sail to the Cape of Good Hope and India on a voyage that was to last eighteen months (see next chapter). He set out still refusing to believe that his passion was as hopeless as his father thought; he remained either unaware of or unwilling to face the reality of Charlotte's state of health. Obsessed, he occasionally poured out his feelings to his journal: '. . . to my bed I now go and there, I can forget the inquietudes of the day, the disappointments [*sic*] of the past, the apprehension of the future, in short everything, but the one object which sleeping or waking asserts its indisputable empire over my mind.'

He returned to Plymouth from his long voyage on 21 March 1807. Before he could take leave of his ship and visit his family and his beloved in Ireland he received on 4 April a joint letter from his father, mother and sister Louisa, telling him that Charlotte was in the last stages of an obviously fatal illness. She died three days later.

He could trust himself only to reply, 'Need I say more! God giveth, and God taketh – Amen,' before turning desperately to write of another profound grief, the refusal of the Admiralty to confirm his temporary appointment, received overseas, to post-captain (see Chapter 14).

What is inexplicable, however, is that he had not written to Charlotte on his arrival or during the two weeks thereafter. Maria Edgeworth, writing[7] to her father the day after Charlotte's death, said: 'Tell my mother [i.e. her stepmother, Fanny] that every day since the *Woolwich* [Beaufort's ship] came to England dear Charlotte expressed her astonishment at not hearing from Francis; that she always expressed greatest interest in his promotion & welfare. . . .'

Astonishing indeed. It is hard to believe that Beaufort's love – not to mention his manners – had vanished during the long absence. On receiving word of Charlotte's impending death, he wrote more than a dozen letters in the next several hours, an act suggesting that he was trying frantically to force his concentration elsewhere. One, to a woman who had become something of a confidante (Mrs Lestock Wilson, wife of his first captain and mother of the woman he was to marry five years later) clearly impressed her as having been 'written

under the great depression of Spirits, the Cause of which I am un-
acquainted with. Disappointments in your profession though truly
vexatious, yet I think . . . something else preys upon you, and destroys
your Peace.'

One possibility suggests itself for his failure to communicate with
Charlotte: Beaufort had been designated acting-captain some months
before by the admiral commanding Naval forces in the Far East. He
had every reason to believe that Whitehall would confirm the promotion and appoint him a post-captain. Hoping to announce this
glorious bit of news to his beloved, making his homecoming triumphant, he may have postponed writing until he had received the good
word he expected from the Admiralty. At almost the same time that
he heard of their Lordships' refusal, leaving nothing joyful to write
about to Charlotte, came the tragic news from Ireland.

ABOVE: Lestock Wilson
(*artist and date unknown*)

ABOVE RIGHT: Alicia Wilson
Beaufort as a young girl
(*artist and date unknown*)

RIGHT: Richard Lovell
Edgeworth (*a painting in oils,
probably by H. Howe, 1785
reproduced by permission of the
National Portrait Gallery*)

FRANCIS' PARENTS

Daniel Augustus
Beaufort (*artist and date
unknown*)

Mary Waller Beaufort
(*artist and date unknown*)

Francis Beaufort (*A Daguerrotype of 1848*)

12
Woolwich:
'A Bad Beginning...'
(1805-1806)

To a storeship! Good Heavens! Is it for the command
of a storeship that I have spilled my blood, sacrificed
the prime of my life, dragged out a tedious economy in
foreign climates, wasted my best hours in professional
studies.... For a storeship, for the honour of carrying
new anchors abroad and old anchors home! For a ship
more lumbered than a Dover packet, more weakly
manned than a Yankee carrier – three fourths of her
arms and ammunition on shore, three feet deeper than
her trim, and with jury masts and sails! – so that she
can neither fight nor run; in short, for a ship where
neither ambition, promotion or riches . . . can be
obtained!

BEAUFORT's journal[1]

As Lord Barham had bluntly told him, Beaufort was to have no
promotion. But at least he was restored to active duty and was notified,
on 5 June 1805, of a new appointment: the command of the *Woolwich*,
built twenty years before as a Fifth Rate with forty-four guns but long
since converted to a storeship, armed *en flute*, i.e. only partially – if
Beaufort was not exaggerating, it was fitted with only one quarter of
its original armament. As such it rated a commander, not a post-
captain. The difference was enormous.

Beaufort was humiliated. The railing in his letters and in his journal
was encyclopedic and continual except when the tedious routine of
long voyages and long waits in port was interrupted by episodes of
heavy duty, furious activity and new experiences. But for too many
of his days he wallowed in a depression compounded of self-pity and
self-righteousness.

As he awaited the completion of the refitting of the *Woolwich* at Deptford, Beaufort spilled his anger and chagrin into his journal:

Why, had I been made a commander for being the son of the First Lord of the Admiralty's bailiff or housekeeper, by the interest of some great Jew contractor for pursers' shirts or dutch caps, or by any other back door means, a storeship, I say, would have been a proper, a suitable and almost honourable appointment. . . . I do think that an appointment might have been offered which might have been less galling to my own feelings, and which would not have produced this natural exclamation from those who know me: 'What the devil has B—— been doing to be blackstrapped?'

But he realized, arguing the point out for himself in his journal, that he had no acceptable alternative. First, he had asked for employment and had resolved to take what was offered. Secondly, he had been too long unemployed: seven months of 'laying about the Admiralty, the operas, the institutions, the collections of paintings, and Miss This's Squeeze and Miss That's Piano, make the idea of even a storeship appear a Paradise'. Third, employment might help towards the attainment of the 'important object I have in view' – presumably marrying Charlotte Edgeworth – and idleness would not. Finally, if he refused the *Woolwich* there would be no chance of getting anything better.

And so, on 10 June, Beaufort received his commission 'from that most insolent of all the Admiralty clerks, Mr Wright', proceeded to his ship, 'and commissioned her with the assistance of the old carpenter who was too drunk to belay the Pendant halyards after he hoisted it'.

To his father he tried to present the matter in the best light he could, writing that although being a storekeeper was not what he aspired to there was nevertheless some sugar in the cup: the ship was comfortable, a good sailer, in thorough repair and fit for a man-of-war. And because men-of-war were much wanted abroad, he might even be able to convince some admiral overseas whom he was supplying to arm the *Woolwich* as a cruiser and post him, as captain, into her. But to his brother Beaufort confessed that a 'store-ship was looked upon as the worst thing in the Service'.

A month after taking command, Beaufort noted in his journal that he had been paid a visit aboard by the Misses Sneyd, sisters of Edgeworth's second and third wives, and by the thirteen-year-old daughter of the latter, 'little Honora, who, if I mistake not, will one day be the heroine of a more interesting tale than this'. The prophecy was valid, if delayed, but the tale was still Beaufort's: thirty-three years later he married her.

In early July the storeship moved downriver to Woolwich, the great Naval depot from which the vessel took her name, for further fitting out and loading of cargo for Bombay and Madras; she remained in the Thames for almost three months while her commander fretted. Beaufort's finances were in miserable shape and he was desperate for money, some £300 to £500, he estimated, for his own foreseeable needs on the long voyage to come. The pay due him for his work on the Irish telegraphs had not come through; he feared he would not even be able to buy a few live cattle to carry aboard but would have to do entirely on salt beef.* Worst of all, his books were held up by some misadventure in Liverpool, 'which makes me really insane'.

The Admiralty was also doing its part to drive Beaufort mad by, for example, denying the *Woolwich* carronades, admirably suited as armament for a storeship, and even refusing a slide carriage for a carronade in the ship's launch although he had cogently argued that it would convert a useless piece of lumber into a serviceable and very effective gun carrier.

Is it to be supposed [he exploded in his journal] that captains will go without these things which they consider useful and already in their power, because forsooth the admiralty gives a dictatorial No, or because it is against the system of the Navy board? They certainly will not. They will also shew by what improper means they are too frequently obtained, and continually enforce that golden saying: *'C'est la premier pas qui coûte.'* Once force a captain to put his name to a fictitious expense for things that are necessary & he seldom feels much compunction afterwards in gratifying his whims and fanciful prodigality in the same manner. . . . I may add that restraining the wishes of captains in distinguishing their ships, and checking their ingenuity and inventions by throwing cold water on all experiments except coming through themselves, has done and will do our Service most injury. Those two imperious boards [i.e. the Admiralty and the Navy Board] become every day more disobliging in granting the applications of men even of character and credit – and more dogmatic in their opinions . . .

*A commander paid out of his own pocket for any amelioration of the ship's rations for his own table. About all that was feasible were wine, spirits and livestock, to be slaughtered en route.

For sufferers from every bureaucracy before or since, Beaufort's cry rings with universal truth.

In his then mood no superior authority seemed able to do anything right:

Death and destruction is threatened to a Captain who permits his private signals ever to be seen by any officer, or his numeral signals etc. to be known or copied. Yet this mighty Admiral [Bartholomew Samuel Rowley, in command at the Nore] and his Drudge sent me off *all* my signals loose and open by a junior lieutenant who tied them up in a pocket handkerchief and who might for aught he knew have left them in a tavern or brothel half the time he was on shore!

The *Woolwich* was jinxed, even at her moorings: a seaman fell overboard and was drowned, a marine deserted, a gun was knocked overboard, a boy fell from the rigging and was gravely injured. Beaufort himself got off on the wrong foot in a quarrel with Captain Joseph Short, aboard HM Storeship *Porpoise*, commodore of the squadron to which the *Woolwich* was to be attached. Worse, Beaufort learned that his two lieutenants had been appointed to the storeship as punishment, 'sent to this newfashioned penitentiary house to do mortification for their wickedness!'

Both escaped by transfer before the *Woolwich* left England, with Beaufort deeply regretting the loss of one of them, John Macredie, a fine classical scholar, with the *Iliad* at his fingertips, and a good mathematician and geometer. Beaufort's lament, speaking so many volumes in so few words about the tedium of life at sea for a man of sensitivity and active mind, seems as poignant today as when it was written in his journal: 'What an acquisition such a man in a long passage to India! To have had some fund of conversation besides the weather, the beauty of the dolphin, the last sail that was seen, etc. would really be worth a great sacrifice of some desirable qualities in an officer, which he certainly wanted.'

When at last the cargo was loaded and a crew embarked, the *Woolwich*, ordered to Portsmouth, sailed down the Thames to worse trouble. An 'old dog of a pilot' came on board at Gravesend, ignorant or obstinate to the point where Beaufort had to take over from him to haul inside the Nore light lest the tide drift the ship to disaster. Beaufort was angry but thought it would be cruel to send the man ashore. A day later the *Woolwich* entered the Flats at daybreak in a light breeze.

Two hours later Beaufort saw that the pilot was worried about having enough water and proposed since the ship was not yet halfway across that they turn back towards deeper water. On the reverse course the tidal stream would be in their favour. The master agreed with the captain but the pilot refused. Thereupon the breeze failed entirely and the ship became becalmed. Frightened out of what few wits he had had, the pilot proposed a series of impossible expedients and then insisted on anchoring. Beaufort realized, however, that they were over the shallowest part of the Flats and argued that matters could not get any worse if they continued to drift since the tide could only carry the *Woolwich* into deeper water, possibly one of the holes known to exist. 'No, No, No from the pilot.' Confronted with the choice of complying or sending the pilot below, Beaufort took the former and the wrong option. The *Woolwich* anchored. Shortly, a breeze arose, the anchor was hoisted and the ship was about to make sail when the forepost grounded before the vessel could pay off.

With relief after the crisis was over, Beaufort set down his feelings: 'In a large and deep laden ship, with only a sloop's complement (121) and they having been on board one night [and I being] therefore totally ignorant of their merits, what a situation! The breeze freshening at the NE [the most adverse direction possible] and exposed to the fury of the North Sea should it rise!'

Beaufort broke out the extra spars and used them as temporary piles to support the ship upright; he shifted guns to maintain an even keel. He was too busy to be miserable, 'much too engrossed to admit melancholy or depressing reflections', but he found time for 'sources of real pleasure: 1st, the ship lay quite still – not a thump. 2nd, the wind brought up no sea as yet, and above all I observed my new crew placed in difficult circumstances, all active, zealous & willing. They exerted themselves to their utmost and have given me the most flattering hopes of their future conduct.'

Thanks to those efforts the ship was perfectly supported and neither heeled nor strained when the tide was at its lowest. By 9 p.m. she floated clear and sailed to anchor in deeper waters. Next day was clear sailing, though in a tricky channel which the captain, not the pilot navigated. He wrote in his journal: 'This old sinner, the pilot, was like an evil genius, deluding us into every scrape that it was possible to entangle the ship in. . . . At last, Heaven be praised, I packed him off to the Downs, giving him (wicked man that I am) as good a certificate as it was possible, for he had a wife and six children.'

However compassionately intended, Beaufort's failure honestly to report the pilot's incompetence *was* a piece of wickedness: Beaufort was obliged to write later, on the opposite page from his original journal entry, that a month afterwards the same pilot put another store-ship on shore not far from where he put the *Woolwich* aground. This time the pilot lost his licence.

In Portsmouth at last, Beaufort wrote to Edgeworth at the end of September that he believed more accidents had happened in the *Wool-wich* in four months than he remembered having experienced in other ships in as many years. He prayed that the proverb 'A bad beginning makes a good ending' might be exemplified in his case.

While her captain's frustrations mounted by the hour, the *Woolwich* dawdled for three more months at Portsmouth without orders to sail for India. Beaufort's books finally arrived, to his huge relief, and he found enough to do about the ship to keep him occupied from dawn to past midnight. The delay was nevertheless infuriating. From June to the end of September he had run through a ream of paper, 480 pages, just writing letters, by which time, he complained, he could have been in Madras had orders only been forthcoming. Instead, he was stuck in port 'lying idle, inactive, disappointed and degraded while *mes compagnons d'armes*, my old mess mates, the youngsters even who were brought up under my wing, are gaining reputation, promotion and riches and sharing in the immortal glory of their chiefs.'

This last outburst was prompted by news of the victory at Trafalgar. On 8 November the first of the ships-of-the-line in that momentous engagement sailed into Portsmouth, to be greeted with a *feu de joie*, a ceremony – in this case misnamed to the extent that the joy was damped by Nelson's death – in which the vessels in harbour fire their guns successively, making a continuous volley lasting for hours. Deeply moved, Beaufort wrote to his father a passionate eulogy of the fallen leader (which Daniel Augustus thriftily put to his own purpose in a thanksgiving sermon):

Never had we such an illustrious commander! No man amongst the num-ber of our victorious admirals had ever united in himself so many of the attributes of a great Captain as did that most admirable man; prompt to conceive, and instant in execution, the resources of his capacious mind always rose to the emergency; possessed of the most extraordinary coolness and presence of mind in the most trying & overwhelming moments (witness Copenhagen and Teneriffe) yet no man could rush with more fervour and enthusiasm when enthusiasm was wanting to carry the point or to animate his companions. . . .

His spirit seems to have alighted on us all; it has animated the sluggish minds of the most dull, it has swelled those of his followers there who had been honoured with his knowledge to a pitch of madness to revenge his fall, and it must enlighten, excite, nerve and invigorate every heart and every head for centuries to come!

On the day the news came Beaufort wrote in his journal:

Who says that sailors have no feeling, neither national pride nor personal affection? I solemnly declare that when I read the *Gazette* to my ship's Company I could hardly observe a countenance in which the flush of glory did not mount, nor in whose eye the tear of regret did not stand. Never had men a more just cause for honest pride, nor ever did I see men more honestly and distinctly express it. Never had men to mourn a greater loss, and never was there a more sincere tribute to it.

Oh! Nelson, what a triumph is this: to make the most sunburnt, weather-beaten faces of thy brethren glow with admiration of your great deeds, to wring from the hardest of their hearts a tear of sympathy, of rapture and of anguish for your *glorious* fate, and for your country's loss! Immortal Man!

In eulogistic mood, Beaufort went on to write to his father of

another great man, for great indeed do I at least allow Bonaparte. With the most perfidious heart, with the most ferocious tyranny and with the utmost depravity of principle, yet he is a most justly great and renowned general. His instant and vigorous action, the skilfulness of his manoeuvres and the happiness with which he seizes the proper moment constitute him a great man in spite of the hireling abuse or degrading adulation of his contemporaries. Good God! who can read his address to the army previous to his last astonishing victory [over the Austrians on the Danube] without confessing he deserved to conquer, without almost finding their wishes go with him in spite of their conviction? Who could have *heard* it without being stimulated to more than mortal efforts!

As the inaction continued, Beaufort's temper steadily worsened, and he took to lashing out physically as well as with words. In early October, he had urged his crew to act so that his cat-o'-nine-tails, until then unused, would stay idle, but warning them 'that when I did punish I punished like a devil, and never forgave a *first* fault'. A few weeks later his purser's steward and a marine got twelve lashes each, for disobedience.

His pen, in letters and in his journal, was equally lacerating: how outrageous the growing practice of private companies to attempt, through subscriptions and donations, to reward individuals in the armed services!

Any body of men, much less Tinkers and haberdashers, presuming publicly to reward the army and navy is I think very wrong. Still, while they conferred their freedoms in gold boxes it was bearable . . . when they give swords, however, it is *impious*. What, a taylor, for instance, giving an Admiral a Sword! . . . But what will you say when they at last have dared to offer money, MONEY to officers!! . . Now indeed may our troops and sailors be called mercenary! And now may the French epithet of a nation of shop-keepers be justly applied to us.

What madness of the Admiralty, at this doubtful period of the war, to waste time

in chusing black and white sword hilts for undress and dress swords for the Navy, and selecting pretty swordknots in the milliners' shops for the differ-ent ranks of officers! Shame, Shame! This is not the spirit or essence of our service. . . . What would Admiral Benbow have said with his round wig and red waistcoat, to the Admt^y.'s interfering about the dangling frippery of our swords. . . . If the Duke of Kent* was made Lord High Admiral it would not astonish me if models of tails were to be sent round to all our fleets, and the number of hairs in each whisker be assigned according to the rate or number of guns in the ship.

How idiotic, with the prospect of the winter westerlies, and 'how worthy indeed of our sagacious Board of Admiralty' to have sent warships from Plymouth back eastward to St Helen's Road, on the Isle of Wight, to form a flying squadron under Sir John Borlase Warren to chase French squadrons said to be on the loose! True, St Vincent was capricious, vindictive and despotic and 'I have felt most severely his cruel injustices . . . but it no less eases my indignation to hear his administration of the Navy compared to the present milksop board, a composition of old women once clever but now totally out-grown it.'

Beaufort's invective was by no means without foundation, but what

*Fourth son of George III and father of Victoria. He had been retired as a general because of his fanaticism about discipline and displayed a 'pedantic, almost supersti-tious insistence on the minutiae of military etiquette, dress and equipment'.

was really gnawing at his entrails was seven months without orders to sail from England to what had been his destination from the beginning, India. The autumn months, with their favourable winds for leaving the Channel, had slipped by. The cruellest blow of all, however, fell in mid-October when Beaufort was ordered to accompany, on the first leg of the voyage as far as the Cape of Good Hope, Captain Joseph Short, with whom he had tangled in the Thames months before, and the newly appointed Governor of New South Wales, Captain William Bligh, notorious as a result of the mutiny of HMS *Bounty* in 1789. Short, as commodore, commanded the storeship *Porpoise*; Bligh was sailing in the convict transport *Lady Sinclair*, bound for Botany Bay. With them were to be some slow-sailing merchantmen, a combination that heaped Beaufort's misery high as a mountain.

'I thought that my evil genius would attach me to those fellows,' he wrote when he received the news in mid-November. 'I am nailed. The devil take his Excellency.' Ten weeks before he had had a premonition that such was to be his fate, and had exclaimed in his journal at the 'singular choice' of Bligh as the new governor: 'The inhabitants there have complained of the ill temper and tyranny of the present governor and petitioned for some person of gentle disposition who may conciliate the dissentions and factious interests of the colony – and so they have appointed Capt. W. Bligh the Governor!!!'

But to picture Beaufort in this period as a man as foul-tempered as Bligh, as the foregoing passages might imply, is to mistake him. His tirades were against real abuses and assaults to the Service and the country. His attitude towards duty, towards maintaining the honour and integrity of Crown, country and Navy cannot be denigrated or discounted.

Nor can his decency and humanity, or his pre-Dickensian enlightenment. The following entry in his journal speaks for itself:

A midshipman stealing money! What shall I do? Punish him, disgrace him and turn him out of the ship is my duty – but if I do I know I seal him in his guilt for his whole life.

How many wretches who crowd our prisons, who are banished from their country . . . how many miserable females who prowl about the streets like beasts of prey, who realize the fable of the harpies, who are by turn the victims and the scourges of our feelings and unbridled passions – how many of these would have lessened the enormous catalogue of unfortunate or of wicked beings had justice sometimes been tempered with lenity, had the hand of reconciliation been sometimes stretched out . . . if, in the moment of shame . . . forgiveness had been offered as a bait for repentance and virtue. Ah! no, that is not the disposition of mankind: the revenge of injuries is a more powerful stimulus to prosecution than example to society. . . .

At present, though many in the ship guess, no one knows the thief – but myself. If I set before him a picture of the misery and wretchedness he escapes by escaping public detection, if I persuade him that he cannot escape either a second time, and if I can shew him in as strong a light what an opposite conduct may lead to, it is possible I may reclaim him. And should I fail, I shall only have robbed the gallows of a victim for a few months or years.

Beaufort failed. The subsequent entry in the journal reads: 'I am happy now that I have turned a thorough-faced scoundrel, though only 14 . . . on shore. Alas, I have no hopes: his heart is too hardened or my eloquence too impotent. . . . Professions he was profuse in; I would rather have wrung a few tears from his eyes.'

Delays while the favourable easterlies blew themselves out and the prospect of a slow passage to the Cape with two disagreeable superiors drove Beaufort to an act of splendid madness, tinged with high comedy. The drama begins with a prelude.

Knowing that he was destined for a long voyage, Beaufort reported in mid-November to the admiral in command at Portsmouth, Vice-Admiral Sir George Montagu, that 'That sagacious board yclept the Lords Commissioners of the Admiralty forgot to order this ship to be victualled', and asked that Montagu give the necessary authorization for provisioning. The admiral, however, said there was nothing he could do about it. Beaufort's journal carries on the story:

'But, Sir, orders will come in a hurry, perhaps to sail with some ship. I shall be obliged to wait then two or three days for my prog [victuals] etc. . . .'

'Well, well, I can't help it,' was all I could get from him.

'But, Sir,' I answered, 'suppose you were to mention it to them either privately or publickly. Consider how much my already long detention here may harm the Service in the East I[ndies] etc.'

'No, Capt. B., I will not say a word about you. I got twice a rap over the knuckles for interfering in what they call their own department, and I won't do it a third time.'

My God, when Admiralty and their Admirals are on such terms what is to become of the Service! . . . As for patriotism – ha! ha! that is a thing pretty nearly forgotten in this country, indeed the word itself would be equally so like any other unmeaning symbol or hieroglyphic were it not for a few members of Parliament who make constant use of it (the word, I mean) and for the pamphleteers who like long words to fill their columns. But all this will not give me provisions . . . I must now wait the return of the post from the Admt^y. for it is too foggy for the Telegraph.

Five weeks later, by then presumably provisioned, the *Woolwich* was transferred to the command of Sir John Borlase Warren, a dashing admiral with the stomach for a fight. Then at St Helen's Road, he was to protect outgoing convoys to the West Indies and the Mediterranean and thereupon cruise the Atlantic in search of French raiding squadrons. Beaufort wanted to remain with Warren, in whose company some action could be expected, but he knew that his latest orders were purely administrative, merely for the period while he was waiting for Bligh at St Helen's Road. It was well understood that he was to go with the new governor as far as the Cape and then sail for India.

But the Admiralty forgot, as the days passed, to countermand Beaufort's appointment to Warren's command. Very well, orders were orders, lack of orders were no orders, as Montagu so recently had made clear. Thus, on 12 January 1806, when Warren made signals to his squadron to sail, Beaufort complied. The procedure took six hours, but Montagu's 'bright officers' did not notice. If Montagu had new orders for the *Woolwich* and forgot to communicate them, 'I know better [than] to remind you of them. You gave me a letter on that head a short time back,' said Beaufort fiercely to Montagu, albeit in the privacy of his diary.

His little piece of daring almost came off. But the hideous westerlies had by now set in and Warren's squadron, after battling against them for five days, returned to Spithead. Beaufort now knew that he was 'nailed' to Short and Bligh. He was hardly at anchor before he was summoned to Montagu. The journal continues:

As I went on shore to wait upon the Adm^l. every body told me the Adm^l. had been mad at my going out, that he had been stamping and swearing at the Signal Post.

Scene 1. Adm^l.'s office. Sentinels, clerks and Lieut^s. at their bureau. Enter Ego.

Lieut^t.: 'Oh, here is Captain Beaufort. The Adm^l., Sir, has been very anxious to see you again.'

'I am come to wait upon the Adm^l., be so good as to inform him.'

Scene 2nd. Enter Captain B. The Admiral, turning briskly: 'Well, Capt. B., where the deuce have you been? It is very fortunate that you have been driven back. I am very glad to see you here again.'

'Sir, in pursuance of orders forwarded to me by *you* a fortnight since (here they are, Sir), I went to sea with Sir John Warren. The winds have forced us back in spite of the Vice-Admiral's endeavour to beat down, and I hope you will pardon me when I say I am right sorry to find myself again under your flag.'

'Aye, aye, but the orders are nothing. You know you were not going to go with Sir John.'

'I know nothing but my orders, Sir.'

'Well, but did you not know that the *Woolwich* was to accompany the *Porpoise* [Commodore Short's ship]?'

'To put myself under the command of Sir J. Warren was the last order I received, and consequently it I obeyed.'

'But did Sir John ever give you any orders?'

'Yes, Sir, an order about fresh beef.'

'Aye, but I mean did he ever give you sailing orders, or rendezvous, or . . .?'

'No.'

'Well then, surely you know, *Sir*, you were not to accompany him. It was clear that if he meant to take you under his orders that he would have given you the usual ones. His not doing so spoke for itself, and it was, I must say – '

I stopped him; he might have said something unpleasant.

'What, Sir! Was it my business to remind him of his arrangements, or you or the Admt^y. of my destination?' (He understood my allusion very well.) 'But I just beg leave to say that I received these orders (the above ones from the Admt^y.) to place myself under Sir John's orders, that I waited upon him, gave him my weekly accounts, answered all his signals at St Helen's, followed all his motions – and on the 12th if he did not intend that I should go with him would he not have answered the signal to unmoor, the signal to weigh, the signal rendezvous of[f] the Lizard, to the *Woolwich*, and particularly when he saw me not only answer them but comply with them, with all the alertness my little crew were capable of. But whether or not, I must repeat, Sir, that I obeyed the last order, indeed all the orders I had received, that I *think* I acted for the good of the Service, and that I am sure I acted with perfect propriety.'

Adm^l., smiling: 'Well, well, I believe, Capt. B, I can make nothing of you – very well.' (What the devil did he want to make of me? A fool?)

'Indeed, Sir, after lying four months ready for sea I was too happy at the prospect of getting out to throw the slightest impediment in the way.'

Perhaps Beaufort improved the account of the interview with a touch of *esprit de l'escalier*. But he was entitled to be pleased with himself: he had taken an outrageous step, almost succeeded in getting away with it and escaped scot free.

13

Wind Scale
(1806)

There are at present 1000 King's vessels employed.
From each of them there are from 2 to 8 Log books
deposited every year in the Navy Office; those log
books give the wind and weather every hour . . . spread
over a great extent of ocean. What better data could a
patient meteorological philosopher desire? Is not the
subject, not more in a scientific than a nautical point
of view, deserving laborious investigation?

BEAUFORT to Richard Lovell Edgeworth[1]

Alexander Dalrymple, the Admiralty's first Hydrographer and an early
discoverer of Beaufort's talents as a chartmaker, once wrote to him for
additional details on some observations he had sent in about the
approaches to Montevideo. Dalrymple apologized for making the
request, explaining that he feared he was himself 'priggishly precise'.

Beaufort would hardly have considered such an admission self-
deprecatory; he might even have deemed it a boast. Such complaint as
there was of his own prodigious chart-making in later years when he
became the Hydrographer was that his charts were, if anything, too
neat; that in his insistence on perfection he fell behind in the volume
of his output.

A 'natural philosopher' in the best nineteenth-century sense, he was
fascinated by almost every bud that grew in the garden of what was
to become modern science; the influence of Richard Lovell Edgeworth
had been decisive. But one aspect of his wide-ranging scientific
interests, developed long before he met 'the ingenious Mr Edgeworth',
was meteorology. Even as a midshipman he expanded his journal from
the required notation of the weather every twelve to twenty-four hours
to reports of it at two-hour intervals; he soon began with considerable

success to set down his own weather forecasts. By 1806 he was chronicling in thoughtful detail unusual weather conditions and speculating about them.[2] From then until the last entry three days before his death at eighty-four, he kept a daily weather journal, with notations of wind, temperature and barometric readings.[3]

Beaufort was unhappy at the ambiguity and subjectivity in the weather notation systems standard during his days at sea for the officers' log books and the log boards on deck. These called for noting at frequent intervals the direction of the wind, which was clear enough, but also for its force, any statement of which, without instruments, would be necessarily subjective. A 'small gale' to one ship's master or lieutenant might seem a 'fresh gale' to another.

As appears in a letter to Edgeworth at the head of this chapter, Beaufort sensed the need, if ever the behaviour of weather and its mysterious causes were to be understood, of thousands upon thousands of roughly concurrent reports on wind force and direction, cloud conditions, temperature and atmospheric pressure from all over the globe – in short, for the synoptic chart of modern meteorology. But, if they were to be useful, the notations had to be consistent.

Thus, while eating his heart out with frustration and boredom at Portsmouth as he awaited orders for the *Woolwich*, Beaufort devised the wind scale that is the achievement for which he is popularly famed.[4] That it was far from the most significant of his lifetime accomplishments is not to the point: to sailors the world over the name Beaufort calls to mind the wind scale. A yachtsman's casual reference to 'Force 5 winds' or the official daily weather report on the French radio forecasting *'cinq Beaufort'* are acknowledgements of his initiative.

In retrospect it scarcely ranks as one of the world's great scientific or intellectual landmarks. Rather, it is a neat, handy and efficient piece of systematization and, like many other useful things, is so simple and obvious that its chief wonder is why no one ever thought of it before.*

Aboard the *Woolwich*, Beaufort began the entry for 13 January 1806 in his private log book (as distinct from the official captain's log to be sent at six-month or annual intervals to the Admiralty) with the follow-

---

*There is convincing evidence to indicate that it was Dalrymple who suggested to Beaufort the idea of adapting an earlier wind scale by John Smeaton to maritime needs. Smeaton's scale, proposed in 1759, correlated wind speeds in miles per hour to simple verbal descriptions, e.g. 50 m.p.h. = storm or tempest.[5]

ing statement: 'Hereafter I shall estimate the force of the wind according to the following scale, as nothing can convey a more uncertain idea of wind and weather than the old expressions of moderate and cloudy, etc. etc.' There followed his new wind scale and weather notation formula, as he set them down in his journal.

The second portion is pure shorthand, a way of using 'hsq' to mean 'hard squalls', and the first part not much more. For, despite his aims of objectivity and consistency, his scale did not eliminate subjectivity in reporting the wind force. It did not answer the problem of making sure that one observer's 'light breeze' was not another's 'gentle breeze'. He hit upon the solution the following year by correlating the gradations in wind force to the amount of sail that a full-rigged ship would carry in different intensities of wind. Except at times of moderate breezes or less, there would be little argument about how much canvas would be set on a frigate or man-of-war. Thus, in a moderate gale that Beaufort first designated as Force 8, the jibs would be set, the royals not, and there would be double reefs elsewhere.

Over the years, the author tinkered with his creation, simplifying the shorthand to seventeen letters to describe the state of the weather, providing a dot under a letter to indicate extraordinary intensity of whatever it stood for – or merely to mean 'very' – and reducing to twelve the gradations in the force of the wind.

If Beaufort attempted at the time to induce the Admiralty to adopt his definitions for use throughout the Navy, there is no evidence of it. As a humble commander of a storeship, he was scarcely in a position to propose major innovations. It was not until 1829, twenty-three years later, when he became Hydrographer to the Navy, that he had the necessary influence. He seems to have begun by proselytizing individual commanders of the surveying ships under his direction, beginning with Robert Fitzroy when he returned in 1830 from his first South American survey in the *Beagle*. Beaufort's orders to Fitzroy when the latter set out on his subsequent voyage read:[6]

Meteorological Registers may be of use in a variety of ways. . . .
In this Register the state of the wind and weather will, of course, be inserted; but some intelligible scale should be assumed, to indicate the force of the former, instead of the ambiguous terms 'fresh', 'moderate', &c., in using which no two people agree; and some concise method should also be employed for expressing the state of the weather. The suggestions contained in the annexed printed paper are recommended for the above purpose.

Hereafter I shall estimate the force of the wind according to the following scale, as nothing can convey a more uncertain idea of wind and weather than the old expressions of moderate and cloudy &c &c.

0	Calm	7	Gentle steady gale
1	Fair air just not calm.	8	Moderate gale
2	Light airs	9	Brisk gale
3	Light breeze	10	Fresh gale
4	Gentle breeze	11	Hard gale
5	Moderate breeze	12	Hard gale with heavy gusts
6	Fresh breeze	13	Storm

And the weather as follows &c

b	Blue sky	h	Hazy
f	Fair weather	dp	Damp air
d	Dry warm atmosphere	fg —	Foggy
s	Sultry	r	Rain
p	Passing clouds.	sr.	Small rain
c	Clear, i.e. that is clear hard horizon but not blue sky.	dr	Drizzling rain
		hr.	Hard rain
cl	Cloudy	sh	Showers
		hsh	Hard showers
w	Watery sky	s.d	Settled weather
wd	Wild, forked, confused threatening cloud.	sy	Steady breeze
		sq.	Squally.
dk	Dark heavy atmosphere	hsq —	Hard squalls
l	Lightning	bk.	Black horizon & clouds
t.	Thunder.	thr.	Threatening appearance
g	Gloomy dark weather		
gr	Greasy threatening appearance		

First recording, in his *Journal*, of Beaufort's Wind Scale, 1806 (Crown copyright and reproduced by permission of the Meteorological Office).

The annexed paper was, of course, a reproduction of the Beaufort Scale in the form to which Beaufort had by then developed it. Thus the first recorded use of the scale in an official log[7] is that of Fitzroy, with his new savant, Charles Darwin, aboard, on one of the most momentous voyages in scientific and intellectual history. The date was 22 December 1831, one day after the departure of the *Beagle* from Plymouth (it was abortive; contrary winds forced Fitzroy back and the successful start was delayed until 27 December).*

The following year Beaufort began his campaign within the Admiralty for the acceptance of his Scale, but in a circumspect fashion. His principal professional colleague in the Hydrographic Office, Lieutenant A. B. Becher, was not merely a fine nautical surveyor himself but also a man devoted to improving hydrographic knowledge and science. With £50 wheedled from Naval funds and a like amount from the Mercantile Marine, Becher founded the invaluable *Nautical Magazine*[8] (which he went on to edit for thirty-nine years). In an early issue (December 1832) he published a short but trenchant article noting that the 'present method of registering the proceedings of a ship . . . is susceptible of much improvement'. The log board (from which the log books were copied), was simply not large enough for all the writing that was required, 'and "Fresh breezes, and cloudy", in sprawling characters, occupy, with a provoking distinctness, an immensity of space, to the exclusion of some more important remark'. The same purpose could be served by using numbers and letters and indeed, by a method 'which originated with Captain Beaufort . . . [as] a result of long experience. It affords a concise means of expressing fully the meaning of whole sentences in writing.' Several ships, presumably including some in the Navy, were already using the system, the magazine noted.

Whether the article was written by Becher or by Beaufort himself, it was obviously a piece of in-house collusion, designed to put pressure on their Lordships to use some common sense.

Such was the conservatism – to use a polite word – of the Admiralty that it was not until 1838 that it ordered the Beaufort Scale to be put into use throughout the Fleet. Individual captains were not so slow. As early as 1833, Admiral Sir George Cockburn,† then commanding the

---

*Fitzroy, the first man to use the Beaufort Scale in his official log, became the first Superintendent of the Meteorological Office in 1854.

†Americans remember him as the man who burned Washington in 1814; the British think of him as the man who conveyed Napoleon to St Helena the year after.

American and West Indies station, wrote to Beaufort that his system was in general use throughout his squadron and 'answers perfectly'.[9] By 1836 Beaufort was advising Commander Thomas Baldock, one of the earliest proponents and captains of steam vessels in the Navy, on how to adapt the Scale on a paddle-wheeler. The next year Beaufort ordered its use throughout the surveying service.[10]

In 1853 Beaufort's great American opposite number, Matthew Fontaine Maury, was instrumental in arranging the first international meteorological conference in Brussels. One of the British delegates was Rear-Admiral Frederick William Beechey, who had been one of Beaufort's hydrographic officers. He seems to have been influential at the Brussels conference, to the point that Beaufort, a year before his retirement, saw his Scale adopted for international use.

With an anemometer on dry land Beaufort's Scale of Forces 0–12 could be translated into knots or miles per hour. But when he invented the Scale, and even when the Admiralty adopted it thirty-two years later, no anemometer had been developed for use aboard a tossing, rolling ship. In the nineteenth century designations of wind velocity by the Beaufort Scale were the best that could be done at sea and were for the most part quite good enough.

With the introduction of double topsails about 1850 modifications to the Scale became necessary; they were adopted by the Maritime Congress in 1874. But when the age of steam began to supersede the age of sail, the notations based on the amount of sail that could be carried steadily lost their significance and utility; thereupon a notation based on the state of the sea was introduced in addition, to be correlated with the 0–12 gradations. In the new notation the appearance of the sea varied from millpond flat to mountainous waves. But that too was only a development, probably originally suggested by Dalrymple, of Beaufort's work, as is evident from the fact that one early printed version of his Scale included, for each of his twelve gradations, the 'sea criterion'. The range is from 'sea like a mirror' to 'air filled with foam and spray'. More sophisticated specifications for that kind of correlation were brought into official use in 1941. The result is a remarkable uniformity in sailors' estimates.

Beaufort would have been pleased, for that was what he was aiming at in the first place.

14

Woolwich:
The Good Shepherd
(1806-1807)

If a vigorous and clear-headed Admiralty has succeeded Lord Barham and his Psalm-singers, they will
approve my conduct and if the latter keep their
places I am indifferent to their rebukes as to their
praises.

BEAUFORT'S journal[1]

About many things Captain Bligh was no fool. He had suspected
Beaufort of wanting to play hooky and two or three times charged him
with that intent despite his disingenuous assurances. Thus, within two
days of Beaufort's return with Warren's weather-defeated squadron,
someone saw to it that the Admiralty's oversights were remedied:
Beaufort was handed firm and unmistakable orders from Commodore
Short.

'To be tied to that tub will be the devil,' he fumed in his journal.

Ten days later, on 29 January 1806, he put to sea at last, with Short
and Bligh's little flotilla and an enormous convoy of 250 or 300
merchant ships, some bound for the Mediterranean and others for
the West Indies, with a protective squadron of warships under the
command of Rear-Admiral Sir Richard Strachan.

Before the huge convoy was halfway down the Channel Beaufort
realized that in Strachan he had a wild man in command. As with
Admiral Warren, who had succeeded in putting to sea on his second
attempt a few days before, Strachan's assignment was to take his
fighting ships into the Atlantic and, after he had escorted the merchantmen to their turn-off points to Gibraltar and the Caribbean, to seek
out a formidable force of French warships, half of their Fleet from
Brest in fact, which had escaped a month before and were out to create

havoc for British shipping in the South Atlantic and West Indies. Strachan was far more interested in chasing the French than in herding merchant ships. Many of them dropped astern, trailing broken spars and torn sails, as they battled against furious Channel gales.

His first orders to Beaufort verged on the idiotic: the *Woolwich* was made whipper-in. She was not quite the worst sailer of the escort, as Beaufort claimed, but she was deeply laden, under-masted and with a crew of ninety-three instead of the regulation complement of 121, yet she was given the job of sheepdog when Strachan had four swift frigates which might have been assigned to that role. Then, not yet out of the Channel, Strachan apparently abandoned interest in the convoy entirely, letting the vessels struggle on as best they could.

'I take leave to say that if Sir Richard does not close his convoy, which yesterday extended about 14 leagues, he will lose one-half of them', the astonished whipper-in wrote. Two days later he added:

Well, by Jupiter, I never saw such a fellow as that Sir Richard. Never once has he closed his convoy since he sailed! The wind constantly in our teeth and a heavy sea running, does he think 2 or 300 merchant vessels will stick up to windward with him – but whatever he thinks, can he not see? Could he not see some of them Topsails down? No, he can see nothing nor hear nothing. Everything in my power I did yesterday to shew him that there were several sail to leeward of me: I edged down to them, made signals, fired guns, hauled my wind, hove to, bore around [?] up – all in vain. . . . He seemed to care a fig whether I and 15 sail to leeward of me parted company. . . . As I expected, this morning they were the only vessels in sight. . . . Were it my instinct to part company, this would be a charming opportunity.

It is hard to believe that that was *not* Beaufort's instinct. Some days later he did part company and was happy to do so although the parting was not at his instigation. For six days he struggled hard at his chore, rounding up stragglers, rejoining the main convoy and holding it together as best he could. Many ships had been disabled by the weather and Beaufort calculated that the convoy now numbered about fifty less than when they left the Lizard.

Sir Richard is a most gallant, active fellow in fighting and chacing, but in protecting a convoy, the Lord deliver us from him. The other night at 2 o'clock up he came with his squadron carrying a press of sail [and] ran right through the middle of the poor astonished merchant vessels firing musquets at them on all sides to make them sheer out of his way!

Three days later Short, Bligh, Strachan and all but fifteen of the convoy were again out of sight. Although the position was off Cape Finisterre, the north-west corner of Spain, and although all night the wind was from NW or NW by N – perfectly favourable for continuing a course to the south – Beaufort concluded (correctly, as he later discovered) that the convoy must have gone on the port tack during the night, a curious decision. Beaufort could only conclude: 'All madmen have their paroxysms; Sir Richard must have been very mad all the evening.'

Reaching the latitude of Gibraltar, Beaufort detached three of his little flock eastwards and herded the remainder towards Madeira. There he found Admiral Warren cruising off Funchal. Beaufort was delighted, hoping to turn over his merchantmen and be rid of his self-imposed responsibility or, if Warren wanted him to continue to give escort, to know that then he would at least be acting under a superior's orders.

Warren bade the *Woolwich* continue her escort of the merchantmen for another week to the point where they would turn off for the Caribbean. Beaufort thus slogged along, annoyed that he had not been able to go ashore at Madeira to pick up some wine and that Warren had not given him any from his stores. But, on the last day of February, he was finally freed of his Caribbean-bound charges, and was jubilant.

He was also awed at his aloneness and at the same time felt self-important, a combination of sentiments which propelled him, predictably, into a literary paroxysm:

Now for the first time I find myself alone upon the awful ocean, abandoned of all human aid and confiding in our own narrow resources – those resources in the hands of one feeble individual, myself. . . .

I look around me on deck and behold a swarm of valuable officers, aspiring youths, unthinking boys and brave and hardy sailors. . . .

Like children unbothered with schemes for the future or remorse for the past, they gently sink into the arms of repose – while at that moment, perhaps, their captain is pacing anxiously the midnight deck or, stretched upon his softer bed in vain, his thoughts labouring with prescient resolutions & alternations, or his mind oppressed with the discovering of some latest and unsuspected villainy, or studies to conceal their approach to some doubtful, but not less dreadful danger.

And so on, for painful pages.

He discovered later that he had been luckier than he knew in escaping the company of Captain Bligh and Commodore Short. The two men, in different ships, raged at each other by signal, boat-borne messages and personal visitations from the Channel to the Cape. The basic fault was the Admiralty's in issuing highly ambiguous orders as to who was in command of what and when and where. The drama, ludicrous in retrospect, fills pages of the Admiralty files[2] and has been recounted elsewhere[3] but the high spot is worth recalling: Bligh was accompanied by his newly married daughter but her husband, Naval Lieutenant Charles Putland, named as Bligh's aide-de-camp, had been posted to Short's ship, the *Porpoise.* Once on the high seas, Bligh asked for Putland to be transferred to him on the *Lady Sinclair.* Short refused, sending Bligh into a passion. Three days later, Bligh altered course without informing Short or obtaining his permission as commodore of the convoy. Short, with an equally violent temper, directed Putland, who was officer of the watch at the time, to fire shots across the bow and stern of, and, if necessary, into the ship carrying his wife and father-in-law. One shot, according to Bligh's account, actually went through the *Lady Sinclair*'s sails.

Far ahead and alone, Beaufort encountered another situation that tested his resolution, so sententiously worried about in one journal entry after another.

About two weeks' sail south-west of the Canaries, the *Woolwich* overhauled the *Trio,* a cartel (an unarmed ship commissioned to exchange prisoners-of-war) carrying the crew of the British sloop *Favourite*, captured almost two months before by a squadron of French raiders which had sailed in October from Lorient. Their strength was formidable: a seventy-four-gun ship, two forty-gun frigates and a brig-corvette, under the command of Commodore Jean-Marthe-Adrien L'Hermite.

Beaufort's orders were to sail to the Cape. The easy and irreproachable thing to do was to follow them to the letter, sending the cartel on her way back to England. But it was of prime importance, Beaufort knew, that Warren, from whom he had parted only a fortnight before, be made aware of the presence in these seas of L'Hermite's ships and their plans, as nearly as the captives from the *Favourite* had learned them. Beaufort took it on himself to breach his orders and turn about, back towards Madeira in search of Warren. In the event his decision was never challenged.

After a week's sail northward, the *Woolwich* encountered an American ship that had recently sailed from Madeira and whose captain reported that Warren had also left the island, bound who knew where. Beaufort once again reversed course and headed towards the Cape Verde Islands, hoping to find the admiral, but in vain. (Warren ultimately received news of L'Hermite from another source, but neither his nor other British cruisers ever came up with the French squadron.)

Once beyond the Bay of Biscay there were fair winds, smooth water and sunshine, to the point where the captain once lowered a studding sail over the side to provide a canvas swimming pool for the crew.[4]

In sight of the harbour, Porta Santa, on the north side of Madeira, the ship picked up a new passenger: 'Mrs Kelly, the wardroom cook's wife, popped a little damsel. If I am either pastor or gossip [sponsor] to the animal she shall be called Porta Santa', Beaufort wrote.

A few days later, having thought that during his many years at sea he had heard everything, he was confronted by something new: two Welshmen aboard approached him and asked permission to get drunk in honour of St David's Day. The captain refused, fearing the precedent: there were many Irishmen aboard, plus others who would become such for the occasion, and St Patrick's Day was only seventeen days off.

Beaufort was in a good mood which contributed to the lightness if not the literary quality of the essays with which he filled his journal:

I must now [11 March], just by way of breathing, record an event which has happened on board this not yet floating castle which is replete with delight to some of its inhabitants and is fraught with the happiest omens of our safety and success: a rich, fragrant and luxurious fountain has burst out of the bosom of the ship, its exuberant streams, after dispensing life and strength to those parti-coloured mortals, supplying my table with a delicious aliment that I prefer to the ambrosia of the Gods and the nectar of their nymphs. . . .

And so, on and on in mock heroics, over several pages. It seems that 'my beauteous black goat has set adrift in this little world three spotted kids'. Their antics delighted the youngsters and boys in the crew and their mother's abundant milk flavoured the captain's tea and rice puddings.

Once Beaufort had corrected the deficient sailing qualities of the *Woolwich*, and once in the steady Atlantic trades, what else was there to do for a mind that took idleness and tedium hard but to write would-be philosophical essays which were profoundly and sincerely felt? Long pages in his journal, for example, were filled with sentiments that later generations of Wilberforces and Gandhis would subscribe to. They dwelled on the callousness of the insatiable Europeans, exploiting the slaves and the inhabitants of colonial conquests – and of the British soldiers sent there to die of war and disease – all ignorant of or indifferent to the misery so engendered.

He wrote too of the churnings of his own heart, for Charlotte, for fame, for glory, for achievement.

His descriptions, less laboured and affected than his moral excursions, bespeak the sketcher's trained eye and the curious, searching mind of that breed of eighteenth- and nineteenth-century gentlemen-savants some of whom he had met during his period in Ireland and whose company he was to join in later years.

I think last night [he wrote on 13 April – he was between Trinidade* and the South American main] presented one of the most splendid spectacles I ever saw. There was no moon; the sky above ⅔ up all round was obscured by the most dense black cloud that one could conceive. This was contrasted by the sea which was an entire sheet of fire. A fresh gale kept it in continual agitation; each wave that broke had the appearance of an explosion or the irruption from a volcano and the ship, going with great rapidity, left a line of liquid fire for miles behind her and, breaking the water around her, threw up a light which was really dazzling; and the sails, strongly illuminated and opposed to the perfect black of the sky, was, I declare, terrifically grand and beautiful. I held a book out of the Quarter Gallery and when the water broke could make out the words distinctly by its flashes – and indeed this morning a bucket full, that I last night laid by, when much disturbed in a dark cabin was very luminous.

But it had an uncommon effect on the appearance of the sails; they all looked as if aback, and frequently people to convince themselves of the fallacy would go close to them. This I conceive a solution of the case: when a sail is full, to an observer standing abaft it, it is very concave; therefore, as he is always used to the light coming from more or less above, the shadow is always (more or less sharply) situated under the upper part of the yard . . . but when before the sail, the light still from above, the shadow is consequently on the underside. Now those circumstances are so firmly associated in the minds of every sailor that when he sees a sail illuminated & shadowed

*A tiny island in the South Atlantic some 750 miles ENE of Rio de Janeiro; not to be confused with the island of similar name in the West Indies.

(from the underside) when he knows he is abaft of it, he cannot reconcile himself at first (nor indeed at all without reflection) to a contrary experience.

Be this as it may, a more sublime, horrible and unique spectacle I never beheld.

Further south, near Tristan da Cunha, Beaufort found a piece of land unmarked on the chart. He took 'bushels' of bearings, noting that 'Everyone has his hobby or insanity; mine is, I believe, taking bearings for charts and plans'.*

At considerable length in his journal, and also in a letter of great charm and tenderness to his sister Harriet, Beaufort described the last tragi-comic episode of the voyage.

Early in May a series of petty thefts and depredations were discovered. So grave was the crime of theft aboard the ships that it was usually left to 'the people' themselves to execute the punishment of running the gauntlet.†

In eleven months in command of the *Woolwich*, Beaufort had ordered only five floggings, generally maintaining discipline in a more enlightened way. He wrote: 'I do not always consider whether the culprit is deserving of punishment – God knows we all often enough deserve to be chastised – but how far punishment may tend to reclaim him, deter others, or benefit the general Service. If other means will answer the same end, I fly to them with pleasure.' Now, however, on detecting the thief, he ordered that he run the gauntlet but that a known accomplice be left for the moment without being sentenced so that he might worry a few days about what punishment was in store for him, 'for reflection, when added to punishment, is often of more service than [punishment] itself'. Beaufort had already resolved to let him off lightly, for he was a feeble, sickly old man, a broken sergeant of

---

*Beaufort's propensity and talents for marine surveying were recognized even at this early stage of his hydrographic career. Before his departure from Plymouth, Alexander Dalrymple, the Admiralty's first Hydrographer, had ordered a chronometer to be issued to him – by no means standard equipment at that time and reserved, apparently, for only those officers capable of cartographic work. Dalrymple also specified those areas in the Indian Ocean for which he most needed observational data.

†The thief, stripped to the waist and preceded by the master-at-arms to prevent his moving too fast, walked or was dragged between a double line of the crew, each with three tarred rope yarns twisted and knotted at the end into a 'knittle' or 'nettle', who flogged him as he passed. At the end his whole body, not excluding the head, was flayed. After one, two or at the most three such ordeals, a few days apart, the culprit was deemed purged of his offence and it was never mentioned again.⁵

marines, 'and in his bitter circumstances had already drunk deep of misfortune'.

The captain had chosen to delay the sentence for another reason as well: he wanted nothing to interfere with the pleasurable events foreseen for the next day — and here one has some indication of where Beaufort found his pleasure. It was the witnessing of the occultation of Jupiter by the moon, to determine longitude. It was his sister Harriet's birthday and he meant to observe it, he wrote to her, by having

all my pupils [i.e. the midshipmen] rise from their slumbers at 7 in the morning and do homage to their master. . . . My mind was then unembarrassed. It bid fair to be a lovely day. A thousand charming associations of you. . . .

Well, up I rose. I rushed upon deck anxious to greet the first beams of Aurora . . . only to be told by the officer of the day, 'Sir, I fear Armstrong has jumped overboard.'

Never shall I forget how those words rung in my ears. Armstrong was the old man, and I supposed was so harassed by his concern, or so dreaded the severity of my punishment that he preferred death to them! To see a fellow creature voluntarily deprive himself of life for fear of my cruelty was a bitter reflection. . . . So ended your birthday, so terminated a day which my romantic or rather frivolous heart had looked forward to with gaiety and satisfaction for a week before hand.

The captain had the ship searched, but in vain. Armstrong had last been seen two hours before, going to the heads (latrines) from which he had apparently let himself down into the sea. But in fact he had not:

Hunger and thirst did more than our searches. On the 3rd night he came up from his hiding hole and crawled forward to the galley to obtain some refreshment. A tall Irishman who slept there happening to put his head out of his hammock saw him. Frightened out of his wits, he covered it immediately with his blanket and bellowed out, 'A ghost, a ghost!' The alarm was instantly general and in 3 minutes our drowned ghost was safely lodged in the bilboes.

Ironically, it was Beaufort, not Armstrong, who seems to have felt himself most punished. He wrote in his journal:

Two days ago I should have embraced with ardour anyone who could have held out a hope of the possibility that Armstrong might be saved. And yet today I feel almost vexed when I add here that hunger at last forced him from his hiding hole and that he is now deep in limbo! So unaccountable is it to the mind to be violently excited by nothing.

One is obliged to admire the self-confidence – even arrogance – of the British Establishment of the day. In deciding in the autumn of 1805 to instruct Short's squadron to call at the Cape of Good Hope, the British government acted in the face of the fact that the colony was then held by an enemy (the Dutch) with an army of 5000 men. It simply assumed that by the time Bligh and Short arrived, an expedition previously sent out would long since have retaken the Cape. Of course it did, with a minimum of trouble, early in January 1806, a few days before Short's squadron left the Channel. But Short's men obviously could not have known the result when they left.

Yet at no time did Beaufort ever allude in his journal, where he worried about almost everything else, to the possibility that he might be sailing into the arms of Napoleon's allies. Only in his long letter to Harriet does he mention, and then only casually, that he landed at Simonstown on 15 May, 'having ascertained that the English were in possession of the Cape'.

Despite the time lost in his vain search for Admiral Warren, he arrived only two days after Bligh and Short. At once each of the two feuding grandees sought his support.

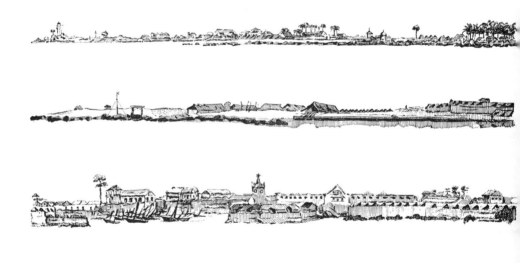

Each spoke in the most bitter terms of the other [a journal entry reads], each had written the most violent representations to the Admt^y. demanding courts martial on the other, and each claimed command here. . . . The question now was for me to decide, i.e., who should I acknowledge the Senior Officer of the Port? I was forced really in spite of my [berth?] to peruse their acrimonious statements. Which, my opinion was not long in forming: they were both wrong, both had acted intemperately and foolishly, both had laid themselves open to censure, which both will probably meet with, and both were equally resolved to stick to what they had already done and not to retract a single expression.

I afterwards attempted to conciliate a little but in vain . . . flint and steel would be easier united. The first thing, however, was to decide on whose supremacy I was to acknowledge. I immediately pronounced for Capt. Bligh.

His decision, insofar as it was based on the documents each had to show him, was that which the government (and most subsequent historians of the affray) came to. But he had another reason as well: the British military commander, Governor David Baird, had let him see secret orders from the Admiralty about some important business (not specified) which the senior officer would have to decide upon, 'and

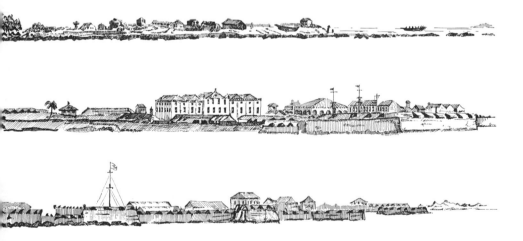

Beaufort's drawing of the Bombay waterfront, from a page in his sketchbook (now in the Hydrographic Department), summer 1806. Redrawn from the original by John Lanigan and reproduced by permission of the Hydrographer of the Navy.

whatever I thought of their mutual conduct, I perceived that one was a man of talents and the other an ass'.

The *Woolwich* was in good repair, her crew healthy, and Beaufort needed only a few days to provision and refit. In the interim he made friends with Baird and saw much of Bligh. The latter, grateful with good reason to Beaufort, sent him on his way to India on 2 June with a cordial and fatherly letter of advice on wind and track.

Beaufort's journal lapses abruptly with his sailing from the Cape; the next volume in the papers that have come down to us begins several years later. Conceivably he simply abandoned his personal chronicle for that period, although that is unlikely for such a conscientious and voluminous chronicler. But we have no more of his descriptions, observations and introspections to flesh out the bare bones of the log of his next voyages. His surviving correspondence over the next several months is also sparse.

From the *Woolwich*'s log, however, it appears that the three-week passage to Bombay was fast and uneventful except for one horrendous punishment. A seaman was first flogged and then made to run the gauntlet twice in three days for theft.

After reaching Bombay, three weeks were spent in the swapping-new-anchors-for-old kind of tasks for which a storeship was destined. Beaufort sketched the harbour and waterfront and took the soundings and bearings to which he was addicted. 'I seem to understand surveying harbours and shoals better than philosophizing,' he wrote to his father, 'and what people do best they generally like best.'

On receipt of orders overland from Madras, he sailed on 1 August, rounded the sub-continent and moored in Madras twelve days later to receive his next assignment from the commander-in-chief of the Indian Seas, the renowned and redoubtable Rear-Admiral Sir Edward Pellew.

A lasting friendship between the two men, based on mutual esteem, developed at once. Beaufort had come to Madras at the height of a monumental battle between Pellew and Rear-Admiral Sir Thomas Troubridge over the geographical extent and relative authority of each in the Indian Ocean. The controversy, originating from Pellew's one and only speech in Parliament two years before, was intricate, of almost unprecedented bitterness and needs only a word here.[6]

When Pitt was out of office and was trying to secure the fall of Addington by attacking the Admiralty, Pellew's speech, supporting the government, made an enemy of him. On Pitt's return to power he engineered a scheme to strip Pellew of the most lucrative half of his command in the East, and give it to Troubridge, who was sent out for the purpose. But on Pitt's death and Grenville's succession the situation was reversed, Pellew was restored to his full command and Troubridge was ordered to the Cape as admiral-in-charge there.

Pellew was not to hear of his triumph until the autumn of 1806. Thus, as far as he knew, the issue was still in the balance in the summer, when Beaufort arrived, and it may be assumed he was trying to make all the friends he could, the *Woolwich*'s captain for one. Moreover, Beaufort carried a strong letter of introduction from Sir Evan Nepean, a man with influence in high places in Whitehall, whose goodwill to Pellew might also be useful.

By October Beaufort had reprovisioned at Madras and taken aboard a new cargo – not 'old anchors' this time but old guns – plus seventy invalids from the Naval Hospital, fifty dragoons and many other supernumeraries. The ship must have been crowded to bursting. At the same time, Pellew resolved to attack the Dutch in Batavia before they could be joined by what was reported (inaccurately) to be a new French Fleet in the Indian Ocean. He was unwilling to spare a seventy-four-gun ship-of-the-line to escort the annual homeward voyage of the large, richly laden East India Company 'Opium' Fleet. But well escorted it had to be: French cruisers based on Mauritius had been successfully preying on the China trade.

Accordingly, what Beaufort dreamed of more than a year before when he was first made a storekeeper now came to pass. Pellew ordered the *Woolwich* to be reclassified as the frigate she once had been and re-armed to bring her up to strength. Her commander was breveted – with a splendidly glowing order – to be acting post-captain. The *Woolwich* was to accompany Pellew's squadron from Madras as far as the established rendezvous point for the China convoy, Trincomalee in Ceylon, and thence to escort the merchant ships back to England. Another frigate, the *Duncan*, was placed under Beaufort's command as far as the Cape and then was to return to Pellew.[7]

No first-hand word about Beaufort's sentiments has survived, but he must have been overjoyed. A nomination by as powerful a commander as Pellew, now restored to good graces by the new ministry, and a successful escort of fifteen rich Indiamen back to Britain should guarantee his confirmation to permanent post rank.

The squadron set sail from Madras on 22 October and reached Trincomalee a week later. Pellew and his warships turned eastward to capture Batavia, while the newly glorified frigate *Woolwich*, along with the *Duncan*, turned south-westward to the Cape. Once Beaufort had arrived at the Cape, Baird told him that the British station at St Helena was in desperate need of grain. Since some of the East Indiamen were loaded with rice, Beaufort determined to take the convoy there and relieve the incipient famine. He sailed from the Cape on 10 January and reached the lonely island in the South Atlantic two weeks later. He had no way of divining that he was about to serve himself badly by his mission of mercy and his sense of duty and responsibility.

Leaving the Cape just five days behind him and in hot pursuit was the frigate *Sampson*, which had recently arrived from Montevideo. A day or two before, a smaller vessel had arrived at Simonstown from India carrying what were represented as the most urgent dispatches from the commander-in-chief at Ceylon, Lieutenant-General Sir Thomas Maitland. They were at once transferred to the *Sampson*, which was ordered to overhaul the *Woolwich* if she could and have the latter take them on to England.

The documents were not all that important. Maitland was over-reacting to an insurrection on the west coast of India which he thought presaged an uprising of the whole sub-continent. He mistrusted the authorities in Madras to meet the threat properly. As it happened, a few troops whom Maitland dispatched to the scene to reinforce those already there handled the trouble effectively.

But Maitland's appeals for speed in getting his warnings back to London could not be ignored. The Governor of St Helena ordered Beaufort, who was still watering when the *Sampson* caught up with him, to take off with maximum haste, leaving the convoy behind for the slower sailing *Sampson* to escort the rest of the way home.[8]

On his return to England Beaufort reported to the Admiralty[9] that he had departed at once, 'aware of the high importance of the mission entrusted to me . . . all the canvas that HM's ship could support [was] invariably carried by day and by night; and all my officers being animated by equal zeal, the same sail had been constantly set and the same means resorted to as if we had been in continual and anxious chace'.

But his luck had again been reversed. 'Perverse and baffling' winds dragged out the passage home for almost two months. He arrived at

Plymouth on 21 March at 7.30 p.m., rushed to London by coach with his dispatches and had them in the Admiralty's hands by midnight the next night.

His detachment from his convoy cost him the £500 of plate customarily given by the East India Company to every captain who safely shepherded home a convoy of its ships. He complained of the loss in later years in stories to his children, forgetting, it seems, his one-time lofty indignation at the idea of officers of His Majesty's Navy accepting emoluments from shopkeepers. But he had much more to lament at the time: had he brought into Plymouth, without loss or cripples, fifteen fine ships, confirmation of the promotion which Pellew had breveted him could scarcely have been denied.

As it was Beaufort immediately laid Pellew's commission before the Admiralty with a request that his promotion be confirmed. A reply from William Marsden, First Secretary, was equally swiftly returned: 'I have it in command to acquaint you that as Sir Edward Pellew had not received their Lordships' directions to alter the Establishment of the *Woolwich*; they cannot confirm the Appointment.'

Lady Lavinia Spencer, one of the most prominent woman in British society, a relation of Beaufort's mother and the wife of the former First Lord of the Admiralty, politicked on Beaufort's behalf. All negotiations failed. 'I needed not that blow,' he wrote.

A few days later came word of Charlotte's death and simultaneously news that the *Woolwich* was to be converted to a hospital ship. He wrote to his family:

To be posted first into a storeship and then converted to a Hospital would at any other time have excited the most exquisite rage and mortification, whereas now, surrounded by drugs and plaisters, by the ghastly looks of the sick, the cries of the wounded, the groans of the dying and the half stifled sighs of despair, I shall every moment be convinced that there are people as miserable as myself. . . . I hope you will allow me to doze away the remainder of my life in peace, in indigence and in proud obscurity. What motive is there left to do otherwise? Neither love, ambition . . . gratitude or zeal.

He reflected on what he had written and added a last line: 'Don't imagine I intend quitting my ship – no such idea.'

Despite everything, he was the Navy's man.

15

Woolwich: 'Interest' (1807-1809)

I have seen Lord Mulgrave & 20 others to whom I
went bowing and smiling & came away frowning and
cursing. You may grasp therefore that I am where I
was, and where I shall probably remain unless I take
the trouble to have my throat cut again to oblige the
courteous Premier of the Admiralty who hinted on
most polite and *friendly* terms that was the way to get
on now.

BEAUFORT to his brother[1]

Beaufort was spared the worst of his anticipations. Orders were issued
cancelling the conversion of the *Woolwich* to a hospital ship. She was
needed instead in her old role to rush supplies to British forces in the
River Plate, attempting an invasion that was soon to turn into a
humiliating rout.

Beaufort supervised three months of refitting at Plymouth by day
and wrote letters of misery by night, cursing the loss of the £500 that
he might have had from the East India Company and which he might
have used judiciously with Members of Parliament to advance his
cause. He tried vainly to reassure his father, who had been complaining
to him for not trying harder to enlist 'interest', that he had done all
that was possible, and that he would press no more.

Yet he continued. His correspondence shows him appealing to his
father's and Edgeworth's long-time friends and Irish neighbours,
Lord Longford, Lord Courtown and John Foster, a Member of
Parliament and Chancellor of the Irish Exchequer.

Edgeworth himself asked the help of another Irish peer, Lord
Palmerston, then just beginning his political career as a Member of
Parliament and junior Lord of the Admiralty, and promised to intercede

with his friend W. W. Pole, the new First Secretary of the Admiralty. Beaufort asked his brother to recruit in his cause Thomas Pelham, the second Earl of Chichester, currently joint-Postmaster General. He himself asked help from Admiral C. P. Hamilton, father of the mid- shipman who had eased his wounds at the capture of the *San Josef.*

All efforts were vain. Still in what he viewed as the 'equivocal' rank of commander, Beaufort sailed in 'this Pandora's box of miseries' on 18 May 1807.

Not a sail was seen in the six weeks' smooth passage to South America. But the behaviour of the crew was turbulent enough. In six months eight men deserted and eleven were flogged. One of them was administered forty-eight strokes. A curious log entry on the outward trip records: 'Convicted the gunner of telling 37 lies in 2 minutes', a virtuoso performance.

Between the time Beaufort sailed from Plymouth and anchored off Montevideo, disaster had overwhelmed the British Army.

The expedition to take Buenos Aires and Montevideo had begun in April 1806 and, ill-advised though it was, met with success in the beginning. Sir Home Popham, swelled with his easy victory late in 1805 at the Cape of Good Hope, received word from the captain of an American merchantman – in such a matter not the most reliable source – that the inhabitants of Buenos Aires and Montevideo would offer no resistance to a British force. The admiral set sail from Table Bay and in short order took Montevideo and received the capitulation of Buenos Aires. But within weeks an insurrection in the latter city, supported by troops deftly sidled in by a French colonel in the Spanish service, obliged Popham to surrender the city. He was called home to be severely reprimanded.

The Naval forces withdrew to an anchorage east of Montevideo. London thereupon decided to send a good cheese after a bad: a large Naval, marine and military force set sail from Britain in May 1807, some days before Beaufort was ready to follow. On 5 July, attacking Buenos Aires, the British were miserably defeated by the same French officer. The British suffered 2500 killed, wounded and prisoners. The victor offered to give up the prisoners if the British would evacuate the River Plate in two months. Whether they had an option is debatable, but in the event they agreed to pull out.

This was the situation into which Beaufort sailed, three weeks after the defeat. It affected him, if we can judge by the tone of his letters, almost more agonizingly than his own woes.

He wrote to his sister Harriet: 'There is nothing to be seen here but wretchedness and disgrace, nothing to be done here but to reflect either on my own miseries or on those of my country, defeated and laughed at in all quarters, and no vigour or activity displayed but the vigour and activity of running away.'

The *Woolwich* was ordered to take aboard more than a hundred disheartened troops and join the humiliated convoy that evacuated the river on 10 September. In a month they were back at the Cape of Good Hope.

There Beaufort made a curious proposal, born, it would seem, of desperation. He requested the new admiral in command, Rear-Admiral Charles Stirling, to be allowed to exchange positions with Edward Thomas Troubridge, acting-captain of a frigate, part of Pellew's forces, then at the Cape. Beaufort's idea was to rejoin Pellew, the friend he had made the year before and with whom there might be a prospect of action in the Indian Ocean. Troubridge, depressed by the loss of his father, the Admiral, wanted to return to England.* He was, in fact, invalided home three months later.

Admiral Stirling refused the request, noting that the proposed exchanges 'would be unprecedented in the Service'.

Frustrated, Beaufort sailed back to the Downs in convoy with ships and troops from the South American defeat. It was a stormy voyage. Two men were lost overboard in gales, some of the invalids died en route and the captain was kept busy taking one after another storm-damaged ship in tow while repairs were effected. The *Woolwich* reached home at the end of January 1808.

Beaufort had one piece of business to attend to at once with W. W. Pole at the Admiralty:

Downes [*sic*]
Jan 27, 1808

. . . . Soon after the arrival [of the *Woolwich* at the Cape] in October last, one of her crew (John Fortune, a man of colour) who had entered the pre-

---

*Having lost his political battle with Pellew and transferred to the command of the Naval forces at the Cape, Admiral Troubridge sailed from India in his unseaworthy flagship, the *Blenheim*. She went down with all hands in a tremendous gale in January 1807 off Réunion.

ceding January at the Cape, and who had received the King's bounty in England, was demanded by the Fiscal of that colony as being a slave, the property of Christopher Smith, an English inhabitant.

The case was referred to Rear-Admiral Stirling, by whom I was directed to discharge him on the property being proved. But when Mr Smith came on board to do so, the man was missing. The most earnest but fruitless search was immediately made by the first lieutenant and other officers, and it was supposed that, eluding the vigilance of the sentinels, he had escaped from the ship.

The horror, however, which he had uniformly expressed to the returning to his old master led me to suspect that he might still be secreted in the ship . . .

And indeed he was. Beaufort retold the story in less guarded terms years later to Edgeworth and Fanny, who had heard that he had been accused of 'imprudence and foolish good nature'. The then civil governor, Lord Caledon, had ordered Beaufort peremptorily to give the man up. When Smith came aboard and the slave was not to be found he 'humanely asked me to let him have a spike to *poke* him with if in any of the Casks or ballast! Other inhuman threats also of this gentleman who swore he would whip him every day of his life, etc. made me openly rejoice in his disappointment.'

Beaufort promised that if the man were in fact aboard and should be discovered after sailing, he would 'prevent a second occultation'. But, provoked by the asperity of Caledon over the matter, Beaufort responded in kind, saying: 'I had hoped to find it the pride and boast of Englishmen, whether Governors or Captains, to share their freedom with the inhabitants of every clime where their influence extended to protect the adopted sons of G. Britain as well as her native subjects, and to make the abolition of slavery a fact as well as a law.'

Two days after sailing, the half-starved black man – a favourite of the crew and a fully qualified seaman – appeared above hatches. The captain put him in chains, as he had promised to do. Once back in England, he took advantage of an order to discharge twenty men into another frigate bound for the West Indies to include John Fortune among them. Then, when he was out of the reach 'of the Gentlemen of the black robe' and would not be back until he had served a full two years on board a King's ship (and would thus be absolutely enfranchised beyond any legal question), Beaufort asked the Admiralty what was their pleasure. He must have known beforehand the answer to be expected: the Somerset Judgment of 1772 set free former slaves who made their way to England. Retain John Fortune as a mariner who had voluntarily entered the King's Service and received the King's bounty, said the law officers of the Crown.[2]

For almost six months the *Woolwich* lay in the Thames, for refitting and provisioning for the next voyage, while her captain at once resumed his politicking. The only result was to make him hate himself.

He enlisted the aid of those who had tried to help him before. From them he received encouragement and from most of them their best efforts. These were insufficient. Stopford, though newly made rear-admiral, lamented that he no longer possessed influence. Pellew wrote his best wishes for promotion, adding: 'I know of no man who merits it more with whom I would sooner serev.'

All of which buttered no parsnips. 'Impotence and civility,' Beaufort concluded, 'have unfortunately in my friends preserved a direct ratio to each other.' His trouble was that he was 'without a parliamentary or a petticoat interest'.

He had, of course, again called on the First Lord, Henry Phipps, First Earl of Mulgrave, for whom by now he had developed an obsessional hatred.

Mulgrave told Beaufort that there was a prodigious number of officers on the post-captain promotion list, 'all gallant and with claims for preferment', and that he was lucky even to retain his ship. Entitlement to promotion, Mulgrave said, came as a 'right' only as a consequence of 'some of those affairs of *éclat*'. In other words, as Mulgrave had implied to him almost a year before, Beaufort had better 'have my throat cut' in some further deeds of daring if he expected to win advancement. Yet he knew that Mulgrave had just promoted to post-captain an actor's son because Mulgrave fancied himself to be a 'great theatrical connoisseur'.

Impressed by Beaufort's surveying in the River Plate, Dalrymple, the Hydrographer, asked the Admiralty for the *Woolwich* to be assigned to survey the English, Dutch and Danish coasts. The ship was for the moment without other orders, was 'most admirably adapted for the Service . . . and her Commander unquestionably as fit as any Man now living to be entrusted with the execution of the Service. I mean Captain Beaufort.'[3] But Beaufort's ill-luck held; the Admiralty declined the proposal.

From his distant observation point in Collon, the Reverend Dr Beaufort kept chiding his son to exert himself more energetically in soliciting support. The son exploded:

> HMS *Woolwich* at Woolwich
> April 5, 1808
>
> .... Let me just remark *en passant* that your reproaches – no, not reproaches, but kind expostulations – about asking and bowing and so forth were rather unexpected. I had almost looked for a certain portion of praise for having exchanged my antient reluctance to begging and cringing for a degree of sturdy beggary that could have done honour to a North Briton.
>
> Have I not patiently sat to hear the unmeaning nothings of some lordly folk about cold winds and cold weather while I could feel nothing cold but their cold hearts? Have I not besieged other great men's doors, stretched myself in their lobbies and antechambers, counted the squares in the carpets or the leaves on the Wall Paper for hours, just to be admitted to one condescending nod?
>
> Have I not after staying in the august presences two minutes been telegraphed off by a significant yawn or a busy search for some paper with their back to me?
>
> I will add no more ... but let me just seriously ask you, would an immediate Post Commission at my age and with my prospects be sufficient repayment for that continually undermining of my self esteem, and thus doing every day what produces a blush on my pillow every night?

The *Woolwich* set sail again in mid-July 1808 for nine months of shuttling between Gibraltar, Malta and Sicily, mostly in vile weather. Barely a week out the floggings began again. As an indication of relative degrees of iniquity in the Royal Navy of the day, it may be noted that Beaufort ordered twenty-four lashes for a marine who struck a sentinel, but only twelve for a seaman convicted of 'beastliness'. Captains could be and usually were blind to sodomy, there being so much of it, but bestiality, when apprehended, had to be punished, even if not as heavily as some other crimes.

Beaufort was dejected throughout. His letters suggest spiritual lassitude, close to defeat. He was back in England by mid-April 1809, having done nothing, he confided to William, to entitle him to promotion and with no more going for him and his cause than when he left. The only difference was that he was now – he said – indifferent whether he succeeded or failed. He felt sure the ship and he would be paid off.

He made a final attempt with the First Lord, and reported the results to his father.

I have seen my Lord Mulgrave and have talked to him and as I swear and declare that [as] I had not the *very slightest* expectations of inducing him to do the *very slightest* favour to me I have not felt the very slightest disappointment but I do feel more than slightly stung at the cold blooded apathy with which he listened to my 'tale' and with some fulsome and frivolous compliment seemed to wish to cut it short.

I would be heard out, pleaded my long services, my character, my wounds, my former promotion, etc. The first of which, my long services, he candidly confessed was *'no claim nowadays!'* . . . To be told with a cold freezing unfeeling look that Services are no claim to protection does really move my indignation more than I can collect bile enough in my pen to write. . . .

Ah! my dear father, that accursed asking has been the ruin of my happiness. Had I never danced attendance nor bowed my cringing back to [Mulgrave], nor to Lords Courtown, or Stopford, or Longford, or to Lord and Lady Spencer or to any body else, I should have been just as far as I am, but with this proud difference of having never to reproach myself with being a poor discarded supplicant.

I hate myself for having been an unsuccessful beggar, and I declare that I would as soon that the world knew that I had bribed Mrs Mary Ann Clarke, or employed Captn. Huxley Sandon,* as that I had ever been whining at any planhandler's footstool. . . . The truth is that my Lord Mulgrave's reply has been a spark that has set all my feelings in a flame or in a fever. I reflect on the prospects I once had afloat and of which the d——th System of parliamentary influence and Corruption has deprived me, and I look forward – to what you do not expect me to insert here – to happiness.

Yes, I am resolved to be happy – absolutely resolved.

The resolve may have lasted the night, but no more. As before, when he forecast happiness in moments of despair, Beaufort could not have convinced himself of his prophecy for more than an hour.

---

*The outrageously extravagant mistress of Frederick, Duke of York, then commander-in-chief of the Army, Mrs Clarke was the centre of a volcanic scandal of the day, having induced her easygoing lover to give commissions to Army officers in return for large fees to her. Sandon was one of her procurers of applicants, also for a fee.

16

Blossom
(1809-1810)

If I obtain anything besides honour and credit in the
service, it shall be by the means I achieved my first
post, Industry.

BEAUFORT to his father[1]

In May 1809 Lord Mulgrave tossed Beaufort a bone: the eighteen-gun
sloop* *Blossom*. At least she was a ship of war and her commander was
no longer manager of a sea-going warehouse.

Beaufort was entitled to something better. He was convinced that
Mulgrave had ordered the transfer 'to throw dust in the eyes of my
friends . . . and to have the answer ready for them: "Oh! See what a
fine sloop I have given him!" '

The First Lord did indeed try to make capital out of the appoint-
ment, writing to Admiral Hamilton and Lord Stopford (the Earl of
Courtown's eldest son and Admiral Stopford's elder brother) assuring
each, separately, that his intercession had been the determining factor.
Beaufort took pains to tell each of the other's letter from Mulgrave:
'Lord S. was enraged, and the Admiral gave him a damn.'

Beaufort believed that he could have had command of a sloop at
any time in the last few years had he asked to be transferred. He had
not, as he told his family a year before, because, 'first, I have always
considered my being placed in a storeship a disgrace, and therefore till
I am voluntarily removed from her I prefer remaining', and second, his
claim for promotion would be undermined: the Admiralty could have
cited his transfer as the answer to any further appeals.

---

*In the Navy at the time, a sloop was a full-rigged, three-masted ship. It is not to be
confused with the single-masted fore-and-aft rigged sloop of today.

Vile old ship he may have thought the *Woolwich*, but it was a wrench to leave a home in which he had sailed 60000 miles in three years. He shook hands with his crew and declared he wanted to go through no such ordeal again:

Poor fellows, it was most gratifying yet distressing to see the tears running down their coarse and rugged cheeks. . . . I could only squeeze their tarry hands, and may I lose my power to squeeze whenever I am ashamed to do so, or whenever I shall feel more gratification in squeezing the delicate fingers of a virgin of nineteen than the rough but honest paw of a faithful, brave and warmhearted shipmate.

He had mixed feelings about the *Blossom*: 'My little morcel of a sloop is tolerably well, too. She sails decently, but is wretchedly crank, that is, with any wind she leans over very much.' He also discovered that in any wind her decks were constantly wet, bringing endless colds and discomfort to his lead-burdened lungs.

The first voyage, beginning in June 1809, was as escort to a convoy to Corunna, where troops were put ashore to reinforce Sir Arthur Wellesley in the early stages of his Peninsular campaign. The *Blossom* returned with dispatches telling the good news of Marshal Ney's evacuation of Corunna.

Beaufort's views of the Spaniards were mixed. Referring to one general, he wrote:

He is a sensible man, I think, and though not very bright is staunch, which in the present politics in Spain is as rare as a black swan, particularly among the lower class, who take arms today and tomorrow disperse upon the slightest check. They throw their English musquet and Ball into a ditch and, having no other symptom of military costume about them, return to their hut and swear to the French that they were only at the neighbouring village to sell a pig or to confess. The next time, however, that they do confess the priest sends them off again into the armies (or want of work or a momentary scarcity in the district carry them there) and this sort of circle many of them perform over & over again, & which is much facilitated to them by the long chains of mountain on which they keep.

He was pessimistic about the chances of the Spanish and English forces and morose about war in general. Gone from his correspondence was what had once been the focal word, 'glory'. Reintroduced to the scene of war again for the first time since the rout at Montevideo two years before, he saw it at its worst and was sick of it.

The change in attitude had begun at least a year before. He told his brother that although war was his trade, his 'soul sickens at seeing all the world cutting or endeavouring to cut each other's throats, for what, they know not'. He was, he said, inclined to subscribe to the principle 'that War, hatred & the lure of mischief are more congenial to the human mind than Peace, friendship and kindness'.

There was some comfort to be taken, however, when a change of orders assigned the *Blossom* in mid-July 1809 to escort a convoy to Quebec. Beaufort's first (and only) visit to North America awed and excited him. He had only three days ashore to satisfy his 'restless curiosity' but they were enough to provide rapturous descriptions to his sisters:

. . . . that great feature of the American world: the river St Lawrence! A thousand miles from its source and 4 hundred from its mouth, my little bark was moored – 20 fathoms of water below me and the city of Quebec twice as many fathoms above me. In one direction high rocky precipices torn and shook in all directions as if Deluge and Earthquake were the only agents employed there by nature; in another, immeasurable plains of grass & corn, studded with smiling cottages & clumps of trees, and bounded by the high blue mountains whose primeval forests still nod upon their summits – making puny the efforts of man, whose numbers and resources must increase so much before his axe is applied to them.

To his brother he wrote of agriculture and minerals and the exciting vision of economic development.

The *Blossom* shepherded a convoy safely back to England in early November. By mid-February 1810 she was again in the Mediterranean and for three months served as escort, sentinel and courier from Cadiz to the mouth of the Channel. Beaufort felt himself growing old in such service: 'Alack, my dear father, a constitution once thoroughly shook is easy to discompose and hard to repair. I tell you all this beforehand that you may not be much astonished when you see me to see a little, wrinkled, sallow, parched old fellow. . . .'

What he saw on his occasional days in port in Spain and what he heard of the progress of the Peninsular War – then in its most discouraging days – likewise did little to cheer him. He wrote to Fanny:

The nobles and priests . . . do certainly keep up a large portion of animosity to the French but the people have seen . . . that a real emancipation is not the object of their leaders, and that the difference between the two tyrants is not worth the continuance of the struggles. Such is the language of many Spaniards, and such I believe to be the sentiments of the majority. They are indeed somewhat like my own.

Fortunately Sir Arthur Wellesley, now Lord Wellington, was of another opinion.

The Admiralty's unjust dealing with Beaufort and his resulting frustrations were not unique. In evidence is the rhyme attributed to Captain Marryat about the famous anteroom of the First Lord, where so many kicked their heels in weary and forlorn waiting:

> In sore affliction tried, by God's commands
> Of patience, Job the great example stands.
> But in these days a trial more severe
> Had been Job's lot, if God had sent him here.

In Marryat's novel *Peter Simple* there is the episode of a newly appointed captain rushing from the waiting room – ante-chamber to each assignment-hunter's private hell or heaven – to take command of the ship just given him before some rival captain brought 'interest' to bear and changed the First Lord's mind.

Conversely, the accounts are almost as abundant of those who *had* 'interest' making the rank of post-captain after ludicrously short service. To be sure, some had done dazzling deeds but there were legions of others who advanced almost as rapidly without any such accomplishments.

But if Beaufort's experience was not the worst example of the iniquity of the 'interest' system it is surely a textbook illustration. His seamanship, the esteem he won from his superiors and associates, his history as an effective, humane commander, his capture of the *San Josef* – all these were entitlement in themselves. But beyond that was his reputation widely known among his colleagues and validated by his contributions to the Admiralty, as one of the Navy's ablest surveyors, 'scientists' and – to use another term not yet coined – technologists.

From his teenage days Beaufort had continued steadily with his 'hobby or insanity' of taking bearings and soundings. Even as a midshipman, his extravagances were his purchases of observational instruments – and from none other than Edward Troughton, the foremost instrument maker of the age. As early as 1803 Beaufort was in lengthy correspondence with him and two years later Troughton wrote to him one of many highly technical letters (in his splendidly idiosyncratic spelling and syntax) about the use of his instruments: 'I am conscous of being writing to a Gentelman with a mind at least as clever and powerful as my own, and much better educated, but I am more harkened in such recerches.'

On his first voyage in the *Woolwich* Beaufort filled a book with his sketches and bearings of lonely islands and rocks he encountered in the South Atlantic, and sent them back to Dalrymple; a few months later he also charted in the Indian Ocean. Dalrymple persuaded Mulgrave to supply him on the next voyage with *three* chronometers, 'an extraordinary compliment conferred on no one but discoverers and navigators', Beaufort proudly explained to his brother. The result was the first reliable survey of the approaches to Montevideo and off-lying banks and (gratuitously submitted in the hope of winning a few extra credits) plans for attacking the fortifications should the need arise. He did the work, he said, 'to keep the devil out of my mind'. Generous Admiralty thanks were forthcoming and Dalrymple in particular was very impressed. Two years later, he wrote to the Admiralty implying that Beaufort's promotion was long overdue.

In another letter to the Admiralty Dalrymple cited the testimony of Captain Duncombe Pleydell Bouverie, who stated that Beaufort 'did more in the month he was in the River Plate to acquire a correct knowledge of its Dangers, than was done by everyone together before'.[2]

Beaufort's letters to Richard Lovell Edgeworth in the years following their joint work on the Irish telegraph show him speculating on a wide range of technological subjects. He was also probably putting his ideas to some of his service colleagues and other 'natural philosophers' (he had, for example, brought back a unique specimen of phosphorescent jellyfish for the collection of Sir Joseph Banks from his first voyage in the *Woolwich*). He asked Edgeworth to bend his mind to the invention of a permanent odometer to gauge a ship's speed and distance travelled inasmuch as the centuries-old device of casting a log was awkward and discontinuous; he himself was getting nowhere on the project. He sent Edgeworth and his father a steady flow of descriptions on new industrial and farm machinery he had seen, critiques of other inventors' devices to curb the recoil of carronades and even – with the utmost solemnity until he saw at the end that he had been ridiculous – instructions on how best to employ a razor: 'I have long been aware of the decided superiority of the pushing oblique movement of shaving. . . . The push is attended by a degree of lateral pressures on the face which keeps the edge steady to the roots of the beard and facilitates cutting in a two-fold ratio, whereas. . . .' and so on for two long paragraphs.

How, he demanded of Edgeworth, can one measure current from *aboard* a ship? The standard method – which his logs show he tirelessly employed – of launching a boat, lowering from it a weighted bucket (to moor it, so to speak), and calculating from the angle of the line the drift of the craft, was a nuisance. (It was, in fact, more unsatisfactory than he suspected. The unvoiced and erroneous premise of the procedure was that there was no current below certain depths and that, accordingly, the bucket would remain motionless while the boat drifted with what current there was.)

To the Admiralty Beaufort sent plans for adopting 'Simple Paddy', the semaphore device he and Edgeworth used in Ireland, to Naval signalling (the machine was by no stretch of the imagination simple, though its awkwardness may have qualified it as Irish). He also devised a set of signal flags on the same principle, although with different execution, as those used by today's ships, and a system for signalling at night with lamps.[3] Much more usefully, he prepared a codification and index to standing Naval Instructions, which was received gratefully, and a list of *errata* for correction of the Instructions, for which he was also thanked. Both documents were ordered to be printed and distributed. Their Lordships expressed their pleasure at his 'zeal' in transmitting reports to the Hydrographer.

Two of Beaufort's ideas are worth noting in more detail, if only as illustrations of his appreciation of the right principle and his invariable choice of the most clumsy means of execution. One was a proposal for transporting heavy artillery over swampy ground. His solution was in essence caterpillar tracks, assembled around the gun on the same principle as a First World War tank, but in monstrous proportions.

Suppose it was an octagon, each side about twice the length of a Field piece, the platform part made of trussed planks across, with railway planks, the joints to detach occasionally to let out the gun. I thought of connecting the planks so that as the motive power pushed or pulled the Gun, so should the next platform descend and the last ascend.

The drawing suggests a horror ten storeys high. But the idea was right, fifty or more years before the first track-laying vehicle was constructed.

Beaufort's sketch of a device for transporting cannon across swampy ground;
a page from a letter to Edgeworth, 5 May 1808.

The second useful notion – with its awkward construction – was a
sighting device for shipborne guns. These were tapered from breech
to muzzle, so that a gunner sighting along the top would at all times
be directing the missile to a spot below the actual target. Beaufort
proposed building up the rim of the muzzle to a square, the top of
which would be as high above the centre of the gun as was the top of
the breech, so that the line of sight would be parallel to the axis of the
bore.

He was also one of the earliest investigators, beginning in 1806, of
the mysterious phenomenon of a daily 'flux' of the barometer which
rises to a peak of about one-tenth of an inch above its low point twice
a day, roughly two hours before noon and midnight. He gave his first
results to Dalrymple, who passed them on to the celebrated chemist,
Henry Cavendish. He pursued the study, until by 1826 he had amassed
a great volume of observations of his own and other captains whom he
interested in the subject. Much later he was receiving reports of the
same phenomenon from a set of new friends, the great British Polar
explorers of the second quarter of the nineteenth century (much to his
surprise, for he thought the manifestation was confined to tropical
latitudes).*

*The diurnal variation was the subject of active speculation for many years; its
explanation did not come until 1890, when Lord Kelvin demonstrated that two great
pressure waves, thermally induced, flow around the earth from east to west in twenty-
four-hour cycles. Soon afterwards daily atmospheric vibrations were identified as pul-
sating to and from the Equator and the Poles.

There is ample evidence that both the injustice done to Beaufort and his exceptional talents as a scientific investigator were widely recognized by the Naval Lords and elsewhere in the Navy. Admirals Pellew, Stopford and Hamilton were outraged at the Admiralty's neglect of him. But the most impressive piece of evidence of general indignation is a letter written by Captain Peter Heywood to a friend, David Malcolm.

Heywood was the sixteen-year-old midshipman on the *Bounty* who had been left behind by the mutineers on Tahiti and was later brought back to England and sentenced to death by a court-martial. He was pardoned by the King and ultimately rose to the rank of post-captain. From his own bitter experience, he recognized injustice when he saw it.

As early as 1807, when he probably first met Beaufort in the River Plate, Heywood had noted in his log that but for Beaufort the true nature of two major hazards, the Archimedes and English banks on which the two warships had previously struck, would not have been established.[4] Heywood's letter to Malcolm was written in June 1809 from Chatham when he was in command of the frigate *Nereus*. The context is not entirely clear but the schoolboy Latin is easily interpreted:

My dear David,

... The Captain he referred me to & of whom I spoke & think more highly in point of professional ability, whether practical or scientific, than of almost any man in the service, & whose rare qualities both as an officer & a man I have met with very few and who possess in anything like degree, is only a poor Commander ...

He has been most hardly & illiberally dealt with because he would not condescend to belong to the family of 'Kisarcii of the Low Countries' in the reign of a certain noble Lord of the Admiralty. His name is Francis Beaufort & he at present commands the *Blossom* sloop. Why? I'll tell you, David. I will go much further and say of him that Beaufort has, I firmly believe, no equal in the King's naval service in any of the various qualities requisite to constitute [a] thorough seaman; a perfect navigator & an officer full of gallantry, zeal & clever judgement in everything that relates to his profession. ...

Yrs faithfully
P. Heywood

17

Post-Captain
(1810)

... for though I would rather have *frayé le chemin* by
my sword or have had it the result of the accumulation of every gazette in Europe, yet it is sufficiently
flattering, to render it infinitely more acceptable, than
if the merits of a vote or the partiality of a faction had
given it to me twenty years ago.

BEAUFORT to Edgeworth and Fanny[1]

In mid-May 1810 Beaufort was at the nadir of his hopes. The masters
of the world, he wrote to the wife of his first captain, Lestock Wilson,
judge increasingly on 'things to be given & got'. Since he had nothing
to give, 'neither venal votes nor party support . . . I shall get nothing'.
The old ties to the Navy, he wrote unconvincingly to his sister Fanny,
were slackening fast:

I often ask myself, *à quoi bon?* What object can I now have? Riches?
There is nothing more to be gained and if there were, to serve merely to
fatten on plunder and robbing is but a base idea. Promotion? It is now too
late to enjoy: post me today, yet some years must elapse before I could
obtain a decent frigate. And at just the same age [he was now thirty-five]
that Lord Nelson and Adm¹. Stopford hoisted their Admiral's flag.

Five days after his assurance to Mrs Wilson that he would get
'nothing', he crowed a different song. He reported that Mulgrave had
been removed and replaced by the learned and experienced politician,
Charles Philip Yorke; that Yorke at last had given ear to the Naval
Lords – in whose judgement Beaufort's lack of advancement was by
now almost certainly a scandal – and that he was about to be posted.
Confirmation was soon forthcoming. He began his report of the news
grudgingly: the epaulet 'was once an object of immeasurable pleasure',

and then exploded with what was in his heart: '. . . but the delight is unspeakable, ineffable, sublime and almost passing comprehension of owing my promotion to my own character without the intervention of friends!!!!!!! If this is so I shall really be pleased.'

His conclusion of cause and effect was not overstated. Yorke told one of Beaufort's advocates that there was no need of his pressing on Beaufort's behalf because 'every other person has [already] borne such full & universal testimony of his merit' that Yorke 'gladly embraced the opportunity of rewarding so meritorious an officer'.

Beaufort's was among the first promotions made on Yorke's taking office.

There was even better news to come. On 30 May 1810 Beaufort was told he would be given command of the *Fredericksteen*, a thirty-two-gun frigate captured from the Danes at the Battle of Copenhagen. The ship 'is far above the rate generally conferred on a young post. Indeed to be unsolicitedly posted, employed and appointed to a desirable frigate of 32 guns . . . is a most gratifying confirmation of many mighty civil speeches that their Lord^s. have lately used about me.'

There was still more news for his family: 'I am desirous to communicate with you, my dearly beloved friends, another circumstance [which] is of far greater importance than any ship or rank that Fame or Fortune can bestow. In a few words, I have a matrimonial scheme on hand.'

His fiancée was Alicia Magdalena Wilson, eldest daughter of his captain on the *Vansittart*. As we have seen, Lestock Wilson had taken at once to his 'Guinea Pig' of twenty-one years ago, followed his career with the deepest interest and regarded him with fatherly affection. So also had his wife, whose surviving letters to Beaufort, long before he was a suitor for Alicia, showed that she had become a confidante and warm friend. Alicia herself had cast what the times called 'a feminine eye' on Francis for several years. It is probable that, encouraged by her parents, it was she who made the running. For at least a decade, during intervals between voyages, Beaufort had been an escort, dinner and breakfast guest at the Wilsons.

He reported his intentions to his family in surprisingly matter-of-fact terms. Alicia, he wrote, 'is about 27 [she was twenty-eight and a half], much in proportion to our own family [i.e. small], no beauty, but a good though very delicate figure. Her principles are incomparable, her education laboured though mismanaged, her temper excellent though quick, her head strong, but her heart weak as she had sacrificed it to me.'

Wilson, he continued, had settled some property on her – £2500, to be matched by a like sum on the marriage – and 'will do what is right', consonant with his obligations to his two sons and two other daughters. But money was never Beaufort's deity, he proclaimed, 'and no one considers it less indispensable to happiness than I'. With that the letter turned to the price of bricks and tiles on the Isle of Wight.

However lacking in ardour and romantic sentiment the thirty-six-year old swain appears to have been at the outset, his love for Alicia mounted during their twenty-one years of marriage to a consuming passion. He idolized her – quite literally, to the point of worshipping at her tomb one or more times a year after her death until he was too feeble to make the pilgrimage.

Wilson had been able to provide his daughter with the conventional upbringing of a young gentlewoman. Far from being penalized for the loss of the *Vansittart*, he was given command of the largest and finest ship of the East India Company, the *Exeter*, and plied her with profit until 1800. Thereupon he was appointed arbitrator for the Company and at the same time founded, with an associate of long standing, a shipping company, Palmer, Wilson & Co., and operated it successfully for the next two decades.

Despite incessant moving from hither to yon, Alicia did what was orthodox for young ladies of some means in the latter years of George III's reign. She made the usual social calls on the houses of the gentry, attended salons and balls and exhibitions, saw Mrs Siddons in *The Gamester* at the theatre, and, at seventeen, took her first sacrament and made her debut 'at a Route' given by an aunt. She emerged as a lovely and cultivated young woman – as her letters later in life amply show – humourless but intelligent, intensely loyal to her husband and singularly liberal and advanced in her attitudes, especially towards education and social responsibility.

Although her letters never carry a burden of religious piety, she was nevertheless extremely devout in a quiet and unvoiced way. It was clearly her deep faith and utter resignation to Providence that sustained her, cheerful and indeed happy, through the last terrible years of the cancer that destroyed her in 1834.

When Francis and Alicia became engaged she and her family lived part of the year in London at 31 Harley Street and the rest at their large country house and nine-acre estate at Epping. In her social rounds she had met the two Miss Sneyds, sisters-in-law of Edgeworth – she pronounced them 'specimens of Irish tabbies' – and probably through them also Beaufort's elder sister, Mrs Edgeworth, and Maria. Letters between members of the Edgeworth family[2] suggest that they thought Francis was marrying beneath his social class – after all, he was a clergyman's son and a post-captain in the Royal Navy with a Noble of the Holy Roman Empire for a great-grandfather, while her father was just a bourgeois merchant. But they lived to change their minds and adore her.

On hearing of his son's promotion, but before he knew of his engagement, Dr Beaufort (inexplicably flush at that moment) offered Francis a loan of £1700. To modern eyes the son's reply is over-blown, but touching nevertheless:

. . . it nearly made me weep at your kindness. But here and at once, my dear father, I disclaim your generous bequest. You formed my heart and im-proved my head: you brought the one to despise and the other to surmount any difficulties I could meet in my profession. You ballasted my little bark with solid principles, you rigged me with the best education that time would permit, you furnished me with the anchor of Hope and Resignation, you instructed me in steering by the Cardinal points of the Compass of virtue, and then launched me gallantly into the world.

And if I have not yet found a quiet haven or hit upon the right rhumb to riches and renown, it is my fault and my misfortune, but can be no reason that I should plunder my dear little sisters whom the customs of the world oblige to keep their lights under a bushel, and to let their talents remain un-improved and buried. No, no, my dear father and 'My dear friend', I will have none of it. May God be pleased to permit their enjoying it these 50 years. . .

The wedding was deferred until Beaufort returned from his next tour of duty. He set off in the *Blossom*, to transfer to the *Frederickssteen*, then at Smyrna (the modern Izmir), at some indefinite future date, and meanwhile to engage again in the tedious activities to which he was used in the Mediterranean. It was understood that one of his ultimate duties would be as a surveyor, and he picked up his three chronometers as a matter of right. Before he left he found time to send to Thomas Hurd, who had succeeded Dalrymple as Hydrographer, an elaborate scheme for penning up Portsmouth Harbour with locks, so that the waters trapped by high tide could lift ships in and out of dry dock and on the release of the accumulated water, scour out the mud and generate mechanical power. The idea is appealing but, doubtless for good reasons, has not yet been acted upon.

After three months on the *Blossom*, still awaiting passage to Smyrna, Beaufort was given temporary command of the *Ville de Paris* while her regular captain was on home leave. The appointment was, perhaps, no more than a sop from the Admiralty for past neglect, but it was a handsome one: the ship was the largest in the Navy, a First Rate of 110 guns. She was stationed off Toulon as flagship of the British Fleet, spoiling for a fight. The French Fleet, safe in harbour, clearly was not. That was too bad, the eager captain lamented, for it would be 'a mighty fine thing' to take the most powerful British man-of-war afloat into battle.

On 20 October Beaufort at last found passage to Smyrna aboard the frigate *Salsette* and at once began to rue the days of his youth when he had so firmly resisted learning Greek and Latin and whatever else might equip a traveller to a classical landscape. He appealed to his more learned brother, to send him a 'well thought out' letter on the region he was about to enter; he would repay it with 'some beautiful rusty bit of antiquity'.

18

Frederickssteen: Terra Incognita (1811)

What barbarous Greeks are these Turks!

BEAUFORT'S journal[1]

The war at sea was won, or nearly so, at Trafalgar and the absence of fleet action thereafter was itself a sign of British mastery.[2] With an eye to the future, the Admiralty could spare a frigate in the Eastern Mediterranean to bridge 'a serious chasm in geography'.

The lack of anything but inaccurate charts of the south Turkish coast, almost 400 miles from the mainland north of Rhodes to the then Alexandretta (today's Iskenderun), was a reproach to British exploration. Moreover, what trade there was suggested that the coast might provide valuable Naval stores and supplies and possibly fleet anchorages for ships of a nation with steadily growing commercial and imperial interests in the rich Levant. Also, and not to be underestimated, was the historical and archaeological appetite of England's 'enjoying classes' – the wealthy, the titled and the classically educated – into whose lives the war had scarcely entered.[3] As the Society of the Dilettanti was to announce in explanation of its origin in 1734, 'Gentlemen who had travelled in Italy [were] desirous of encouraging *at home* a Taste for those objects which had contributed so much to their Entertainment abroad.'[4]

A vanguard of British travellers reported treasures of antiquity even beyond Greece, on the western shore of Asia Minor, from the Troad to Cnidus. They were not without influence: one of them, William Richard Hamilton, Elgin's secretary on the voyage that first carried him to Constantinople in 1799 (and whom Beaufort had thought to be 'without even an ostensible employment'), was by now Under-Secretary for Foreign Affairs and an ardent sponsor of his fellow antiquaries.

At the time of his promotion in May 1810, it was hinted to Beaufort that he would be sent to the Eastern Mediterranean on surveying duties. Later, when he was officially assigned to spend two seasons charting the south coast of Turkey, he said he felt flattered. It was a job perfectly suited to his talents, as important as it would surely be interesting. But very soon, even before the task was successfully completed, Beaufort resumed his all-too-frequent role as an injured party. Later, when he was enraged at what he felt was shabby treatment by the Admiralty on his compensation, he began to complain that he had accepted the duty only out of gratitude to Yorke.

It is hard to understand his change of attitude and none of his papers casts light on the reason. Conceivably he was unhappy at losing prize money that might have come his way had he remained senior officer at Smyrna, the post to which he was initially appointed; in later years he told his children that he thought he lost a potential £20 000. The estimate is not to be believed: when he was first ordered to Smyrna he told his brother that there was very little in the way of prize money to be had in the Archipelago.

He must have guessed that the survey would result in a splendid cartographic achievement and must have hoped that if he could only find some of the archaeological treasure trove known to exist in his survey area his reports of them would propel him to fame in scholarly British circles. And far from being *ultra vires*, there is evidence that his investigation of ruins was encouraged by the government, with priority second only to the hydrographic work.

Every university graduate in the British Isles at the time knew from his inescapable diet of the Greek and Latin authors that the coast must be studded with the remains of the rich and famous cities of antiquity. Writers and historians from Herodotus on, through Arrian, Cicero, Livy, Pliny, Strabo and two dozen others, had proclaimed the treasures in art and architecture that had been there. But since early Byzantine times there had been almost no reports of what was to be found on the south coast; those Crusaders who passed that way (or even those who for a time maintained principalities there) were blind to Graeco-

Roman remains or at any rate silent about them, and once the Ottoman curtain was lowered information dried up.

Only a dozen knowledgeable Europeans had crossed inland Turkey in the eighteenth and early nineteenth centuries[5] and those few who reached the south coast saw only Adalia (modern Antalya), near the middle, and the region to the east around Adana and Tarsus. Elsewhere on the coast of the whole stretch eastward of Cape Krio, the south-westernmost point of Asia Minor, only two classical sites had been visited by Europeans and reported on in any detail, Telmessos (Fetihye) and Antiphellus (Kaş), and even that was misidentified.[6]

In 1800 William Martin Leake had seen a great deal of the area Beaufort was to travel in 1811 and 1812 and had identified scores of ancient sites. But he did not publish his *Journal of a Tour through Asia Minor* until 1824 and Beaufort had no knowledge of his findings. The book did not offer duplicate descriptions of places Beaufort had already reported.* Rhodian, Greek, Cypriot and Egyptian sailors knew the coast, of course, but in their own terms, which most certainly did not include an interest in old pieces of stone and marble. Thus, to scholars of the early nineteenth century the treasures of Lycia, Pamphylia and Cilicia were like Montezuma's gold mines to Cortes: they must exist but they had not been discovered.

From the viewpoint of a hydrographer, the potential was equally rich. The most useful chart available to explorers was made by that passionate geographer, Jean Baptiste d'Anville. His map, of 1780, was by no means mere fantasy, but it was somewhere between an outline and an approximation and was, on average, 15' to 30' out in both latitude and longitude. Charts and descriptions of a scattering of coastal travellers – Miletus, Cellarius, Sonnini† – were of limited use, often being nothing more than attempted extrapolations of Strabo's *Geography*.

Beaufort, then, would have the pleasure of producing the map of an old land and writing on a slate long ago bleached clean.

---

*If Leake was vexed that Beaufort had beaten him to publication and identification of sites he had seen a dozen years before, he gave no indication of it. Rather, Leake's book is replete with praise for Beaufort's 'minute and accurate delineation of this coast'.

†Of the productions of the last, who travelled in the Greek islands in 1777–80, Beaufort wrote: 'Whenever I touch upon Sonnini's route, I find his descriptions fabulous.... Many of the islands which he describes I conclude that he never saw and that either he was sea sick in his hammock or took his information from some of the Greeks who, to do him justice, tell lyes even faster than he could write them.'

He took command of the *Frederickssteen* on 12 December 1810, but it was eight months before he began the survey. His other duties were crisply laid out by Stratford Canning, in charge of the British Embassy at Constantinople at the age of twenty, and in the early stages of a career that was to elevate him into the 'Great Elchi', ambassador *par excellence*. Canning knew exactly what had to be done: counter French influence in the area and at the Sublime Porte, prevent war between Russia and Turkey, and protect British maritime and trading interests. The orders he gave Beaufort as senior officer at Smyrna were exactly those Beaufort wanted to hear: to stop known privateers fitting out at Constantinople (Canning sent precise intelligence on them), to prevent the Turks from holding British Navy deserters on the excuse that they had turned Muslim, to allow Turkish authorities to unload British ships that had illegally taken on cargoes of grain but to forbid them to hold the vessels, for 'His Majesty will never suffer any Power, at whatever distance from his dominions, to invade with impunity the right and property of his subjects'.

Beaufort expressed happy agreement, and on his part Canning was delighted with a copy of the orders Beaufort issued on procedures to follow when boarding strange vessels. The document is a masterpiece of clarity and common sense.

Beaufort reached Turkey at an interesting if troubled time. The Ottoman Empire had been on the decline ever since the sixteenth century;[7] inside Anatolia itself, the Sultan's authority had weakened and the local 'valley-lords' exercised strong powers in their own territories, so that the *firman*, or royal decree that Beaufort carried from Constantinople, was not always a sovereign *passe partout*. And although French influence was giving way, under the skill of Stratford Canning, to a treaty with England (1812) and to a change of public opinion in its favour, those were matters which scarcely affected attitudes in the regions that Beaufort was to travel. What he found instead was the historic predisposition of the Turks: xenophobia and contempt of everything (except military techniques and material) about the infidel 'Franks', under which term the British were included.

Cruising in the Aegean in April 1811, Beaufort captured a neutral polacre, the *S. Nicolo*, with a French cargo worth more than £8000, but it took months of wrangling before a prize court at Malta and two trips to Rhodes to threaten the Turkish Bey, bribed by the polacre's captain to withhold a list of the vessel's cargo, before the complications were resolved.[8]

Beaufort was ready to set out in mid-July on the survey when more urgent business intervened: a Neapolitan privateer had captured a richly laden Maltese brig, and carried her off to Syra (Siros), an island about 120 miles WSW of Smyrna. The *Frederickssteen* captured the brigand and his prize 'but unfortunately a Turk[h]. Frigate with broad pend[t]. lay at anchor in the harbour and he was conseq[y]. temporary governor – and still more unfortunately this Turkish Commodore was both knave and fool. After much discussion we sealed up the property which had been landed. . . .'

Beaufort turned about to carry the news of the ambiguous situation back to the British consul in Smyrna. The wind was adverse and he chose to put in at Sigacik, on the south coast of the peninsula forming the southern side of the Gulf of Smyrna.

Returning to Syra – 'a wretched little island with 3 advantages: snug port, good grapes and not a Turk on the island' – the *Frederickssteen* set out again on her surveying mission in late July and was again forestalled. About to round the south-western corner of Turkey to proceed along the south coast, Beaufort spied a small lateen-rigged craft off the island of Stampalia (Astipalaia) and judged her, correctly, to be a privateer. The vessel headed between two small rocky islets where the crew abandoned her and scrambled for shelter in the rocks.

Beaufort ordered a broadside to be fired and then sent in his boats to reconnoitre.

The next thing was to get hold of her rascally crew. To have landed and marched up in their teeth would have been quite impossible. So I sent a white flag to tell them that if they did not surrender directly I would land in the morning and leave their carcasses to feed the vultures and their bones to bleach. . . . This magnificent message had the desired effect and, except 6 who remained on the Summit, they came down before dark.

Hearing of a larger privateer in the area, Beaufort set off vainly in pursuit. Two days later he returned to the islets where the six who held out, without food or water for forty hours, meekly surrendered. The larger boat that escaped, he learned, was commanded by

a desperate fellow who had been made a slave at Const[ple]. and generally revenged himself on every Turk that fell his way. A few days only before, they had carried a Candiot Turkish Caique into a small island near which we were then at anchor and murdered the six musselmen who were aboard. Indeed, Mr Gammon [the *Frederickssteen*'s first lieutenant] had seen and smelled their remains in pulling past the place.

After receiving the thanks of the Stampalians and dressing the wound of a Turk who had had one ear severed by the pirates, Beaufort headed for Rhodes to browbeat the Bey who was frustrating British claims to the *S. Nicolo*.

I sent word to the Bey that I wanted an audience (and I offered to salute for an equal No. of guns, but he good humouredly replied that we had better keep our Powder for our enemies). . . . He received me in a dirty room, the floor surrounded by Sophas, the walls by blunder-busses, and himself by twenty of his ill-looking ruffians, but to do him justice, with that dignity which all the better kind of Turks possess.

After threatening to tell the Porte that the Bey had pocketed a 10 000-piastre bribe from the *S. Nicolo*'s captain, Beaufort at last sailed back to the mainland on 6 August to begin his survey.

He quickly reduced the procedure to a system: he himself rose daily at 5 a.m. and in one gig took bearings and soundings, staying out until sunset, occasionally making a rendezvous with another of the ship's boats for midday food and a fresh crew; the *Frederickssteen*'s surgeon and marine officer explored along the shore with the interpreter to discover and translate local names; the purser and pilot ('a Sclavonian [Slav] . . . to the prevaricating subtlety of the Greeks he adds the brutality of his native country and, what is infinitely worse in my eyes, or rather in my nose, is that he smells like a soapboiler's shop') went ashore to buy fresh food; the first lieutenant completed the ship with wood and water, while the master, in the other gig, sounded the bays that the captain was obliged to pass by.

From the beginning of the voyage Beaufort kept a detailed journal, obviously intended as a first draft of a book he already had in mind, *Karamania* (the medieval name of the southern area), published in 1817. It shows that however bitter were his later complaints he enjoyed himself enormously at the time. If at the beginning he did not have the 'true Antiquarian taste', before long he was an obsessive prowler of ruins, begrudging his obligations as a surveyor which gave him too little time for the quest.

The first site to be explored was a bonanza. It was Patara, lost to

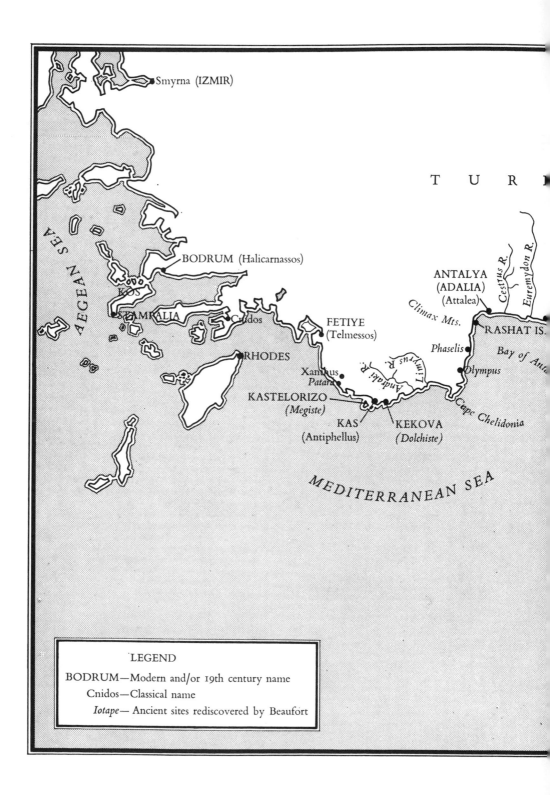

Smyrna (IZMIR)

T U R

ANTALYA
(ADALIA)
(Attalea)

BODRUM (Halicarnassos)

Cestus R.

Euremydon R.

KOS

Climax Mts.

STAMKALIA

Cnidos

FETIYE
(Telmessos)

RASHAT IS.

RHODES

Phaselis

Bay of Anta

AEGEAN SEA

Xanthus
Patara

Andaki R.

Limyrus R.

Olympus

KASTELORIZO
(Megiste)

KAS
(Antiphellus)

KEKOVA
(Dolchiste)

Cape Chelidonia

MEDITERRANEAN SEA

LEGEND

BODRUM—Modern and/or 19th century name

Cnidos—Classical name

Iotape— Ancient sites rediscovered by Beaufort

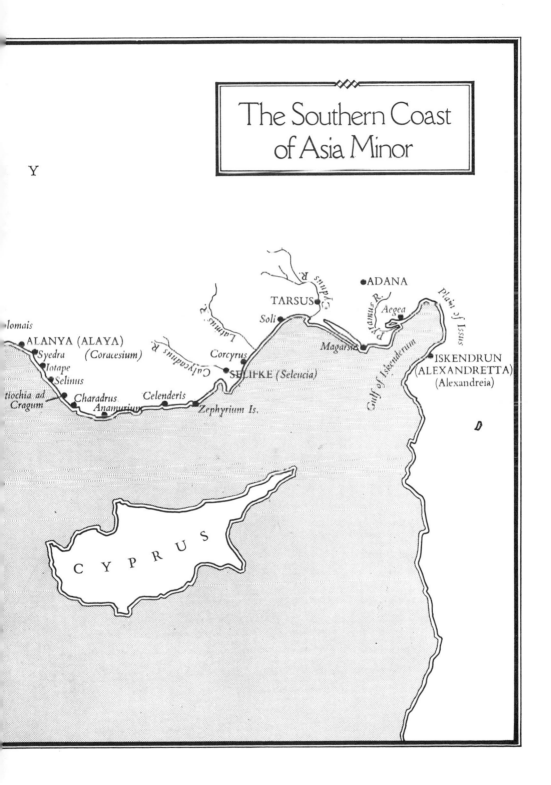

The Southern Coast of Asia Minor

Y

•ADANA

TARSUS•

Soli

Aegea

•lomais

ALANYA (ALAYA)
•Syedra   *(Coracesium)*
•Iotape
•Selinus

Corcyrus

Magarsa

ISKENDRUN
(ALEXANDRETTA)
(Alexandreia)

•SELIFKE *(Seleucia)*

•tiochia ad
Cragum   Charadrus
         Anamurium

Celenderis

Zephyrium Is.

Gulf of Iskenderun

Plain of Issus

D

C Y P R U S

Western knowledge for more than a millennium. Beaufort stole a day to search for the oracle of Apollo described by the ancient historians and thought he found it in the huge circular pit cut deep into the crest of a hill behind the splendidly preserved theatre. It was actually only a water cistern[9] but so impressive that his error is understandable.

Beaufort sketched, and philosophized vigorously, and lamented the vandalism:

> At every step we took I heard some of my companions exclaim: 'What barbarous Greeks are these Turks! See their sarcophagi a prey to their cupidity. Look at these columns and temples, trampled under their prophane feet or carried away to build their hovels!'
>
> But I should like to know what nation could resist the temptation of jewels or money buried with the dead, and if the Turks, ignorant of history and taught to despise the learning, the taste and the monuments of all other religions than their own, are so culpable in converting the remains of antient buildings to their use or convenience, what shall be said of those who, educated in the highest veneration for the antient Greeks and Romans, rob, pillage, break and steal away their most valuable fragments, to gratify a momentary whim or childish caprice?

Beaufort went on to repay with caustic words the kindness shown to him a dozen years before by Lord Elgin:

> What shall be said of an English Nobleman, availing himself of his situation as Ambass[r]. at Constantinople, to plunder Athens of its most beautiful remains and even tear down one of the large sides of the temple of Neptune placing a wooden post in its room, which must soon rot and consequently accelerate the ruin of the whole!* How selfish of all these travelling gentry thus to deprive others of seeing on those sacred spots what gives them their value. . . . It would be more becoming if the rich and noble of Europe were to join in subscriptions for renting the ruins of Athens from the Grand Signor, where they might . . . employ their idle persons and plethoric purses in . . . replacing the fallen columns, and preserving the tottering temples from yielding to the hands of time and European robbery.
>
> Or if it is impossible to persuade the Turkish Gov[t]. to preserve their magnificent ruins, let their removal be a national work. The French have a plan, I understand, for removing one of the buildings *in toto*, numbering each stone, and setting them up exactly in the same order at Paris. Such a system of Pillage would be infinitely less vile than the piecemeal plunder of

---

*The reference is probably to Elgin's removal of one of the columns of the east portico and one of the caryatids of the Erechtheum.

The following is part of the inscription on the right hand or West scroll — That upon the third from it on the left is the same as well as we could see it.

ΠΟΝΡΟΥΦΩΝ ΠΑΤΑΡΑΜΕΜΤΙ.
ΜΟΔΕΣΤΟΥΗΓΕ٭Ε٭·٭
ΜΟΝΟΣΛΥΚΙΩΝ·٭·
ΤΟΚΟΙΝΟΝ·————

upon the fourth we made out the undermost,

ΝΕΤΥΠΟΜΦΡΟΝΕΟΝΤΟΝ
ΠΑΤΑΡΑΜΕΤΗΠΟΥΜΟΛΕΝΤΟΥ
ΠΑΤΑΡΕΟΝΥΜΝΤΡΟΠΟΝΟΝΣ
ΟΥΛΥΚΙΩΝΕΟΝΟΨΣ
ΟΝΜΕΤΤΙΟΥΜΟ٭٭٭ΟΥΡΑΤΕ

Η ΔΥ

The Great Gate at Patara; a page from Beaufort's *Journal*, 1811.

inconsiderate travellers who knock off a head, a hand, a leaf or volute without comprehension and merely to show to their equally inconsiderate friends at home.

Already, even on the better known west coast, Beaufort had begun to copy in his journal every inscription he could find. By the time his survey ended he had amassed scores.* His lack of Latin and Greek must have made the task frustrating. He could usually puzzle out the names of emperors and, when luck was with him, the city in whose ruins he was wandering. He was helped by advance knowledge from classical historians and geographers of what cities lay in his path. A hand-written English translation of Strabo's Book XIV, Chapter 5 is among his surviving papers along with some other miscellaneous geographical material. He was undoubtedly also briefed by the new chaplain to the English 'factory' (trading station) at Smyrna, George Cecil Renouard, a scholar whose lifetime contributions to classical and Arabian studies were to earn him distinction. He was in a position to give Beaufort a detailed précis of the appropriate sources – almost none translated into English at that time – beyond his linguistic reach.

The problem, though, was to reconcile those authorities which so often disagreed. On his return to England Beaufort took counsel with whatever experts he could to refine his initial identifications; but what is remarkable is how accurate were those he made on the spot. For sixty features on the coast from a few miles east of Antiphellus to just north of Alexandretta – cities, rivers, capes and bays – which Beaufort identifies with classical names in his journal and on the map included in his book, today's best classical map of Asia Minor[11] disagrees with him in only seven cases, giving different identifications in four instances and omitting three that he postulated. For the first European in a thousand years to attempt identification,† almost ninety per cent accuracy was a formidable achievement.

---

*As a consequence, he rates as one of the most prolific contributors to that monumental four-folio-volume compendium, *Corpus Inscriptum Graecarum*, published in Berlin between 1828 and 1877.[10]

†Except Leake, whose work, as noted, had not been published.

19

Frederickssteen:
A Matter of Mercy
(1811)

... they were perhaps grateful, but their gratitude did
not seem to be addressed to us; in their eyes, we were
still infidels; and though the immediate preservers of
their lives, we were but tools in the hands of their
protecting prophet.

Karamania

Although Beaufort knew from his Strabo that Xanthus, greatest city
of Lycia, must be only a few hours' ride north of Patara, he rejected
the temptation to visit it. His mission was to chart the coast – and
Xanthus was inland.

As his duty demanded, he proceeded eastward to the island of
Kastelorizo, and correctly identified it as Livy's, Pliny's and Ptolemy's
Megiste. Just opposite it, on the mainland, he visited Port Vathy
(Kaş) with its Lycian tombs and its well-built, seaward-gazing theatre,
and found it as interesting as Kastelorizo was dull. He identified it
accurately as ancient Antiphellus.

There, and to the east, he discovered, as usual, that all the tombs had
been broken into and ransacked.

The Turks are always on the lookout for hidden treasure and whenever we
were seen carefully reading or searching amidst ruins, some of them would
ask if we expected to find it there. I directed that they should be uniformly
answered that the only method of finding, when treasure was scented, was
by comparing the inscription on the stones; therefore when they came across
new ones to preserve them carefully and that we or succeeding travellers
would then be able to inform them if such might be found.

This innocent ruse may perhaps save some curious fragments from the
disdainful violence of the Turks, who generally think any writing but their
own wicked, and any of their own except the Koran useless.

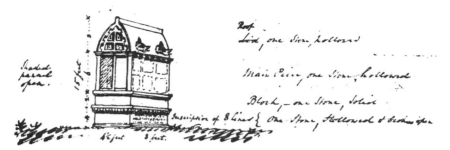

A Lycian tomb, Telmessos (Kaş); a page from Beaufort's *Journal*, 1811

From Kaş the *Fredericksteen* sailed to Kakava (Kekova), whose singular charm somehow escaped the captain. He was struck only by the crumbling Turkish castle at the top with its few small cannon 'which from their appearance would be destructive to those only who might fire them', and the rows of ancient house ruins on the long island of Kekova, across a spacious channel from the mainland village. Fronting the water with steps leading down, built on extremely rugged slopes and with no sign of roads behind them, they could have communicated one with another only by small boats, Beaufort observed. He correctly identified Kekova as Ptolemy's Dolchiste.

Three miles further east he found the immense Roman granary at the mouth of the river Andraki, site of Adriace and harbour of the ancient city of Myra a few miles away. Again he failed to press inland and thus missed the fourth-century city of St Nicholas.

Beaufort had only a week in which to survey a coast 'that would take a month to survey accurately'. He pushed on to Finike, with another good guess that its river was the ancient Limyrus, and there went on in a boat to Cape Chelidonia, the tip of the 'Sacred Promontory' of classical times. When the ship caught up with him, Beaufort turned north into the Bay of Adalia (modern Antalya). He passed the tiny barren Chelidonian Islands remarked on by Scylax, Strabo and Pliny and filled his journal with speculations about their curious geology, the mystery of the strong westward current, the grand scenery of the white and red cliffs rising perpendicularly from the sea, the majestic peak of Adrachan (Tahtalı) towering to almost 8000 feet as the southern anchor of the great Climax range which extends the length of the west side of the Bay.

It was a rich archaeological hunting ground. Almost at once, under the northern foot of Tahtalı, Beaufort touched at Deliktaş ('Perforated Rock') and stumbled on the beautiful ruins which, inscriptions made clear, were the remains of Olympus.

Further north, at night, the *Frederickssteen*'s crew wondered at a steady light in the hills. On shore the next morning, they were told it was a *yanar*, or volcanic flame. Beaufort took to horse and after a two-hour ride across the fertile coastal plain and up a rocky glen came to a ruined building, with an aperture in one corner like the mouth of an oven.

> ... from thence the flame issues, giving out an intense heat, yet producing no smoke on the walls. ... Our guide asserted [that] it was never accompanied ... by earthquakes or noises; and it ejected no stones, smoke, nor any noxious vapours, nothing but a brilliant and perpetual flame, which no quantity of water could quench. The shepherds, he added, frequently cooked their victuals there; and he affirmed with equal composure, that it was notorious that the *yanar* would not roast meat which was stolen.

Beaufort realized that he had found the reputed tomb of Pliny's Chimaera, the fabled fire-eating monster with lion's head, goat's body and serpent's tail, slain by Bellerophon.

Riding back by a different path, past small summer settlements of herdsmen, Beaufort was moved to return to one of his favourite themes, the nature of the Turks. At times he loathed them, and on other occasions admired their pride and manliness. This day, in high summer, in the lovely foothills of the Climax mountains, he was inclined to be mellow:

> In the Turkish character there is a striking contrast of good and bad qualities: though insatiably avaricious, a Turk is always hospitable, and frequently generous; though to get, and that by any means, seems to be the first law of his nature, to give is not the last.
>
> In this point of view, the character of the modern Greeks would ill bear a comparison with that of their oppressors; such a comparison, however, would be unfair, for slavery necessarily entails a peculiar train of vices; but, it may be hoped, the growing energy, which must one day free them from political slavery, will also emancipate them from its moral effects.

A few miles north of Olympus Beaufort passed Pliny's three barren islands of Cypriae and then was lured ashore by gleaming white marble. The ruins were those of Phaselis, whose three harbours, olive-

The Chimaera, or perpetual flame, near Olympus: a page from Beaufort's *Journal*, 1811. In the script on the right Beaufort relates a local legend about nearby Mt. Tahtalı. The French text is a translation of Pliny's account of the Chimaera.

overgrown theatre, splendid main street, graceful aqueduct and scattered tombs captivated him, as they have every visitor since. As with Olympus and the *yanar*, no educated European had beheld this important Rhodian foundation for centuries. Beaufort filled pages of his journal (and book) with enthusiastic descriptions and made a sketch which remains today on the Admiralty Chart of southern Turkish anchorages.

As Beaufort knew from his almanacs, an occultation of a star by the moon and a lunar eclipse were approaching, both events important for determining longitude. Beaufort wanted to make his observations as near as possible to Adalia, then as now the principal city on the south coast until Adana, 250 miles to the east. He wanted to set up his instruments on Rashat, an islet a few miles south-west of Adalia, when he heard the sound of distant guns. A vessel brought word that during an absence of the ruling Pasha of Adalia, a rival had secretly introduced a small armed force and taken over the city.

The episode, which Beaufort had to piece together during the following months and which he described in detail in *Karamania*, was of Oriental complexity. It involved slaughter, theft, bribery and intrigue (for the Sultan was probably backing the usurper). Beaufort heard enough at the outset to realize that he should in no way become involved. He explained in his journal:

> The Turks are quite barbarous enough without the additional ferocity incited by civil commotion. Besides, both parties would probably annoy us; one would beg for powder, the other for ball; the weakest would seek for refuge on board, the victor would claim his prey. In short, I might embroil myself . . . and last and worst commit the flag.

For a few hours Beaufort still thought that he might be able to proceed to Rashat undisturbed.

> But vain were our hopes. The city was recaptured by the former Pasha, and the unsuccessful party were flying in all directions. The following day, a large body of them came down to the beach abreast the ship, and begged of our watering party to protect them from the fury of their pursuers. This was of course refused: we had no right to interfere in their disputes. . . . Exhausted, however, as the fugitives were . . . I could not resist their importunity for a little bread, and for surgical assistance.

Beaufort also urged them to flee to the mountains. The vanquished party replied that such a course was impossible: there were no roads, a price had been put on their heads, all the inferior aghas (local headmen in the Pasha's province) were hostile, and finally 'their religion taught them to rely upon God for their deliverance, or to submit without repining their fate'.

A few hours later the compassionate captain tried again: an un-manned large sailing launch, or *caique*, was seen drifting out to sea. As the Pasha's pursuing cavalry were already seen descending the plain, Beaufort proposed to let the fugitives escape aboard the launch. 'Again they declined – none of them were seamen; they knew not how or where to steer: if their hour was come, they preferred dying like men, with arms in their hands on shore.' Nonetheless, about half the unsuccessful rebels stowed themselves aboard the craft while the rest stayed on shore.

Next morning one of the Pasha's vessels was seen rounding the cape and the cavalry, until then checked by the sight of the British frigate, resumed its advance. Beaufort wrote in his journal:

This was the critical moment of the wretches' fate – 30 of them on shore, and 30 more in the *caique* would in less than an hour be headless, without any chance of escape except through me or through a miracle.

I confess I was barbarous enough to try to reason myself into a confirm-ation of my resolution to abstain from any interference. . . .

But I thank my God that those calculating cold-blooded arguments kept possession of my mind for a very few moments. A more generous batch succeeded them. . . .

For fear I should waver I ordered the boats away immediately [to pick up both sets of refugees and bring them aboard the *Frederickssteen*] but I have never for a moment repented it and shudder at the bare possibility of my having decided otherwise.

He continued the story in *Karamania*:

Since the day before, the fugitives had betrayed no signs of despair or impatience: . . . when our boats landed, they were found sitting under the shade of the neighbouring trees, with an air of resignation that bordered on indifference. They now displayed neither exultation nor joy; they came on the quarter deck with much composure . . .

Beaufort was in no physical danger, of course – the Pasha was not about to take on a thirty-two-gun frigate with his ramshackle fleet –

but however certain the captain was of his state of moral grace, his political skirts were by now considerably soiled. Whether or not Sultan Mahmud II in Constantinople had given secret support to the attempted usurpation of the Pasha at Adalia, it was the Pasha who had won. He would not be pleased at a British frigate's having given succour to his enemies; at a minimum, the frigate's hydrographic survey of his coast-line would be impossible for a time and her captain, who had indeed committed the sin of involving His Majesty's flag, would have some explaining to do to the Admiralty. The Pasha could make unpleasant representations to the Porte which in turn might do the same to Stratford Canning. An ugly diplomatic *contretemps* was a real possibility.

The issue was about to be joined: Beaufort dispatched his first lieutenant in a boat to meet the oncoming Turkish ship and was suddenly fired on with a single shot which missed. The incident gave Beaufort a fine excuse to take the offensive in the game to follow.

Two officers from the Pasha's polacre went ashore to take counsel with the commanders of the cavalry and then came aboard the *Frederickssteen*. Beaufort's journal continued:

> To overawe these gentry I received them with a good deal of hauteur, and much in the way their great Pashas treat inferior folk. I sat still on my sopha in full uniform and, slightly bowing my breast toward my hand, waved to them to sit down. I resolved to begin the battle and by way of the first shot sternly asked them how they could presume to fire at my boat. They deluged me with excuses and apologies without meaning or consistency. After they had sworn and lied and averred their compunction sufficiently I dryly said that it was fortunate indeed that neither the boat nor crew had been touched. Had they, I should certainly have sunk their ship first and afterwards inquired into the cause. . . .
>
> Secretly enraged at having been foiled of their prey, yet they addressed me with the most courteous respect: menaces indeed they were not in a condition to offer; persuasion gave them the only chance of success.

Coffee, precursor of all business in Turkey, being finished, the negotiating concert-piece commenced, beginning *legato* and ending *con fuoco*. The Turks first insisted that only the Pasha's ignorance of the *Frederickssteen*'s presence in the area had prevented his offering compliments and hospitality long since. Then they gently hinted that it might have been more gracious for the captain to have begun his business in the capital. The notion was thereupon introduced that the captain could not possibly condescend to be interested in local quarrels and that obviously he knew nothing of the whereabouts of 'the band of robbers'. Step by step they continued, sometimes alluding to the displeasure of the Porte at the rebels' escape, sometimes hinting at the magnificent presents that might be expected from the Pasha if his enemies were turned over to him. At last, casting pretence aside, the two Turks flatly demanded their return.

Perceiving that unconditional surrender was the sole object of their instructions, and that nothing but indiscriminate slaughter would satisfy their vindictive master, I here put an end to the conference, and civilly dismissed them from the ship.

In departing, they offered my interpreter a large sum if he could induce me to give up, at least, the Bin Bashy, or chief . . . but, disappointed in all their intrigues, they at last begged for a small stock of coffee and rum . . .

Shortly afterwards, the polacre set sail after a vessel the rebels had dispatched while still masters of Adalia, carrying off the Pasha's treasury. Beaufort soon made sail as well, knowing that it would be impossible for the time being to carry on his survey in the Pasha's domains and, of course, obliged to rid himself of his sixty passengers somewhere out of reach of the Pasha's vengeful arm. He returned to Kaş but found it was still within the Pasha's jurisdiction. Sailing on to Rhodes, he discovered that the slippery Bey was also one of the Pasha's confederates. It was at last resolved to land the rebels on the island of Kos, off the south-western tip of Turkey.

On the way Beaufort made of necessity such virtue as he could, diligently surveying, charting, describing, and copying inscriptions from the north and south entrances of the Ceramic Gulf and exploring the great sites of Cnidus, of Kos and (after landing the refugees) of Bodrum, ancient Halicarnassus. He was by no means the first latter-day European to bring word of those remarkable treasures of antiquity but his descriptions – and of course his charts – were far superior to anything produced before.

He tried to enter the great Crusader castle of St Paul at Bodrum, by then converted to a Turkish fort, suspecting, correctly, that within it were some of the marbles that once embellished the famous Mausoleum, one of the seven wonders of the ancient world. But this time, it was he who was bested by the Turks.

What cunning rogues are the Turks. I had promised [the local Bey and his officials] a little fine powder for shooting, and under a hundred pretexts they had screwed it from me before their refusal [of entrance to the castle] was announced. My writing master often impressed on my mind . . . 'Experience teacheth', and with this recondite aphorism in my mouth I put on my hat, pulled off in my boat, hove up my anchor and made sail. . . .

20

Fredericksteen: Survey to Syria (1812)

An old blackman . . . gave me a good deal of information, and what was very singular (as 48 hours afterwards proved) advised us to beware of the inhabitants to the Eastward [saying], 'Tell your Captain not to trust himself on shore, for he will not be the first that they have killed or carried away.'

BEAUFORT's journal[1]

The *Fredericksteen* was back in Smyrna by December and sailed to Rhodes on 7 January 1812 in company with the frigate *Salsette*, commanded by Commodore Henry Hope, who succeeded Beaufort as senior officer at Smyrna. At Rhodes the two officers paid a call on Lady Hester Stanhope who had just embarked on her career of awe-inspiring eccentricity by losing everything but her life in a shipwreck. Beaufort upbraided the Bey 'for not having treated her with more gallantry & hospitality' – after all, she was the daughter of an earl and the niece and treasured confidante of William Pitt. Hope offered to convey her and her companions to Constantinople but the noble lady refused: her physician and future biographer, the long-suffering Charles Lewis Meryon, had just sailed off to fetch new clothes for her and without them she declined to move.

Beaufort took his ship back to Smyrna to show the flag to a Pasha momentarily threatening the British trading station there; the trouble once ended, he set sail for Greece, calling at Chios, Samos, and several islands in the Cyclades en route. He sensed that it would be his last time in the area of Smyrna and dwelt in his journal both on the magnificence and grandeur of the coast and – what had been his most obsessive speculation ever since he first touched Asia Minor – on the brutal, inexorable workings of nature, destroying here, creating there:

Notwithstanding the outcry against revolutions, Nature herself seems to be one of the greatest revolutionists of any age or time. . . . The revolu\^y. mill is always at work, and though the effects are not always so sudden & sanguinary as at Catania or Lisbon or Paris, yet when slowest they are not the least powerful. . . . The degradations of the mountains, the filling up of the seas, the changing the course of rivers, the alluvial increase of territory on this shore and the robberies of the sea on another are amongst her silent but invariably acting tools of revolution.

Four years earlier, his cartographic accomplishments already recognized, Beaufort had been invited to be an honorary member of the new Geological Society. Accordingly, he now expatiated for six long pages in his journal on the evolutionary processes at work on rivers and the shoreline. The passage bespeaks far wider reading and interests than the theological volumes of the days before he came under the tutelage of Richard Lovell Edgeworth.

The age prescribed that a 'natural philosopher' embellish his conclusions with a moral gloss: 'It is beautiful thus to observe Nature providing antidotes against her own poisons, to see in the physical as well as in the moral world ambitious encroachment defeating its own Machinations.' Those lofty considerations occupied the right-hand pages of the journal; on one left-hand page, however, a totally different note appears. It is an unexpected paragraph in cipher (the first known recourse to his old schoolboy code for many years and this time written, as in early Greek inscriptions, in lines reading alternately from right to left and left to right).

O Smyrna what I have suffered within your walls! The beastly cunning of one woman, the seductive charms, the dangerous follies of another and the strange mixture of my own vices, virtues and weaknesses have thrown my mind and body into a state whence they must have long to emerge. Oh God let me turn this bitter lesson to account: reclaim the one, and forgive the other, heal me, oh God.

In subsequent pages, written later, there are two other short ciphered entries, too cryptic to provide any explanation for the strange outburst. If Beaufort wrote 'reclaim' and 'forgive' respectively to 'mind' and 'body', he was not in need of the attentions of the ship's surgeon.

But why the anguish over having seemingly doubled the traditional sailor's delight, with not one but two girls in port? We can only guess that the 'reform in manners' led by Wilberforce and Hannah More that was to convert the cheerfully reprobate late Georgian society into the Victorian one was already making a certain impact on a minister's son and one who, indeed, had pledged his solemn troth to a lady in London.

The *Frederickssteen* anchored in Piraeus on 29 February, summoned there purely for antiquarian research. In September of the previous year, William Richard Hamilton, the patron of the Dilettanti and Under-Secretary of State for Foreign Affairs, had asked Beaufort to help two friends in Greece who were bound for Karamania; one of them was Sir Richard Gell.*

Meanwhile, Gell himself had written a 'demi-official' letter to Beaufort, stating that he was acting under the patronage of the Prince Regent and asking for geographical coordinates and other particulars of the south coast. Beaufort noted that a passage in the letter was *verbatim* in his own instructions, demonstrating that Hamilton, as well as the Admiralty, had had a hand in ordering the Karamania survey. He was less than exhilarated by Gell himself: 'This Mr Gell seems a shrewd fellow. He is Eng^l. Consul at Voulo Gulph. . . . He was, I believe, an artist employed by L^d. Aberdeen – but industry and talents are not always plants of the same soil, and he prefers an indolent existence amongst the *chef-d'oeuvres* of Greece to using them as a model at home.'

Beaufort oh-ed and ah-ed at Athens' treasures but concluded that they had been so learnedly described by everyone from Pausanias to Gell himself that it would be impertinent for him 'even to endeavour to describe their effect upon my feelings'.

The visit was not without its troubles. During a terrible thunderstorm, lightning struck one of the masts of the frigate and Beaufort had

---

*This was the Gell of Byron's *English Bards and Scotch Reviewers*:

'Of Dardan's towns let Dilettanti tell,
I leave Topography to Classic Gell.'

In his MS Byron had written 'coxcomb Gell' and by the fifth edition had changed it to 'rapid Gell', noting that he had 'topographised and typographised King Priam's dominion in three days' in exploring and delineating what he thought, incorrectly, was the site of Troy.

to return to Malta for repairs. It was mid-April before they were completed.

He was at last in a position to resume the survey interrupted seven months before. Again reaching the coast opposite Rhodes, he searched for Charles Robert Cockerell, in later years to become one of England's finest architects and already renowned for his knowledge of Greek sculpture and architecture. He too had instructions from Hamilton and, after two fruitful years in Greece, was known to be coasting Lycia in a Greek *caique*.*

Beaufort was concerned for him, as a solitary traveller 'in this infrequented & barbarous country'; giving Cockerell a safer passage would be doing a service to the public, a kindness to a deserving man and a pleasure to himself, he noted.

Find him he did, on the west coast of the Bay of Adalia, thus fulfilling his hopes and making a friend for life as well. At first sight, however, Cockerell's crew had been terrified, thinking the *Frederickssteen* a Turkish cruiser. For, as Beaufort noted in his journal:

> The Turkish vessels of war on meeting a Greek *kaik* invariably exact some present or, on failure, ill treat & rob. If one of the Barbary Coast cruizers meet a Greek vessel they take away all the young men for soldiers or slaves & plunder besides.
>
> [The captain of] Mr Cock's. *Kaik*, on seeing us, alarmed as usual, sent his boat on shore on pretence of obtaining some wood and hid the money which he had to purchase his corn cargo in the sand.

Beaufort proceeded slowly northward, revisiting Phaselis. Coasting under the mighty Climax range, he discussed in his journal, as he was later to do in his book, Arrian's famous account of Alexander's progress along the shore, wading waist-deep in water with a divine and rare north wind providing a shallow passage.

On 1 May he arrived at Adalia. Stratford Canning had written to him that he had heard of his 'adventure' there the year before but that no minister at the Sublime Porte had made an issue of it or, in fact, even mentioned it. Beaufort was not sure, however, of what reception he would receive on the spot from the masters of Adalia.

The reception was cold enough. Gun salutes and presents were exchanged but the captain was received suspiciously by the new Bey,

*His superb drawings and water-colours of Greece, Constantinople and Asia Minor are now in the British Museum.

son of the by then deceased Pasha. The young man refused to visit the frigate, but on trifling pretexts a Turkish officer came aboard several times every day and a telescope was kept trained on the ship. Beaufort deduced that the son of the late Pasha suspected that the Sultan might still be intending to displace him.

... they thought it probable that the next expedient of the Sublime Porte would be the common and summary one of assassination. ... Whatever cause the father had for alarm, the apprehensions of his son were still better grounded: he had formerly supported his refractory father, he now openly claimed succession as a right, and above all, he had taken possession of his father's riches. In this anxious posture of affairs, while in doubt whether to expect the tails* or the bow-string, we had arrived.

Beaufort discovered later that when he anchored off the city troops had been called out, the gates secured, and the guns trained. Except for his one visit no one from the *Frederickssteen*'s crew was allowed within the walls. He was disappointed, for he had heard that the city contained 'many remains of antiquity'. Only from a distance could he note the upper part of the Fluted Minaret, arguably the most beautiful in Turkey, the fertile 'gardens' and the thriving bazaar.

To the vast relief of the young Bey the *Frederickssteen* departed after a week, sailing eastward. Beaufort identified the mouths of the Cestrus (today's Aksu) and Eurymedon (Köprüçay) Rivers and proceeded a short distance up each in boats, hoping to see whether substantial ruins of Perge and Aspendus remained. Beaufort felt he could not give more time, and so missed the huge gates, walls, and stadium of Perge and the theatre (the best preserved of the ancient world) and splendid aqueduct of Aspendus all only a few miles from the coast.

But Cockerell and Beaufort had their reward in the discovery of Side, queen city of Pamphylia. Its enormous theatre rose so loftily above the flat land of the little peninsula on which the city was built that the visitors thought at first that it was the acropolis. Beaufort was ecstatic over the site. He drew the first map of the city and its peninsula, devoted several pages to its splendid second-century B.C. walls, the agora and the carvings (some now vanished) of its fallen tholos temple, the artificial harbours, the aqueduct and a number of other ruined structures. Although he was greatly impressed by the nymphaeum just outside the main gate, perhaps the finest and largest in Asia Minor,

*Horse tails on a standard, denoting office.

he was completely at a loss as to its function as the city's ceremonial (and practical) water distribution facility. So was Cockerell, who consequently thought it a piece of 'absurd architecture'.[2]

But it was the theatre that principally captured Beaufort's admiration. It is the largest on the south coast and of the most interesting construction. He was a little apologetic in devoting such space to it in *Karamania*: the reader, he hoped, would 'excuse any want of perspicuity in details which are so foreign to the general pursuits of a seaman'. Beaufort also made an elaborate calculation of its original seating capacity – 15240 he reckoned – which today is still the best estimate: the late Professor Arif Müfid Mansel, doyen of Turkish archaeologists who spent two decades excavating Side, never attempted to refine it.[3]

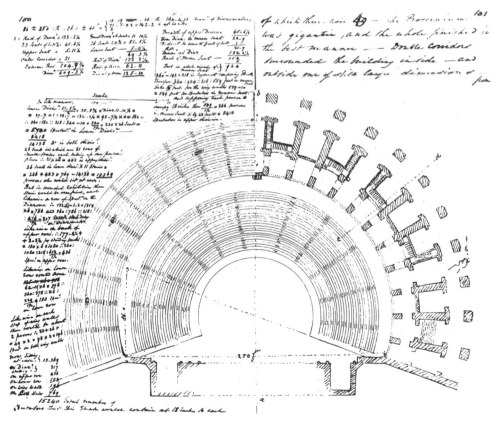

The theatre at Side, with calculations of its dimensions and seating capacity; a page from Beaufort's *Journal*, 1812.

The local agha paid a cautious courtesy call and, Cockerell noted, offered 2000 piastres for a young midshipman who had taken his fancy. Beaufort must have felt it beneath his dignity to record the matter in his journal, much less in his book.

With a sheaf of water-colours, sketches, charts and plans to show for his work, Beaufort pressed eastwards on 13 May. Forty miles down the coast he raised the great promontory of Alaya (Alanya), which put him in mind of Gibraltar. He knew it to be ancient Coracesium, once a Hellenistic fort, subsequently the seat of the tyrant-pirate Tryphon the Voluptuary whom Pompey defeated in a sea battle under the cliffs of the fort. Few remains from classical times were visible; what Beaufort saw was essentially the thirteenth-century construction of the greatest of all Seljuk Sultans, Keykubad I, who made Alaya his winter capital.

If Beaufort was aware that architectural and artistic masterpieces were created in the Byzantine, Seljuk and Ottoman periods he neglected to mention them. The passion of the times was for 'antient' remains, which is to say Greek and Roman. All else was considered inferior and usually described as 'modern'.

Nevertheless, he accepted an offer from the city council to climb up to the walls and visit the fort. At this point the narrative in *Karamania* changes from its almost unvarying use of the first person to the third person. In making the change the author contrived an unworthy piece of dissembling.

'A large party of officers, accompanied by a guide furnished by the government, set out the following day to walk up the hill,' Beaufort wrote. The implication is clear: that it was some of the ship's officers *not* including the narrator. Yet Beaufort's journal shows beyond all doubt that he was among them. He cannot, perhaps, be accused of an outright lie: he did not say in his book that he was *not* of the party, but he surely intended to leave his readers with that impression.

The group had gone only a little way when it was surrounded by a rabble of small boys, 'the sure forerunners of a tumult in Turkey. . . . The low murmur of Ghiaoor, of Infidel, was first heard; a few stones were then thrown, and the guide became so alarmed, that the officers consented, at his entreaty, to turn back. The signal was made for a boat, and they embarked.' 'They' included Beaufort, and in full uniform, as Cockerell noted.

The captain wrote that he was incensed. 'To have been invited by the government to go freely on shore, and then to be insulted and driven back was not to be endured.'

A severe remonstrance was therefore sent to the Mekemeh [town council], and their present of bullocks, which had just been received on board, was relanded on the beach. The scene was presently changed: [the most cosmopolitan member of the town council] came off loaded with apologies for the barbarians, as he called them, of that country; he assured me that several of the mob had been already seized and bastinadoed; and he offered to inflict any further punishment that might appease me. Whether this was strictly true, or not, it was enough; they had been brought to their senses; I professed myself satisfied; and the officers proceeded up the hill without any further molestation.

This time the captain was *not* among the tourists. 'I could not risk a second visit,' he wrote in his journal. 'Everybody was exposed to the attack of fanaticism, but none but a fool to its repetition.'

The excuse was valid – more trouble would have required retaliation – but Beaufort's public account was shabby. Without more details, it is hard to condemn him for his initial retreat: he probably had to heed his guide's appeal but to conceal his own role in print was less than honest.

The most charitable explanation is that Beaufort felt it simply would not do to portray the captain of one of His Majesty's warships being routed by a juvenile rabble. A less charitable explanation is that he was ashamed of his retreat and embarrassed by his decision (although it was correct) not to return on the second excursion, and could not bear to reveal it.

His conscience was anything but easy about his behaviour. Three weeks later, when he still cherished plans to retrace his route from the proposed end of the voyage at the Syrian coast, he listed in his journal tasks he had omitted and wanted to complete. One of them concerned 'the rock of Alaya which haunts me every night'.

Cockerell and the officers who made the second sortie up to the fort reported that 'little had been found to repay their toil'. The walls were ruinous and without cannon. 'Some remains of a Cyclopean wall, and a few broken columns, were the only vestiges of antiquity which they discovered.' This, in the finest example of Seljuk military construction in Turkey.

Beaufort sailed off next day in a huff, returning all presents and telling Cockerell that although he bore no personal resentment, 'his character as a British officer [had] been insulted [and] he would neither accept their presents or visit the town'.

Charting, sounding, sketching and stealing time for a bit of archae-ological prowling, Beaufort pushed on. His speculations on wind and weather led him back to the dream he had first written about to Edge-worth, three years before: how easy and how useful, he thought, to obtain information about weather from ships at sea; it could create a new branch of science.* Naval officers, if only they were sensibly treated, could be induced to provide the necessary data:

A careful examination of Log books – might those [not cast] light on the theory of the wind. . . . Once convince the officers of the Navy that their remarks may be of use, flatter their reasoning on the observations, and en-courage them by giving them a few books or instruments like [premiums?], by attaching some degree of credit to their names and by (in a very few instances) making scientific industry a chance to promotion, and as there are abundance who have talents sufficient, if rightly developed, so there would be abundance of valuable sketches, remarks and astronomical obser^s. carried by every post to the Adm^y.

He was impressed by Anamur castle, at Anamurium, finding that it 'much resembles that class of old castles in England which are I believe called Saracenin. Indeed the coincidence of many points in their style makes Cock^1. think they must have had a common origin.' They did, but Saracenin is a misleading word for it: Anamur castle, like so many of the period of the Crusades, was designed by 'Frankish', which is to say European, architects. Beaufort and his companions were the first appreciative westerners known to have set sight on the old city and the superb castle since the last Lusignan knights boarded ship in their little private harbour under the walls and sailed to Cyprus five hundred years before.[4]

The *Frederickssteen* anchored in early June in the harbour that served Silifke (ancient Seleucia). Beaufort was pleased with his progress but, as usual, considered joy subversive:

So rapidly have I advanced lately . . . that I begin to hope that I shall complete the whole of this South Coast as far as the commandment of Syria,

*Lamarck, Laplace and Lavoisier had begun compilations of weather observations as early as 1800 but the birth of synoptic meteorology in Britain was still ten years in the future.

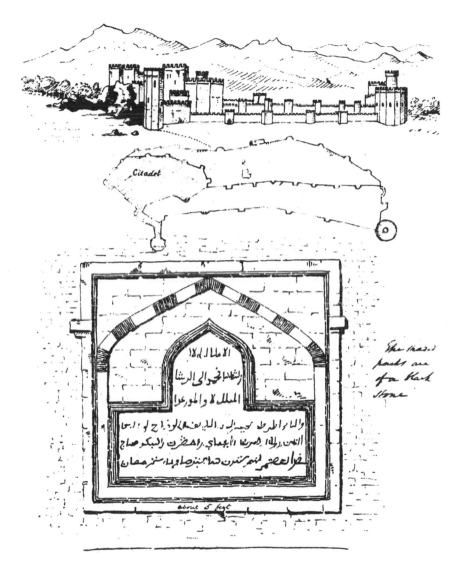

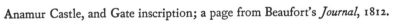

Anamur Castle, and Gate inscription; a page from Beaufort's *Journal*, 1812.

but for that purpose I must waste no moment of time. I can have no inter-mission of toil and I must rigorously debar myself those amusements of antiquity-hunting in which I formerly indulged, and which excepting this strong and generous feeling of devotion to one's duty could alone have reconciled me to these dry, wearying and probably thankless efforts. Division of labour is the only method of working rapidly. Therefore to the accidity [sic] and good taste of Cockerell aided by my industrious gropers (from the gun room) I must yield labours and the harvest of the land whose sandy beach or rocky coast I may pace and explore with about as much hopes of ultimate profit – i.e. credit – as of present gratification.

The pages of his journal belie the lugubrious and sententious declaration. They show instead that for more than two months, from Adalia to Silifke, Beaufort had been happy, because profoundly interested in every geological anomaly, every inscription – in Greek, Latin, Arabic, Armenian or indeterminable language – every column and foundation, every duck, lizard and turtle. He could not have been relaying only what Cockerell and the 'groper' lieutenants found: the entries are written in a way that demonstrates personal observation.

He and his officers copied Greek and Armenian inscriptions there and, in reproducing one of the latter from Silifke in a pretty vignette he used to head a chapter in *Karamania*, pleaded in a footnote for scholars to attempt decipherment and offered, in fact, to lay before anyone interested his whole collection of inscriptions.*

The exploring went on at Soli,† or Pompeiopolis, an archaeological treasure-trove which delighted Beaufort and of which he produced a characteristically elegant plan and a long description of the finds. Further on, off Tersoos (Tarsus), Beaufort had to forgo a twelve-mile ride inland to the famous city, but sent some of his officers.

Further along the flat coast, rounding what the captain identified as Magarsus and surveying the mouths of the Pyramus, the *Frederickssteen* at last sailed into the Gulf of Iskenderun (Alexandreia of classical times). Beaufort was excited at the prospect of 'entering on a part of the coast which surpassed in interest all that we had explored', the plain of

*The offer was taken up after publication of the book by several epigraphers and by the Austrian Joseph Hammer-Purgstall, the outstanding pioneer and pathfinder of old Near East languages.

†Whence the word 'solecism': Alexander, so Arrian relates, was annoyed to the point of punishing the inhabitants, descendants of Athenian colonists, for having corrupted their Attic tongue.

Beaufort's sketch of the island castle (facing a second one on the mainland) at Korykus, east of Silifke. It shows the punctilious detail of his description, typical of all his drawings. A page from his *Journal*, 1812.

Issus, site of Alexander's victory over Darius. But all his hopes were disappointed.

On 20 June the ship's company watered on the flat shore of a little cove west of Ayas (Aegeae, near present-day Yumurtalık) and those in the boats revelled at the sight of 'the greatest number of fish and fowl I ever saw together', catching for the mess tables turtles '[in cipher] in the act of copulation which seems a very slow affair'. Beaufort was also ashore, taking observations. Other officers and Cockerell were exploring the country nearby, including a ruined castle, in company with unusually friendly and good-humoured villagers. But one of them, 'a blackman', gave Beaufort the warning that appears at the head of this chapter. It was all too exact.

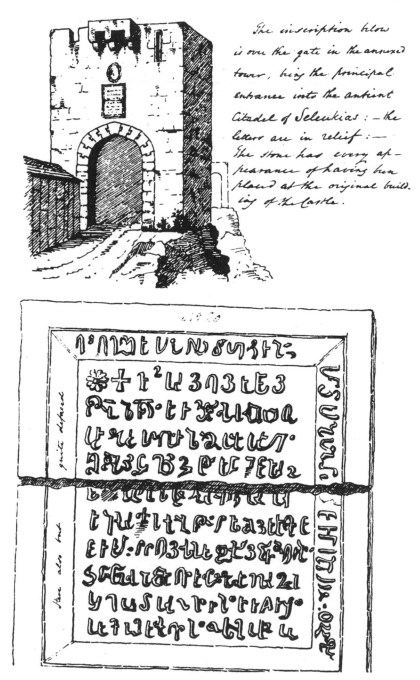

The inscription below
is over the gate in the annexed
tower, being the principal
entrance into the antient
Citadel of Seleukias : — the
letters are in relief : —
The stone has every ap-
pearance of having been
placed at the original building of the castle.

Gate and inscription of the crusader castle at Silifke; a page from Beaufort's
Journal, 1812.

As Beaufort was embarking his instruments after his observations, a number of armed Turks were seen advancing. There was no particular reason to be alarmed for, as he knew, all Turks habitually carried arms. But as they approached,

an old dervish was observed haranguing them; and his frantic gestures, with their reiterated shouts of 'Begone', 'Infidel', and other offensive expressions, left the hostility of their intentions no longer doubtful. The interpreter was absent with the officers, and all my little store of friendly words and signs seemed to irritate rather than to appease them. To quit the place seemed, therefore, the most probable means of preventing a fray; and as the boat was ready, we quickly shoved off. The mob now rushed forward; their voices assumed a shriller tone; and, spurred by the old fanatic, they began to level their muskets: the boat was not yet clear of the cove; and if they had succeeded in reaching the outer points, our retreat would have been cut off. It was, therefore, full time to check their progress, and the unexpected sight of my fowling-piece had for a moment that effect; but as they again endeavoured to close, I fired over their heads.

'That expedient saved us,' Beaufort continued in his account of the affair in *Karamania*. The mob fell back, 'the dastardly Dervish' ran away and the boat had time to get its head around and almost disentangled from the rocks, 'when one ruffian, more resolute than the rest, sprang forward to a rock on shore, which covering his person allowed him to take deliberate aim'. The ball hit Beaufort in the groin, damaged the femur and emerged near the rectum.

Fortunately, for the moment no other marauder fired and the boat drew clear. The pinnace, with nineteen men aboard, was nearby. Before Beaufort fainted from loss of blood, he ordered her to rescue the other officers on shore and to protect the cutter, lying a little distance to the east near the old castle. But before the pinnace could reach the cutter the dervish's party approached her from the shore and fired, killing a highly esteemed young midshipman in command. The pinnace collected the rest without further loss; the major difficulty of the lieutenant in command was 'to curb the natural fury of the boats' crews, which, if unrestrained, would speedily have taught these miscreants a dreadful lesson in retaliation'.

Had the *Frederickssteen* been near, Beaufort was sure, 'her appearance alone would have prevented our disaster', but she was becalmed, five miles from shore. The boats rowed to her and put the captain and the various parties aboard. Cockerell, on first glance, was pleased that

Beaufort's wound was no worse and 'not less astonished at his coolness & moderation even in this extremity'. But Beaufort burst into tears on learning of the death of young Olphert, the midshipman, and was 'more affected by that blow than his own'.

For a few days Beaufort was able to retain command. When a breeze sprang up, he ordered the ship in to shore and anchored under the ruined castle at Ayas, 'the inhabitants precipitately flying from their houses, persuaded that retribution was at hand'.

Yet some allowance was to be made for the bigotry and ignorance of these poor wretches; and perhaps some credit was due to the assertion of the villagers, that none of the inhabitants of Ayas had been concerned in this outrage. They alleged it was entirely the act of the mountaineers. . . . They seemed fully sensible that we possessed the means of inflicting a summary and exemplary chastisement; and I, therefore, flattered myself that for-bearance would be ultimately attended with more beneficial effects than could have arisen from a vindictive display of power.

Beaufort did, of course, write as menacing a letter to the Pasha of Iskenderun as he could compose and declined to be put off by a reply that the castle and local population were not under his jurisdiction but that of the Pasha of Adana, and that the offenders would be brought to justice. He sent another letter[5] to Iskenderun, warning the Pasha that a British squadron would arrive within a fortnight 'to assure itself of the Punishment of the Offenders' and to act as the circumstances might indicate if the culprits had not been seized. 'For in consideration alone of the Friendship which exists between my most powerful King and the Sublime Porte I have not burned the castle, destroyed the country, exterminated the inhabitants of a place which treated us as Enemies and you will I am sure be sensible of this moderation.'

The ship then turned westward and fell in with Captain Hope in the *Salsette* who, as promised, at once put in to Iskenderun. Hope was under orders from Stratford Canning not to antagonize Turkish authorities, since the Porte was now at war with France and increasingly inclined to the British cause.[6] He therefore refrained from drastic action.

Beaufort conceded in a letter to his father a month later that firing his gun 'was very imprudent and against my own orders'. He declared to Hope[7] that although he felt some strong steps should be taken, yet 'the discovery of my having undoubtedly been the first aggressor, &

the pitiable ignorance and barbarity of these people, requires that much more allowance should be made for them than if the murder of my young friend had been first in the order of time, and consequently without provocation, which with the utmost mortification I confess that my conduct afforded them'.

After some few days at sea Beaufort was no longer able to exercise command. He relinquished it to the *Frederickssteen*'s excellent first lieutenant, W. S. Gammon, who set a return course to Malta. A few days later, the captain's condition deteriorated badly: the oppressive heat of high summer militated against recuperation; the wound became infected and the shattered bone began to exfoliate. Beaufort felt that he could not survive and, three weeks after he was shot, painfully inscribed a letter to Lestock Wilson:

To whom can I apply to perform the request in the following papers but to you. The reasons are obvious. . . . That I shall recover I have the strongest dependance & assurance upon that Almighty & Merciful being who often reduces us to the last stage of calamity to render us worthy of his other favours – but as appearances are against me, and my body & mind may equally weaken it [behoves?] me while strength remains to do my last duty. On the 20th of last month as a just punishment for my many sins I received, a shot from a Turk in the thigh and . . . there are too many reasons to fear that it may prove mortal. If so I beg you will with the utmost caution convey the intelligence to my Alicia, and that then you will also impart the fatal intelligence to my dear & excellent friends in Ireland . . .

He enclosed his will and asked Wilson to send all his observation books, survey charts and notes to Captain Thomas Hurd, who by then had succeeded Dalrymple as Hydrographer to the Admiralty. He asked that all his other books and his small pocket telescope go to Alicia and that his other instruments be distributed to members of his and Wilson's family. 'All this is a melancholy task indeed but I feel myself quite unequal to the task of writing to take leave of friends I love and who love me so much.

'May we meet again if not here, hereafter.'

21

Author and Chartmaker
(1812-1817)

*I envy you the satisfaction of having done a great duty
in this service to mankind. To have established this
step in science, fixed the bounds of the oceans, thus far
shalt thou go and no further, is no small boast.*

CHARLES ROBERT COCKERELL to Beaufort[1]

The danger was over by early August when the ship came to anchor
in Malta. The bone splinters emerged neatly and the captain was able
to move about on crutches. 'I eat and drink and sleep like a Welch
parson,' he wrote cheerfully to his brother.

Beaufort brought his frigate home to Deptford without incident in
mid-October, which was none too soon: the usual late autumn gales
would have gravely jeopardized a ship which, on inspection in port,
proved to be in such poor condition that she was paid off at once and
broken up.

Beaufort made his courtesy calls on the Lords of the Admiralty and
from them heard 'many civil nothings', but he also received from them
praise 'that the apparent discipline of the *Fredericksstein* [*sic*] has been
such as to require so trifling an infliction of Corporal Punishment in
the space of four months'. In the second season's voyage along the
southern Turkish coast there had been only one flogging.[2]

When Beaufort stepped ashore his career as a sea-going officer was
forever ended. He did not know it, and later, in fact, applied for other
appointments afloat. But at the moment different matters occupied his
attention – his forthcoming marriage to Alicia, months of desk work
for the Hydrographic Office and the book on his travels.

The marriage took place at St Mary Le Bon Church in London on 3 December 1812. It initiated more than two decades of a profoundly loving attachment.

Good as his word, Lestock Wilson settled £5000 on his daughter (which she at once passed to her husband), and also gave the couple the use of his handsome country house on a large estate, 'The Grove' in Epping Forest, and his town house at 31 Harley Street when they chose to live in London. These arrangements continued for almost ten years, somewhat to Beaufort's embarrassment but not so much as to cause him to forgo the substantial monetary saving of free lodging.

He fell to work at Epping to record his survey and begin his book, working on the first by day, the second at night, and forgoing for almost a year the introduction of his wife to his parents and friends at Collon and Edgeworthstown. He also began a correspondence with prominent antiquarians, travellers and scholars which was to continue throughout his life. Within a few months of his return from Asia Minor his reputation as a man of science had grown so much that when Edgeworth proposed him for election to the Royal Society, the President, Sir Joseph Banks, replied that Edgeworth's sponsorship was supererogatory: 'He has not need of favour of any kind, but will come amongst us on his own sole account, as he ought to without owing thanks to any one.' He was elected unanimously in July 1814 and uncharitably gloated to his father that 'an emminent DD who followed [in the balloting] was blackballed 48 to 13'.

Completing the charts and accompanying textual material took more than two years; the final product was presented to the Admiralty at the end of April 1815. The work was masterly and is still referred to with reverence in the Hydrographic Office. The eleven basic sheets, ranging from 16 in. to 24 in. wide and 16 in. to 30 in. deep, and the index chart were so perfectly executed that unlike any before and few if any since they went directly to the engraver for transfer to copper plates without the intervening hand of a draughtsman.[3] The basic charts, on a Mercator projection, were on the scale of two miles to an inch, the index map of twenty geographic miles to an inch. The basic sheets were then condensed to six. Their quality may be judged from the fact that Beaufort was quoted by the Hydrographic Department as the principal authority for the surveys of the southern coast of Turkey until 1972, and in 1976 he was still given as the authority for its eastern part; another current chart, compiled from his drawings, is of eighteen anchorages on the south coast of Turkey (plus three from another hand). All told, Beaufort presented the Admiralty with forty-eight charts, plans and topographical sketches of sections of the coast as they appear to an observer on a passing vessel. Some of these are of shores and anchorages on Rhodes, the west coast of Turkey and nearby Aegean islands which Beaufort also surveyed during his two-year stint in the Eastern Mediterranean.

Beaufort also wrote a *Memoir* of seventy-five printed pages (published by the Hydrographer in 1820). It is a textual companion to the charts with an explanation of the methods and nomenclature used and a summary of the geography and other phenomena of interest to seamen. Most of the volume consists of a detailed description of the whole coast, its harbours, reefs and shoals, fortifications, currents, availability of supplies and other features, even the disposition of the natives. Beaufort extended the *Memoir* to give a similar report on the other Eastern Mediterranean areas that he had surveyed.

He had made his basic observations of longitude, he explained, at three places, Makry, Cape Avova (before he turned about with his cargo of Turkish fugitives) and Anamour, ascertaining the positions by eclipses of the moon and of Jupiter's satellites, observed with a two-foot reflecting telescope. Longitudes of the remainder of the coast were deduced by successive triangulations or by the three good chronometers he carried. Latitudes, much easier to determine, were done from shore observations 'with an excellent circle of Troughton's'.

Finally, he devised, and proposed for the future, a better set of symbols for indicating the height of mountains.

According to the usual mode, [he wrote in the *Memoir*] their comparative altitudes can be inferred only from the depth and force of the engraving; and the several gradations of abrupt descent or gentle slope are altogether omitted, though the face of a hill may change to every variety of inclination. It is therefore proposed that the strokes [radial from the crest] of which the shading consists, should be broken into a number of parts; that, each of these parts should signify a given measure of altitude, suppose a hundred feet; and that they should just occupy the space in which the face of the hill rises that number of feet. These several zones of short lines may then be said to shew horizontal sections of the hill at every hundred feet of altitude: and thus, the relative inclinations of all sides of the hill will be manifest, as will also the entire elevation, by reckoning the number of zones.

Here is still another manifestation of Beaufort's correct approach to a problem and his usual failure to hit upon a solution that was exactly right. What he was groping for were the contour lines now in almost universal use. The failure is doubly strange, for he used nothing more nor less than contour lines to show the depth of water.

Beaufort ventured one political suggestion in his *Memoir*: the island of Kos (now a Greek free port) facing Bodrum was, he saw, the spot most frequented by merchant vessels in the archipelago. Therefore:

> Many circumstances appear to point out this island as the proper place for the establishment of a British vice-consul; provided always that he is a British subject. The miserable and venal natives, who now fill that important office in most parts of the Levant, disgrace the national flag. . . . The situation of vice-consul might be a desirable retreat to many retired officers.

The proposal was never accepted.

John Wilson Croker, the famous Tory politician who was then First, or Parliamentary, Secretary of the Admiralty, wrote to Beaufort that their Lordships were greatly pleased even by their first slight inspection of the work 'and have given directions for your full pay being continued to you, up to the date of the letter announcing the completion of the survey'.

Beaufort exploded. He had expected much more. His sense of justice – and his vanity – were outraged. There ensued a short but furious controversy with the Admiralty in which his action was considered 'impatient and petulant' by his brother-in-law Edgeworth but fully justified by his old commander, Admiral Stopford, to whom Beaufort appealed for counsel. There were indeed two sides to the case.

In letters to the Admiralty Beaufort argued that he had accepted the appointment instantly and without demur, and that he had stepped down from a potentially lucrative post as senior Naval officer in the Eastern Mediterranean, taking instead a mission 'which must be considered as partly extra-professional and which is usually consigned to those who offer their services in that line'. That was overstating the matter: little prize money or glory could be expected from the Smyrna station. But Beaufort believed that other officers assigned to survey work had received as much as two guineas a day extra pay, and that such a payment would have brought him £2000 more, rather than the

£200 which was the difference between half-pay and the full pay the Admiralty proposed to give him.

Administrative records cast no light on Beaufort's assertion. He probably would not have claimed that extra pay was customary without grounds for his belief, but it was not until 1817, two years later, that extra surveying pay – £1 a day for captains and commanders and lesser amounts for lower-ranking officers – was formally established; and then only for the time actually spent in surveying.[4]

In short [Beaufort wrote to Croker], unless their Lordships should be pleased to confer on me such a recompense as would throw a lustre on my work, and such as would not degrade me in the eyes of my brother officers, I must beg permission to decline any further reward than their Lordships' gracious approbation, and the proud confidence of having contributed to the credit and resources of my country.

Their Lordships replied firmly but politely – surprisingly politely in view of the fact that Croker, who was handling the matter, was no friend of hydrographic work during his twenty-one-year tenure as First Secretary. Croker declared that their Lordships intended the offer of full pay not as a reward but as a generous interpretation of Beaufort's activities, conceiving that he had been fully active on Naval work even when ashore and without a command. More important, they would never accept Beaufort's inference that officers of the Navy were entitled to refuse hydrographic work when ordered to do so or that such employment constituted any higher claim than regular service. Naval officers were to do as they were told.

Their Lordships were more gracious than they might have been after Beaufort's admitted 'bullying' of them. 'My Lords trust', Croker wrote, 'that this explanation will be satisfactory and will convince you that quite the contrary of any slight or neglect of your Services was in their Lordships' contemplation.'

Beaufort sulked like a child and refused the full pay. He ended the matter with a snarl at the Admiralty: 'I have only further to express a hope that the Survey may one day prove as beneficial to the Service as it has been unproductive to me.'

The Admiralty could have taken Beaufort's rejection as an insult, but the new First Lord, Viscount Melville (son and eventual successor at the Admiralty of the man Beaufort so detested fifteen years before), was placatory: hearing that Beaufort had nearly completed his book,

Melville offered to have it published by the Admiralty or, if Beaufort wanted to publish himself, to arrange for the Admiralty to engrave the charts for it.

In preparing his book Beaufort made the 'priggishly precise' first Hydrographer, Alexander Dalrymple, look positively slapdash. He rewrote *Karamania* endlessly and agonized for months over the title. For precise readings of inscriptions, translations of ancient and medieval travellers, of Greek and Turkish place names and other geographical information he pestered his old friend, the outstanding scholar George Cecil Renouard, chaplain of the Smyrna factory, and his interpreter on the voyage, and conducted correspondence with other travellers and scholars. Among them were Major James Rennell, the foremost geographer of Britain and a pioneer researcher of ocean currents; the traveller Edward Daniel Clarke, who had touched on the Karamanian coast before Beaufort but who did not publish his *Travels* until many years later; Robert Walpole, himself about to publish an anthology of reports on Turkey; and, of course, Cockerell. But in particular, he called on his classically educated brother, William, in Cork, to adjudicate on such questions as should it be 'Faselis' or 'Phaeselis', and what was the authority for saying that Cleopatra entered the Cyndnus below Tarsus? In two years William supplied his insatiable brother with scores of pages of translations and commentary.

The correspondence was not entirely one-way. Rennell increasingly drew on Beaufort for information for his own publications (and came to depend on him heavily for counsel and criticism in later years when a deep friendship developed); Walpole first proposed to publish in his own travel anthology whatever Beaufort wrote and, on being turned down, begged successfully for geographical crumbs.

Beaufort gave all his earnings from *Karamania* to his publisher, a decision which appears downright perverse in the light of his earlier bitter campaign for extra money from the Admiralty. Edgeworth thought he was pushing professional purity to an idiotic extreme. Beaufort argued that he would 'stand higher in the eyes of the world, but partic^y. those of my profession, by not appearing to make a trade of authorship'; that in making any further claim on the Admiralty he would not be haunted by profits made on the book, and that since the material of the volume was derived in the course of public service, it should go before the public at the lowest possible price, i.e. without any royalties to the author. But he ended his argument on a feebler note: he could not expect much from the publisher anyway and therefore 'it would not be worth while to sacrifice these principles, although a larger sum might perhaps provide a temptation'.

The text, a chart (he rejected the Admiralty offer to engrave it) and vignettes for the chapter headings of *Karamania* were finished in May 1816 and the published version appeared a year later. It was an instant success and went into a second edition in 1820. A happy combination of geographical and archaeological information, travel narrative and personal reactions, especially to the grandeur of the scenery, the wonder of nature, the beauty of the antiquities and characteristics of those strange people, the Turks, puts *Karamania* into the top flight of nineteenth-century English travel books. It is, as well, a splendid and historically important account of discovery. It was the direct instigator of several later expeditions to Asia Minor, and remains to this day the most charming *vade mecum* for any seafarer along the southern coast of Turkey.

Letters of congratulation poured in. His unpublished inscriptions were seized upon by European philologists. The great astronomer John Brinkley, Yorke, Croker and many others wrote enthusiastically. Highly favourable reviews appeared in *The Times*,[5] the *British Critic*,[6] the *St James Chronicle* and elsewhere.

Sir John Barrow, Second or Permanent Secretary of the Admiralty, who claimed to have been responsible for selecting Beaufort 'out of the of the whole Mediterranean fleet' for the Karamania survey and for selecting him years later to be the Hydrographer, called the book 'superior to any of its kind in whatever language'.[7] This, from the founder of the Royal Geographical Society, was praise indeed.

22

Interim
(1815-1829)

I cannot bear that his fine talents, enterprising spirit
and noble principles should be left in oblivion and
inaction. His ambition, like his patriotism, is of the
true sort, ardent, yet chastened. And I feel confident
that had it but scope for action, his family, his country
and his species would be graced and benefited by its
exertion.

ALICIA BEAUFORT to Fanny Edgeworth[1]

In the fourteen years between his completion of *Karamania* and his
appointment as Hydrographer Beaufort led a life without a specific
focus, fragmented by conflicting concerns – his word was 'vortices' –
of family, business and science. Much of the period was rendered
melancholy by his realization that his ability was being wasted. To be
sure, his family life was for the most part happy but his business affairs
were marked with little success and much frustration. Such comfort as
he gathered outside his home came in his increasing activity in scientific affairs.

The beginning of a family came hand in hand with a succession of
crises of finances and ill-health. Alicia gave birth to a boy on 10
February 1814 (christened, inevitably, Daniel Augustus) but within a
few months the infant fell dangerously sick with erysipelas and recovered from it looking like a cadaver. By the end of the year the
financial difficulties of the senior Daniel Augustus set a new record in
horror; Francis ultimately saved his father from a humiliating bank-
ruptcy by lending his own money and negotiating a loan of £3000
from Lestock Wilson; the interest kept him in painful straits for years.
As if that burden was not enough, the old man saddled Francis with
a scheme for the shipment from Holland of the library of a long-dead

Beaufort relative, to be auctioned in London and thus to recoup the family fortune. The sale, at Leigh and Sotheby, was a disaster, the proceeds falling short of defraying even the shipping costs. Incredibly sacrificial in any matter concerning his sainted parent, Beaufort made good a £200 or £300 deficit from his own meagre funds, blaming himself for having misappraised the market.

Within a few years 'DAB' prodded his son into a similar piece of idiocy. He bludgeoned Francis to find a publisher for a manuscript written by a silly Irish woman friend. Francis knew the work was worthless but felt himself forced to contract for its printing by his own (and Maria Edgeworth's) publisher, Hunter. Predictably, the book was a catastrophe and under the contract the author was liable for the costs. Francis paid them himself, to the tune of £124.

A second son, Francis Lestock – his parents had hoped for a girl, to be named Anatolia or Karamania – was born in June 1815 and remained in precarious health for months. Alicia had a difficult recovery and Beaufort himself began spitting blood, possibly from the old wound. Within a few months, his father's financial position again sank into dreadful difficulties. Once more the two sons forwarded every penny they could raise. Francis wrote to his sister Fanny: 'We may, and most likely will scorch our feathers, but they will grow again. The strength of the wing will, I trust in Providence, escape injury. The simple and beautiful code of Moses places filial duties first of all in social duties – and few children have parents more entirely worthy of their exertions.'

In time the health of the new baby and his parents mended, but irremediable tragedy struck with the birth of a third boy, Alfred, in January 1817. He soon proved to be hopelessly defective mentally. Beaufort tortured himself with the fact that he had asked Maria Edgeworth to be a godparent without having initially revealed to her the depth of the child's malady. Alfred was cared for at home for some years until the task proved impossible, whereupon he was sent to a private asylum outside London. He lived, with the mind of a child, until he was fifty-two.

The family grew with relentless regularity: in 1819 a daughter, Sophia, was born; next year another daughter, Rosalind Elizabeth; then in 1823 another son, William Morris (the middle name after Beaufort's captain on the *Phaeton*), who became his father's favourite; and finally a third girl, Emily Anne, born in 1826.[2]

Meanwhile, death struck at older members of the family circle. Richard Lovell Edgeworth, the brother-in-law who broadened Beaufort's vision from the Quarter Deck to the world of science and technology, 'my warmest and most anxious friend', died in the summer of 1817. 'Whatever improvement I have made in my mind,' Beaufort wrote to his bereaved sister, 'must be ascribed to the impact he gave it. It was he who taught me that true education begins but with the resolution to improve, and it was he alone of all my friends who tried to wind me up to that resolution and to sustain it.'

A few months later the other great friend who had played such an important role in determining Beaufort's future and who had sustained him in both success and family disaster was stricken. Lestock Wilson suffered what seems to have been an apoplectic attack towards the end of 1817 and lingered half-alive in body and not at all in mind for four more years.

Finally, also in 1821, the man whom Beaufort had treasured since childhood as 'my dearest, dearest father' succumbed in his eighty-fourth year. His death was a blessing, for his debts had by then mounted to the point where the two sons could not hope to rescue him again. When death came to Daniel Augustus Beaufort, Francis and William were debating whether to try to contrive a flight for him to France or resign themselves to seeing him go to prison.

The old man had ultimately become contrite about the burdens his fecklessness had placed on his children. A year to the day before his death he wrote to Francis.

The ancient Trunk, which addresses you, no longer serves to nourish or support its various branches.... And yet, so far it differs from the vanquished hollow oak of the forest, that what little sap remains in it has for a long while been [supplied?] by those separated and extended branches.

No wonder then, that the greatest pleasure of my life arises from the close and intimate connexions that subsist between those branches and the old stem.

Beaufort's correspondence for the next several years tells a story of melancholy. One of the reasons, surely, was that after *Karamania* was finished, his talents were not fittingly employed.

That was no fault of the Admiralty, which had excuse enough from his waspish behaviour to put him on its blacklist, but did not. He was offered a handsome appointment, ideally suited to his talents. Against his own interest, and for the most honourable reasons, Beaufort turned it down. The proposal, made to him by Croker late in 1815, was to survey the entire coast of Ireland, a congenial task that would have occupied him for at least ten years during which he could have been in frequent contact with his family and friends. He was greatly tempted, but made such high-handed demands that Edgeworth, for one, feared he might be cutting his own throat and his mother pleaded with him to follow the motto (changed by now from the original) on the family crest: *Suaviter in modo*. But, quite remarkably, the Admiralty yielded. Discussions continued for several months. Suddenly, at the end of May 1816, Beaufort wrote to Croker that the whole idea was wrong. A geodetic survey of Ireland itself, he said, should precede a coastal one; triangulation from precisely determined points on land would be much a more accurate way to chart all the shores than by trying to fix key coastal features by celestial observation. The great Ordnance Survey of England was nearing completion and soon such a survey would have to be made of Ireland; a maritime survey made before it would soon be outdated as inaccurate. The argument was unassailable and Beaufort was not being self-righteous in writing to Croker that 'by discarding from my mind every idea of present and personal advantage, I am making the best return in my power for the flattering performance with which you have honoured me'.

Years later the Ordnance Survey of Ireland was carried out and the coastal survey followed. As Hydrographer Beaufort had the satisfaction of supervising it. But for the present he had no job. He was offered other surveying appointments, but of coasts such as West Africa where he could not have taken his family and which his health would not bear. Alicia dreaded that he might have to accept such an offer.

One day after the death of Thomas Hurd, in May 1823, Beaufort applied for his position as Hydrographer but the Board of Admiralty told him that it had no immediate intention of filling the vacancy. The decision was almost certainly that of the First Secretary, Croker. He viewed the department as an insatiable money-eater and was determined to keep its direction in his own hands. He had constantly fought Hurd's attempts to exercise the independence that was the Hydrographer's by regulation and he wanted no repetition of such a battle with a new and strong-minded chief. In an otherwise painfully discreet history of the department L. S. Dawson declared that it may have had other enemies 'but certainly none holding so prominent a position' as Croker.[3]

> It has been said [Dawson continues] that he imposed upon the traditional credulity of the naval members of the Board, using the oft repeated arguments so dear to the naval mind – that they had managed to navigate ships and conduct operations without such scientific charts in their day; why, therefore, should not the navy of the period, and posterity, do the same?

Beaufort's promptness in applying for Hurd's job before the body had time to grow cold suggests that he was tremendously eager for it. After the rejection, however, he pretended as he had often done before that the grapes were sour. He wrote to his brother how the matter had been decided, 'to the great disappointment of my friends but I must say to the secret satisfaction of myself; . . . the being confined to an office would be a heavy drag around my neck.'

Six months later the Admiralty appointed Captain William E. Parry – 'Parry of the Arctic' – to the post. He held it, with two considerable interruptions to do what he was really interested in, namely, exploring Polar waters, until mid-1829. On occasion, he tried to fight against Croker but had only small success: the office stagnated into not much more than a depot for issuing such charts as it had on hand or had copied from other sources.

Despite Beaufort's surliness Croker always held him in high regard. In September 1826 Croker proposed his employment in inspecting the Greenwich Pensioners' institution but the letter failed to reach Beaufort and the offer was withdrawn. Two months later Croker asked Beaufort to participate in some new surveys and bade him call by. For unknown reasons Beaufort declined to accept whatever it was that Croker was suggesting. Two years later, it appears, Beaufort turned down what would have been a magnificent job for him: a project for surveying the Gulf Stream, still incompletely studied: long afterwards Beaufort disclosed to a colleague, Colonel Edward Sabine, that 'five & thirty years ago I was offered to command an exp^n. for that purpose'.[4] Yet in 1817 he had told his friend Rennell, the British pioneer in the study of ocean currents, of his eagerness to survey the Gulf Stream. Why did he turn such an offer down a few years later? Perhaps it was not only Alicia who dreaded long separations; her husband also, by the time he reached his fifties, was probably loath to leave what he once called his 'lamentably' growing family or to exchange the comforts of his father-in-law's splendid mansion for the rigours of lonely seafaring.

With the death of Lestock Wilson in 1821, however, those comforts were no longer freely available: Wilson's eldest son reclaimed his father's houses for himself. Francis and Alicia knew they had not the means to run a household themselves but were forced nevertheless to find them. Preparing to leave Epping, Beaufort wrote to his brother, 'How shall we manage only Heaven knows on about £700 a year [from his half-pay, pension and the income from Alicia's marriage settlement]. The Horizon is black, but please God the Sun may break through the darkest clouds.' His 'one huge benefit', he told Fanny, was that he 'owed not and will not owe a shilling'. Paying off his father's debts had prevented any saving; now he was obliged to provide at least £100 a year for the boys' education. At the same time he was paying £100 for the annual support of his mother and youngest sister, Louisa.

Somehow, he made do. He found a house in London at 51 Manchester Street, which was hardly big enough for his by then large family. (It carries today the blue plaque of the Greater London Council, marking his residence there.)

He then set out to make some money. His letters over the next eight years afford only fleeting glimpses of his ventures but enough to show that most of them – in Irish mining, manufacturing and canal projects, plus the sugar refining systems that brought business failure to the statistician George Richardson Porter – seem to have been unsuccessful. They kept him fearfully busy in the City and from time to time he fancied himself an important entrepreneur – he was director of several companies. He may have been paid some fees but he received little if anything on his investments. Putting his money into Irish shares, it was appropriate that he received what used to be known as Irish dividends, i.e. further assessments as a price for holding on to his equities. Even worse, he induced his relations and even Maria Edgeworth to invest in his ventures.

His correspondence in the 1820s gives touching glimpses of his generosity while he himself was in such straits.

In 1822, aghast at the financial problems his brother William was then encountering, he gave him £50, on the stipulation that the gift must be kept utterly secret; it was an unconscionable alienation of seven per cent of the family's annual income. Five years later, when the financial demands of his children's education were even more intense than before, he tried to give a further subsidy to his eighty-eight-year-old mother (but the good lady would have none of it, insisting she was 'rich' in what he gave her already).

In the light of the unpleasantness over his Naval pay, where the record shows Beaufort as petulant and unduly aggrieved, it is only fair to his reputation to recall these acts of generosity, in time and effort as well as money. Over the decades, his was a history of unremitting kindnesses.

At almost the nadir of his financial resources in 1819 when he was overwhelmed with his father's debts, he received a pathetic letter from Duncan Campbell, the Marine lieutenant who boarded the *San Josef* with him and was wounded in the assault: he needed £140 to resettle in Cape Province. Without a shilling to spare at the moment, Beaufort nevertheless promised to have the money for Campbell by the time he needed it, a year hence, although he had no idea how he was going to scrape it up. 'I have already four little *brats*, yet I do not consider their claims as interfering with the duty of assisting a friend,' he wrote to Campbell. 'The most valuable legacy I can bequeath them is the precept and example of doing as they would be done by.' Happily, Campbell found funds elsewhere.

Years later, when matters were easier, Beaufort repaid some of his relations in full for the losses they sustained in following his investment advice.

A diary entry in 1845 shows him buying Johnson's *Dictionary* from the effects of a deceased aunt of Alicia – herself long dead – to give to the woman's daughter: she had yearned for it but her mother had refused to give it to her.

More profound charities, perhaps, were those entailing not the expenditure of money but of himself. The 'In Letters' of the Hydrographic Office for a quarter of a century spill over in a cascade of gratitude from the officers for whom he campaigned to secure promotions, desired appointments, reinstatements and pensions, or to whom he had merely taken the trouble to write words of encouragement and approbation – apparently not a common practice elsewhere in the Admiralty.[5] The letters of thanks, from widows and parents as well, are touching accounts of the services he did them.

One revealing act, when he obtained his first command, was taking on board the *Woolwich* at the behest of the Edgeworths and rather against his own better judgement an Irish village lad, William Henry Quin, with the intent of making him an officer. The boy was bright so that the technical training would be no problem, Beaufort thought, but it would be a different matter to convert a peasant's child from Edgeworthstown into a gentleman at home on the Quarter Deck. The effort succeeded: the youngster rose to be a gallant captain; his son, named after Beaufort, also became an able Naval officer.[6]

Beaufort's kindnesses to his own relations were full and forthcoming. We find him standing for many years *in loco parentis* to Fanny Edgeworth's two elder sons when they were being educated in England. He became Maria Edgeworth's agent in dealings with her publisher and himself her editor and proof reader. (Maria seems to have accepted his editing without demur, once writing to him in gentle irony: 'Pray in future spare yourself the trouble of so fully illustrating and illuminating your observations, my dear friend. This is love's labour lost with me for I assure you I am not attached to my errors & have no affection for my own sentences.') He was saddled with the consequences of tending to two of Edgeworth's sons who inherited the family trait of mental instability: for William Edgeworth he had the task of finding an asylum when he went mad in 1818 and of overseeing his welfare while he was institutionalized; seventeen years later he had to do the same for his old friend Sneyd Edgeworth who, according to an enciphered entry in Beaufort's diary, 'was taken up for exposing his person'. For books, instruments and materials not available in the Hibernian backwoods, he seems to have been purchasing agent for every relative and acquaintance in Ireland.

One sees acts of grace best, perhaps, through the eyes of recipients. A set of fourteen letters written over a span of forty-four years speaks for itself. The correspondence begins in Quebec in 1809, when Beaufort was in harbour with the *Blossom*. An impoverished widow there, Maria Lennon, wrote to him of her plight: her husband, an Army surgeon, had died two months before, leaving her with three little girls and no resources. She was in desperate need of a passage back to England to escape another winter in Canada. A faithless servant had embezzled such money as she had managed to give him, intending it to buy food, bedding and other provisions for the voyage. The convoy that Beaufort was to escort across the Atlantic was her last chance that year.

Beaufort arranged the passage, aboard one of the merchantmen. He did much more: Mrs Lennon's letters, sent to him periodically by boats plying between the ships, show that he sent the children toys and dolls, not to mention essential provisions, as well as small delicacies and books from his own library. When the mother and one daughter fell seriously ill, he dispatched the *Blossom*'s surgeon across to their ship. Her thanks were the only return she could make: 'The remembrance of your kindness to us often sustains us in the midst of our sufferings. . . . My little ones, if they knew how, would send you ten thousand blessings for the nice bread you send. . . . Anna Maria sends a small cake and hopes you will excuse the Liberty.'

Maria Lennon somehow made her way to France and a kind of living as proprietor of a small school for girls. The daughters left her to an old age of loneliness. At intervals through her life she continued the correspondence, always recollecting that Beaufort had been her salvation. In a final letter, when she was almost eighty and living alone in Boulogne, she wrote: '. . . never, whilst my Heart beats or Memory holds her seat in my brain, never can I forget your unbounded Care & never failing humanity to me & my helpless children . . . never did I meet with such a friend since in my long voyage through life. . . .'

Beaufort met her once when he was rowed over to her ship in mid-Atlantic. They never met again.

23

Recognition
(1815-1829)

The first person to whom I happened to be introduced
[at l'Institut de France] was the great mathematician
La Place and his *accueil* was very flattering. . . . He
instantly said, '*Je suis charmé de vous voir ici, où votre
nom et vos travaux son bien connus*,' and he added a few
questions about Asia Minor to show that they were,
at least to him. . . . Humboldt also was peculiarly civil.

BEAUFORT to his sister Harriet[1]

For a boy who went to sea at the age of fourteen, and whose only
formal introduction to exact science was five months in the Dunsink
Observatory, to become the professional associate of the foremost
British scientists of the age was a triumph in self-education. With only
a few – although notable – exceptions, the great men with whom he
worked, from the astronomer Airy to the chemist Wollaston, were
university-taught; Beaufort's schoolrooms were the cramped and
turbulent cockpits and gunrooms of frigates.

Before 1814, when he was elected a Fellow of the Royal Society,
he had given little real evidence that he was anything more than a
gifted surveyor and keen observer of natural phenomena. He was not,
even in the loose parlance of the times, a qualified man of science.
Yet he soon became one.

In the category of simple description rather than theoretical science
was Beaufort's short account of an earthquake at sea which he experienced in 1810 in the Eastern Mediterranean while sailing to Smyrna in
the *Salsette*. He submitted it sixteen years later to Sir David Brewster,
a scientist noted for his research in optics – he was the inventor of the
kaleidoscope – and editor of the *Edinburgh Journal of Science*. Beaufort

must have felt that what he had to report was too slight for submission to the Royal Society's *Philosophical Transactions*. Brewster, however, deemed it one of the most interesting accounts on the subject that he had ever read and promptly printed it.[2] It had, indeed, some vivid elements:

At 11 a.m. solar time, while tranquilly standing to the southward, the ship was felt to quiver violently from stem to stern, – the masts, yards, rigging partaking of the general tremor, and even the guns being strongly affected. The agitation, which commenced with considerable force, seemed rather to increase for about two-thirds of its duration, and then gradually subsided until it became insensible. According to the general opinion, it lasted between two and three minutes; but . . . a minute and a half will probably be the safer estimate. The sensation it produced will be accurately recognized by any person who has been launched in a boat over a rough beach of gravel; indeed, the resemblance was so alarmingly manifest, that the leads were instantly thrown overboard; but no bottom was found with seventy fathoms of line, and I have since sounded in the same spot with 500 fathoms without reaching the ground. . . .

We afterwards ascertained that, on the same day, earthquakes had taken place both in Candia and the Morea; and as the ship was nearly in a line connecting the extremities of those countries, it was probably the same great convulsion which had extended throughout that space.

In the entirely different dimension of exact rather than descriptive science was the correspondence that Beaufort began as early as 1817 with John Brinkley, first Astronomer Royal of Ireland. Brinkley very soon made Beaufort one of his principal confidants in his monumental controversy with the Greenwich Observatory over his claimed discovery of the parallax of Alpha Lyrae (Vega),* a very technical, very mathematical bit of business, filling pages of Brinkley's letters.

In 1829, the year it was founded, the Royal Astronomical Society elected Beaufort a Fellow in recognition of his stature as a nautical astronomer. Accordingly, he was at once thrown into association with such outstanding figures as Sir William Rowan Hamilton, a subsequent Astronomer Royal of Ireland; Sir George Airy, later to become Astronomer Royal; Sir William Herschel, greatest of all nineteenth-century British astronomers; Francis Baily, also of great eminence, and Charles Babbage, the remarkable mathematician who envisaged

*He was wrong but Greenwich could not prove him so. Parallax of the fixed stars was not demonstrated until 1848 by F. W. Bessel.

the principles and constructed the prototypes of modern computers.

By 1825 Beaufort had also established a close friendship, lifelong in its duration, with the gifted astronomer Sir James South, despite the latter's notoriously contumacious disposition. He made free use of South's splendid private observatory in London. On one occasion he visited South for two weeks in Paris and was taken to a session of L'Académie des Sciences de l'Institut de France (counterpart of the Royal Society), there to be seated as a 'distinguished foreigner' and given the flattering reception indicated in the passage opening this chapter. In 1836, Beaufort testified on South's side in what the mathematician Augustus de Morgan called 'the most remarkable astronomical trial which ever took place in England'.[3] It was an arbitration of a suit, arising from a dispute lasting five years, brought by the great instrument maker Edward Troughton for payment of a telescope mounting for South, who claimed it was a failure.[4] On losing the case – which he deserved to do, for Troughton's work was good – and some £8000, South broke up the instrument and sold the parts at public auction, placarding the walls with venomous denunciations of the maker. The action effectively shattered both men and also, it would appear from the lack of any further mention of Troughton in Beaufort's papers, destroyed the friendship that had begun thirty years before when Troughton descried in his young customer 'a mind as clear and powerful as my own'.

Also during the 1820s and well before he became officially involved in their activities, Beaufort developed close relationships with the principal Arctic explorers of the age. Among Beaufort's correspondence in the Huntington Library are letters, hitherto unpublished, from three of the principals in four ambitious ventures of Arctic exploration (all aimed explicitly or implicitly at the goal of the North-West Passage) during the years 1824–7. The contents and tone bespeak intimate friendship.

One of the thrusts, that furthest north, was made by William Edward Parry. We find him writing to Beaufort from aboard the *Hecla* in Davis Strait on 1 July 1824, on the threshold of his third and final entrance into the Canadian Arctic. He had received two letters from Beaufort about Beaufort's years-old favourite puzzle, the diurnal variation of the barometer, and promised to read his own barometer twice a day to see if the phenomenon existed in high latitudes as well as tropical ones. (As good as his word, he sent Beaufort pages full of his observations on his return.) He went on to discuss the abundance of his supplies and to tell of his hope that 'we may be enabled to perform something worthy of so liberal and complete equipment'. The hope was only partly justified: he brought back valuable new knowledge but lost his companion vessel, *Fury*, and fell short by 400 miles of his furthest point west reached five years before.

The second voyage was that of Commander George Francis Lyon, in his clumsy brig *Griper*, on orders to pass through Hudson's Strait to the south of Baffin Land (hundreds of miles south of Parry's course in Lancaster Sound at the north end), and on to Repulse Bay at the south of Melville Peninsula. Thence he was to strike out on land towards a reputed body of water to the north. He too wrote to Beaufort, on 4 August 1824 from somewhere off Hudson's Strait, and also promised, like Parry, to study the daily 'aerial tides'. He added his hope that Parry would be able to turn southward through Prince Regent Inlet – as Parry at that moment was earnestly but futilely attempting – and that the two of them would meet, or that at least Lyon would find his markers. In the event, whatever study Lyon was able to accomplish of the weather was for purposes of survival: after horrible storms and harrowing escapes he had to abandon his attempt and return to England five months later.

The third expedition was that of Sir John Franklin. He was to move overland from the American frontier and through Canada to Lake Athabasca and Great Slave Lake and thence down the Mackenzie River to what is known now – it was not given the name until thirty or thirty-five years later – as the Beaufort Sea. He was then to press west as far as he could in the open boats that he carried with him and thereby meet the fourth explorer. This was Captain Frederick William Beechey who, by way of Cape Horn and the southern Pacific, was to sail through Bering Strait in Beaufort's old sloop, *Blossom*, and to push eastward along the northern coast of what is now Alaska. In fact the *Blossom* never got beyond Captain Cook's Icy Cape, on the north-west shore of Alaska; her master, in her barge, managed to push on another 130 miles north-eastward to what was christened Point Barrow. Franklin never progressed that far west.

Even so, that second North-West Passage venture of Franklin – unlike his appalling first and fatal third – was relatively (the word must be emphasized in describing any Arctic venture of the nineteenth century) easy and successful. He did indeed go down the Mackenzie, twice, and westward along the hitherto unknown coast to within 160 miles of Beechey's thrust in the other direction.

Two of his letters survive among the Beaufort papers. The first, written on 21 April 1825 from a settlement on Lake Huron, is a cheerful travelogue describing his happy reception in the United States, his esteem for the good people of America, the kindness shown him by New York's governor, De Witt Clinton, and above all the stupendous impression made by Niagara Falls,

the grandest object in Nature. The only feature I have seen which can be compared to them is the immense Iceburg attached to the shore of Spitzbergen, 1¼ miles in length and 300 feet above the water. That, however, is a still scene but at Niagara the mind is overpowered. . . . All other recollections give place to amazement, awe and reverence.

Franklin bade Beaufort write to him once a year and assured him that mail would be forwarded. He added: 'I hope you will do me the kindness of calling on Mrs Franklin as often as you can.' There was a tragic postscript on the last page: '8 pm – I have this Evening received through the newspapers the distressing intelligence of my dearest wife's death.'

The second letter, four closely-written folio pages, dated 6 February 1826, was from his winter quarters, Fort Franklin on Great Bear Lake. He told of the provisioning he had done along the Mackenzie the previous season, the enormous quantity of fish – and the lack of game – being taken every day to feed the large party of Indians and Scottish voyageurs assembled at the fort (fifty-eight were in one room during one of his Christmas revels), his sanguine hope for Parry (whom he supposed to be by that time as far west as the mouth of the Mackenzie), his enormously high regard for Beechey's talents and character and his own buoyant hopes of meeting Beechey far to the west.

His 'sufficiently monotonous' situation, that of the inactive winter season, had been greatly relieved, he wrote, by the delivery by Indian couriers of a large bundle of mail and journals. Included was a letter from Beaufort full of a mass of miscellaneous news about scientific developments since Franklin left home and, apparently, the usual appeal to study the daily variation in atmospheric pressure. Alas, Franklin replied, his barometers had been broken. He was fascinated, though, at what Beaufort had to tell him about the French physicist

Arago's experiments on the effect of copper on the compass needle and reported a strange magnetic phenomenon of his own discovery:

> Our observations lead us to suppose that the motions of the needle often depend on Atmospherical changes. On three occasions for instance an Easterly Gale has produced an increase of variation as shown by the needle which we have placed on the Magnetic Meridian and which recovered its usual position on the subsidence of the wind or on its changing to the westward. I have no doubt that these as well as other effects which we have noticed have been occasioned by the state of Electricity in the Atmosphere being changed.

Beaufort later sent the letter to Rennell, who, sensible man, remarked that if a strong east wind had such an effect it would have been observed long since in 'our Parallels'. He wondered if the effect was purely local and asked: 'Are there any effluvia arising from it, which are wafted by the motion of the Atmosphere; & in different quantities, under different circumstances?'

Rennell's speculation was wide of the mark, Franklin's much closer to it. The compass needle is *not* affected by the wind but *is* affected by electrical conditions in the atmosphere and so, on occasion, is the weather. Electrical changes in the atmosphere (as evidenced by Franklin's frequent observations of the Aurora Borealis) doubtless caused the easterly gale as well as the compass change.

No record is available, but it is possible that Beaufort was concerned with Arctic expeditions in some official capacity as well as that of personal friend of the leaders. The Royal Society was deeply involved in planning expeditions and Beaufort was an energetic member, with particular interest in meteorological investigation. He also may have been a consultant to the Admiralty, as was the case in early 1828 when it called on the Royal Society to set up a committee to draw up instructions for what turned out to be a particularly fruitful scientific voyage. Beaufort served on the committee with the President of the Society, Herschel, and a few others[5] to lay out a programme for Commander Henry Foster in the *Chanticleer*. He was to do magnetic and gravitational research in the South Atlantic, with the aim of finding a more accurate value of the ellipticity of the earth and 'the laws of the variations of gravity in different points on its surface', by pendulum observations both at the Equator and in high southern latitudes.[6] Foster's death by drowning off Panama in 1831 prematurely ended the brilliant career of one of England's outstanding scientific officers. The Beaufort papers contain a last letter from him before he sailed. It showed that the two men were close friends.

In 1826 Beaufort embarked on a project that put to work at least some of his talents. It was a labour of love – or a sense of social duty – which continued for two decades: the preparation of a series of maps to be sold for trifling sums by that remarkable institution, the Society for the Diffusion of Useful Knowledge. The organization was the creation of a remarkable politician and social and educational reformer, Henry (later Lord) Brougham. A founder of the highly influential *Edinburgh Review*, the moving force behind the creation of University College, London, Brougham was at the centre of reform movements in Britain after the Napoleonic Wars.

The SDUK was created to bring education to the artisan and burgeoning middle classes. Its initial prospectus, prepared in 1826, called for it to impart educational material 'of elementary works upon all branches of useful knowledge' by periodical publications at modest cost to all classes, but 'particularly to such as are unable to avail themselves of useful teachers or may prefer learning by themselves'.[7] It was a goal which Beaufort, recollecting his own self-education, backed enthusiastically. Asa Briggs characterizes the Society as 'noisy and inefficient' and suggests that the novelist Thomas Love Peacock did more to preserve the memory of what he dubbed 'The Steam Intellect Society' by his biting satirical attacks than did any of its own intellectual achievements.[8]

The SDUK produced an enormous volume of educational literature, including the *Penny Cyclopaedia*, over its twenty-two years of life. Beaufort was associated from the beginning with all its varied activities but principally as map-maker, a role which he hoped 'would be useful to mankind'. He explained to his brother in Ireland: 'In every house you will find a few books of some sort; in scarcely any house will you find a map of any sort – and as [the new maps] will be . . . engraved in the best manner and cheap as dirt I hope to see them in every house.'

The SDUK proposed to sell the maps for a shilling; Beaufort furiously opposed the price, insisting they should go for sixpence apiece. He won his point by volunteering to produce them without any recompense to himself.[9] Thereupon, year after year, he rose at 5 a.m. to work on the Society's maps before going to his desk at the Admiralty.

He was still at it in 1845 and probably until the dissolution of the institution in 1848. The original programme for the maps announced in 1829 called for sixty plates, to be finished in four years. Taken together, they would presumably constitute a world atlas. It is not known how many Beaufort finally turned out, but in 1840 he had produced 172. He was nevertheless abused in *The Times* for not having completed the series promised initially. The complaint, which seems outrageously unfair, had nevertheless a sliver of justification. What had happened – and was to happen in the Hydrographic Office itself – was that Beaufort carried his passion for perfection so far that he spent months instead of weeks on a map. Schedules fell far behind. Nevertheless, for at least ten years his maps provided almost the only income of the Society. By 1841 25 000 copies had been sold.

A collection of a dozen SDUK maps in various stages of completion among the Beaufort collection at the Huntington Library gives some idea of the enormous work he devoted to the project. Some he drew himself, working no doubt from existing maps and correcting and augmenting them with further data; for others he took an existing map as the base and embellished it with mountains of additional detail and corrections. One of the latter, apparently a previously published map of north-west Ireland, covering portions of four counties and measuring about 6 in. by 8 in., contains more than 200 corrections, additions and instructions to the draughtsman, written by Beaufort in red ink and the tiniest of characters.

By the latter half of the 1820s, to judge by the company he was keeping, Beaufort had 'arrived'. The fact must have pleased him so much that he indulged in some name-dropping for his private pleasure: among his papers there is a list covering the years 1825–9, probably compiled by one of his children but proudly headed in Beaufort's own hand, 'Remarkable people constantly at the House'.

The names are indeed sufficiently impressive for an Irish country parson's son to boast of. The Arctic explorers included Franklin, Lyon and James Clark Ross. William Stephen Jacob, who was credited with having corrected the positions of 317 stars in the *British Association Catalogue*, was listed together with the astronomers Herschel, Baily and South. In addition to those scientists already mentioned as Beaufort's associates – Babbage, Rennell, Davy and Wollaston – there were Davies Gilbert, then President of the Royal Society; Peter Mark

Roget, the physician and compiler of the *Thesaurus*, who was its secretary; the geologist William Henry Fitton; the mathematician, physicist and designer of the system to correct ships' compasses, Peter Barlow; the Scottish anatomist Robert Knox, who was later to incur the condemnation of the right-minded for buying the cadavers he dissected from the 'resurrectionists', the professional grave robbers.

Along with Heywood and Foster there were two other great geodetic and nautical scientists, Basil Hall and Henry Kater, and also the surveyor-general of India, George Everest. As might be expected, among the 'remarkable people' were a flotilla of knighted admirals who fought the Corsican Ogre: Beaufort's old captain, James Nicoll Morris; Thomas Ussher, son of his old astronomy mentor: Edward Hamilton, Nesbit Willoughby, Byam Martin, Controller of the Navy, and Henry Prescott.

For cultural leavening there were Beaufort's old Asia Minor travelling companion, Charles Robert Cockerell, by now a renowned scholar of classical architecture and soon to complete the Fitzwilliam Museum in Cambridge; Thomas Hofland, the painter; Edward Daniell, the archaeologist who was to die at Adalia in search of antiquities; and Thomas Bellamy, singer and theatrical impresario at Drury Lane and Covent Garden.

Not yet on the list but soon to be frequent visitors were Darwin and also Ricardo, who became a particularly treasured friend.

If Beaufort at first had need of a list of his prominent friends to reassure himself of his reputation, the offer to him in November 1827 of one of the two Secretaryships of the Royal Society made such bolstering unnecessary. Sir Humphry Davy had just stepped down from his forty-one-year reign as President and Davies Gilbert, more of a politician than a scientist, was about to take over on an interim basis. Beaufort had served on the Society's Council for the previous year. Although he did not conduct original research or publish scientific dissertations, his breadth of knowledge in hydrography, astronomy and meteorology must have recommended him to Davy for a seat on the Council and later to Gilbert for the Secretaryship.

Beaufort was enormously flattered but nevertheless declined. It was not because the honorarium was so poor – about £100 a year at the time[10] – for he told his brother in one of his more pompous declarations that lucre was not what philosophers set out to gain and,

besides, science should not be a trade. Rather, it was because the
Society's Secretaries would have to represent British science to every
distinguished foreigner and he simply did not feel qualified for such a
responsibility. How incompetent he would feel if Laplace visited
London and asked him about developments in British astronomy!

It is impossible to know whether that was the real reason: the argumentation sounds a trifle amiss. Beaufort knew that his own talents
and knowledge were considerable; he knew also that other Secretaries
in the past had been no better qualified than he. It is possible that given
his woeful financial situation he could not afford the time – with £100
or without it – that the post would require. It is also possible that he
sensed that a battle royal over the Society's basic organization was on
the horizon and would find him on the opposite side from Gilbert.

The right offer came eighteen months later. Edward Parry's interest
in the Hydrographic Office was never a flaming passion and although
he made sporadic attempts to bring the organization to life, he felt
himself chronically frustrated by the Admiralty's First Secretary,
Croker.[11] When Parry was offered the Commissionership of the
Australian Agricultural Company at a huge salary and pension he
decided to quit his post as Hydrographer. The next day, 14 May 1829,
the First Lord, Melville, offered the post to Beaufort, 'with a few kind
words which were a great deal from a cold person like him'. Beaufort
was fifty-five, the age at which, today, the Hydrographer of the Navy
is obliged to retire. He accepted on the spot.

He described the interview to his brother, conveniently forgetting
the number of Admiralty survey proposals he had rejected:

... before we parted, said I, 'Now, my Lord, I closed with your offer without
hesitation because I never refused any service which it is possible for me to
perform and if the appointment were but 50 £ a year I would work as
zealously and cheerfully as if it were the 500 – but I think to one who has
made the sacrifices that I have etc. etc. that that order in Council which
prohibits an officer receiving his ½ pay who takes a civil office is most cruel.'

After an argument Melville eventually secured a special dispensation
for Beaufort's half-pay to continue. Beaufort felt himself in clover. In
addition to his half-pay, pension and the £500 salary, he was soon
given a residence by the Admiralty at 7 Somerset Place which was
valued at an additional £300 a year.

For once his automatic listing of drawbacks was buried beneath his exultation. At last he could stop dipping into capital; he need no longer cheat his children out of a decent education. But mostly his exuberance was over getting the job he had so long desired, and 'without interest, intrigue or even asking'. He wrote: 'I think I can be of use in my generation, and that is a charming feeling. 2dly It is a proud situation for an insulated unconnected individual like me to find myself absolutely at the *head* of a department, and that in a country which . . . places her hydrographical department at the head of all others.'

The candidates, as Sir John Barrow recalled in his *Auto-Biographical Memoir*, were Beaufort and his friend Captain Peter Heywood; Melville was reluctant to decide between them and asked Barrow and Croker for a recommendation. 'We had little or no hesitation in assigning the palm to Captain Beaufort,' Barrow wrote. 'It could not be otherwise, as far as I was concerned, that my mind should at once be made up. In Mr Yorke's reign I had, at his request, selected Captain Beaufort and his ship, out of the whole Mediterranean fleet, to be sent to survey an unknown portion of the coast of Syria.'

Heywood's widow, however, remembered the matter differently and perhaps more credibly. In a letter to the *London Daily News* on 26 January 1858, she declared that her husband had been offered the post on the death of Captain Hurd in 1823 but, for reasons she did not specify, he declined. On the resignation of Parry he was again offered it by Melville 'who sent especially to Heywood for the purpose'. But he refused again, 'at the same time stating that Captain Beaufort was the fittest person to fill it'.

Whether Beaufort was first or second choice, Barrow had no reason to regret his selection. He gave the Hydrographer his full and ardent support for as long as he remained Permanent Secretary. Writing while Beaufort still held the post, Barrow said he was persuaded that no other man could have carried out the laborious duties 'in that clear, precise, and efficient manner in which they have long been and still are executed. . . . Beaufort has no equal in that line, and not many in most other branches of science.'

24

Hydrographer:
The Right Man

Took possession of my new Hydrographer's room.
May it be a new era of industrious & zealous efforts to
do my duty with sincerity, impartiality & suavity &
that not from worldly motives but from a sense of the
far higher duty I owe to that Providence who placed
me in this vocation.

BEAUFORT's pocket diary 12 May 1845

From his seven-room domain on an upper floor of the Admiralty in Whitehall, Beaufort described his work for his brother in Ireland a few weeks after he took up his post in 1829.

My duty there consists in directing and examining the construction of new charts of all parts of the world, digesting the information communicated in the Remark books sent home by every ship in commission . . . issuing sets of charts to every ship and receiving back old sets; watching the process of and investigating the operations of all the surveying expeditions of which there are 12, and of each of which I keep an abridged history in a large book, and another of the merits of all the surveyors; corresponding with . . . all the foreign hydrographers, of France, Spain, Denmark, etc . . . replying to minutes sent to me by the Board [of Admiralty], the charge and issue of all instruments belonging to the Admt^y., and lastly the whole of the Chronometer business of the Navy goes through my hands . . .

In painting a picture of a sharply focussed and tidy set of duties he was being naive, innocent of the welter of other tasks that were to fall to him in the next quarter-century. But even without the additional burdens soon to come, the direction of a dozen or more Admiralty surveys under way at any one time and the preparation of the charts and sailing directions entailed more than enough work for the small staff the Hydrographer commanded: one lieutenant who was in effect indexer, curator and issuer of the charts, another who acted as secretary, an assistant to each, one man to draw up sailing directions, four draughts men and, as needed, an outside bookbinder, a lithographer and an engraving-printer.

On hand, to be issued to Naval ships or to the Admiralty Chart Agents for sale to merchant ships, were copies of something less than one thousand charts. Only a small minority of these were engraved in the Hydrographic Office from Admiralty surveys; the rest were either engraved from foreign surveys or printed from plates purchased from private chartmakers. Some of the British engraved charts were indeed distinguished pieces of work, such as those of Cook, Spence, Flinders, Murdoch Mackenzie, Jr., Owen, Beechey, Smyth and Beaufort's own charts of the south coast of Turkey. But most were hasty 'running surveys' by ships bent mainly on regular duties or exploration and discovery, certainly not on detailed chart-making. On Beaufort's coming to office, 'there was scarcely what could be termed a correct chart of any portion of the globe in existence',[1] even of the shores of the United Kingdom itself, excepting only the Channel.

The Hydrographic Office had been born thirty-five years before but it had been an unloved and stunted child. The Order in Council that created it in 1795 instructed it 'to take charge of such plans and charts as are now or may hereafter be deposited . . . and to be charged with the duty of selecting and compiling' information useful for the Royal Navy for navigation. Nothing was said about doing any surveying on its own, and no great amount was done.

Naval captains had, however, been under explicit instructions since about 1760 to make observations of foreign shores and harbours and were directed early in the nineteenth century to keep special Remark Books, to be returned to the Admiralty. Thus a mass of material, unsorted and of varying utility, was available to the first Hydrographer, Dalrymple. He spent years trying to make order of it and was able to engrave some new charts from the data before him. On Admiralty instructions he also purchased such charts as he could from private publishers, including a considerable number of his own privately printed earlier ones. His office accordingly grew into something of a chart depot but not much more. Hurd, who succeeded Dalrymple in 1806, did vastly better, regularly issuing charts to each station; he expanded the staff in 1817 and gained the right to select and appoint some surveyors himself. Yet even as late as 1810 there was not one Admiralty surveyor afloat. Matters improved and by Hurd's death in

1823 he had succeeded in building a programme of some substance: four Admiralty surveys in home waters and eight abroad.[2]

In the next six years, however, activity declined disastrously: the number of surveys was sharply reduced and one of the most expert surveyors, W. H. Smyth, was dismissed after his voyages before he could convert his data to completed charts. During periods when the office of Hydrographer was left vacant during Parry's expeditions to the Arctic, John Walker, long serving as principal assistant, did what he could when Admiralty lack of interest was at its most profound. Years earlier, and on his own initiative, he had bought back and preserved some of Dalrymple's own copper plates which had been sold off as scrap metal.[3]

Hurd's successor, Parry, was as we have seen usually 'playing another game than mere Hydrography',[4] and for two and a half of the next six years he was away on his own expeditions. Parry succeeded during the brief period the Duke of Clarence served as Lord High Admiral in hiring six additional draughtsmen and re-instituting considerable surveying activity, but when the royal prince left office First Secretary Croker regained control; his penny-pinching and resistance to the whole idea of hydrography were once again decisive. Parry left in disgust when the lucrative Australian offer came his way.

When Beaufort was appointed in 1829, the Hydrographic Office 'was a kind of hybrid institution, the one branch of it inviting as it were the opposition of the civil element at Whitehall, the other calculated to encounter the ill-will of authorities afloat, from the circumstance that it was necessary the officers composing it should be in a measure independent of their authority'.[5]

Not until 1831, two years after Beaufort's arrival, was the Office established as a separate department of the Admiralty, controlled by its own chief. That – and Croker's departure in the same year – provided the conditions necessary for take-off. But what was also essential was a strong leader; happily one had been found. In her anthology[6] of British surveying achievements Mary Blewitt concludes: 'Sometimes in history the right man fills the right post at the right time and no more perfect example could be found than the appointment of Francis Beaufort.'

Despite the Office's past deprivation, Beaufort was not, of course, starting from scratch. The admirable Lieutenant (years later Rear-Admiral) Alexander Bridport Becher remained as the Hydrographer's right-hand man, as he had been since 1823; John Walker kept working almost until his death in 1831, to be succeeded in Beaufort's office by two of his four chart-making sons. Most important of all, a dozen of the most gifted surveyors and maritime scientists in the history of British hydrography, several already crowned with accomplishment and the rest soon to be, were eager to continue with their work.

Time too was in Beaufort's favour. Looking back over 150 years of his organization's history, a subsequent Hydrographer, Rear-Admiral A. G. N. Wyatt, observed:

It must be confessed that neither the advent of the great Hydrographer, Francis Beaufort, nor the departure of the arch-enemy Croker was the real cause of the achievements of the half century following 1829. The inexorable pressure of economic expansion would have forced some such results from any authorities . . . . The Surveyor and the Merchant went hand in hand while British commercial prosperity was leaping to its peak . . .[7]

Beaufort's was a period of huge expansion of the merchant fleet; tonnage more than doubled. Steam power began to drive out sail and brought with it new navigational demands; the Empire was rapidly expanding, the home country was steadily depending more and more on food imports. To all those developments, inadequately charted waters at home or on the far-flung trade routes were a menace that could not be allowed to persist.

The number of surveys in operation was not immediately increased but the work of the Hydrographic Office was nevertheless enormously enlarged. Beaufort soon found himself heavily involved with the affairs of Trinity House, which controlled pilotage, lighthouses and buoys; with harbour improvements and protection of navigable waters, especially against the encroachments on rivers and ports of the rapidly proliferating railways; and with the opportunities of new aids and techniques and investigations in maritime surveying arising from the work of the scientists and industrial technicians.

It was the high noon of British hydrography. R. T. Gould, a historian attempting in the 1930s to write about the Hydrographic Office in the 1820s, gave up struggling to chronicle its myriad activities after Beaufort became its chief, declaring that the canvas had become too large.[8] The task is no less impossible today; from the tens of thousands of incoming and outgoing letters and the accompanying minute books in the archives of the Hydrographic Office at Taunton only a few illustrations can be presented to suggest the variety and flavour of the work in Beaufort's era.

Once his office was established as a separate department of the Admiralty – the first to be so designated – Beaufort appears to have operated with relative independence. He was, of course, limited by the decisions of the Lords of the Admiralty in his budget, pay scales, accommodations, etc., and his directions could be undone by acts of caprice – mercifully rare – from above. Also, the ships of his surveying service could be redeployed by an Admiralty order.

Beaufort was not often thwarted in selecting areas for surveys and deciding how much time should be spent on each. His judgements doubtless reflected the military and commercial emphases of the moment and were not likely to be overruled.

Thus, Beaufort assigned the ships at his disposal according to need, arranged for their refitting and provisioning, chose their captains and officers, drafted their instructions and sent them on voyages that – except for surveys of home waters – usually kept them abroad for two or three years and on occasion five or six.

The surveyors were expected to make frequent interim reports with tracings of completed portions of their surveys; these were returned to London by whatever transport could be found;[9] in turn, Beaufort sent out to his widely scattered commanders a continual flow of comment, further instructions, notations of omissions and, always, encouragement. Above all, he demanded precision and detail from them.

When at the completion of his voyage the surveyor turned in his charts and accompanying sailing directions, Beaufort gave them intensive scrutiny. His office diaries[10] show that he spent from three days to more than a week perfecting the charts of each incoming survey. On his retirement he left behind an enormous mass of material, the publication of which had not kept pace with its accumulation. It is true that threat of war in the Crimea during his last years in office forced him to drop everything else in favour of charts of the Black Sea and Baltic, but it is equally true that he could not break the habit of the early days of his office when his intense personal supervision was essential,[11] nor could he trust others to be as perfectionist as he. 'What he had at heart had to be done by his own hand.'[12]

Once Beaufort had finished his review of the surveyor's harvest the draughtsmen would process it, on whatever scale Beaufort specified, to

beautifully finished charts and sketches. Those would flow in turn to
the copper-plate engravers and ultimately the printed copies would be
run off, to be distributed to the Naval ships needing them and to the
Agent for Admiralty Charts, for sale to the public.

Beaufort was held in strong affection and esteem by his surveyors,
but he certainly did not let them off with easy tasks. A typical set of
orders for a new survey in the West Indies in 1837, by Lieutenant
Edward Barnett in HMS *Thunder*,[13] runs to twenty-seven folio pages
under nineteen different subject headings. Some of the instructions
were standard, dealing with the nature of the shore and the appearance
of the land, sketch 'views', drawings and descriptions of the terrain
behind the coast, soundings near shore and in the deep, details of
current and tidal flows, chronometer records and sailing instructions.
These, it might be thought, would keep any survey ship busy enough,
but Beaufort also demanded reports on matters not hitherto considered
an integral part of a surveyor's duties: magnetic observations, reports
on Sargasso Weed, extremely detailed recordings of wind and weather,
other aspects of meteorology, and findings in the field of natural
science.

For example, under the headings of magnetic variations, divided between 'local attractions' and 'dip and intensity', Beaufort ordered that:

No possible pains should be spared which may throw any light on the
inexplicable forms of the curves which unite the degrees of equal Magnetic
Variations, or on the annual motion of those curves to the East or to the
West. The diurnal arcs of variation should also occupy your attention in
favourable situations, and it will be interesting, if by multiplying observations you can either confirm or refute the assertion that there is a constant
difference on the East and on the West sides of an island, independent of
that due to the space it occupies. . . . No subject can be of greater importance
to Navigators than the laws which affect their compass and none should be
pursued with more perseverance.

Surveying vessels were ordered to keep an exact register of the
barometer at its two daily maxima and minima, and to record the
comparative temperatures of sea and air.* The readings were to be
made 'with a view of assisting to provide authentic data collected from

---

*Beaufort did no less himself on land, in London or wherever he was travelling. He
kept a weather diary every day of his adult life, the entries ending only four days before
his death, showing temperatures, barometer readings and wind force directions. Surviving diaries are in the archives of the Meteorological Office.

all parts of the world, and ready for the use of future labourers whenever some accidental discovery, or the direction of some powerful mind
should happily rescue that science from its present neglected state'.
Exactly such a reporting procedure had been Beaufort's dream twenty-
five years earlier. He listed eight other specifics, including such recondite phenomena as solar and lunar halos, to test the assertion that they
were not always circular. Accordingly, 'a general order may therefore
be given to every officer of the watch to measure their vertical and
horizontal diameters whenever they occur day and night'.

Other instructions were tailored explicitly to the individual missions
and areas to be charted. Documents in the Hydrographic Office
archives and entries in his diaries show that Beaufort usually spent
several days, in addition to the *viva voce* discussions with the captains
before departure, in gathering on his desk all existing charts and descriptions of the area to be surveyed. These he digested and reduced to
specific tasks of investigation.

One example suffices; it is the instructions to a surveying officer of
the *Mastiff* in the Gulf of Arta (Greece) in 1831:[14]

The first and principal object will be the hydrographic contour of the Gulf
with its islands, roads, shoals and soundings . . . an accurate examination of
the entrance . . . and judicious marks for passing over the bar in the deepest
water. These marks are always best conveyed to the seaman by addressing
them to his eye, that is by sketches of the objects when in the desired position.
The height of all headlands, isolated hills and remarkable peaks should be
trigonometrically determined and inscribed on their summits on the charts –
as they afford the seaman a ready means of ascertaining his distance by the
dip table.

The nature of the shore, whether high cliff, low rock or flat beach, is of
course inserted on every survey – but much more may be easily and usefully
expressed – for instance the general elevation of the cliffs and their colour,
the material of the beach, mud, sand, gravel or stones etc.

Advantageous landing places and their nearest point of approximation to
the known roads should be distinguished.

Where alluvial deposits have carried out the mouths of the rivers, or
wherever accumulations of sand and mud have advanced the line of the coast
the apparent ancient boundary should be likewise marked; and if you can
assign the causes of the gradual changes so much the better.

In the Eastern Mediterranean the tides are imperceptible but I should be
glad if you would take some pains to ascertain to what extent the Lunar
influence may be traced in the gulf.

Beaufort was emphatic on the matter of nomenclature. He told his surveying captains:

Experience has shown that the love of giving new and generally unmeaning names tends to confuse our geographical knowledge. The name stamped on a place by the first discoverer should be held sacred by the common consent of all nations, and in really new discoveries it would be really more beneficial to make the name convey some idea of the sense of the place, or some allusion to the inhabitants, or still better to adopt the native appellation, than to exhaust the catalogue of public characters and private friends.

That last exhortation was one that few of the surveying officers followed to the letter, for none were completely indifferent to what a little judicious flattery might accomplish for their future careers. Prime Ministers, Admiralty Lords and Secretaries could not all be so monkishly self-effacing as to object to a brave captain in far-off seas honouring them when he christened some new-found headland or anchorage. Thus one sees in the atlases any number of Peel and Palmerston islands and inlets, Minto heads, Auckland islands, Barrow straits and points, and no less than eighteen Melville features named with, it may be safely assumed, the goodwill in mind of the First and Second Viscounts, for long years First Lords of the Admiralty. Beaufort went through the motions of resisting the tendency when he himself was the person to be honoured. On one occasion he struck out 'Beaufort Land' in the Arctic which an explorer had written on his chart, changing it to 'Queen's Land', on the grounds that it would be 'too presumptuous to let a humble Hydrographer's cognomen stand'.[15] Yet he apparently acquiesced in having his name given to a dozen or so geographical features, including Beaufort Sea in the Arctic, Beaufort Islands in the Antarctic and several others similarly christened by his captains and friends during his lifetime.[16]

In the 1830s Britannia ruled not only the waves but also – such was her Empire – many of the shores on which they broke. In addition, there were vast stretches of coastline where suzerainty was more nominal than real and accordingly where no great political or military problems stood in the way of operation by British ships. Permission to survey sometimes had to be requested of the rulers, as in the Eastern Mediterranean and in Spanish possessions in the West Indies; it was usually granted. In some places, notably the China Seas, surveying rights were included in negotiated concessions. Only rarely were there difficulties, as when the Emperor of Morocco caused a British survey to be broken off. Even on the west coast of North America there was no barrier against British surveying although Beaufort once told W. F. Beechey (whose instructions for the survey of the *Sulphur* and *Starling* to the Americas in 1835 filled *forty* folio pages) to break off surveying in the Columbia River if the Americans objected. But in that case more than ordinary prudence was needed because Beechey also carried secret orders for detailed military reconnaissance.[17]

In a world that was open to British surveying and hugely inviting to British trade what was needed was not exploration – for most of the world's coasts had long since been visited – but exact surveying. Except for Beaufort's work in the River Plate and that of Peter Heywood, who was surveying there at the same time, both coasts of South America were sparsely charted by British surveyors and quite inadequately described by the Spanish. Since Cook's and Vancouver's voyages in the previous century, only two or three British surveyors had worked along the Pacific Coast of America. W. F. W. Owen's 1821–8 African surveys, rendered harrowing by fever and 'drawn and coloured with drops of blood',[18] constituted a mammoth achievement but left a great part of that huge coastline still to be charted. Little or nothing had been done in New Zealand in the almost sixty years since Cook.

Most astonishing of all, except for the Channel and parts of Ireland, charts of the home waters of the greatest maritime power in the world were 'totally inadequate for the safety of shipping' at the time Beaufort took office.[19] As early as 1808 Dalrymple had pleaded in vain with the Admiralty for some surveys of the British coasts, or at least the area from the east coast to Holland (and had asked that Beaufort, idling in the *Woolwich*, be the surveyor).[20] It was a request that, considering the then locus of marine hostilities, was hardly unreasonable. Dalrymple succeeded in getting some further work done in the Channel but new coastal surveys were still in their infancy by the end of the 1820s. Beaufort took them in hand and fostered them throughout his career as Hydrographer.

Beaufort inherited a dozen or so surveys in operation when Parry resigned.* In succeeding years, the number of ships and surveys

---

*The records are somewhat discrepant: Dawson lists fifteen in progress in early 1829; a sheet of expenses incurred for that year shows thirteen;[21] Beaufort reported to his brother (see above) twelve as of October 1829.

fluctuated markedly according to the Admiralty's alternating moods of generosity and miserliness. In 1832 thirteen surveys were being carried on by Beaufort's own ships plus one by a hired schooner and four by hired boats. In 1842 Hydrographic Office records show that its fleet had risen to twenty,[22] not including *Erebus* and *Terror* on James Clark Ross's famous Antarctic voyage. A sharp reduction was forced four years later when all six of the service's steam vessels were withdrawn from surveying to carry grain to famine-stricken Ireland. Giving them up was painful; always forward-looking in matters of technological development, Beaufort had never doubted – in contrast to so many of his die-hard Naval contemporaries – that steam would supersede sail, and had begun to deploy the little paddle-wheelers in the early 1840s. Though he could not object to their use in relieving the Great Hunger, he was outraged when, with the crisis over, they were not returned to him, leaving four of his captains on half-pay. The steam vessels had revolutionized maritime surveying, taking over much of the work of small hired boats in home waters, permitting surveyors to run direct lines of soundings in weather impossible for sailing craft.[23]

For almost a decade after 1846 the average number of ships employed was eleven and in 1851 there was a further unexpected cut of £10000, or fifteen per cent, in the Hydrographic Office's former budget of £70000.[24] Crushed, Beaufort wrote a letter to the Secretary of the Admiralty ending, 'I will not trifle with your time by repeating here the hackneyed truisms about the comparative expense to the country in the cost of surveys or in the loss of ships and cargoes, but I will just entreat you to weigh the small sum you propose to save against the large amount of mischief which may be the result.' Although documentation for it is not to be found, Beaufort is often quoted as the author of the aphorism, 'The natural tendency of men is to undervalue what they cannot understand'. If he did say it, that must have been the moment.

But better days ensued: by 1855, his last year in office, the records show that his fleet had been built back to seventeen vessels and, with hired boats, were conducting ten surveys in home waters and ten abroad.[25] Beaufort could view his achievement with satisfaction.

25

Hydrographer:
The Admiralty Chart

Your last letter is really all Hebrew to me: ransoms
and dollars; queens; treaties and negotiations? What
have I to do with these awful things; they far trans-
cend my limited chart-making facilities. . . . The
harvest I look for at your hands does not stretch
beyond the reach of a deep sea-line and all the credit
I crave for you, and through you for myself, must be
won in the Kingdoms of science and reaped in hydro
graphic fields.

BEAUFORT to Sir Edward Belcher[1]

Beaufort's were the years of the great surveys and great surveyors,
recollected with awe and admiration by hydrographic professionals
ever since, even if they are unknown to or forgotten by the public
who remain their beneficiaries. The charts of Beaufort's surveyors
constitute the first coherent panorama of the world's coastlines and,
in so many individual portraits, provide flesh and features for what
until then had been so largely mere skeletons.

Today's public does, of course, remember Robert Fitzroy's second
voyage of the *Beagle* (1831–6), but only because of its famous naturalist Darwin, whose findings in fields other than hydrography brought
about the greatest intellectual revolution since Copernicus. Yet within
its own terms Fitzroy's work was also a monumental achievement.
From the River Plate on the east coast of South America, around Cape
Horn and through the Straits of Magellan to as far north as Ecuador on
the west side of the continent, Fitzroy charted major sections of the
coast, continuing the surveys started in 1826 under Captain Phillip
Parker King in the *Adventure* and Commander Pringle Stokes in the
Beagle. He added necessary detail to such few good earlier charts as
there were, and made new ones for areas either uncharted or, more
usually, inaccurately charted by the Spanish whose representations of

the whole coast of Chile were twenty-five miles out in latitude. Charged with measuring meridian distances (the distance in longitude between established locations and new ones), he returned with a whole chain of them around the world that exceeded 360° of longitude by only 8.25′ of arc, an error of one part in 2600.[2]

A letter from Beaufort to Fitzroy written at a relatively early stage of the voyage (5 September 1832)[3] is typical of those he kept flowing to his surveyors. One notes the easy tone, the unlaboured encouragement and praise – with a compliment from someone else artfully tucked in – together with agreeably stated instructions for a new task and, finally, an explanation of what was being done with the material so far sent back:

I am well satisfied with everything that you have yet done. Your *daring* return to Bahia [Fitzroy had turned back from Rio to remeasure a meridian distance which differed appreciably from that of Baron Roussin, a French admiral who had surveyed the coast in 1818–21 but with only two chronometers]* was I am free to say exceedingly judicious, for however subsequent events might have justified a reliance on your chron^s. in preference to Roussin's still such a striking difference at the beginning of your labours would have hung like a dead weight round your neck for the remainder of the expedition.

I shall be exceedingly anxious to learn your Merid^n. D[istance] to King's station at M. Video and the Straits of Mag. I will not however alter the Longitude on his chart, even if your difference should be material, the difficulty of obliterating the lines on copper is so considerable, but I will note in the title the result of your observations. . . .

Commodore Shomberg has just been here. He speaks in the most flattering terms of you, and desires me to remember him to you most kindly. He has also been talking of some rocks off the Cape Horn of which he gave you an account. He does not remember their distance offshore, so that I can say nothing about your taking a peep when in the neighbourhood. Your own judgement will suggest what should be done, and indeed will give you a better clue to the probability of the story than the sanguine temperament of our friend the Commodore.

I have been looking at your log as you desired, and I think by two more columns you would make the business of Winds and Weather much clearer. Enclosed is a fabricated day's log to show my ideas. I add also a paper of our abbreviations for soundings.

*Almost worse than none at all, for if they disagreed there would be no clue to which was in error.

I had many other things to say but a series of cruel interruptions all this morning only leave me time to add the sincere good wishes of

Yours ever

F. Beaufort

Dozens of other surveys during the Beaufort era were no less competent, no less important. Few were without drama, several were inordinately hazardous, many were haunted by sickness and death. The histories of some of them, usually in the biographies of their commanders, have received the book-length treatment they deserve* but the full chronicles of the others remain buried in the eighty-seven folders and eight bound volumes of letters – 6000 to 7000 items in all – in the Hydrographic Office archives. Only a few of the great surveys can be mentioned here. They provide, at best, a pale shadow of the reality.[4]

Edward Belcher, one of Beaufort's most brilliant and flamboyant officers, surveyed the west coast of Africa, the China Seas, East Indies and west coasts of Central and North America, producing therefrom almost sixty new charts. He interrupted his enormous surveying commitments with prolonged episodes of fighting, diplomacy and secret missions – in the Pedro–Miguel struggle for power in Portugal, in China's first Opium War with Britain and in the turbulent affairs of Sir James Brooke, the 'White Rajah of Sarawak', in Borneo. Belcher was knighted for his exploits. Although hated by his officers for his vile treatment of them, he was hugely admired by Beaufort as a brilliant nautical scientist and superb surveyor. Beaufort's view of his diplomatic diversions, however, may be seen at the head of this chapter. By rights Belcher deserved to have a surveying ship named after him, as has been done in honour of so many of his contemporary captains. His unfortunate name, one assumes, is forever a deterrent.

Another renowned surveyor of the West African coast was A. T. E. Vidal, triumphing over prolonged periods of ill health in a dreadful climate. He was also distinguished for his measurements of meridian distances there and in the Cape Verde Islands.

Still another who worked in the same area was Henry Denham,

*For example, Captain Robert Fitzroy's *Voyages of the* Adventure *and* Beagle *in 1825–36*; Admiral Sir Edward Belcher's *Narrative of a Voyage around the World in HMS* Sulphur; T. and W. Boone's *Voyage of the* Rattlesnake; H. B. Robinson's *Narrative of a Voyage to Explore the Shores of Africa, Arabia and Madagascar under the Direction of Captain W. F. W. Owen.*

later to make his name even more distinguished for twenty years of surveying in home waters. Among his achievements was saving the port of Liverpool by dredging a new channel. For seven further years he mapped the Fiji Islands and Australian waters. It was at Denham's initiative after six years of surveys in the Gulf of Benin and Niger Delta that light local craft were sent up the rivers for exploration and mapping. The project was enthusiastically supported by Beaufort and, after several expeditions and much travail, at last established intercourse by sea with the interior.

Like Belcher, Henry Kellett moved from surveying African coasts to fighting in the war in China, but thereupon reverted to his *métier* and charted the north-west coast of South America between Guayaquil and Panama, a stretch of 500 miles or more then known only from accounts of navigators a century before him.

Also on the far side of the globe were the famous surveys of Owen Stanley. His apprenticeship included a survey in the Eastern Mediterranean where he was away from his ship for eighty-four days in a small boat which he had ultimately to haul overland across the Isthmus of Corinth. Stanley was to work himself to death at only thirty-nine in charting the north-east coast of Australia, the Arafura Sea, the Torres Strait and south-east New Guinea. It was aboard Stanley's ship, *Rattlesnake*, that a penniless assistant-surgeon, barely into his twenties, became fascinated with tropical sea life and thereupon made a career of biological research. His name was Thomas Henry Huxley.

The first major survey work in New Zealand since Cook was that of John Lort Stokes, beginning in 1848. It was continued by a five-and-a-half-year effort by Byron Drury in a sailing brig of only 400 tons, the *Pandora*.

Scarcely out of his teens after seven years' service in the Napoleonic wars, Henry W. Bayfield began in 1815 a career of forty years in Canadian waters by surveying in the Great Lakes. The work was extended later to the St Lawrence River and Gulf, the Strait of Belle Ile, much of the coast of Labrador and Nova Scotia, and Anticosti, Prince Edward, Magdalen and Cape Breton Islands. His two-volume sailing directions for the Gulf and River of St Lawrence remained the authority until late in the nineteenth century.

Valued as much by succeeding generations of classical scholars as by navigators were the fruits of ten years' work in the Eastern Mediterranean by Thomas Graves, mostly in the *Beacon*. For some of the time he

had the help of two other devotees of archaeology aboard, the renowned naturalist Edward Forbes and, as first lieutenant, Thomas
Spratt (later to become a brilliant surveyor himself, particularly admired
by Beaufort, and to distinguish himself further for his pilotage and
intelligence operations in the Crimean War).

Graves' work was cut short, but not before he produced the material
for nearly 100 charts of the Greek archipelago, whence the Admiralty
recalled him without even consulting the supposedly-responsible
Hydrographer. Beaufort's only known public remark on the affair was
that the order seemed to him an 'inscrutable measure'.[5] His private
comments were doubtless more positive.

In 1841 the *Beacon* was given a special assignment to carry Sir
Charles Fellows to Xanthus, in south-western Asia Minor, and bring
back to England the fine marble sculptures he had discovered there
two years before. This time, it may be assumed, the order had Beaufort's heartiest concurrence: he had been within a few miles of the site
thirty years earlier and remained fascinated by the area's archaeological
treasures, and he knew that his book had in good part inspired Fellows'
travels. But once on the scene Graves refused to transport the marbles
without further instructions from Whitehall and, disputing Fellows'
proposed methods for dismantling the monuments, gave orders that
no one was to touch them. From Fellows' account,[6] the ensuing
quarrel must have been bitter. After months of delay, the stones were
removed and sent to England, where they are now assembled in the
magnificent display of the Xanthian Marbles, including the famous
Harpy Tomb and Nereid Monument, in the British Museum.

There is scarcely one of a total of more than fifty-five officers – in
command of surveys or with major surveying responsibilities – whose
results fell short of excellence or whose harvest was not of enormous
importance to navigation in the half-century or more that followed.
Their achievements, though, were too often accompanied by personal
tragedies. Like Owen Stanley, destroyed by his work in New Guinea,
Lieutenant G. B. Lawrence died of fever in the West Indies at the age
of thirty-eight; so also did Lieutenant David Gordon on Borneo, not
yet thirty, and Commanders T. Boteler and Bird Allen, from fever
contracted while surveying African coasts. Commander James Wood
died at forty-seven, weakened from many years' exposure in the tropics
and ultimately brought down by the harsh conditions of the seas
north-west of Scotland.

Graves fell to an assassin's knife in Malta. W. G. Skyring, only a few years into his career as a surveyor, worked barely three months after succeeding Belcher off the west coast of Africa before he was horribly murdered by natives while ashore making observations. Henry Foster, made a Fellow of the Royal Society when he was only twenty-four and, to judge by his earlier work with Parry in the Arctic and elsewhere, on his way to becoming one of Britain's most brilliant nautical scientists, was thirty-six when Beaufort (described as the young man's 'most intimate friend')[7] helped him obtain the command of the *Chanticleer* to carry out an intricate and highly specialized expedition to make geophysical observations in the South Atlantic. Its elaborate instructions had been framed by a committee of eminent scientists of the Royal Society, including Beaufort. The *Chanticleer* carried seventeen chronometers and quantities of other instruments; her pendulum experiments were to obtain values of gravity, from the variations of which the ellipticity of the earth could be determined. As a result of Foster's findings, new theories on the earth's figure emerged. Tragically, before the voyage was completed, Foster was drowned off Panama, falling from a canoe after returning from making observations.

The most harrowing disaster – Beaufort's pocket diary reflects his agony of uncertainty over several weeks before the tragic truth was known, and his shattering grief thereafter – was the loss of the survey vessel *Fairy* with all hands in a tremendous North Sea gale in 1840. Her captain was William Hewett, also a gifted nautical scientist and the author of an outstanding survey of the North Sea, conducted over a period of eight years. It was Hewett's ingenious observations which confirmed the existence of a previously suspected amphidromic point (a position of no vertical tide movement) in the North Sea.

In Dalrymple's day the Hydrographic Office had been engaged only in sorting and engraving such surveys as had already been deposited in the Admiralty, in issuing Admiralty Charts to the Fleet and in choosing the most useful privately printed charts. In a crucial advance Hurd persuaded the Admiralty in 1816 to set up a permanent surveying fleet manned by specialist officers so that the Hydrographer could initiate his own surveys. Some splendid surveys were conducted during his fifteen years (1808–23) as head of the department but by 1825, when the first Admiralty Chart catalogue was issued, only just over half the charts were based on British surveys and many of those were indifferent.

By 1829, at the end of Parry's term, the catalogue had grown to 986 items. At the start of Beaufort's reign nineteen new charts were published in 1830, a modest improvement on previous years.

A tally sheet found in Beaufort's private papers, reveals subsequent explosive growth. It shows that the number of charts produced annually by his office rose to thirty after five years and to sixty three years after that. The total fell significantly only once, to thirty-nine, in 1842. It had risen as high at 106 the year before and to 101 in 1848. (Beaufort's successor, Captain John Washington, reported that in 1855 130 charts were published. A large proportion of them, it can be assumed, were completions of the huge backlog of surveys that had accumulated and were awaiting Beaufort's final scrutiny.) In all, Beaufort could boast of having published 1446 new charts, at an annual average of sixty-eight, once the organization hit its stride in 1835.* In sheer volume, it was a staggering accomplishment, especially since there were never more than seven and usually only five draughtsmen and five or six Naval assistants, a staff only slightly larger at the end than that when Beaufort took office a quarter of a century earlier.

Beaufort was as starved of working space as he was of staff. His cramped quarters were a scandal to visitors and were far exceeded by the hydrographic departments in Paris, St Petersburg, Copenhagen and Washington. If, on one occasion, the grant by the Admiralty of a little more room evoked the piously dedicated diary entry quoted at the head of the previous chapter, its removal by the Lords a year later also brought forth a religious diary notation, bitterer and shorter: 'Matt V:11 and 12'.†

Quantity is only one part, and the grosser one, of evaluation. But the other criterion, quality, resists precise tabulation; judgements

---

*Somewhat different figures are cited by Dawson and Day but the discrepancies are not significant. Collins points out that at the end of Beaufort's term the Admiralty Chart series had risen to well over 2000, more than doubling the number at the end of the Parry era. Some 300 were copies of foreign government charts and 200 were from East India Company surveys, but the remaining 1500 were made from Admiralty surveys.

†'Blessed are ye, when men shall revile you, and persecute you, and shall say all manner of evil against you falsely, for my sake.

'Rejoice, and be exceeding glad: for great is your reward in heaven: for so persecuted they the prophets which were before you.'

about the degree of excellence of that mountain of charts must necessarily be subjective. Certainly the best equipped to judge the results of Beaufort's efforts were the professionals in his field and the men who sailed the seas, the ultimate users of the Hydrographic Office's product. Their contemporary verdict, undisputed, was that the Admiralty Charts had no rival for reliability and usefulness. 'Trust in God and the Admiralty Chart' is a precept that has been recommended to Naval cadets through the years.[8] As an indication of his own reputation, surveyors of his time commonly gave the nickname 'Beaufort' to any native guide or pilot who was particularly knowledgeable of hidden hazards.[9]

The Hydrographic Office was as highly esteemed abroad as at home. The *Revue des Deux Mondes*, for example, carried an article in mid-century describing the Office as 'the first great emporium of hydrography in the whole world' (although the author was scandalized that it was 'cooped up . . . in some half a dozen rooms').[10] The famous German chemist Robert Wilhelm von Bunsen wrote to Beaufort in 1849 that the equally famous German archaeologist Ernst Curtius, tutor to the future Emperor Frederick III of Prussia, adopted the principle 'always to follow the English charts whenever they are posterior to the French' and even when they were earlier, still to prefer them unless the French ones had 'undeniable claims' to superiority.[11]

The honours that came to Beaufort from foreign professional and learned societies* – including election to the United States Naval Lyceum, the American Philosophical Society and the Académie Royal des Sciences de l'Institut de France – necessarily showed their esteem for the work of his department as much as for his person. The King of Denmark, a nation advanced in surveying, insisted that Beaufort receive, first, a gold chronometer and, second, a gold medal. Beaufort's most astonishing honour – for what service the records provide no clue and the imagination falters in trying to conceive – was a bejewelled sword from the Sultan and Imam of Muscat. The recipient solemnly thanked the potentate, with the assurance that 'I shall always be ready to unsheath it not only in defence of your Majesty's Person but in support of those noble principles which have thrown such a lustre on

---

*Among honours from within the United Kingdom were election to the Irish Academy, the Society for the Arts in Scotland, the Royal Society of Literature, and the award of a DCL from Oxford.

Your Majesty's throne.' The weapon is now in the National Maritime Museum.

Some impression of the quality of the beautiful nineteenth-century surveys is to be had from the collection of them reproduced in Mary Blewitt's *Surveys of the Seas*, each one a gem cut with infinite care and labour. The cartographic standards set by Beaufort have been faithfully observed ever since. The Admiralty Charts of today and the techniques that go into their making remain unsurpassed throughout the world.

Charts are merely the most obvious creations of a hydrographic office. They are the consumer product unfolded on the ship's bridge and beside the helm of the yachtsman and pleasure-boat skipper, or reflected in the landsman's atlas. But the safety and efficiency of larger ships, Naval or otherwise, depend not alone on charts but also on much other information that only a specialized and professional institution can provide. For navigation more substantial than that involved in weekend boating, additional descriptive and tabular aids are imperative.

In one form or another, publication of such non-cartographic data of concern to the mariner has been going on ever since Moses reported fluctuations in the water level of the Red Sea and Homer described certain meteorological and geographical hazards to navigation in the Mediterranean. Descriptive and statistical material about seas and shores, gradually growing more specific and hence more useful to a subsequent voyager, increased over the millennia in the accounts of explorers and discoverers; by the end of the fifteenth century they began to multiply at an almost geometrically progressive rate. It was not until some 300 years later, however, that the oceanic and coastal explorers began systematically to accompany the charts they published with what could be called technical navigational information: sailing directions, tables of distance and location, data on tides, winds and currents. Yet, since governmental hydrographic offices were only beginning to be established, no nation committed itself to issue such material, except perhaps for home waters, on a systematic basis.

Some sort of beginning of that process was made in Hurd's term as Hydrographer with the publication of sailing directions issued abroad. It was Parry, however, who took the major step forward of publishing *Sailing Directions*, i.e. verbal guides, supplements and explanations that could not be presented graphically. At about the same time, the Hydrographic Office began to issue *Light Lists*, in which the position and distinguishing characters of lights exhibited from lighthouses were listed.

Such were the meagre non-cartographic publications of the Hydrographic Office (besides, of course, its catalogues of charts for sale) when Beaufort came to head it. If anyone had entertained doubts about the vigour and innovative temperament of a new chief already on the wrong side of fifty-five, he was speedily reassured.

First, in 1831, Beaufort effected a piece of empire-building by taking over the superintendence of the Nautical Almanac Office from the Royal Observatory. Its annual publication and *raison d'être*, the *Nautical Almanac*, gave the day-to-day positions of the sun, moon and prominent stars throughout the year which, with the use of the chronometer and Hadley's quadrant, was the indispensable tool of the mariner for determining his location.*

Its publication by the Hydrographic Office was in fact only a continuance of what had been done before. But a real innovation came the following year with the publication of the official *Nautical Magazine*, edited by Beaufort's assistant Becher as a commercial proposition but initially given a small yearly subsidy by the Admiralty. In the beginning it printed reports of newly-learned navigational information; two years later these were promulgated more officially and in greater volume by another new Hydrographic Office publication, *Notices to Mariners*, carrying changes to navigation information for users of Admiralty Charts and their sailing directions. Thereupon, the *Nautical Magazine* assumed the role which it has today: publishing reports of interesting voyages – first-hand accounts and thus valuable, and not merely entertaining, reading at that period – feats of navigation and seamanship and miscellaneous maritime topics of great variety. We have seen how Beaufort used it to promote his Wind Scale.

*The transfer followed a period when the *Nautical Almanac* had fallen into disrepute and was under heavy criticism for inaccuracies in its tables of the sun and for gross omissions in lunar distances from the planets, and of occultations and daily planetary positions. In a fiercely critical pamphlet James South declared that W. H. Smyth was obliged to use the ephemerides produced in Paris, Milan, Bologna and Florence, because of errors in the *Nautical Almanac*. Wishing on one occasion to show politeness to a Spanish captain, South said, Smyth gave his copy of it to him: 'Captain Smyth with his foreign ephemerides found his way to England; but there is an awkward story afloat that the Spanish captain has not since been heard of.'[12]

In 1833 came the first publication of the *Admiralty Tide Tables*, at
its outset a mere pamphlet giving the times of high water at five major
English ports. Recognizing its inadequacy – and the lack of observational data to permit not only its expansion but also the development
of scientific theory on tidal flows – Beaufort promptly organized
systematic readings at coastguard stations and brought about an
international effort to record tides on both sides of the Channel, the
North Sea and the Atlantic Ocean. Coverage in the *Tide Tables* grew
with the years; by 1858, not long after Beaufort left office, they contained predictions for twenty-three home ports and one colonial
one. The foundations were thus laid for the present *Admiralty Tide
Tables*.

Beaufort soon developed standard symbols, markings and abbreviations for the Admiralty Charts. These in turn led to the publication
in 1855 of the first *Abbreviations used in Admiralty Charts*, still in
general usage.

The last new publication launched during his regime, somewhat
scantily treated by historians of the Hydrographic Office, is one which
nevertheless may hold most interest for the landsman. It was *A Manual
of Scientific Inquiry* for use by Naval officers and, as the title page
stated hopefully, for 'Travellers in General'. Beaufort's guiding hand
is apparent. His role as link man between the Admiralty and the scientific bodies in Britain must have impelled him to have such a volume
prepared and enabled him to enlist authorities in contemporary British
science to write it. He was convinced that reports on every subject
from astronomy to zoology supplied by ships' officers around the
world would fill the alembic from which 'some powerful mind' would
distil the elixir of truth. Ready to serve in his data-gathering squadrons
were, he hoped, Naval officers in far-off and exotic parts of the globe
who would report their observations if only they could be encouraged
by admonitions from on high.

Even for its time the notion was old-fashioned, reflecting more the
attitudes of Sir Joseph Banks' era than the newer trend towards mathematical and analytical methods. But it had been the prevailing method
during those earlier years when Beaufort was schooling himself; as
far as it went, there was nothing wrong with it.

The first edition of the *Manual* appeared in 1849 – it was to go
through four more in the next forty years – and carried an opening
memorandum in a prose suspiciously like Beaufort's:

It is the opinion of the Lords Commissioners of the Admiralty that it would be to the honour and advantage of the Navy, and conduce to the general interest of Science, if new facilities and encouragements were given to the collection of information upon scientific subjects by the officers, and more particularly by the medical officers, of Her Majesty's Navy, when upon foreign service. . . .

Hence the issuance of a manual

giving general instructions for observation and record in various branches of the science. Their Lordships do not consider it necessary that the Manual should be one of very deep and abstruse research. Its directions should not require the use of nice apparatus and instruments; they should be generally plain, so that men of good intelligence and fair acquirement may be able to act on them [yet still serve] as a guide to officers of high attainments.

The thirteen sections that follow are not merely 'instructions for observations and record', but splendidly organized introductions to the several sciences. The names of some of the authors suggest the quality of the material.

The editor and the author of the chapter on meteorology was Sir John Herschel, the greatest astronomer of the century. Sir George Airy, then Astronomer Royal, was responsible for the section on astronomy and Charles Darwin for the one on geology. The monograph on tides was written by Sir George Darwin, a successor to Airy as Plumian Professor of Astronomy at Cambridge and one of the pioneer theorists of tides. Sir Edward Sabine, perhaps the foremost authority on the subject in Britain and for ten years President of the Royal Society, wrote the monograph on terrestial magnetism. Another Royal Society President, William J. Hamilton, wrote on geography; James C. Pritchard, an early authority in his field, wrote on ethnology, and Sir Henry De La Beche, who conducted the geological survey of England, contributed the chapter on mineralogy.

The book was revised and reissued several times in the half-century after its first edition and remained in the Chart Catalogue until 1913. The Admiralty and the British scientific community must have concluded that it served a more productive purpose than merely providing intellectual diversion to relieve the tedium of long voyages.

Whether or not it was the *Manual* that stimulated them, Beaufort's surveyors for many years provided a creditable proportion of the papers that filled the publications of British learned societies.

26

Private Life

I believe that both Happiness and its more humble
dependant, Pleasure, consists far more in expectation
or anticipation than in actual enjoyment.

BEAUFORT to his brother[1]

With his appointment as Hydrographer in 1829 the tempo of Beaufort's life speeded up sharply; his activities became much more varied
and the circle of his friends and associates greatly expanded. Within
a year or two he was cheerfully complaining that his responsibilities
left him time for only five and a half hours' sleep a night. Along with
the exigencies of his job his heavy involvement in the affairs of the
Society for the Diffusion of Useful Knowledge as well as his map-
making for it, his advisory and administrative duties for the Royal
Observatory, the obligations of his membership on the Tidal Harbour
and Pilotage Commissions and the multifarious activities of the several
learned and professional societies to which he belonged combined to
make certain that he had few idle hours.

He soon involved himself deeply in plans to create a new school to
train Naval officers and at almost the same time he was immersed –
almost certainly through his association with the principal founder,
Lord Brougham – in the creation of University College, London. He
became at once a member of one of its academic committees and attended frequent meetings of its Senate.

Well known as a non-party man, Beaufort wrote to his brother
that 'one half my friends revile me for being a Whig and a Radical and
the other half despise me for being an old Womanish Tory'. He was
thus an obvious choice of Sir James Graham, then Beaufort's superior
as First Lord of the Admiralty and a member of the Prime Minister's
committee of four to draft the great Reform Bill, to serve on Thomas

Drummond's Boundary Commission. Its function was to define the new parliamentary constituencies established under that monumentally important legislation.

Beaufort's advisory role to the government thus extended well beyond the scientific areas where recourse to him became, over the years, automatic. A reference five years after his death in the *Naval and Military Gazette*, which took pains to claim knowledge on this particular matter, declared that his opinion

was courted, not only by the First and Naval Lords, but we also know was referred to on very critical matters by Ministers of State, even those not appertaining exactly to his office. He was, we may affirm, the secret adviser of both political parties, and everyone respected him, not only for his ability, and for his graceful and persuasive mode of conveying an opinion, but also loved him for the amiability of his disposition.[2]

Beaufort grumbled at the demands on him, but his protests were hollow: he enjoyed work and variety. The tasks for the most part were happy ones, matched in the first few years by a generally happy family life and a mercifully eased financial position. To be sure, there was scarcely a time when one of the children was not suffering one ailment or another, some of harrowing severity, and Beaufort himself was often the victim of various sicknesses. But recoveries always followed and the children's growing-up process was a source of satisfaction. The eldest son, Daniel Augustus, was accepted at Oxford and won a small scholarship; the second, Francis Lestock, was placed in a school to prepare for service in the East India Company and distinguished himself in languages. The father's reputation in professional and governmental circles increased with each year; honours showered on him; the family's social life enlarged and grew more interesting and rewarding.

A bright future opened up – but at once was blighted by the most crushing blow in Beaufort's life. In the late summer of 1832 Alicia detected a lump in her breast and within six months it was clear that the cancer would be fatal. Her physical agony, intense at a time when the only analgesic was laudanum, lasted more than two years. Yet her profound religious faith, her certainty that her trial was ordered for her own benefit by an all-wise and all-loving God, sustained her and suffused her with a serenity and even a cheerfulness almost incomprehensible to a generation less certain of eternal salvation.

The march of my disease is slow but sure [she wrote to her brother-in-law William in 1833] and the work of destruction, however long it may, for wise and merciful reasons, be protracted, is as palpable as it is inevitable. I am not often free from uneasy sensations; and never pass a day without more or less acute pain, but my nights are generally refreshing; I still have much physical enjoyment; and for the mind, I can truly say that Heaven has taught me to 'rejoice in tribulation'; for I have blessings without number – Oh! how many more than I deserve, & how doubly dear to me since I have the constant prospect of losing them – while every shaft of pain comes fraught with the conviction of its utility, and of the protecting love of a redeeming Providence.

Death came on 27 August 1834, ending a marriage of more than twenty-one years. Alicia was buried in Hackney churchyard where, except for one year when he totally forgot, Beaufort made a pilgrimage on the anniversary day until he was himself too feeble to leave his house. In the early years after her death Beaufort also went to the grave on other occasions, often taking his daughters with him to kneel in prayers that Alicia's virtue might forever guide them.

Beaufort was shattered by her sickness and death. According to an obituary of him based on material furnished by his youngest daughter, 'he came out from the long trial so much changed that it seemed doubtful whether he would ever regain his health and buoyant cheerfulness'.[3] The problem of raising his children appeared overwhelming. Although the two elder boys were settled in their schools, the question was what would become of the three girls, respectively fifteen, fourteen and eight, and of 'Little Morry', aged eleven. The distraught father chose the only answer available to him, importing his two spinster sisters, Harriet and Louisa, from Ireland to look after the children.

Ever since his own childhood Beaufort's relationship with Harriet had been particularly close. It was principally to her that he wrote his longest and most subjective travelogues during his seafaring days. She in turn adored him to a point of idolatry. Unmarried, far away in Ireland, she felt herself forlorn, living an empty life, starving for affection from her hero-brother. Once, during the earlier years of his marriage to Alicia when he made a business trip to Ireland and failed to make a detour a few miles north of Dublin to spend a day with her, she wrote him a letter revealing her sense of insignificance and longing:

. . . if you had allowed only one day to poor old Allenstown, to wander about with me in my ancient haunts . . . we should – at least poor little I should – have had one whole day passed with you there to think of ever after. Since 1804 we were never in that house together for more than a night – 22 years! A long & varied time to look back upon: joy & bitter grief, gloom and brightness, failure & success all appear in one's [illeg.] view of such a time. But in all these lights & shadows our friendship remains un-clouded, unbroken, & you are still, as you say in your last command to me, my old friend & brother & Master – and when the vanities & flatteries of life have passed away, it will be one pleasure at least to us to look back on the unchanged affection of our whole lives – to me indeed greater than it can be to you, because I know well my worthless inferiority.

When at last she came to join her brother in London in 1835 he had been without a sexual partner for more than two years. Her presence was too great a temptation.

The first record of incest comes in a ciphered line in his pocket diary on 26 November, five months after the arrival of the two sisters: 'Fresh hor[r]ors with Har[r]iet, O Lord forgive us.' Two months later: 'Again I employed Har[r]iet O Lord take pity upon me and strengthen my mind now.' He was sixty-one, she was fifty-seven.

In all, there are thirteen such coded entries, continuing for almost three years until a few months before his second marriage, explicitly or implicitly recording sexual acts. Most of them include his terrible cries of remorse and resolves to sin no more, as for instance on 16 December 1837: 'My poor sister again tempted by me – but the shame I feel now wil[l] I hope preserve for ever from further temptation. O Lord as[s]ist me to receive thy holy sacrament worthily.'

As can be seen, the anguish derived largely from his sense of the enormity of the sin, intensified by his religious convictions – he had by then long since abandoned his adolescent doubts and had become almost obsessive in his devotions – and probably secondarily from his feeling of having betrayed his dead wife. Only at the end of the affair, a month before his marriage to Honora Edgeworth, is there a diary notation, this time *en clair*, of his realization of the iniquity done to his sister: 'Long conversation with H.B. about [Honora] – and I did very wrong. *Heaven have mercy on me.*'

Ever since Beaufort left the sea, married Alicia and resumed his visits to Collon and Edgeworthstown, the little girl about whom he remarked so singularly many years before when she visited his first command at Woolwich was never far from his mind. Letters to Fanny at Edgeworthstown seldom failed to inquire of her stepdaughter, 'that tender plant', 'that truly aimiable and affectionate friend', Honora Edgeworth. With a zeal that went far beyond the duty of a step-uncle and which endured over many years, Beaufort acted as middleman in an interminable correspondence in which Fanny reported on Honora's various ailments – mostly heart irregularities, digestive difficulties and a deaf ear – and Beaufort responded with prescriptions, diagnoses and recommended treatment from his London physicians. It was also Honora who accompanied Beaufort and his son on an excursion around southern Ireland in the summer of 1826.

Within eighteen months of Alicia's death Beaufort's diaries show that he had fixed on Honora with a passion. It is probable that his attraction for her was enhanced, subconsciously it may be, by the magnetism that the Edgeworth family exerted on him. One senses that the poor parson's son always longed to join, as more than a friend, the charmed circle of the scholarly, widely connected and well-known country squire and of his famous novelist daughter.

For a time the courtship was star-crossed. Beaufort's diaries are full of ciphered cries of desperation at prospective failure: Honora felt herself obliged to remain in Ireland to take care of the aged and last surviving sister of her mother. At the same time, Beaufort himself struggled painfully with the notion that a second marriage would somehow betray his pledge to his first wife. Ultimately, he felt that Alicia had released him from his vows, while Honora, by what means is not clear, was freed from her responsibilities. The marriage took place in Edgeworthstown on 8 November 1838. Beaufort was sixty-four, his bride forty-six. Maria Edgeworth described the event in a letter to a friend:[4] the night before the wedding, the bridal pair went to the room of the eighty-nine-year-old aunt and received her blessing; then, at the marriage ceremony, Beaufort was more affected than any man Maria had ever seen in similar circumstances, 'yet in the most manly manner'.

In an obituary of Beaufort twenty years later[5] the well-known Victorian writer Harriet Martineau declared that in marrying Honora Beaufort 'secured a friend to himself and his daughters for many of the later years of his life'. We can be certain that it was rather better than that. Dozens of ciphered diary entries, continuing until he was seventy-nine and always accompanied by passionate cries of contrition and vows of continence, testify to the strength of his sexual drive, but they appeared only during Honora's occasional long absences and, ultimately, when she became an invalid.

Although such representations of Honora as can be found – a sketch of her as an adolescent and a skiagram[6] – are not particularly revealing, it is certain that she had been a very pretty young woman. British friends spoke of her a few years before she married Beaufort as 'the tall thin elegant looking young lady with a high colour and with such a remarkably lady-like manner'.[7] By the time of her marriage, she described herself as being 'as grey as a badger'.[8] Edgeworth family letters make it clear that she was much beloved by her half-sister, Maria; Christina Colvin, an editor of those letters, draws the conclusion from them that she was possibly less vivacious than most of Richard Lovell Edgeworth's other children, but had the role of conciliator in the family, 'retiring and dependable', 'everybody's confidante and councillor'.[9] She helped Maria extensively with her children's books, copying, editing, correcting proofs and advising on the texts, a role Beaufort later assumed.

On her death, one of Fanny's daughters, i.e. a much younger stepsister of Honora, recalled her as 'the guardian angel [of] our childhood, putting everybody right & being always the sympathiser in all sorrows & joys & all difficulties – & her gaiety & grace'. Another younger stepsister remembered – somewhat emotionally but probably not inaccurately – 'all the many years of imperturbable kindness & justice & constancy – & sprightliness & grace . . . joined with such peculiar feminine & diffident composure and gentleness. . . .' At the end of his own life, when Honora was still alive· but paralysed and mindless, Beaufort referred to her 'retiring delicacy', 'charming disposition', her softness combined with firmness and with the 'strong judgement of her father' Richard Lovell Edgeworth.[10]

As a wife, Honora appears to have been attentive, devoted, devout enough to elicit no complaints from her punctiliously observant husband, avid for music (for which Beaufort had, if anything, a negative passion) but more inclined to a life of balls and dinner parties than to the scientific lectures, demonstrations and inspections of new technology on which her spouse doted.

Withal, it was an amiable marriage if not an exhilarating one. Five years after the wedding Beaufort could boast that 'neither unkind word or look have escaped from either of us', and five years after that he was still writing Honora loving and tender letters. He was forlorn when she left him on her annual return visits to Ireland, which grew longer and longer with the passing years. During her increasingly severe sicknesses, beginning seven or eight years after the marriage, he was a paragon of attentiveness and solicitude.

Yet Honora was far from being another Alicia, for whom Beaufort's longing grew as the years went on; the emptiness left by her death was never filled. 'Grateful as I am to my beloved wife', he wrote in his diary on his eighth annual graveside visit, 'I cannot but look back to the virtues, the devotedness & the dreadful death of my lamented Alicia.' The same year, on receipt of a joyful letter from his second son telling of his happiness at the prospect of marrying a girl in India, Beaufort wrote to his brother William the passage on the greater joys of anticipation compared to those of realization that is quoted at the head of this chapter. Sensing the implication of his words, he hastily backtracked, protesting his present happiness. But both there and more often when he declared his felicity to his diary he was protesting too much.

Life in the house at 11 Gloucester Road* (to which he had moved in 1839 from 7 Somerset Street) settled into a busy and crowded pattern of family and social activity but with a certain regularity and comfortable stability. On more evenings than not, Honora and Francis dined out as guests of friends or were hosts to them. Their circle included as before Beaufort's scientific and Naval cronies but broadened also to a multitude of distinguished and well-placed figures in government and the lesser nobility. Now and then the excessively social life became too much of a good thing. Beaufort fumed in his diary one day during the annual summer 'season': 'How horrid dining abroad every day, wasting time, learning nothing, seeing less, eating & drinking too much, talking nonsense etc.'

The unmarried aunts having returned to Ireland, Beaufort's daughters found their new stepmother much to their liking. To the father's mild annoyance, Honora was forever taking the girls to balls that lasted until the small hours or to recitals at the Society for Ancient Music or simply 'gallivanting about the globe in the carriage' with them. Once to his real dismay the ladies visited 'those horrid waxworks', assuredly those of Madame Tussaud.

---

*Now replaced by a large block of flats.

For Beaufort himself there were many late nights of work at the Admiralty when he usually dined at the Athenaeum or occasionally at one or another of his several professional societies. There were the annual June voyages down the Thames to Greenwich for the visitation to the Royal Observatory, the yearly Trinity House dinners where Wellington (always 'very civil to me') or some other noble lord was in the chair, the prescribed huge dinner party of the First Lord of the Admiralty on the Queen's birthday, and endless other meetings and dinners at the Navy Society, the Society for the Diffusion of Useful Knowledge, the Royal Society, the Astronomical Society, the London University Senate and other such assemblies.

Without fail, unless his periodic illnesses prevented, Beaufort took his family to Sunday service at Portman Chapel of which, and of its controversially ritualistic Tractarian minister, William James Early Bennett, Beaufort was a devoted and admiring supporter. In due time, when his eldest son, Daniel Augustus, came down from Oxford with a good record and was ordained, he was installed as Bennett's curate and often took the afternoon service and delivered the sermon. His father carefully noted the subject of every sermon he heard and pronounced his judgement in his diary. He usually found them good but was infuriated with Bennett's frequent attacks on the impiety and heresy of the geologists with their implicit challenge, even before Darwin, to Bishop Ussher's cosmic chronology. Of one sermon by his son, on circumcision, Beaufort thought it a topic 'better left alone'.

After church, with equal regularity, the family paid its Sunday calls – on the Babbages, the Fitzroys, the Souths and scores of other friends. On weekdays their own house was constantly full of visitors – Irish members of the family passing through London, friends in for breakfast or tea and, as noted, constant guests for dinner. During the 'season', the Beauforts entertained frequently and, if not lavishly, then hugely: diary entries of '18 dined here' or '19 dined here' (often on successive nights) recur again and again.

Beaufort's own indulgences, in which the wife and daughters whom he dragged along may not have been as thrilled as he, were excursions to see new scientific and technological developments: floating bridges; more powerful steam engines; an Archimedes screw adapted for ship propulsion; John Ericsson's rather more practical propeller; the electric light in Trafalgar Square; a test model of the Menai Bridge; the great tunnel being driven under the Thames with its builder, Isambard

Kingdom Brunel, as guide; the first British demonstration of Foucault's pendulum, changing 'its plane of vibration according to the diurnal movements of the earth – simple and beautiful', and the electro-magnetic telegraph, 'at present a very pretty toy, but I have little doubt that it will come into general use'.* A birthday gift to himself was a subscription to a set of lectures on electricity at the Royal Institute by Faraday. At eighty, he went to the Great Exhibition at the Crystal Palace to see 'the most interesting materials gathered from the whole world'.

The Admiralty gave its Hydrographer an annual holiday of six weeks which Beaufort usually took at the end of August. With the family in tow he would tour Wales one year, Northumberland and Yorkshire another, or the Lake District, the southern coast, the Scottish Highlands or Gloucestershire. Frequently, the vacation was spent in Ireland whither Honora usually retreated for weeks – and later, for months – beforehand. After her enfeeblement in both body and mind, her husband took his annual time off with his unmarried daughters on the Continent. His diaries record endless rounds of sight-seeing, walking, visiting friends and, inevitably, sketching and making water-colours by all the family. Fascinated by the new world of steam power, Beaufort meticulously recorded travel times by rail and boat from each point to the next, awed, one senses, at the revolution in transportation from the sailing ships and stage coaches of his younger days.

Back in London the family were far from sedentary. They were frequent visitors to exhibitions, galleries, and often went to Kew Gardens where the senior Hooker, Sir William, conducted their tours. There was the theatre – 'With all the children . . . to Cov. Gar. to see Macbeth murdered by Macready' – and one splendid day, 'Regents Park [was] finally open to the public. Ho[nora] . . . and I walked there to take triumphant possession of it. Met Darwin who showed us some curious facts about the bumble bee.'

---

*Possibly the telegraph on view was that invented by Beaufort's friend Charles Wheat-stone, but more probably it was that of Edward Davy, on exhibition at Exeter House in the Strand.

27

Hydrographer:
'In Addition to
Other Duties...'

. . . but business if it be not quite overwhelming is
really an ingredient to happiness and though it often
robs me of great pleasure, and cramps my endeavours
to administer to the taste of the little fold round me as
well as to my own, yet I would not exchange it for the
largest fortune or highest dignity if they should compel me to sit still and do nothing.

BEAUFORT to his brother[1]

Twenty-five years of Beaufort's office correspondence, copied and
filed in several score of volumes and folders in the Hydrographic
Department archives, reveal the immensity and bewildering variety
of his labours. No count of every memorandum and letter has ever
been made or is ever likely to be, but an estimate is possible.

A conservative figure for out-going letters is between 21000 and
22000, copied out on 7734 folio pages. The total does not include the
voluminous private correspondence Beaufort somehow found time to
conduct from his Admiralty desk (and for which he brought to the
office his own pens and letter-paper).[2] Except during his annual six-
week holidays all mail was signed by Beaufort; given his small staff
and his known punctiliousness about what went out over his signature,
he must have drafted most of the letters and read all of them before
they were dispatched.

In-coming letters retained in the files (there is considerable evidence
that several thousand other letters were never kept), including 6000 to
7000 from surveyors in the field, can be estimated at about 17500.

Finally, the files contain 3418 pages, comprising about 9000 individual items, of official minutes of the department: records of decisions

reached, proposals made, policies, procedures and actions recommended and adopted and informational material supplied to the Board of Admiralty.

In all, there are some 40000 separate pieces of correspondence and memoranda, some of a few sentences only, others of substantial length as, for example, a minute arguing to the Board why it should resist a Parliamentary demand for the Hydrographer to appear in person before a committee considering the construction of the Thames embankment;[3] or forty-four pages of instructions to Commander John Clements Wickham of the *Beagle* on surveying the west coast of Australia,[4] or a vocabulary of the language of the Amerindians on the banks of the Columbia River.[5]

Beaufort lacked modern office aids; every member of his small staff of Naval assistants had a specific task – calculating tide tables, issuing charts, compiling sailing directions, etc. – and only one of them was concerned with correspondence (and that, one must conclude, in his spare time, since he was also in charge of accounts, estimates, Remark Books, surveying instruments and the issuance of barometers and the *Nautical Almanac* to the Fleet).[6] Accordingly, dealing with the mountain of paper – reading what came in, preparing what went out and acting on the information and requests received – seems an utterly impossible task by itself; one wonders how Beaufort had time left over for his principal responsibility of supervising the compilation of charts and navigational material.

He did find time for it, as the record of achievement shows, and for a great deal else of major consequence. And, in 1848 he took on another demanding burden, in effect becoming chief of staff to Sir John Barrow in directing the successive searches for Sir John Franklin, lost in the Arctic.

Yet, as if that was not more than enough, the records show that he was called on to perform an encyclopedic array of other duties. His assignment to the Parliamentary Boundary Commission has already been noted. In 1835 he became a Commissioner of Pilotage and in later years a member of the Committee on Tidal Harbours,[7] the Committee on Lifesaving Rockets and the Harbours-of-Refuge Commission. In 1833 Trinity House was consulting him on centralizing the control of lighthouses, on the jurisdiction of the Cinque Ports and on the conservancy of the Thames.[8]

Included in his duties were the planning of lights, beacons and buoys in ports and their approaches. Surveying captains were called on to recommend to him the constructions of lighthouses abroad and Beaufort himself was responsible for bringing about the installation of the lighthouses in the Orkneys and Shetlands. He had hardly settled into his chair before he found himself the Admiralty authority to be consulted before Parliament sanctioned new works in harbours, canals and docks to meet the needs of steam propulsion. In his first year he noted that surveys of all small creeks and river mouths on the south coast of England would be necessary. With steam, he declared, these hitherto neglected waterways 'could be used for smuggling and hostile purposes'.[9] In asking for new charts to be made of them, it probably did not occur to him that up-to-date ones would probably be of more use to the smuggler than to the customs officer.

Beaufort brought on himself what was to be his most hateful task when he insisted that any proposed extensions of the railways to the coasts, port areas or over navigable waters first obtain Admiralty approval. Like the cosmos a few seconds after the 'big bang', so in Beaufort's time were railways at their point of explosive expansion. Beaufort soon found himself knight-defender of navigational interests, battling against promoters (and their friends in Parliament) seeking to obtain rights-of-way, bridges and harbour facilities, however much they might injure the efficiency or safety of maritime operations.

Beaufort was obliged as well to address himself to the new navigational problems to which steam vessels gave rise. In 1836 he was making recommendations for the adaptation of his Wind Scale, calibrated until then on the amount of canvas carried, to steam vessels,[10] and in 1848 for the number and nature of lights that they should carry.[11]

The introduction of iron into ships' structures brought him different problems. He soon suspected that the metal affected ships' compasses and might affect chronometers as well; he recommended, therefore, the creation of a committee to advise on compass improvements which, after some years, led to the establishment of the Compass Department of the Admiralty, where a standard Naval compass and a standard system of swinging ships to determine compass deviation were first evolved.[12]

Beaufort was called on to perform such diverse duties as to recommend map styles, scale and colours for the Ordnance Survey of Great Britain (a Treasury request);[13] to stock the ships of the Fleet not merely with navigational material but with the books of its general library;[14] to present the Board of Admiralty with eight pages of navigational data – winds, currents, relief harbours – plus estimates of number and location of defensive batteries, as part of a contingency plan to force the Dardanelles, reduce Constantinople and enter the Black Sea;[15] to lay down routes for postal steamers to Australia;[16] to arrange a continuing exchange of charts with Russia's greatest navigator, Admiral Krusenstern,[17] or to coordinate efforts on a tidal survey of the Bay of Fundy with the American hydrographer, Lieutenant Maury.[18]

Browsing through the Hydrographic Office's archives raises the question of whether there was any subject with the most remote or far-fetched connection with navigation, exploration or geography in general on which Beaufort was *not* asked for advice or action or carefully informed about. For that matter, was there any in which he did not take the initiative himself?

He appears as the authority on classical geography: Thomas Arnold, the celebrated headmaster of Rugby, is using Spratt's charts and drawings of the Eastern Mediterranean in his next edition of Thucydides, but would Beaufort answer a question about Minoan Crete? And could Arnold be given any Admiralty Charts the better to understand the geography of Carthage and the location of ancient Lilybaeum?[19] The captain of the *Meteor* reports on inscriptions at Philippi;[20] Lord Byron's old friend, the renowned historian George Finlay, would like some maps for a new edition of the topography of ancient Athens.[21] The classical scholar George Long wants help in determining the exact spot where Caesar landed in Britain,[22] and the Astronomer Royal needs to find the route of Agathocles' ships in the war against Carthage.[23] In a search for information of a somewhat later date, the First Secretary of the Admiralty, Croker, wants to be shown Pope Alexander VI's line of demarcation between Spanish and Portuguese possessions in the New World.[24]

Remarkable natural events must be investigated: would Graves give Beaufort information to enable him to confirm or deny a report of a 'singular phenomenon', viz. that submarine rocks are growing upwards in the Bay of Santorini (Thera)?[25] Would the *Mastiff* investigate the report that a fall of dust, possibly volcanic, persisted for several hours in the Orkneys?[26] From Pago Pago comes a report of violent tidal fluctuations a week after a slight earthquake shock.[27] Thomas Henderson, first Astronomer Royal of Scotland, reports details of his observations of Halley's Comet the night before.[28]

There are needs for new surveys, new settlements: for meteorological reasons, Fitzroy argues, Port William is the best settlement in the Falklands and 'without easy and frequent intercourse with ships the Falklands are not worth notice. With that, they are invaluable.'[29] Lieutenant Dayman suggests a settlement at Cape York for succouring ships wrecked on the Great Barrier Reef and in Torres Strait, because earlier survivors have been massacred by the natives.[30] James Brooke, newly established as the 'White Rajah', argues the political and commercial importance of Sarawak and pleads for a survey.[31] So also legislative bodies of Nova Scotia and New Brunswick want action on their long-ignored appeals for charting their coasts.[32] The shipowners of Peterhead demand no less, on behalf of the fishing and whaling industry, for Spitzbergen and Novaya Zembla.[33] Captain William Allen has been able to win Lord Palmerston's support for improving the port at Rhodes,[34] but Captain Charles Bethune considers Singapore not suited for a Naval station as it would be difficult to defend (a judgement validated only too disastrously a century later).[35] Macgregor Laird, pioneer explorer and trader of the upper Niger, points out the advantages of high land in the Cameroons for white settlement, above the level of tropical fever.[36]

Some matters are weighty enough: Lord John Russell, the Prime Minister, requests Beaufort's judgement on the applicability for its intended purpose of 'certain calculating machinery' constructed by Babbage.[37] Beaufort's reply is not known. One wonders whether he saw that his old friend had an intimation, a century early, of today's computer.

And some are wonderfully trivial: Her Majesty's Stationery Office will not pay the higher price necessary for decent pens and the draughtsmen are having to buy them out of their own pockets.[38] Captains on home surveys have no business interrupting their work just to see the Great Exhibition at the Crystal Palace but, on second thought, very well, permission for leave is granted.[39] Fitzroy is outraged that Roman Catholic priests in the Pacific Islands are making converts by means of threats and intimidations.[40] For storage at sea, what is the optimum shape for ships' biscuits?[41]

The needs of the scientists are ever present, and so are the demands on them: Sir Charles Lyell, perhaps the greatest geologist of his age, asks Beaufort if he can obtain the latest information on the geology of Patagonia from Darwin, then in New Zealand, almost a year before the *Beagle*'s return to Falmouth.[42] Faraday expresses regrets but he 'cannot undertake the examination of the water', as Beaufort requested; he must devote all of his time to his own researches which have been so constantly interrupted.[43] Sir Joseph Hooker, newly appointed assistant to his father at Kew Gardens, comments on the botanical collections brought back by surveying captains and would like to have more.[44] Thomas Huxley, four years back from the *Rattlesnake*, promises faithfully to complete his work on the results of his zoological researches within another year.[45]

On occasion, the Palace itself needs the Hydrographer's help. The royal yacht, *Victoria and Albert*, is to make her maiden voyage and the Queen her first trip abroad. Who is to advise Prince Albert on the best sailing arrangements, first to the Isle of Wight to choose the site for a private residence for the Monarch and her consort, and then to France for a stately meeting with Louis Philippe of no small diplomatic significance?[46] Beaufort, obviously. He has a preliminary discussion with Prince Albert on 5 August 1843 at Windsor and is asked to come again two days later with his 'cogitations' in memorandum form. His journal entry for the 7th reports the event:

Finished my plan. Off again to Windsor. Long explanation with the Prince from 3 to 4 (Taken by mistake to H.M. boudoir). Sauntered about the castle and town & read till dressing & at 8 assembled in the drawing room. At 8½ the Queen swept in with all her train, bowed to all & at once proceeded to the dinner table. 26 in all. H.M. sat but a short time after dinner & we $\frac{hove}{2}$ after her. Royal round game & 2 whist tables. Broke about 11 when the Queen went round to those who had been near her before & said something to each of them, to me amongst the rest & then she retired & I followed not her but her example. Sleeping in the York Tower.

Queen Victoria had occasion to call for his help once again. Her 'place of one's own, quiet and retired', had been established on that maiden cruise at Osborne, by the shore on the Isle of Wight. But, two years later, Her Majesty let it be known that she was 'desirous of having some means of landing at Osborne without passing through the inquisitive stares at Cowes'. Beaufort at once ordered his surveyor in charge on the south coast to investigate, but the files are blank on how the delicate problem was solved.[47]

However much those heterogeneous tasks and that magpie collection of communications may have irked the Hydrographer on some occasions – or kept him from being bored on others – they were by their nature only on the periphery on his main undertakings. The great majority of the thousands of letters and minutes make clear where and how he devoted his greatest and most earnest efforts: to the surveys, the improvement of surveying instruments and ships, the welfare of his officers, the nurture of the observatories, the promotion of the expeditions and the support of the scientists. By the mid-century those efforts endowed British hydrography with the strength and lustre that have marked it ever since.

As if the work in his office did not provide him sufficient variety, Beaufort undertook a private venture, apparently late in life, on a sea almost totally foreign to any he had sailed since he was a teenager: stegannography. The remarkable consequence was that just as his name is in the vocabulary of every sailor as a standard of wind force, so in the repertory of every cryptographer it is a standard for a cipher. Both the Beaufort Wind Scale and the Beaufort Cipher are renowned and have been widely used, but there are two significant differences: the wind scale is a good one and justly credited to its conceiver; the cipher is rather less good and Beaufort did not invent it.

The first identifiable publication of 'Sir Francis Beaufort's Plan for Secret Correspondence' was in the *Nautical Magazine* of August 1855, seven months after Beaufort's retirement. It can be assumed that he had given it to his office-mate of a quarter of a century, A. B. Becher, the magazine's editor, to be made public. In a note preceding the exposition of the cipher, the editor declared that it had 'appeared many years ago in a scientific journal, but it is by no means commonly known, nor that the author of it is the late Hydrographer to the Admiralty'.

Its next publication, in the identical version of the cipher, was on a 4½ in. by 5 in. stiff paper card, folded into an envelope half as wide, offered for sale by a London printer for sixpence. It is undated, but it probably appeared soon after Beaufort's death. On the cover is the legend: 'Cryptography, a system of Secret Writing. By the late Admiral Sir Francis Beaufort, KCB, adapted for Telegrams, and Postage Cards.' On the reverse were a few paragraphs by his youngest son, William Morris Beaufort, declaring that the cipher was 'invented and published many years ago by my father . . . and I have been induced to republish it in a cheap and portable form, to affirm and to preserve the claim of the inventor, which has recently been overlooked or disregarded.' The cipher was claimed to be 'inviolable'.

The publication was timely. The use of telegrams was expanding rapidly and the postcard – curiously, a later invention – was coming into its own. Both were felt, probably needlessly, to be irresistibly tempting to the prying eyes of strangers.

No trace can be found of the earlier publication mentioned by Becher and William Morris Beaufort has been found and, curiously, there is no mention of its conception or development in any of Sir Francis' surviving papers, nor any reference to it in his pocket diaries, preserved without a break from 1835 to his death at the end of 1857. But the cipher *was* published, in only unimportantly different form, by Blaise de Vigenère in 1586 and by Giovanni Sestri in 1710. According to the magisterial history of cryptography, *The Codebreakers*, by David Kahn (1967), it is 'probably the most famous cipher of all time'.

Known as the Vigenère,* it is the archetypical method for substituting cipher text for plain text by using a tableau of several – conventionally twenty-six – alphabets, each with the letters in different positions and each separately selected, to encipher each letter in the message according to a key word agreed upon by the sender and recipient. Elementary as it now seems to cryptanalysts, it was almost impervious to attack until well into the nineteenth century. But it was slow and cumbersome to use and susceptible to inaccuracies; thus it lapsed into disuse for almost three centuries until Beaufort and others of his period revived it. Easily susceptible to solution by today's methods, it was nevertheless for its day a significant improvement over systems previously in use.

It is impossible to know how Beaufort hit on it. It was an enormous step forward from the puerile cipher he and his brother developed as youngsters. The leap from a simple substitution cipher to polyalphabets with a keyword is about that from a sling to a musket. Moreover, Beaufort did not have a creative mathematical mind. At least two of his frequent companions were much more gifted in cryptography: one was Charles Babbage who, had he concentrated on a subject that he

---

*The name is an injustice to Blaise de Vigenère's talent and memory. It was invented before his time; his great achievement was its conversion by the autokey, which he *did* invent, into something infinitely more subtle and secure.

only amused himself with, would have been one of the greatest crypto-graphers of his age; the other was Sir Charles Wheatstone who invented (besides the Wheatstone bridge) the much handier and more popular Playfair cipher, erroneously named after one of his friends. Yet it is hard to believe that Beaufort fell upon some earlier exposition of the Vigenère and deliberately tried to pass it off, with a theoretically unimportant modification, as his own invention. Above all, he was an honourable man. Many years before, he related to Richard Lovell Edgeworth how he was about to make public plans for a device he thought he had originated only to discover at the last moment that someone else had anticipated him, and how thankful he was that he had escaped the charge, if not the act, of plagiarism.

The mystery remains.

28

The Scientists' Middleman

There are so few opportunities for serving those
whom we admire and esteem that when they offer I
seize them with avidity.

BEAUFORT to John Herschel[1]

Serving for the first time on the Council of the Royal Society in 1827,
Beaufort was appointed to a committee of eight to consider the apparently bland question of 'the best means of limiting the members
admitted to the Royal Society'. It was in fact an extremely controversial
issue concerning the fundamentals of the organization's structure,
operations and purpose. The proposal for limiting the membership,
put forward by the incurably abrasive astronomer James South, was in
reality an attack on the practice by which, for five decades under the
amiably despotic reign of Sir Joseph Banks and the passive one of Sir
Humphry Davy, almost everyone proposed for membership was
admitted, the election procedure being virtually *pro forma*.[2] The
consequence was that, except for some physicians who made worth-
while contributions, a large majority of the Fellows were not scientists
by any modern definition, which is to say professionals in the 'hard'
or exact disciplines. Rather, they were persons more or less associated
with what would be thought of today as the humanities or – most of
them – gentlemen with at best a vague interest in 'natural philosophy'
or at worst no interest at all, including men of title and wealth who
enjoyed the prestige that membership brought them. In a copy of a
proposed 'Letter to the Editor' among his papers[3] – it is uncertain
whether it was ever published – Beaufort denounced what he implied
were a large proportion of 'dunces' in the Society plus those who by
their 'venal motives . . . endeavour to increase their professional
practice, or give *éclat* to some silly book by the imposing appendage to

their names of FRS'. This large majority made a proportionately minuscule contribution to the Society's *Philosophical Transactions* but nevertheless dominated the Council and the institution's affairs. Its prestige had thereby greatly diminished over the years.

With the impending resignation of Davy a group of the Society's science Fellows grasped an opportunity for reform. Besides South, whose intemperate style rendered him less effective, the leaders were Herschel and Babbage. Their purpose was to transmute what had become a club run by amateurs into an institution of professional and practising scientists.

Beaufort's own roots in science – from his father and Richard Lovell Edgeworth – were those of the old-fashioned observers, describers and collectors rather than of analysts and precisionists. Yet he was at once on the mathematicians' side and, it appears, tirelessly active in the 'kitchen cabinet' of Herschel and Babbage. Among his personal papers is a draft in his handwriting of the report of the committee of eight containing its key proposal: that the Society elect only four new Fellows a year. This suggests that he was either the author of the final report or the secretary of the reformers' cabal.

The report was presented to the Council in June 1827 but was not considered until December, by which time Davies Gilbert had succeeded Davy as President and, in a discreditable manoeuvre, secured the election to the Council of Lord Colchester, one of the most formidable advocates of his age. He was able to prevail on the majority to reject the committee's report. Thus the proposal lapsed.

Beaufort was enraged and when, the next year, Gilbert asked him to continue on the Council he refused in a sharp letter.[4] Gilbert returned a soft answer; the social relations between the two men continued. But, without referring Beaufort's refusal to the Council or making it known to the membership, Gilbert simply substituted as a nominee Sir John Franklin, so that no one who did not have inside information would have known that Beaufort had been proposed initially. But a letter-writer to *The Times* of 30 January 1830,[5] who signed himself 'Argus' (probably Babbage), *did* know and laid bare the whole story. Gilbert did not deign to answer, hoping the matter would blow over. Instead, Babbage went into a scathing frontal attack with his famous treatise *Reflections on the Decline of Science in England*, denouncing the Royal Society. The battle continued and Gilbert soon felt obliged to resign from the Presidency. But he sought to guarantee that the Society would continue in its old form by trying to arrange that the Duke of Sussex* should succeed him.

The reformers put up John Herschel in opposition. Babbage, the Cambridge-trained geologist William Fitton and Beaufort managed the campaign,[6] but badly. They came to believe that Herschel was sure of election and at the last moment relieved a number of his supporters from coming to London to cast their votes. The result was 119 for the royal amateur, 111 for the great astronomer.

The reformers, their hopes blighted, promptly founded the British Association for the Advancement of Science. (For unknown reasons Beaufort, an inveterate joiner, did not become a member of the new body.) Ultimately, however, they were victorious within the Royal Society. In 1847 they succeeded in pushing through membership regulations similar to those they had proposed twenty years before.[7] The group, including Beaufort, thereupon created the Philosophical Society, ostensibly a dining club but basically an organization to defend the professional nature of the Society against any backsliding.

This early liaison of Beaufort with Cambridge scientists – Babbage, Herschel, Airy, George Peacock and others – continued throughout his years as Hydrographer and was to have profound results in fostering the work of several branches of British science. As the 'Cambridge Network's' ally, strategically placed in a vital government department, Beaufort was in a position to support their research with money, talent and facilities.

Another institution with scientific interests which Beaufort helped to found, and for which he obtained significant and continuing government support, was the Royal Geographical Society.

It was Beaufort's old friend, James Rennell, 'to whom the blanks on the map were eyesores',[8] who was first to discuss the idea of a society for the encouragement of geographical exploration, research and study. The editor of the *Literary Gazette* made the first formal proposal in its pages in 1828; others joined in support, including several members of a travel-minded dining group, the Raleigh Club. Of these the most effective was Captain W. H. Smyth ('Mediterranean' Smyth), an outstanding sailor-scientist. As a friend of Beaufort, perhaps his closest, Smyth enlisted him in the cause. Rennell died before his idea could

---

*This was the same Augustus Frederick, sixth son of George III, whom Beaufort, as first lieutenant on the *Phaeton*, had accompanied to Leghorn and back in 1793–4.

become a reality; the promoters felt it essential that John Barrow, his successor as the foremost geographer in Britain, should launch the project. At first Barrow was reluctant but later yielded, he wrote in his memoirs, to the persuasion of William Sotheby, a wealthy patron of the arts. Barrow's memory was faulty, however: Smyth insisted in a long review of those memoirs that Beaufort was the effective arm-twister. Barrow proved invaluable in obtaining royal patronage for the Society and he, more than any other, moulded its form and purpose.[9]

Others of Beaufort's friends were also instrumental in its first period. Besides Smyth and Barrow, there was George Cecil Renouard, the chaplain of the Smyrna trading station, who advised Beaufort on his Karamania survey; William Richard Hamilton, Lord Elgin's secretary when Beaufort had sailed on the *Phaeton* with the ambassadorial party to Constantinople thirty years before; the astronomer Francis Baily and the maritime scientist Captain Basil Hall. Beaufort himself served on its first Council and frequently thereafter. He was often asked to stand for the Presidency but invariably declined on grounds of lack of time.[10] He remained on its Committee, however, until almost the end of his life.

The reports of his surveying captains fill the *Proceedings* of the Society, especially in its early days. Some were transmitted directly by Beaufort, others by Barrow and some were submitted by the authors' themselves, with Beaufort's encouragement. Faithfully, the Hydrographer presented the Society annually with copies of the charts produced by his office, kept up a vigorous correspondence with its secretaries, edited several of the contributions of his surveying captains and – a most generous donation of his time – served as reader and judge of papers submitted from other sources.

Serving both in a government department and at the same time as an officer, council member and activist in three of the most important scientific institutions of the period – the Royal Society, Royal Astronomical Society and Royal Geographical Society – Beaufort played a double role, unexceptionable then but which if attempted today would raise serious questions about conflict of interest. It turned out to be of inestimable value to British science. Beaufort was the principal link between the geographers, astronomers, oceanographers, geodesists and meteorologists and the one agency in the government best able to

The Arctic Council. An oil painting by Stephen Pearce, 1851. Beaufort is seated in the centre. Standing, left to right, are Sir George Back, Sir W. E. Parry, Captain E. J. Bird, Sir James Clark Ross, John Barrow Jr., Lieutenant-Colonel Edward Sabine, Captain W. A. Baillie-Hamilton, Sir John Richardson, and (seated) Captain W. F. Beechey. The portraits above show, from left to right, Sir John Franklin, Captain Fitzjames and John Barrow (*reproduced by permission of the National Portrait Gallery*).

SKETCHES BY BEAUFORT

TOP: An unidentified hilltop village in the Eastern Mediterranean.

BOTTOM: Kingstown Harbour, Dublin, 1828. The Martello Tower on the left later made its own appearance in literature as the setting of the first scene in James Joyce's *Ulysses*.

Greenhill's
Church

a Memorial of Lichfield for Aunt Mary August 18.th 1828

DRUMGLASS COLLIERY
Sept.r 21/32

TOP: Lichfield Cathedral, 1828.

BOTTOM: Drumglass Colliery, 1832.

A chart, reworked by Beaufort for the engraver from an existing map,
for publication by the Society for the Diffusion of Useful Knowledge.
It shows his immense concern for detail.

champion their research projects. It was the Hydrographic Office that had administrative and financial jurisdiction over the Royal Observatory at Greenwich and its branch at the Cape of Good Hope; it was the Admiralty, to which Beaufort became *de facto* scientific adviser, that had the resources to mount or carry through expeditions not only for geographical purposes but also for studying tides and currents, terrestial magnetism and geodesy; it was the Admiralty whose officers Beaufort ordered to make observations and keep records for the infant science of meteorology; whose ships were encouraged to carry the naturalists (or, usually, surgeons trained to function as naturalists) to report on and collect specimens for the geologists, zoologists and botanists.[11]

Wearing one hat, that of a Fellow of a learned society, Beaufort could enlist himself, or be enlisted, in the cause of one or another scientific enterprise; thereupon, wearing a second, official hat, he was in a position to forward it by furnishing ships, officers, equipment, instruments and, most important, finance. The dual role was crucial: in the first half of the nineteenth century the Navy was the principal governmental subsidizer of science. To be sure, Parliament made direct appropriations to such special institutions as the Royal Gardens at Kew, the Army was in a position to help some scientific research through the Ordnance Survey, and by mid-century a Meteorological Department under Fitzroy was established in the Board of Trade, but otherwise such money as was forthcoming for 'pure' or even applied science came from private sources, and there was not much even of that. The funds of the learned societies such as the Royal Institution and the British Association, or from that would-be popularizer of learning, the Society for the Diffusion of Useful Knowledge, were much too meagre for vast expeditions; at Oxford science languished, and at Cambridge, Dublin and Edinburgh there was money enough in most cases only for the work of their own scientists on their home grounds. But the Navy could make its normal functions – and its ships – into vehicles to carry scientific ventures.

Thus, for example, and as mentioned above, in response to the urging of the Royal Society the *Chanticleer*, under the tragically-fated Henry Foster, was sent by the Admiralty from 1828 to 1831 to the South Atlantic to determine by gravitational measurements more definite conclusions on the earth's density and not-quite-spherical figure. Beaufort sat on the Royal Society committee that drew up the instructions; a few years later, as Hydrographer, he received their results.

Similarly, we find Beaufort as a Fellow of the Royal Geographical Society vigorously urging a new attempt to find the North-West Passage and thereupon, when the Society formally presented such a proposal, in a position as Hydrographer to lobby the Admiralty from within to accept it.

One of Beaufort's most dramatic services to the scientists, especially those at Cambridge, in obtaining government support for their objectives was in mounting the great voyage of 1839–43 of James Clark Ross to the Antarctic. The purpose was to obtain an extended series of observations of terrestial magnetism in southern latitudes, to be co-ordinated with efforts at stations in Europe and Asia which would be making similar readings, almost minute-by-minute, on certain specified days. The enterprise was in a sense a smaller-scale precursor of the International Geophysical Years of today. The chief instigator was Edward Sabine, an Artillery officer who, like Beaufort, was an ally of the scientists inside government and Britain's foremost authority on terrestial magnetism, standing towards that branch of science as Rennell had towards geography.

Impressed by the pioneering work of Gauss and others on the Continent and knowing of the system for simultaneous magnetic observations already operating in Germany, Sabine proposed to the British Association for the Advancement of Science in 1838 that Britain enlarge the number of fixed observatories throughout the Empire and at the same time dispatch what would amount to a large, lavishly equipped floating base for magnetic instruments to the area where the data were most lacking and would be most interesting, as close as possible to the South Magnetic Pole. The Association at once appointed a committee to consider the matter, with Herschel as Chairman and Peacock and William Whewell among the members. The committee, heavily weighted by those Cambridge mathematicians, could count on Beaufort and Sabine as allies within the government departments.

The committee drafted a memorial embodying the arguments in favour of the enterprise and presented it to the Prime Minister, Lord Melbourne. He in turn referred it to the Royal Society (with Beaufort strategically placed on its Physics and Meteorology Committee) which gave it full support.

There were two enemies to be overcome. One, within the Admiralty, was Barrow, obsessively and almost exclusively interested in the Arctic. The other was time: Melbourne's government, beset by Irish, colonial and budgetry problems, was on the verge of falling; a new First Lord of the Admiralty might well have meant the cancellation of the entire project. The conniving of the promoters, to be read in the Sabine–Herschel papers of the Royal Society archives,[12] was successful: Ross was given command of the *Erebus* on 8 April 1839; 'their Lordships gave directions to proceed with the equipment of the expedition upon the most liberal scale'.[13]

Beaufort sighed with relief in his diary. The Melbourne government fell just thirty days later.*

The Council of the Royal Society presented Ross with a volume of 100 pages (drafted by its Committee on Physics and Meteorology) alluding to his instructions and containing 'a detailed account of every object of inquiry which the diligence of that learned society could devise', with 5000 words on the topic of terrestrial magnetism. Beaufort, meanwhile, had drafted the Admiralty instructions, just as he had a hand in those of the Royal Society, with 2000 words of specifics, in addition to the usual standing instructions.

Ross, the Navy's outstanding expert on terrestial magnetism, and his companion captain, Francis Crozier on the *Terror*, succeeded magnificently on the famous voyage. They established their fixed observatories and took voluminous readings on the special days set for the simultaneous international observations; their ships became observatories often superior to those they set up ashore or in the ice pack.

Nevertheless, the expedition is remembered more for the discovery of the gigantic Ross Ice Barrier and for the mapping of hundreds of miles of the hitherto unknown coasts of the Antarctic continent than for its great scientific accomplishments (of which not the least, as the botanists and zoologists appreciated, was the dazzling work of the young assistant surgeon on the *Erebus*, Joseph D. Hooker).

But out of sight for four years and five months was out of mind: the return was greeted with less acclaim than might have been expected. Sixty-two years later, Hooker wrote to another famous Antarctic explorer, Captain Robert Falcon Scott, that Ross had been 'coldly'

*Only to be restored when Peel refused to form a ministry because of his rebuff by Queen Victoria over the 'Bedchamber Question'.

received.[14] Not, however, by Beaufort, who realized from the interim reports the tremendous importance of the expedition's discoveries. Earlier, in August 1841, he had been outraged when Ross's first report was received of his discovery of the Great Barrier and his penetration to 78° south longitude – far higher than had ever been reached – and the Admiralty declined to have it published. He raged in his diary on 16 August:

Sir John Pechell [one of their Lordships] dissuaded the Adm^y. from yielding to my entreaties to publish Jas. Ross's letter in [the official] *Gazette*. There appears to be no sufficient merit in his eyes to be given to the public under the sanction etc. of the Government but cutting throats. The capture of a wretched [gun?] boat with a 2 lb. swivel & 5 frightened lazzaroni is given there but an act which enobled the age & even the board that excogitated it may find its way to the world through a newspaper paragraph.*

Underlying the Admiralty's support of scientific research were surely not just the blandishments of science-minded insiders like Sabine and Beaufort, nor even a recognition of a moral and cultural obligations akin to those which today bring public financing to a National Science Foundation or an Arts Council. A more profound, if unspoken, inducement must have been the pressures of the times: the imperatives of British trade and colonialism demanded ever-wider efforts from maritime surveyors and cartographers.

Moreover, government interests were handsomely rewarded. The Hydrographer was able to obtain on demand the counsel and help of Britain's finest scientists. We have seen how Beaufort could enlist them in the preparation of his *Manual of Scientific Inquiry*. The collection of the John Herschel papers in the Royal Society archives illustrates how Beaufort called on the great astronomer over the years for help of manifold kinds: who was the right man for the new head of the Cape of Good Hope Observatory? Would Herschel review the tide tables at the Cape with a view to judging the notion that a one-inch variation of the barometer means a one-foot variation of the tide? Would Herschel write a preface to a star catalogue? Could he give a judgement on a paper describing a new chronometer? (Herschel did, in a huge, highly detailed reply.) Thomas Drummond was under attack; would Herschel give his opinion of the principles Drummond had

*The reference was probably to recent publicity given to some trifling capture in the Opium War.

adopted? (The reply extended over eight folio pages, closely written.)

Such were the individual returns Beaufort could exact from his scientist friends. The most vivid example of a grander, more institutionalized service to the government from the cooperating scientists – an immensely valuable *quid* for a relatively inexpensive *quo* – was the study of tides (mentioned in Chapter 25) supported by the Hydrographic Office. The principal practical result, achieved with no little speed over a few years, was reliable tide tables not only around British shores but, thanks to international cooperative efforts, for those of the European mainland and North America.

In the eighteenth century, oceanographic research had concentrated on temperature and densities, the work hampered by still inadequate and often misleading instruments; later came Rennell's great studies of ocean currents. But with his death and those of the earlier pioneers, predominantly French, interest in those fields lapsed.[15] It was replaced by investigation of tides and attempts to formulate tidal theory.

Oceanographers, again mostly French, had concerned themselves with the subject since before the middle of the eighteenth century, but practical experimentation and observation remained inadequate. It was not until 1829 that the newly-founded Society for the Diffusion of Useful Knowledge discovered that the tide tables for London – the product of private publishers for their personal profit, with their methods of calculation kept as trade secrets – were inaccurate. One of the Society's members, John William Lubbock, soon to become a Vice-President of the Royal Society, looked into the problem. Beaufort was immediately interested, offering what help the Hydrographic Office could afford including, most valuably, the services of one of his three Naval assistants, Joseph Dessiou. That assistance 'was to be of crucial importance in the development of tidal studies during the 1830s'.[16]

Beaufort wrote some forty letters to Lubbock in 1830,[17] testifying to their cooperation. Reporting on a conversation with Davies Gilbert in 1832, he wrote:

> I assured him, as I do you, that no one can be impressed with a stronger conviction than myself of the urgent necessity of acquiring proper data for the construction of our Tide Tables, that I considered it to be a national object, and that Government sh^d. take it in hand when they found a person qualified like you, disposed to undertake a principal part of the labour without expense to the Country.

The words 'without expense' must have referred to a willingness by Lubbock, astronomer and mathematician by inclination but with a banker's income, to donate his services. The expense of obtaining records from dozens of locations for the computations and for eventual printing had to be met from other sources; Beaufort wheedled some of the money needed from the Admiralty and much of the rest came from the British Association for the Advancement of Science.

The first fruits appeared in the *British Almanac* for 1830 in the form of new tide tables for London. Yet a useful system for more extensive predictions was more difficult to create than Lubbock had expected. He realized that to make his tables more accurate and to improve the understanding of tides in general, observations would have to be greatly expanded. Once again he had the support of the Royal Society for his new proposals and the Admiralty agreed to have observations made at the Naval dockyards; the building of the necessary tide gauges began in 1831 and two years later the first volume of *Admiralty Tide Tables* was published containing predictions for Sheerness, Portsmouth and Plymouth as well as London. According to Margaret Deacon:

Lubbock's determination to rescue the tides from their ignominious position as the most neglected branch of physical astronomy met with a wide response from seamen and scientists alike, so apparent was the need for a better practical understanding of them. Through Beaufort he had the help of Dessiou and later of other members of the staff of the Hydrographic Department. The Admiralty as a whole proved sympathetic – as long as the projects put to them did not involve too much time and expense.[18]

Lubbock's main preoccupation was analysing tidal data, especially in harbours, to understand their workings and to enable predictions. A rather more theoretical interest, the understanding of the general pattern of tides around the globe, was that of William Whewell, Fellow and later Master of Trinity College, Cambridge, Lubbock's former tutor. A renowned astronomer and mathematician, a fellow reformer with Herschel and Peacock in the Cambridge scientists' efforts to import Continental analytical mathematical methods to British science, Whewell ultimately came to overshadow the reputation of his pupil in tidal research.

It was Whewell, again with Beaufort's help in obtaining Admiralty assistance, who expanded the observations at the dockyards into a much more ambitious system of record-keeping at the coastguard stations. That was no sooner put into operation than it was realized that a still broader series of observations, this time on an international scale, was necessary. Beaufort's enthusiasm was communicated to the Admiralty which in turn approached the Duke of Wellington, then Foreign Secretary, to make arrangements with foreign governments. The effort succeeded; a series of observations for two weeks in June 1835 was held on both sides of the Atlantic, at twenty-eight or more places on the American coasts between Florida and Nova Scotia and on the European coasts from the Strait of Gibraltar to North Cape, and at more than 300 points on the coasts of Great Britain.[19]

Copies of dozens of Beaufort's letters in the Hydrographic Office archives[20] to his surveying captains and to Whewell, as well as those to Lubbock, testify to his indefatigable energy. We see him inviting the collaboration of foreign countries, issuing detailed instructions, calling for similar observations in the Pacific and India, encouraging Captain Frederick William Beechey – perhaps the most energetic and gifted tidal researcher in the Service – in his work on tidal streams in the Irish Channel, asking coastguard stations to make renewed observations (this time for a whole month, in 1839), supplying home water surveyors with recording devices developed by Beechey, noting Becher's undertaking to record hourly tidal heights on the Thames, asking the advice of James Ross as late as 1852 about a 'great Tidal enterprise', begging for the use of a fast frigate to conduct tidal research for two years in the Atlantic (the Admiralty refused, balking at the £10 000 cost),[21] consulting Lubbock on the form the *Tide Tables* should take, urging Whewell to put more pressure on the Admiralty in favour of his 'grand scheme of the Atlantic tides', calling for information about a reported fluctuation off Wexford, and, of course, planning with Captain Hewett for his epic tidal studies in the North Sea in the doomed *Fairy*.

It cannot be said that the work of Lubbock and Whewell and the Hydrographic Service captains resolved all the mysteries of the tides. Even today total understanding is incomplete. What they did accomplish, however, was to introduce quite different approaches and set tidal study on a modern course. The practical results, meanwhile, as observations multiplied throughout the world and tide tables were developed and perfected in a process that still continues, were surpassingly useful.

Still another service to science and technology energetically fostered by Beaufort was the testing of new or improved instruments for hydrographic, meteorological and geodetic work. The costs were minimal but the returns must have been very considerable, for the surveying ships were ideally suited as laboratories for evaluating the measuring and observation devices under field conditions. The ships' officers were trained in their use and were charged with exactly those functions in which the instruments were applicable.

Beaufort, whose youthful delight in technological novelty lasted all his life, happily put his captains to the task of trying out every likely piece of new equipment. Scores of letters in the Hydrographic Office files show him calling on his surveyors to determine the extent of magnetic influence of the iron in their ships on the rates of their chronometers, demanding trials of at least a dozen patented compasses submitted to the Admiralty, ordering the *Fairy* to test Becher's new artificial horizon and the *Protector* to try out one invented by someone else. Could Britain's best instrument makers try to construct a theodolite of copper that would be unaffected by magnetism? Tests are authorized for an electric sounding machine invented by the great John Ericsson; they are successful and half a dozen of the devices are purchased. A favourable report is returned on a so-called double sextant to measure large obtuse angles; a magnetic detecting apparatus perfected by Sabine must be examined; the well-known inventor, the Reverend Edward Lyon Berthon, has 'a very ingenious log for showing the rate at which a vessel is moving through the water'. And so on for marine barometers, wind and storm and tide gauges, sounding lines and weights, submarine current meters and a multitude of other specialized kinds of equipment.

Beaufort's special passion was for astronomical instruments. Each new telescope installed at the Royal Observatory at Greenwich received his personal and enthusiastic attention. But he was eager to inspect other instruments as well: a diary entry in April 1837 notes his spending three hours in the Admiralty garden with James Clark Ross, Sabine, the mineralogist William Hallowes Miller and the astronomer George Fisher 'trying Friend Fox's new dip^g. needle'. Their verdict must have been favourable, for it was Robert Were Fox's dipping needle that Ross carried with him to the Antarctic two years later.

Beaufort's fascination with the latest technological improvements never flagged. A few months before his death he wrote to James Ross to ask what he thought of an invention by W. H. Smyth's distinguished astronomer son, Charles Piazzi Smyth, a 'spinning top apparatus for a sea telescope stand, perfectly uninfluenced by any motion of the ship' – in effect, an early gyroscope.[22]

Beaufort's deep involvement for more than twenty-five years with Britain's oldest scientific institution, the Royal Observatory at Greenwich, provides still another example of his functioning as a middleman linking scientific purpose to official performance.

Since 1818, when the Admiralty took over the Observatory's administrative and budgetary control, the Hydrographer was, in those areas, the overseer of the Astronomer Royal. But the Hydrographer also sat, by virtue of his office, on the Observatory's Board of Visitors which, reconstituted in 1830 to consist mainly of nominees of the Royal Society and Royal Astronomical Society (Beaufort was also one of the latter's), directed the Observatory's policy for scientific objectives and duties.

Thus, with great fidelity to his obligation, Beaufort journeyed downriver to Greenwich as a Visitor on the first Saturday in June of every year to determine with his astronomer friends how the Observatory should serve the national scientific interests for the coming twelvemonth. The next Monday or thereabouts, back in Whitehall, it may be presumed that he fell to work lobbying their Lordships to submit to Parliament adequate estimates for the money that the eminent Visitors deemed necessary. And for the rest of the year his duty was to supervise the Astronomer Royal in the spending of the funds appropriated and in the administration of the work at Greenwich and its second observatory at the Cape of Good Hope.

However official its demarcation, the Hydrographer's relationship to the Astronomer Royal could have been difficult. At one moment he was partly responsible for determining the work of the observatories, at another he was special pleader for their budgets, and at still another their controller. In fact, however, during the two decades that Beaufort's term of office was concurrent with that of George Biddell Airy's as Astronomer Royal, the two men worked effectively in double harness. They respected each other and kept closely in touch, as demonstrated by a heavy correspondence between them. The result was a monumental period of achievement and expansion for the observatories at

Greenwich and the Cape, and for astronomy in general. Beaufort worked hard on behalf of the observatories' needs and found his satisfaction in frequent visits to Greenwich to rejoice in the splendid new instruments Airy commissioned and installed.

In the early days of their collaboration, an historian of the Royal Observatory has noted,[23] there was some friction. Airy felt himself burdened with what he deemed an excessive amount of work in checking chronometers for the Navy and Beaufort, to judge from an occasional diary entry, was irritated at Airy's oracular bearing and perhaps a mite jealous of the former Plumian Professor's great reputation. With reference to some dispute – the context is not clear in his diary – Beaufort wrote: '. . . . I left the field to him and his worshippers, discussion being useless when common sense is satisfied at the shrine of great talents.'

Yet controversy was rare. W. H. Smyth, a friend of both men, could say in the obituary of Beaufort he supplied for the Royal Astronomical Society: 'The Astronomer Royal bears his strong testimony to the uniform urbanity of Sir F. Beaufort to himself and his assistants, and to the uniform support given by him to the interests of the Royal Observatory . . .'

A final footnote to the catalogue of Beaufort's fruitful relationship with some of the most productive British scientists comes in the form of an episode which, trifling in terms of the exertion he made, was momentous beyond description in the result produced.

A certain Commander Robert Fitzroy, having been engaged in a hydrographic survey off the western shores of Patagonia, returned to England in 1830 with his frigate, the *Beagle*. The next year he was ordered to take her out again to the same area, to complete the work. He wanted companionship, in the person of a naturalist to study the flora and fauna while he charted the shores. The proposal was not an unusual one; naturalists had sailed aboard surveying vessels since Cook or before. But Fitzroy knew of no one suitable: could the Hydrographer, now settled into his office for two years, find someone who would go as a volunteer, without salary?

It must have been only a moment's effort for the Hydrographer to send off a line to a resident scientist friend at Cambridge, George Peacock. Though a mathematician and astronomer he could be presumed to know the scientists in other disciplines at Cambridge who could make a competent recommendation. Beaufort's letter to him is not on record, but we can guess reliably at its contents – for Peacock could not have conjured up the specifics from his own imagination – from the letter Peacock dispatched in August 1831 to a professorial colleague, the botanist and mineralogist John Stevens Henslow.[24] Peacock wrote:

My dear Henslow,

Captain Fitzroy is going out to survey the southern coast of Tierra del Fuego, and afterwards to visit many of the South Sea Islands, and to return by the Indian Archipelago. The vessel is fitted out expressly for scientific purposes, combined with the survey; it will furnish, therefore, a rare opportunity for a naturalist, and it would be a great misfortune if it should be lost.

An offer has been made to me to recommend a proper person to go out as naturalist with this expedition; he will be treated with every consideration. The Captain is a young man of very pleasing manners (a nephew of the Duke of Grafton), of great zeal in his profession, and who is highly spoken of . . . is there any person whom you could strongly recommend? He must be such a person who would do credit to our recommendation.

The sequel needs no describing here. Henslow recommended Charles Darwin. On 1 September Beaufort wrote to Fitzroy:[25]

I believe my friend Mr Peacock of Trinity College, Camb°. has succeeded in getting a 'Savant' for you – A Mr Darwin, grandson of the well known philosopher and poet, full of zeal and enterprise and having contemplated a voyage on his own account to S. America.*

Let me know how you like the idea that I may go or recede in time.

Within days Darwin made his agreement with Fitzroy and the two young men discussed the voyage with Beaufort. In a letter to one of his family, reciting his negotiations with the Hydrographer about being carried on lists of the *Beagle* at least for victuals, Darwin wrote of him, 'He is too deep a fish for me to make him out.'

What evoked that curious comment remains a mystery. Be that as it may, Darwin and the world had reason to thank the Hydrographer. Without Beaufort, Darwin would never have set foot on the *Beagle*; another man might not have drawn the conclusions that Darwin did from what he saw.

---

*Peacock must have relayed the notion of a planned trip to South America to Beaufort, but whence he derived it is a mystery. Darwin had no such idea, being headed at the time – not very eagerly – for the Church.

One cannot resist speculating on Beaufort's reaction, had he lived another year, to reading the joint paper of Darwin and Alfred Russell Wallace delivered to the Linnaean Society in July 1858 or to reading, the following year, *On the Origin of Species*. Would he, an increasingly uncompromising High Church communicant, have reacted as did Fitzroy at the great Oxford confrontation between Huxley and Wilberforce in 1860, shouting that he had unknowingly harboured a viper in his and the *Beagle*'s bosom? Or would Beaufort the scientist have instinctively recognized a great new truth?

29

'This Sacred Cause' (1847-1855)

Where poor Franklin and his 2 ships may be, or what may be his ultimate fate, no one can tell; that he and they may be now down under the ice is indeed possible, but there are no more grounds for asserting it than that he has been carried up like Elijah into heaven by a whirlwind. Further efforts therefore must be made in order to come to some decisive conclusion. England will never brook the cowardly abandonment of those 2 shiploads of her brave and zealous sons.

BEAUFORT to Captain Horatio Austin[1]

The hope for a North-West Passage as a short cut to the markets of Cathay, cherished for some three hundred years, had vanished by the nineteenth century. The rigours of the ice-clogged channels reported by the early explorers, from Frobisher to Cook, had been confirmed all too impressively by the fur traders of upper Canada and the whalers in Baffin Bay to leave any illusions about routinely shuttling cargoes from Sheerness to Shanghai across the top of the North American continent. Nevertheless, for the geographers, explorers and Naval officers of an adventurous disposition – on half-pay since the defeat of Napoleon and eager for active service – the mystique remained. As Arctic historians have noted, the compulsion was akin to that to climb Everest, but more so: one sought to ascend Everest 'because it was there'; one searched for the passage to prove that it *was* there.

Beaufort in particular was eager for the challenge, but he became involved only at the time of the voyage of Sir John Franklin in 1845. He was intimately engaged in the ten-year effort, begun two years later, to rescue him and, when that hope was gone, to discover what had happened. His important role has hitherto gone largely unreported.

Beaufort was the confidant of at least three of the commanders of major Arctic expeditions as early as 1824. The letters to him of Parry, Lyon and Franklin indicate that he had also been their preceptor in meteorological and magnetic research for some considerable time. Once he became Hydrographer, officially concerned with such enterprises, his relationship became even closer. He had been chosen for the post by John Barrow, whose passion for the discovery of a North-West Passage was consuming. Beaufort could hardly help sharing it, despite the profound doubts of some of his friends who felt that the game was not worth the candle.

Rennell, that wise old man, wrote to him as early as 1818:

How can any one suppose, that a Ship can make her way from Baffin's Bay to Bhering's [sic] Strait in the short summer of the Artic [sic] Region, in less than 3 months; when the Whalers are a Month or 6 weeks, in boring through the loose Ice, 4 or 5 degrees to get to the whaling station, & it is 30 such degrees that a Ship is to go. If she be caught by the winter, adieu. Nor is it probable that the Ice *is* loose. See Cook on the Ice of Bhering's Strait.

Edward Parry's voyage of 1819–20 to the southern coast of Melville Island beyond 110° W was seen by enthusiasts as proof of the Passage via that route. Sagely, Beaufort's old captain, Robert Stopford, told him that on the contrary it in no way strengthened 'Mr Barrow's theory of an open sea near the Pole'. And from France the director of hydrography, Paul-Edouard Rossell, taking thought on Franklin's overland expeditions, wrote: '. . . *il ne faut pas trop tenter la fortune, et surtout on doit s'arretêr dans la crainte de s'abuser de la persévérance ou plutôt de la ténacité.*'

But not even the terrible experience of John Ross, trapped four years in the Arctic ice from 1829 to 1833, dampened Beaufort's optimism. Although the expedition was privately financed by the distiller Felix Booth, Ross took pains to keep the newly-appointed Hydrographer informed and, faithfully every January, wrote from his ice prisons on Boothia Peninsula and North Somerset Island the account of the preceding twelve months' ordeal.[2] Instead of being dismayed by its obvious lesson – that a ship could be tempted by unusually ice-free conditions into a deep penetration and thereupon became locked in for years on end – Beaufort chose to find encouragement in Ross's history: he wrote on the cover of the letter that it 'affords abundant proof of what may be effected by resolution, perseverance and unanimity'.

Thus minimizing difficulties and deeply influenced by Barrow, Beaufort was caught up in the enthusiasts' patriotic visions. In company with Barrow, James Clark Ross, Franklin and his two companions on his overland expeditions, Dr John Richardson and George Back, Beaufort beat the drums at the Royal Society in 1836, importuning its special committee set up to consider another quest for the North-West Passage to importune in turn the Admiralty. He wrote also to the Royal Geographical Society:

That there is an open and, at times, a navigable sea passage between the Straits of Davis & Behring there can be no doubt in the mind of any person who has duly weighed the evidence; and it is equally certain that it would be an intolerable disgrace to this country were the flag of any other nation to be borne through it before our own.

Dreams of national glory had outrun common sense. The rash assertion was in no way typical of a man who all his life punctiliously refrained from exaggeration and overstatement about objective issues. And it *was* rash. In 1836 there was *no* evidence of an open passage 'navigable at times' – at least for ships, and barely conceivable even for boats. Parry had been blocked by impenetrable ice off Melville Island coming in from what was to be named the Beaufort Sea; Beechey, entering the Arctic through Bering Strait in the *Blossom* in 1826 in an attempt to rendezvous with Franklin, was held up near Icy Cape; the sloop's barge was blocked 120 miles further east, at what Beechey named Point Barrow.

Despite the ardour of Barrow, Beaufort and their Royal Geographical Society colleagues, the Admiralty had no stomach for mounting a new North-West Passage expedition. It was not until 1839, when the boat journeys of the Hudson's Bay Company explorers Peter Warren Dease and Dr George Simpson along the northern Canadian coasts disclosed possible connections with the waters far to the north where Parry had sailed almost twenty years before, that interest was revived. Meanwhile, James Clark Ross's magnificent voyage to the Antarctic had, however illogically, added to hope of success in the north. The 'impulse for a final grand effort was gathering force ... the pride of England, the world's greatest naval and commercial power, was again aroused'.[3]

Eighty years old, on the eve of his retirement, Barrow finally won

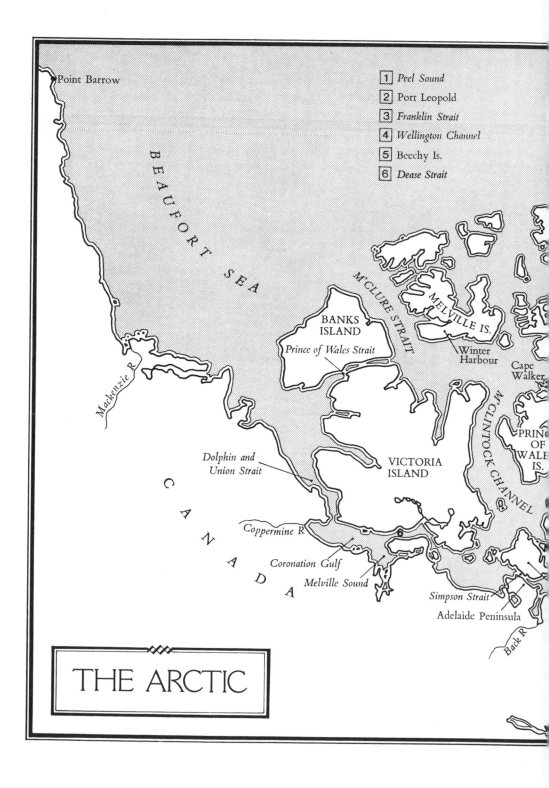

Point Barrow

1 Peel Sound
2 Port Leopold
3 Franklin Strait
4 Wellington Channel
5 Beechy Is.
6 Dease Strait

BEAUFORT SEA

Mackenzie R.

M'CLURE STRAIT

BANKS
ISLAND

Prince of Wales Strait

MELVILLE IS.

Winter
Harbour

Cape
Walker

Dolphin and
Union Strait

VICTORIA
ISLAND

M'CLINTOCK CHANNEL

PRINCE
OF
WALES
IS.

C A N A D A

Coppermine R

Coronation Gulf

Melville Sound

Simpson Strait

Adelaide Peninsula

Back R.

THE ARCTIC

G R E E N L A N D

Smith Sound

Jones Sound

NORTH DEVON IS.

BAFFIN BAY

row Strait

NORTH
SOM-
ERSET
IS.

Prince Regent Inlet *Lancaster Sound*

Fury Beach

hia

BAFFIN ISLAND

DAVIS STRAIT

ING
WILLIAM
SLAND

*Melville
Peninsula*

his point. With the specific endorsement of Beaufort, Parry, Richardson and Sabine he proposed to the Board of Admiralty that a new attempt 'to complete the discovery' of the Passage be made by the dispatch of the *Erebus* and *Terror* which had served James Ross so well in the Antarctic. Franklin, in his fifty-ninth year, was given command. The orders were drawn up by Barrow, but represented also Franklin's, Parry's and James Ross's combined ideas for the attack.

Franklin sailed in May 1845 with supplies that were supposed to be sufficient for the 130-man party for three years. His orders were to proceed through Lancaster Sound and Barrow Strait to Cape Walker at the north-east tip of Prince of Wales Island, thence south or south-west towards the coast of North America rather than due west where, it was correctly judged, he would be blocked by the ice that had held up Parry.

Franklin's orders gave him considerable leeway to act on his judgement but implicit in them was the expectation that he would make his southward turn at the next inlet *after* Cape Walker. The implication, firmly in the minds of those in London who dispatched him, fatally perverted the routes and targets of the major expeditions later sent out to search for him.

Apparently blocked on his first attempts at or near Cape Walker, Franklin sailed up Wellington Channel, as his orders gave him the option to do, to find a westward opening. Thwarted in that objective, he returned to Barrow Strait, spent the winter of 1845–6 at Beechey Island off the south-west corner of North Devon Island, and proceeded again towards Cape Walker in the summer. It is barely possible that he went on round the north coast of Prince of Wales Island and turned south into M'Clintock Strait, but much more probably he turned south just east of Cape Walker and sailed down what are now known as Peel Sound and Franklin Strait. One must assume that freakishly good conditions enticed him, as they had John Ross sixteen years before in Prince Regent Inlet, to voyage 200 to 250 miles southward. Franklin was thereupon beset in September 1846, a few miles off the north-west coast of King William Island. In the following year, instead of being released, the *Erebus* and *Terror* were locked in the pack. But, as revealed many years later by the principal written record from the expedition so far discovered, all was well in May 1847. A month later, an additional entry revealed, Franklin died, of causes unstated, and Captain F. R. M. Crozier on the *Terror* assumed command. Ten months later the officers and men abandoned their ships (a final note showed) and set out for the Back (Great Fish) River estuary on the Canadian coast, 200 miles south-east as the crow flies. Losses had already been heavy: nine officers and fifteen men had died. The survivors perished before the year was out as they made their agonizing way on foot, dragging sledges, along the south-west coast of King William Island. A few were able to cross Simpson Strait and died on Adelaide Peninsula or near the estuary of Back River.

More than 125 years and half as many would-be explanatory volumes later the mysteries of the tragedy still remain: why did the party, beset for nineteen months, not strike out northward back towards Cape Walker where they could expect rescue ships to be searching, or north-eastward across Boothia to a known cache of supplies at Fury Beach; why, with supplies for three years, did they perish of malnutrition before that time had expired? That they were afflicted with scurvy is almost certain. Unlike John Ross, who was able to stave off scurvy thanks to enormous catches of fish* and some game with the help of Eskimos, Crozier was without such salvation (or did not know how to find it) either in the ice or on the nearby shore of King William Island.

In London, meanwhile, Barrow had retired and Beaufort became in effect operations officer for the Admiralty in the most extensive, expensive, perverse, ill-starred and abundantly written-about manhunt in history. In that role he shares no more blame – and not much more credit – than the dozen or so others most directly responsible: their Lordships themselves, the commanders of the rescue expeditions, and a group of Arctic authorities that ultimately became institutionalized in the Arctic Council (with Beaufort as its secretary). Beaufort was at a disadvantage: he had had no experience in Polar waters and of necessity deferred to the opinions of those who had.

With hindsight, it is easy to see their fundamental mistake that set search expeditions awry for years: almost all the planners believed that Franklin had succeeded in sailing much further west than he did, because that was known to be his initial aim and that is what Parry had been able to do. It seems not to have occurred to them – at least for some years – that ice might have blocked him in that attempt before he could even set sail out of Barrow Strait to the west, and that he might

*He wrote to Beaufort in 1832: 'What do you think of 6376 at one haul? I am afraid I must not stick this in my publications – unless I want a worse name than I have.'

have turned south *east* of Cape Walker and sailed down Peel Sound. Even after the first rescue expedition of James Ross had been blocked by ice well to the east of Cape Walker, the notion persisted that Franklin had done what James Ross could not do.

In a memorandum of 28 January 1850 after James Ross's return, Beaufort could still write:[4]

Sir John Franklin is not a man to treat his orders with levity, and therefore his first attempt was undoubtedly made in the direction of Melville Island and out to the Westward. If foiled in that attempt, he naturally headed to the southward, and using Banks Land as a barrier against the northern ice, he would try to make westing under its lee. . . .

If both of these roads were found closed against his advance, he perhaps availed himself of the 4 passages between the Parry Islands [i.e. to the north of Barrow Strait] including Wellington Channel, or lastly, he may have returned to Baffin Bay & taken the inviting opening of Jones Sound.

No mention here of the possibility of doing what Franklin actually did: turning due south.

The searches, accordingly, were for the most part aimed at areas hundreds of miles west – and later hundreds of miles north – of where the *Erebus* and *Terror* were frozen in.

There were, however, some exceptions to those who held to the conventional wisdom. The first and most vehement was Dr Richard King, gifted but offensive in manner,[5] the surgeon of an overland expedition led by Back down the Back River with the hope of rescuing John Ross in 1832–3. Throughout the several years of the Franklin searches he argued for what was in fact the correct area of investigation, the Back River estuary, but his demeanour was so arrogant and his contempt for the Establishment so strident that he doomed his own proposal. Not even Lady Franklin (Sir John had married again), usually more perceptive than the officialdom, would give him an ear.[6] Moreover, as James Ross pointed out,[7] one of the best reasons for rejecting the proposed rescue mission was that it could not have carried sufficient supplies to save any significant number of the Franklin party. It could, though, have discovered their fate many years earlier.

A second exception was Lieutenant Sherard Osborn, later to make a name for himself both as Arctic explorer and chronicler. He adopted much the same idea as King, although a year or two later. In February 1850 he wrote to Lady Franklin[8] that her husband might well have gone down James Ross Strait and that therefore expeditions should search from Back River northward. But, like King, he was not on the best of terms with Whitehall.

A third exception, and the wisest of the Arctic Council experts, was Frederick William Beechey, who had sailed with Parry on the *Hecla* and later with him to Melville Island and subsequently had commanded the *Blossom* through Bering Strait when she sought to link with Franklin's boat journey in 1826. He too wanted a boat party to be sent from Back River north to Boothia and King William Island.[9] But the Arctic Sanhedrin – Parry, James Ross, Sabine, Back and Richardson – were vehemently opposed to the idea, Richardson being almost derisory.[10]

Beaufort was at least foresighted. As early as 20 January 1847 he wrote to James Ross[11] that although he 'would not let a whisper of anxiety escape me' – meaning, of course, that he *was* anxious – 'yet one must perceive that if [Franklin] not be forthcoming by *next* winter some substantial steps must be taken in 1848, and for that certain measures must be set foot in 1847'. He asked what they should be: doubling and strengthening a pair of bombs like *Erebus* and *Terror* themselves, or building two strong and shallow steamers?

Three weeks later, again with a hollow assurance that their Lordships 'have as yet felt no apprehensions' about Franklin's safety, Beaufort drafted an Admiralty letter[12] to James Ross, Parry, Sabine and Richardson asking them, in view of their known intimacy with Franklin, whether they had learned from conversations with him if he had fixed certain places where he intended to leave supply depots and whatever else they knew of his intentions. Repeating what Beaufort had written to James Ross before, the Admiralty asked their opinions – assuming no word was heard from Franklin that year – what kind of ships to send, where they should go and any other advice from them, who had had so much Arctic experience and 'whose feelings must be so deeply engaged'.

The request was curious. One would have thought that Franklin's discussions at the Admiralty if not his orders themselves would have been specific about his intentions and such elementary matters as the proposed location of his fall-back supply depots.

Sir John Ross suggested that supplies be deposited on the south shore of Barrow Strait and that the west coast of Boothia be searched.[13] The first idea was completely logical and the second pointed at least in the right direction. But John Ross was not a man whom the Admiralty was inclined to heed: on a North-West Passage search in 1818 he blotted his copybook fatally in a controversy about some of his observations and, victimized by a mirage, turned about at the very entrance to the Arctic Sea when he supposed Lancaster Sound to be blocked by the non-existent 'Croker Mountains'.

Other replies were wider of the mark. Sabine wanted to have Wellington Channel searched for notes.[14] James Ross proposed two ships to follow what was presumed to be Franklin's course and, anticipating a proposal which Beaufort later made his own, two others to sail eastward from Bering Strait but – the fatal misconception persisting – to search the west side of Banks Land and the south side of Victoria Land.[15] Richardson implied that the search should be first to the west of Barrow Strait and, since he thought Franklin would turn south only as a last resort, an overland expedition from Canada should be mounted only when the need arose, i.e. if the other searches proved futile. Even then, he was sure Franklin would head for the Mackenzie River (a thousand miles or so west of the Back River) and the rescue expedition should therefore be aimed at Victoria Land.[16]

By late autumn, and still without word of Franklin, the Admiralty was stirred into action. A major campaign was ordered, its main element being the dispatch of two ships from the east into Lancaster Sound and Barrow Strait. James Ross – who would have commanded what became the Franklin expedition had he not promised his wife, whom he married after his Antarctic venture, never again to go on a long voyage – was the obvious commander, as the nation's most experienced and esteemed Polar expert. Beaufort had the job of persuading him. In a letter to Ross on 6 November, in which the Hydrographer showed a clear appreciation of what had happened to Franklin – although not where it happened – Beaufort wrote:[17]

. . . The severity of this year must have been a sad blow to our dear friend Franklin, who had probably been coaxed on by the fineness of the former years to entangle himself very deeply in the ice. Still, I trust in Providence that we shall hear of him before Candlemas [i.e. 2 February 1848]. If not, my good friend, you must undertake the painful search for him; to no other person would the country be satisfied to delegate that exploit. . . . The regret and vexation of a whole life would not expiate to your own heart the having allowed any consideration to interfere with what you have nobly called your peculiar privilege. . . .

James Ross bowed to the inevitable but his former good fortune had run out. His orders – Beaufort noted in his diary that he had stayed up until 3.20 one morning to finish them – were doubtless more carefully drawn than Barrow's for Franklin, but although London could propose, it was the Arctic that disposed. Bad ice conditions put his ships, the *Enterprise* and *Investigator*, a month behind schedule. They reached Lancaster Sound only in September 1848. Even worse ice conditions blocked him from making the substantial westing that was contemplated and he was forced to winter at Port Leopold on North Somerset Island, 150 miles short of the pivotal point of Cape Walker. On a sledge journey down the west coast of the island the next spring – in the right direction for Franklin's ships – he was obliged to turn back 200 miles north of what could have been success. In the summer, when the *Enterprise* and *Investigator* were again able to move, Ross's bad luck held: he progressed no further westward; by autumn he was forced by the ice to turn about and head home.

The second element of the campaign was that of Richardson, authorized to carry out his own proposal of a search overland from Canada. With Dr John Rae, an agent of the Hudson's Bay Company, he journeyed by boat down the Mackenzie River and coasted east to the Coppermine River. At their furthest point, Richardson and Rae were a good 400 miles west of the route of the doomed men who had struggled down King William Island towards the Back River.

A third prong of the rescue campaign was the dispatch in February 1848 of the *Plover* to sail through Bering Strait and scout the north Alaskan shore in the tenuous hope of meeting Franklin there. The Admiralty also ordered Captain Henry Kellett, commanding the *Herald* (a surveying vessel), to suspend his work on the lower California coast and sail northward to join the *Plover*. Beaufort wrote to Kellett one of his typically persuasive letters.[18] It was 'vexatious' to him, he said, to see Kellett taken from his surveying, 'But in the present case, I could not even grumble – any effort on behalf of poor Franklin & his anxious friends here, no one with any heart can grudge. Besides which there is no one on that station who has the resources of mind and the physical activity you have.' Beaufort forbade him to enter the ice – the frigate was not strengthened and had only six months' provisions – but called on him to make such observations as he could of the current and take samples of the bottom to cast light on the much disputed issue of whether an open sea or an Arctic continent lay to the north. Beaufort suspected a continent and was wrong. But there was no great open sea either.

Indicative, however, of how persistent was the notion in London of the westing Franklin had made were Beaufort's last words to Kellett: if time and weather permitted, the *Herald* was also to sail as far as was prudent along the north coast of Siberia, 'for who knows but Franklin may be seen on that coast?' Kellett did so the following year and though his geographical discoveries were significant, he found, of course, no news of Franklin.

Mortified, Richardson and James Ross returned to England late in 1849,* the latter to find himself the subject of considerable and unjust criticism for not having remained in the Arctic another year. Lady Franklin (the explorer's second wife) was particularly bitter and Beaufort found himself placed in a role he was to play on and off for the rest of his life, that of placating her and mediating between her and everyone else she believed had failed her. 'Lady Franklin came to town,' Beaufort noted on 8 November. 'She appears v. indignant at the return of Ross & little inclined to listen to the real merits of the case.' (By January, Beaufort had persuaded her at least to dine with him and Ross.) Years later, after his death, Lady Franklin termed Beaufort her 'wisest counsellor'.

By late 1849 Franklin and his crews had been gone four and a half years, and London had no inkling of their whereabouts. Their supplies, it had to be presumed, were long since exhausted. Lady Franklin and some of her (by now late) husband's friends in and out of the Admiralty might still have cherished some hope – had not John Ross survived four ice-bound years? – but everyone, whether believers or despairers, agreed it was imperative to continue the search. Emotions had risen to something close to crusading fervour; much the same feeling, remarkably, prevailed in America, constituting another reason, however unworthy, for Britain to exert herself. Relaying to a friend a report from Richardson that two American search ships were being fitted out largely by private subscription, Beaufort declared:[19] 'What *we* are to do is now the question, for we must not be behind the feeling manifested

---

*Before Ross's return there had been a cruelly deceptive report of success: on his annual holiday in October Beaufort heard from the Admiralty that Franklin and Ross were safe in Prince Regent Inlet. Beaufort accordingly 'sent news to D. of Wellington... and drank dear old Franklin's health in a bumper of champagne'. The report seems to have been a false or garbled account from Eskimos, relayed to London by whalers.

throughout our own country or suffer ourselves to be eclipsed by the humane enthusiasm in America.'

It was for a 'holy object', he explained to Kellett whom he had once again ordered away from his surveying duties to take the *Herald* back through Bering Strait as a support ship, a necessity 'for the satisfaction of those most interested as well as for the consistency and credit of the country'.[20]

In that spirit an unprecedented campaign of search and succour was mounted on both sides of the Atlantic in the last two months of 1849 for dispatch in the following spring. Apparently still not convinced that James Ross had just been defeated in exactly such an attempt by normal conditions whereas Parry's success long years before had been made possible by a freakishly benign season, the Admiralty ordered four ships under the command of Captain Horatio Austin to sail through Lancaster Sound and thence westward.* Lady Franklin financed two ships, commanded by William Penny, a famous Scottish whaling captain, to investigate Smith and Jones Sounds and Wellington Channel, and a third vessel to sail southwards into Prince Regent Inlet. In the United States the merchant-philanthropist Henry Grinnell – 'a noble minded gentleman', Beaufort called him[21] – aided by a grant from Congress, paid for an expedition of two brigs to look into Wellington Channel. Even old John Ross, financed by public subscription, made ready to set out in the steam yacht *Felix* for Lancaster Sound and Barrow Strait.

However much the Admiralty's distaste for the seventy-three-year-old Ross may have persisted since his disastrous turn-about some thirty-two years before in Lancaster Sound, Beaufort remained his staunch supporter, and recommended Ross's venture to the Admiralty:[22]

He is well acquainted with the management of steam. He possesses a singularly hearty constitution. He has acquired much dear bought experience in the ice, is full of inventive resources and would feel a degree of pride in carrying out this, his favourite scheme, which supported by an intrepid and dogged resolution would probably do more in surmounting the difficulties and dangers of this sacred cause than would be achieved by officers of far more brilliant talents.

---

*It was not until 1944 – almost ninety years later – that a vessel, the Royal Canadian Mounted Police schooner *St Roch*, accomplished what the Admiralty intended, i.e. a passage from Melville Island south-west across Melville Sound to Victoria Island. Only one ship has done it since, the 100000-ton tanker *Manhattan*, in 1969.

The various flotillas, ten ships in all, that entered the Arctic from the east in 1850, had little more luck than James Ross. Penny discovered remnants of Franklin's 1845–6 winter quarters – the first positive news of the expedition – on Beechey Island (Beaufort prepared charts of it for the Queen) but beyond that, however valuable their geographical work and however harrowing and heroic their adventures, none of the vessels turned up a clue about where Franklin had gone from his winter quarters.

Beaufort's emphasis and efforts, however, were much more ardently engaged on a quite different approach, an attack in the opposite direction.

His reasoning, set forth in a long memorandum to the Admiralty,[23] was logical enough even if it embodied some fatal misconceptions and ignored the shrewder inspiration of Beechey, Osborn and the rancorous Dr King.

Franklin could have come to grief, Beaufort's memorandum began, had his ship caught fire or struck on rocks, but it was highly unlikely that such disasters would have befallen both vessels. They would not have gone down in storms for the Arctic seas were so encumbered by ice that there were no swells. Finally, if they were crushed beyond repair by the ice, some of the party would have taken to boats and would have reached shores where they would have been discovered by now: if they had come to grief at any intermediary point such as Cape Walker or in the chain of islands north of Lancaster Sound and Barrow Strait, they would have contrived some method of getting word of their position back to those shores; alternatively, if they had reached south of Victoria Island, they would have got word to the Eskimos in the area of the Mackenzie River. Finally, if they had failed to penetrate westward or southward, they would have returned, intending to go up Wellington Channel and, in doing so, would have left word of their intentions by detached parties stationed along Barrow Strait. Inasmuch as there was no evidence that any of those possibilities had been acted upon, the only conclusion that could be drawn was that Franklin must be locked in an archipelago which, Beaufort mistakenly thought, stretched to the west of Melville Island.

There were at least three unvoiced premises, all false, that poisoned the argument, all to be seen with wonderful clarity now but not then. First, Beaufort assumed that Franklin's party, certainly having the 'resolution, perseverance and unanimity' that so impressed him in

John Ross's 1829–33 expedition, could have survived three or four years in the ice and then marched 200 miles to salvation as Ross did; second, that Franklin's orders – and the whole strategy of the search for the North-West Passage – would have led him to sail west of Cape Walker before turning south or south-west; and third, that ice conditions would have permitted him to do just that and therefore the ships must have been beset so far to the west that the crews were induced to head for the Mackenzie and not the Back or Coppermine Rivers.

Faulty though the analysis was, one conclusion Beaufort derived from it was sound: if Franklin had not succeeded in getting word of his whereabouts *to* Barrow Strait, searches starting *from* there could never reach him. Of course, the expeditions ordered to push from east to west must be carried through, and even explorations of Wellington Channel and Smith Sound should be undertaken, though Beaufort thought they were unpromising, 'yet in the fifth year of their absence every place should be searched'.[24] But besides chasing Franklin, why not try to meet him, with an expedition setting out from the goal towards which he was driving?

Accordingly, Beaufort proposed that the two ships which James Ross had just brought back, the *Enterprise* and *Investigator*, be hurriedly made ready and dispatched again, but this time through Bering Strait, to sail eastward along the north coast of Alaska and then to make their way north-eastward to Banks Land and on to Melville Island. At the same time Dr Rae (whose orders came too late for him to carry them out in 1850) was to make a similar attempt by setting out from northern Canada with boats; if blocked by ice he was to fall back – again the fatal misconception – *westward* towards the Mackenzie.

Beaufort had hoped to have approval in time for the *Enterprise* and *Investigator* to leave England before Christmas in order to pass through Bering Strait by 1 August 1850, soon enough to make some foray into it although perhaps 'only skin deep'. The Admiralty, however, procrastinated for a month,[25] deferring approval until 8 December after Beaufort had won backing for his proposal from James Ross, Beechey, Back and Richardson.[26] Notably – the repetition is tedious but the point is crucial – all of them agreed that any search east of the Mackenzie, whether by ships or boats, was not to be considered.

Richard Collinson, a veteran surveying officer and a long-time favourite of Beaufort, commanded the expedition aboard the *Enterprise*, almost certainly on Beaufort's nomination. Robert M'Clure, who had been with James Ross in the Arctic and was newly promoted to commander, sailed under him as captain of the *Investigator*. The venture was very much Beaufort's personal achievement and certainly his darling.[27] His correspondence about it in December 1849 and January 1850 was abundant and his absorption in its preliminaries such as to force him to the most unusual neglect of his pocket diary for three weeks: he scribbled merely: 'Behring Strait affairs and consequent talking and writing so occupied me that I had not time to fill up [the spaces for] these days – never getting home until $7\frac{1}{2}$.'

Some of his busyness bespeaks the continuance of his passion of younger days for gadgetry. His letters show him in a flurry of inquiry and action for equipping the ships with inflatable india rubber balls, bladders (he wanted the price of them by the thousand)[28] and hundreds of paper balloons[29] to be set adrift with messages* to let Franklin know where rescue was to be had. His enthusiasm spilled over into family letters. One, early in January 1850 to his sister Louisa, told how he

wanted to furnish [Collinson] with a balloon to carry him half a mile high from whence with a good telescope he could see ships, huts, smoke or flags for many miles, but the apparatus w^d. occupy too much room. The next thing to seeing them is to make them see those who are in the search, and therefore I am now endeavouring to send out some smaller paper balloons with tails of slow match string [Beaufort here appended a sketch] in which are suspended at six inch intervals little bundles of paper or gutta percha on which will be stamped the place etc. etc. from which they ascended. As the slow match burns it detaches a bundle of them & from a mile high they will fly dispersing to a great distance. One was tried today from the ship in the river, and half Woolwich Common confessed the shower.

Some time later he was intrigued with the possibilities of noise-making by 'cannon speaking trumpet', perhaps with resonance walls behind the gun, and with experiments for sending sound further and louder by undersea transmission.[30] But he rejected as 'absurd' the idea of some unidentified proposer of propelling a balloon by mechanical means.[31] On the more practical side, Beaufort demanded all information available about ice-blasting and recommended its use to his

---

*One of the balloon messages, printed on red silk and launched in June 1853 from the *Assistance*, one of Austin's ships, was auctioned in London in 1976 for £1600.

commanders. The devices were at least no more fanciful than James Ross's 'twopenny Postmen' of earlier years: trapped foxes released with metal collars bearing rescue information.

Of all the Franklin searches that of the *Enterprise* was the most skilful; that of the *Investigator* was the most fascinating – because of its daring, its rigours, its achievements and its disaster, and especially because the motives and decisions of its commander, M'Clure, remain so suspect. But once Beaufort had arranged for the two ships to be towed by a Naval steam vessel through the Straits of Tierra del Fuego to compensate for the Admiralty's dawdling, his involvement with them ended, except for sending letters – and balloons – to Collinson at Honolulu.

The two ships were separated. M'Clure beat Collinson through Bering Strait and, despite every effort of Kellett, short of a direct order, to persuade him to wait for his senior officer, he plunged on and into the ice. He discovered Prince of Wales Strait between Banks and Victoria Lands – thus proving them islands – and proceeded up the west coast of the former to become hopelessly embedded in the ice on the north coast. He sledged across the ice of what became known as M'Clure Strait to Parry's Winter Harbour on Melville Island, left a message and, when his people were near death from scurvy and starvation, was rescued in the most dramatic episode in Polar exploration, but at the cost of abandoning his ship. By reason of his sledge crossing to Winter Harbour, he was credited with being the discoverer of the North-West Passage, having reached, from the west, the point to which Parry had sailed in 1819.*

Collinson, following a year later the route M'Clure had taken, prudently turned back, thinking M'Clure had been sensible enough to do the same; then setting out in a completely different direction, he performed the superb feat of sailing 300 miles eastward through Dolphin and Union Straits, Coronation Gulf and Dease Strait, channels then thought to be navigable only by boat. The following spring

---

*The discovery was less that of a 'passage' than of the fact that interconnecting waterways – although frozen almost solid and impenetrable to ships of that period – linked the Atlantic and the Pacific north of the American continent. If that constituted a 'passage', then one had been discovered five years before by the starving handful of Franklin survivors who struggled across Simpson Strait before they died. To acknowledge M'Clure's feat as *the* discovery of the North-West Passage was to accept a dubious substitute for what England and the world had had in mind for three centuries.

he thereupon sledged up the east coast of Victoria Island. The persuasive argument of Leslie H. Neatby in *The Search for Franklin* is that had M'Clure and the *Investigator* been with him Collinson would have had the manpower to sledge up the west coast of King William Island as well, which he had wanted to do; and he would have had with him the able interpreter (left with M'Clure's ship and never transferred, as had been intended, to Collinson's), who would have understood some Eskimos who were encountered on Victoria Island and seemed to be saying something, barely intelligible and to a prudent man not credible, about a ship abandoned somewhere to the east. In either set of circumstances Collinson would almost certainly have discovered Franklin's fate. Instead, having found nothing of Franklin, Collinson made his way safely back to Bering Strait in 1853.

The empty-handed return in late 1851 of Austin's and the other expeditions that had searched for Franklin from the eastern approach was a deep disappointment, especially to the Hydrographer. Beaufort had been one of the proposers of Austin's voyage,[32] he had had great confidence in Penny,[33] and in particular he had believed that John Ross, in a steam vessel, could succeed in reaching Melville Island if no one else could.[34] Worse than the failure of the expeditions to bring back information about Franklin (except for his 1845–6 winter quarters), was the misinformation with which they returned. Some of the explorers came back convinced – two or three years after that conviction should have been established – that Franklin could not have gone west or south-west of Prince of Wales Island, but none seem to have suggested that he may have turned southwards somewhere east of it. Worst of all, one officer in Austin's squadron, Lieutenant Willy Browne, sledged south along Peel Sound and returned to report it impassable to ships. Unfortunately it *was* passable and it is almost certain that Franklin sailed down it five years earlier.

Where, then, was the search to be continued? The *Enterprise* and *Investigator*, unheard from, were presumably somewhere in the western Arctic and there was no point in making further ventures there, unless to rescue *them*. If routes to the west and south of Barrow Strait were impenetrable, then the only course it was supposed that Franklin might have taken was up Wellington Channel, searching for an opening to the west further north. No one could have known, until the terse written record of his voyage was discovered in 1859, that that was exactly what he had done in his first year, only to return, thwarted, to Beechey Island.

Accordingly, while the persevering Dr Rae set out on another futile journey from the Coppermine River to the south-west of Victoria Island, and while Lady Franklin financed two more ships, one to search Prince Regent Inlet and the other Greenland and Smith and Jones Sounds, the Admiralty sent out four ships instructed initially to explore Wellington Channel. Providentially, orders were changed so that while two followed the original plan, two went west. One, the *Resolute*, commanded by the admirable man Beaufort regarded so highly, Captain Kellett, sailed on a hair-raising journey as far as Melville Island – the first to do so since Parry thirty years before. Ultimately, the note left by M'Clure was found by a *Resolute* sledge party; accordingly a further sledge party was dispatched to his ice prison on Banks Island enabling M'Clure and his mostly disabled and starving crew to be brought back over the ice to the *Resolute*.

Little more needs to be said about that last Admiralty expedition except to note that if Beaufort's greatest achievement in the search for Franklin was fathering the probe of the *Enterprise* and *Investigator*, his worst mistake was his selection of Sir Edward Belcher to command the four ships of the 1852–4 attempt.[35]

So keen was Beaufort's admiration of Belcher, in fact, that he had tried to have him put in command of the Bering Strait venture two years earlier[36] but Belcher demanded to be invited rather than volunteering[37] and the Admiralty, apparently, would have none of it. Somehow, Beaufort and the Arctic Council succeeded in naming him to lead the later attempt. It was an incredible decision: Kellett was the obvious man for the job, Belcher had had no Polar experience and, most significantly, despite his magnificent nautical skills, he had made life a living hell for his officers on every ship he had previously commanded. Usually, he brought one or two home with him after every voyage under arrest or threatened with court martial. His was scarcely the temperament to animate four ships that would inevitably be locked in frozen winter quarters, where high morale was indispensable, for eight or nine months of every year they spent in the Arctic. The correspondence files of the Hydrographic Office are larded with denunciations of him throughout his career and with refusals by

Admiralty officials to countenance him as commander of earlier ventures. 'How unfortunate,' Captain Robert Bethune wrote to Beaufort, 'it is that such a capital fellow for work should be such a devil incarnate with his officers!'[38] How to employ Belcher again in view of his 'violent and overbearing conduct towards his officers', Admiral Cockburn asked as early as 1834.[39]

In the Arctic Belcher ran true to form, winning the hatred of his officers, threatening one with court martial and placing another under arrest. In the end, even Beaufort was angered by him. Belcher, the Hydrographer fumed in a minute to the Admiralty on the last day of 1853, 'expresses his future intentions, in either public or private letters, so obscurely' that no one could know what he was going to do next.

What he was able to do next was, as it turned out, no help in finding Franklin. Wellington Channel and islands to the north were explored, ultimately all four ships were frozen in and Belcher ordered them to be abandoned and their crews to be carried home by relief and supply ships lying within reach. Belcher's decision remains a matter of argument: by that time Franklin's party had clearly perished, the search had become something of a farce and there was little point in keeping Belcher's crews for another winter in the Arctic, where they had already spent two. On the other hand, they were subject to no more hazard than was normal in such voyages, and a supply line to Britain had been opened and was in operation. A grievous humiliation to Belcher came in the next year when wind and weather freed the *Resolute* and drifted her eastward out of Barrow Strait and Lancaster Sound into Baffin Bay. There she was encountered by an American whaler, brought back to the United States, purchased by Congress, refitted and sent back to the Admiralty as a gift from the United States.*

A court martial tried Belcher for the abandonment of his four ships, giving him a 'bare acquittal' in the light of the broadly permissive nature of his orders, but his sword was handed back in deadly silence and he was never given another command. To make the snub more freezing, the two officers against whom he had taken action were promptly promoted.

---

*When she was broken up years later, a massive desk was made of her timbers and sent to President Chester A. Arthur. President Kennedy found it in a White House storage room and used it throughout his Thousand Days. Similarly, President Carter chose it for his Oval Office desk on the day after his inauguration.

By 1853 the Admiralty's search for Franklin was almost over and the next year the crews were officially declared dead. Britain's interest shifted to the Crimean War and, with it, Beaufort's principal attention. His office diaries show him buried from mid-1853 until his retirement in January 1855 in the problem of turning out Admiralty Charts of the Baltic and Black Sea. He did his best, though, to encourage those non-governmental efforts that continued. From the fullness of his heart he wrote an emotional letter[40] to Dr Elisha Kane, about to set out on another Grinnell-financed expedition, sending him memoranda which the Admiralty had requested Parry, James Ross and Richardson to supply, charts, sledge models and all other germane reports 'as a slight proof of my earnest hopes'. In addition, he sent a small pocket compass to be worn under Kane's outer garment, but cautioned that 'the best magnetic compass is but a torpid machine in the vicinity of the pole, & you will therefore find in the little book of tables showing the sun's bearings as he skims along the horizon a far more ready method of preserving your course & of ascertaining the bearings, provided your watch is correct'.

A few months earlier he wrote equally cordially and helpfully to the gallant young French Naval lieutenant, Joseph Réné Bellot, who sailed on another of Lady Franklin's expeditions. Similarly, in letters and conversations, he advised Dr Rae before the latter set off on his last overland expedition.[41]

By the end of 1855 Beaufort confessed that there was no longer hope of persuading the government to continue searching,[42] but he could not resign himself to defeat. It was a 'sacred duty', he wrote to Sir Roderick Impey Murchison,[43] to examine by daylight and in good weather every inlet. If Franklin and his crews were not to be found, 'still we owe it to the character of our country to leave no stone unturned for that purpose, no spot unexamined that might betray their footsteps & no resources neglected that might reveal the place and manner of their fate'.

To the end of his life, even after he retired as Hydrographer, his diary and letters show he was counselling Lady Franklin, supporting her vain requests to the Admiralty for further efforts and, sick as he ultimately became, jumping to her summons.

In the end it was Rae, on an 1854 overland journey more for geographical purposes than for information on Franklin, who heard from Eskimos the fate of the expedition and collected some relics they had picked up. Beaufort heard of the 'dreadful catastrophe' on 23 October 1854 and his first thought was to urge the Admiralty to send an expedition to the Back River to learn the details. The Admiralty had enough on its hands with the Crimean War and it was only through Lady Franklin's expedition, commanded by that fine Arctic sledge traveller, Leopold M'Clintock, that the meagre record and some of the pitiful remains were found on King William Island in 1859. Beaufort was no longer alive to hear the details.

Between Franklin's departure and the grim confirmation of the fears that had haunted eight of the ten years he had gone, Beaufort had done everything one man could have done except sail after him himself – *The Times*[44] had even proposed that when he was seventy-five, saying that he was 'a fit person' to command the search expedition. Without Arctic experience himself he shared with others who had the basic misappreciation of where Franklin had gone. It could have been only cold comfort for Beaufort to know at the end that the one expedition, that of Collinson, which was most truly of his own conception and creation, came closer to success than all others until Rae's.

30

'Yellow Admiral'

And so poor Beaufort is gone! Well, peace be with
him, and may his failings be written in water, his good
deeds in brass. He lived long enough for his fame —
too long for many of his friendships, and probably for
his happiness. His judgement was generally clear but
he often acted from impulse and was susceptible to
flattery. Hence the employment of his favourites. His
professional skill was great and his composition
beautiful. Better than all, he was charitable and
religious.

ADMIRAL SIR GEORGE BACK[1]

There is no more impressive testimony to Beaufort's value to his
office and his country than the fact that when he was in his eightieth
year, deaf, enfeebled, in pain, and racked by a sequence of illnesses, he
could not be spared from his post: in early March 1854 the declaration
of war with Russia was less than a month away and long since determined on; Beaufort, his desk heaped high with the charts for the Anglo-
French invasion of the Crimea, submitted his resignation as Hydrographer but was persuaded to withdraw it by Sir James Graham, First
Lord of the Admiralty.

The proposed resignation had either been announced or rumoured
since January; letters of praise and honour had already been flowing in.
But, as Beaufort recorded on 3 March, 'Sir James Graham tells me I
must not go yet. Rather a nondescript position for me, but things had
better be left to take their course.' He struggled on for another year.

It was probably better for his own happiness that he did. There was
more satisfaction to be had in his office and his work than in his home
which, too often in the preceding ten or fifteen years, had been plagued
by his and his wife's ill health and the misfortune of his elder sons.
Once he did retire, the deprivation of work was a misery to him.

Within two months of his marriage to Honora he noted a sudden thickness of her speech and a sagging of one side of her face. It was, of course, a small stroke, although he did not recognize it as such. She recovered, apparently completely, and a few years of happy if not ecstatic married life ensued. But seven years later came another stroke, again unrecognized, which toppled her heavily and left her with a badly broken thigh. From then on the path led steadily downward. She was hopelessly crippled; other afflictions followed and moments of well-being grew less frequent. Beaufort could write in his diary in 1851 that in the thirteen years of their marriage 'not one cross word [was] employed between us' but, one senses, neither had there been many great joyous moments in the later years. One or more strokes and a fearful leg infection followed. In the last year or two of her life her mind failed completely. She died, at sixty-seven, less than two months after her husband.

His own ailments were even more varied, painful and long-continuing than his wife's, though fortunately they did not affect his mind. For twenty years his pocket diaries chronicle – in horrendous detail – a succession of illnesses ranging from dizziness and chronic gastritis to kidney stones and prostate trouble. The worst suffering and the one longest endured was what can be diagnosed unmistakably today as a classic case of prolapsed or 'slipped' lumbar disc, manifested in backache and acute sciatica. The pain rendered him semi-paralysed from time to time for several weeks on end. His physician, Sir James Clark, was so constantly in attendance on him (and on Honora and the children as well) that one wonders how he had time to care for his other patients, including Queen Victoria. Clark prescribed a veritable pharmacopoeia of multi-coloured pills and, for the sciatica, nitric acid, turpentine, 'galvanization' and ice-cold baths every morning, whereupon the patient was to be bundled into his heaviest coat and made to walk to work, than which scarcely any worse or more painful regimen can be conceived. On one occasion, when Beaufort was seventy-four, he was bowled over by a runaway Post Office cart and badly bruised, but was back at work three days later. At another time he seems to have had a heart attack at his office desk, but nevertheless walked home from the Admiralty, a matter of about two miles, a few hours later.

Beaufort was not a hypochondriac: his descriptions in his diaries leave no doubt about the reality of his afflictions. What is amazing is how he managed to keep at his work with only relatively rare periods of absence and how he survived into his eighty-fourth year.

If Beaufort's children were a joy to him – and he insisted in his letters and journals on their 'excellence' and on the pleasure they gave him – some of them caused him acute anguish as well.

The saddest and least reconcilable tragedy was, of course, that of the mentally disturbed son, Alfred, whom Beaufort self-accusingly regarded as 'a melancholy victim, no doubt, of my sins'.

Another child who engendered more grief than pleasure for several years was the youngest daughter, Emily. She was given to fainting spells, dizziness and hysterics, but seemed to be resilient enough when there was a ball or dinner party in the offing and, in her maturity, was endowed with prodigious physical energy. Of all Beaufort's children, she achieved the most distinction. After her father's death she set off with her elder sister Rosalind on travels in Egypt, Syria and the Adriatic, wrote several passable books about her tours and in 1862 married the Middle Eastern scholar and linguist Viscount Strangford. Widowed seven years later, she studied nursing for four years and thereupon launched herself on a career of founding organizations and hospitals to furnish medical care and relief to the poor in Bulgaria, Turkey and Egypt. She persuaded the Patriarch of Jerusalem to award her the Order of the Holy Sepulchre on the strength of her alleged descent from the Beauforts of the Crusades – a descent, incidentally, which her youngest brother, who devoted himself to the family genealogy, never claimed. She died at sea of apoplexy en route to Beirut where she had arranged to found still another hospital.

Of Rosalind, the middle daughter, we know little except that she died, unmarried, at the ripe age of eighty-four. Her father's diary records not much more about her than her frequent childhood illnesses and that she went into 'violent hysterics' on one occasion from smoking 'Indian hemp'. Parental worry about their children's appetite for cannabis, it would seem, enjoys a considerable antiquity.

The eldest daughter, Sophia, appears to have given least concern, growing up happily and marrying, to her father's great pleasure, the distinguished theologian and classical antiquary, the Reverend William Palmer, a Tractarian writer of religious treatises who ultimately obtained a baronetcy.

No such clerical or secular success was the lot of the eldest son, Daniel Augustus. On coming down from Oxford he served, as mentioned earlier, as curate to the controversial ritualist divine William James Early Bennett, in Portman Chapel. When Bennett was given a new church, Beaufort bought Portman Chapel from him for precisely £2901 and bestowed it on his son, with lamentable results. For reasons unknown Daniel could not hold his congregation together and after five years gave up. There is a vague intimation in his father's diary that the root of the trouble was a liaison with an unsuitable young woman. The Chapel was sold and Daniel Augustus was shipped off to Italy whence he returned after eight months 'improved in mind and body (though not much in estate)'. It took a year of searching and importuning by his father to find him another living in a country parish near Liverpool. He married the daughter of a baronet and produced children more distinguished than himself – one became governor general of North Borneo – and died at the traditional Beaufort age for such an event, which is to say eighty-four.

Beaufort's second son, Francis Lestock, began his manhood inauspiciously. When he was not yet twenty and in training for the East India Company service, he filched his recently deceased mother's jewellery and pawned it in London for £36. On discovering what had occurred, his father was aghast. The boy 'seemed truly penitent', Beaufort wrote in cipher in his diary, 'but I told him distinctly it would be criminal in me to let such a monster go to India to be perhaps a judge there. A melancholy scene.' Four days later, another coded entry discloses, paternal affection vanquished moral scruples: 'Made up my mind not to disgrace him out of the Civil Service. O Heaven, what a question for a father.'

The young man did badly for some years at the East India College but ultimately graduated with honours in Classics and Hindustani and took up an appointment in India. There he was happily married and began to engender a huge family, but within three years he was in trouble for alleged embezzlement. During the following three years his father was engaged in the humiliating task of trying to persuade the East India Company in London to consider the case leniently. Ultimately, the son was found guilty of gross carelessness and negligence in his accounts but not of dishonesty. He was reinstated, rose to be in effect Attorney General of Bengal and produced a highly regarded codification of its laws and procedures.

The youngest son, William Morris, his doting father's 'merry little man', caused no grief except the agonizing one of departure when he too entered the Indian Civil Service. To the old man's almost uncontrolled delight, he returned twelve years later on leave, 'much oldened & yellowed, but his heart in the same spot, his spirits as buoyant & his disposition as full of integrity and good feeling, without a grain of affectation or vanity, as the day he left us'. (His siblings, however, found him impossible, but muffled their antagonism out of regard for their father's intense attachment.) Another harrowing leave-taking ensued three years later when he returned to India for a second tour of duty three months before his father died. 'My son embraced me for the last time in this world at 5 p.m.,' Beaufort wrote, and followed the diary entry with a fervent and emotional prayer. Morris returned after another twelve years, took up bachelor's lodging in Piccadilly and seems to have done little in later life except devote himself to researching his family's genealogy until he too died at eighty-four.

If his children were at some times cares and at other times comforts, his grief over Alicia's death was unremitting. Especially as his second wife's health and companionship failed, he sensed the loss of the first wife more profoundly. Once, thinking he had lost Alicia's 'sacred wedding ring' – it was only misplaced and was recovered a few weeks later – his lament in his diary revealed him as shattered. On the last visit he was able to make to her grave, in 1853 when he was seventy-nine, on the anniversary of her death he wrote: 'How every successive year brings out in stronger light the virtues she possessed and which I have lost! and which 'til that loss I never knew how to appreciate. The Lord bountifully gives & indignantly takes away!'

'Too soon dejected and too soon elated', Beaufort wrote of himself late in life. His was indeed a volatile temperament from adolescence on, shifting from joyful to morose according to what befell him. The changeable disposition continued throughout his life, the fits of depression, however, concealed for the most part from his associates, to whom he appeared as patient, gracious and charming, and revealed only in the privacy of his home and his diaries.

For most of the time his work was his happiness. He referred to it as 'my delight' and, in the terms quoted at the head of Chapter 27, as the essence of a contented spirit. Just how much it meant to him is revealed when he was deprived of it during the three years he survived after his

retirement, as for instance in his end-of-year journal notation for
1855: 'So ends . . . a year that probably embraced the most trying
period of my life, both bodily and mental . . . the sudden change from
the exciting business of office to listless idleness.' The next year he
rejoiced in having 'a mind more inured to the want of active employment as well as perhaps more disposed to make a better use of my
inactive leisure'.

His office had been his joy, despite periodic disappointments and
frustrations. As Sir George Back mentioned in a little obituary note
(quoted above), Beaufort was susceptible to flattery, which meant
that he enjoyed it, and in the office he was flattered by his associates.
Despite occasional diary notations about 'the worthlessness of my long
life', which Victorian piety may have made obligatory at the end of
each year, he could know just how valuable his services were, and
could take satisfaction therefrom. He esteemed some of his superiors
such as Lord Auckland and Sir James Graham, First Lords of the
Admiralty, and Sir George Cockburn, from time to time First Sea
Lord; he found pleasure in working with them and usually felt himself
fairly treated by them.

There were, of course, bad moments. One must have preceded a
dinner with Lord Minto, then First Lord, and half a dozen other
moguls in the Upper House, when he spat out in his diary, in cipher,
the one word: 'Beasts.' On another occasion, after a series of rebuffs to
his proposals, he wrote: 'Thus I labour every day turned over by
caprice & ignorance. . . . My first impression was to resign. . . . How
many destructive things have occurred within these few days . . .
are they not all marks of a kind Providence trying & chastising
me?'

A long memorandum written by his daughter Emily three weeks
after her father's death (it served as the principal source for contemporary obituaries) portrays him as embittered, unsupported by his
superiors, disappointed, overworked and frustrated. Yet the document
is so emotional, so shrill, so much of a tirade, and also so gushingly
adulatory, that it should be discounted. To be sure, as Dawson wrote
of Beaufort:[2] 'He had to endure the affliction, which breaks the heart
of every highly qualified servant of Government – the baffling of his
aims and plans by failure of sympathy in those who hold the power
and the purse – manifested either in opposition to useful projects, or
parsimony in providing for them.' Yet, however studded with out-

bursts of frustration, his letters and diaries of the last decade of his service do not on the whole display such rancorous or despairing sentiments as Emily's memorandum imputes to him. If anything is clear from the records, it was that he was deeply absorbed in his work, cherished it and enjoyed it.

He was made deeply unhappy, however, at being required in 1846, ostensibly by some administrative regulation, to choose between retaining his post and remaining on the Admiralty's active list of officers. The circumstances are murky, but it is probable that by seniority Beaufort was due to be promoted to rear-admiral and that there existed, or was said to exist, a rule preventing an admiral on the active list from heading a largely civilian organization in the Admiralty. Offered a choice between the two horns of the dilemma Beaufort at first submitted his resignation as Hydrographer, but after being much harangued by members of the Board and ultimately by Lord Auckland, the new First Lord, he changed his mind, agreed to stay on at his job and to go on the retired list. 'In short, there is some mystery and all mysteries are dirty', he wrote, 'and the end of it is that this day I am a YELLOW ADMIRAL!'*

Two years later, however, some sort of amends were made for what the Admiralty may by then have sensed was a shabby piece of business. On 28 April 1848 the official *Gazette* carried Beaufort's name in the list of new Knights of the Bath. He wrote in his diary: 'Of the many unexpected events that have taken place in my life whether of good or evil this has been the most unlooked for & I can truly say the most uncoveted.'

In her post-mortem memorandum Emily declared that he felt the knighthood was little compensation for his 'yellow flag' which was 'a source of mortification and pain'. In view of a letter he wrote on the day after his investiture such a sour reaction may be doubted. As might be expected, the letter was to his sister Harriet, sending birthday congratulations. They came from

that knightly and distinguished person who was yesterday invested by the dear and delicate fingers of Her sacred Majesty with the insignia of the most honourable Order of the Bath — wiping her sword in the most sentimental manner across my shoulders, stretching out her royal hand to place in mine the glittering star which thenceforward was destined not only to dignify my

---

*i.e. an officer reaching the top of the captains' list not promoted to rear-admiral on the active list but instead retired and granted that rank on the retired list.

left breast but to derive fresh dignity from the devoted heart which was then (somewhat uneasily) beating in that breast, and then finally placing with those same fairy fingers over my head and round my *neck* (in token I presume of the dire fate that justly awaited any recurrent infidelity) the glowing crimson ribbon and collar. . . . Twice during that awe-fraught ceremonial did she give me her august (but plump little) hand to press with ardour to the lips. . . . Then rising from my knee and looking unutterable things of love and loyalty into her royal eyes, came the first proof of true knightly skill – in retreating *backwards* from the Presence with my sword dangling across my legs (and boldly endeavouring to insinuate itself between them) for the distance of about 40 feet through a lane of the old Grand Cross Knights accompanied by the Herald King of Arms! But all this I happily accomplished without fall or fatal trip, which would have excited perhaps a smile on the royal but compassionate features, and a broader grin from the old hard-a-weather veterans on either side of me.

So terminated that wonderful & unsought page of my life. . . .

The letter is vintage Beaufort in its resort to overblown prose and schoolmasterish humour, to facetiousness and to self-mockery, as a shield against the charge of immodesty and a cloak to hide his pride and pleasure. But that he was proud and pleased, and greatly so, cannot be doubted.

In one respect at least, Back's obituary note told less than the whole truth: Beaufort had indeed outlived a great number of friends but many still remained – the Babbages, Smyths, Souths, Fitzroys, Fellowses, Herschels, Hookers, as well as equally long-standing companions in the Admiralty, the Surveying Service and the Arctic exploration fraternity. There were also new friends and thoughtful visitors such as his American opposite number Matthew Fontaine Maury, the mathematician Baden Powell and – one of his callers in his last year – David Livingstone, a 'fine, tough looking, sensible, modest fellow'. Especially attentive during the last ten years of Beaufort's life were Sir Isaac Goldsmid and members of his and Sir Moses Montefiore's families. Their visitations were frequent and their kindnesses, in the form of dinner invitations and carriage outings, were abundant. In the end, these friendships grew very close, notwithstanding the fact that Beaufort shared the prejudice of the times. Referring to a Goldsmid daughter who was a particular intimate of Emily, Beaufort commented, 'That good soul comes here every day or two. Surely she is a Samaritan & not a Jew.'

Admiralty Jany. 24/55

Having been in HM Naval Service upwards of 67 years, 25 of which I have been employed in this laborious office, I feel that advancing age & severe infirmities make it my duty to retire, & to leave its labours & its responsibilities to younger and more active hands. . . .

F. Beaufort

The old man had stayed on a year to oblige the First Lord. Graham was now willing to let him go, to replace him with the surveying captain he recommended, John Washington, and to grant his single request, the promotion of 'my excellent invaluable assistant', Lieutenant Edward Hardy, to commander.

Beaufort worked on for another month, finishing charts on the Norwegian and Swedish coasts, the White Sea and St Petersburg Bay. His last official letter, to Henry Grinnell, enclosed revised charts of the Arctic and told him that the peninsula north-west of North Devon Island, the name of which had been in dispute, would be renamed Grinnell Land.

The new Hydrographer, others of Beaufort's surveying captains and John Barrow, Jr., son of the late Permanent Secretary of the Admiralty, proposed a testimonial. Beaufort first demurred and then agreed, telling his diary (with the sanctimoniousness to which he was unhappily prone) that he felt 'that there is sometimes more pride in supporting and adhering to one's humility than appearing to be guided by one's vanity'. Some 300 donors, contributing from one to twenty guineas apiece, raised a fund of £540. Stephen Pearce, whose speciality was portraits of Naval personalities, was commissioned to do one of Beaufort; it was completed and hung in the Great Hall of Greenwich Observatory before his death. The remainder of the testimonial fund was used to endow a prize in Beaufort's name, awarded every year up to the present day, to the officer gaining the highest marks for Navigation and Pilotage in the examination for the rank of lieutenant.

At the same time, however, Beaufort became the centre of a much less lustrous affair. On his retirement the Treasury had determined that he was legally due seven-twelfths of his salary as an annual pension. He protested rancorously and with some success. In view of his 'meritorious services' the Treasury amended the amount to £500 annually, equal to his former salary in full (in addition he drew his half-pay as a retired rear-admiral and his pension for his wounds).

Beaufort demanded £300 a year more, the amount he had received ever since 1834, in lieu of a residence hitherto made available to the Hydrographer by the Admiralty. The Treasury refused it.

Beaufort's eldest son, Daniel Augustus, whose pastoral duties apparently allowed him time for such an enterprise, carried on the fight in a series of letters and personal visits to men of influence. He declared that his father had no knowledge of what he was doing, an assertion that Beaufort's surviving papers show to be manifestly untrue. Waxing ever shriller, Daniel appealed to Members of Parliament, Captain Fitzroy, Lords Hervey and Monck at the Treasury, the explorer Joseph B. Pentland and Sir Thomas Erskine May, then examiner of Private Bills for both Houses of Parliament. Sir James South was enlisted to take the matter up with Lord Shaftesbury and plans were laid to bring the issue to Parliament. At that stage Beaufort had a delayed change of mind. Among his papers is a fragment of a note, apparently a copy of a letter to an unknown recipient – who was bidden to 'transmit this paper into the fire as soon as you have read it' – in which Beaufort professed horror at the very idea of the plan. He wrote:

. . . it seems they are now going to make the matter a public affair in the H. of C.! £300 a year for my short term will be dearly purchased by such a means. Whatever have been my faults and follies, covetousness has never been one of them and now on the verge of life I shall be shown up in the four quarters of the globe as being discontented with the flattering expressions & public praises showered upon my [retreat?] from this office and stickling for mammon.

The affair, which shows Beaufort as, at the least, disingenuous, fortunately went no further.

Beaufort's three years of retirement saw the steady diminution of his physical abilities. At periods he was bed- or chair-bound, but there were enough remissions from his ailments to permit him occasional walks and even a night at the theatre to see *Richard II*. Throughout, he received a steady flow of visitors, maintained his customary heavy flow of correspondence and kept up pressure on the Admiralty to assist Lady Franklin in her efforts to have another search expedition mounted to discover further remains of her husband's expedition. The house on Gloucester Place was relinquished and for the last months of his life Beaufort lived in a pleasant cottage at Brighton, where he could be wheeled along the promenade and even take the sun on the terraces. His reading seems to have continued unabated: in 1855 he recorded that he had just finished Macaulay's *History*, the last volume fresh from the press, and was starting a biography of Lord Nelson. Ten days later he was reading Burton's *El Medina*.

But tribute to old age was inescapable. In June 1855 a diary entry read, 'For the first time in my life sat down to shave', and in October, 'in getting up for first time forgot my prayers in 65 years'. Mercifully, his condition improved somewhat in 1856 and 1857 and his letters and diary entries in the last six months of his life show as bright an interest in events of the day and in his reading as ever before. But the notations in his 'little black books' and his daily weather journal ended on 11 December. He died in the early morning hours of the 17th.

In the afternoon of the day before he had chatted with his doctor on the interesting matter of what were the merits requisite for a good historian[3] and according to a family letter by his daughter Rosalind, he astonished the physician 'by the wonderful clearness, memory, spirit and animation in the discussion of a book he was reading'. For most of the day he read – at times without his spectacles – in Charles Dickens' weekly magazine, *Household Words*. In the evening he read a passage from his lifelong *vade mecum*, *Sacra Privata*, announced to his children at the bedside that he was sleepy, and bade them a final goodnight.

He was buried in Hackney Church graveyard in the tomb where Alicia had been interred twenty-three years before. Honora followed him there two months later in February 1858 and, forty-seven years later, Rosalind.

Unique in Britain in being built on a stone pier thrusting into the Thames (its axis therefore running north–south rather than in the conventional east–west direction), there stands at Gravesend a small but charmingly proportioned church dedicated to the memory of Sir Francis Beaufort. Tearfully abandoned in the 1970s when its congregation became too small to support it, its origins forgotten by all but a handful of its former communicants, it is now (1976) scheduled to be converted into a community arts centre.

It arose out of an earlier seamen's mission nearby that ministered to the religious needs of the crews and passengers of the vessels, particularly the emigrant ships to Australia, that waited offshore, often for many weeks, before departure. In 1868 a local minister began a campaign to establish a proper church as near as possible to the river. 'Perhaps someday,' he wrote in a public appeal, 'someone who has lost a loved one would build us a little mission hall instead of erecting a costly marble memorial.'

Hearing of the project, Rosalind Beaufort determined to be that 'someone' and promised to pay most of the costs. There were other contributors as well, a particularly generous one being Charles Dickens. The architect was Sir George Edmund Street, fresh from his work on the new Law Courts and his cathedral restorations. On the saint's name day, 30 November 1871, St Andrew's Waterside Church was consecrated.

The ceiling is of pitch pine shaped to represent an upturned boat, even to the ribs, planks and keel; two cross beams represent the thwarts. On each side of the wall behind the altar are panels of fine majolica tiles; behind the altar itself is a gleaming mosaic portraying Jesus stilling the tempest. Under three stained-glass windows on the west wall is a brass plaque noting that they were placed there by Lady Franklin as a memorial to the crews of the *Erebus* and *Terror* (ninety-six names are listed) who sailed from the Thames in May 1845 'and shared the sad but not inglorious fate of their commander'. She chose to install them, the legend continues, in a church erected in the memory of 'the faithful friend of her husband, the unwearying advocate of the search for the lost ships and her own wisest counsellor'.

It was the custom in the final quarter of the last century for the bells of St Andrew's Waterside to be rung as the emigrant ships left the Thames and stood out to sea, to wish them and their passengers God's speed. The peal was the last sound they heard from English shores. It was fitting that their blessing was being invoked from a church commemorating a man whose life's work had been to make their voyage – all voyages – safer and surer.

Notes

The source of so much of the contents of this book is the Francis Beaufort Collection in the Huntington Library, San Marino, California, that to have given the document reference for each quotation and statement drawn from it would have left the text intolerably pock-marked with superscript numbers. Accordingly, I have annotated only a few passages from papers in the Collection when it seemed useful; unannotated quotations and summaries from the letters, journals, etc. of Beaufort, his family and his correspondents may be assumed to have been taken from the Huntington Library material. A fully annotated manuscript draft of the book with exact references to those documents has been deposited in the Library.

ABBREVIATIONS USED IN THESE NOTES

Persons

Alicia: Alicia Magdalena Wilson Beaufort, first wife of Francis Beaufort.
DAB: Daniel Augustus Beaufort, father of Francis Beaufort.
Fanny: Frances Anne Beaufort Edgeworth, elder sister of Francis Beaufort, fourth wife of Richard Lovell Edgeworth.
FB: Francis Beaufort.
MWB: Mary Waller Beaufort, wife of Daniel Augustus Beaufort, mother of Francis Beaufort.
RLE: Richard Lovell Edgeworth.
Wm: William Lewis Beaufort, elder brother of Francis Beaufort.

Sources

ABB: Parliamentary Papers re Arctic expeditions ('Arctic Blue Books').
ADM: Admiralty records, Public Record Office, London.
DNB: *Dictionary of National Biography*, 1855–1900.
HL: Francis Beaufort Collection, Huntington Library, San Marino, California.
HO: Hydrographic Department (formerly Hydrographic Office) archives, Taunton, Somerset.
MO: Meteorological Office Archives, Bracknell, Berkshire.
NLI: National Library of Ireland, Dublin.
NMM: National Maritime Museum, Greenwich.
RAS: Royal Astronomical Society archives, London.
RGS: Royal Geographical Society archives, London.

RS: Royal Society, London
SPRI: Scott Polar Research Institute, Cambridge.

CHAPTER ONE (pp. 17–25)

1. HL. Unsigned sheet, marked 'Written in 1801'; from the context, by a sister, probably Louisa Beaufort.

2. The history appears in a privately printed book (1886), *The Family of de Beaufort in France, Holland, Germany and England,* by William Morris Beaufort, FB's youngest son.

3. Canon C. C. Ellison, 'Remembering Dr Beaufort', *Quarterly Bulletin of the Irish Georgian Society,* January–March 1975. I have drawn on this monograph, correspondence and visits with Canon Ellison, as well as on DAB's diaries in the HL, NLI and Trinity College, Dublin, for much of what appears here about DAB and FB as a boy.

4. HL. Privately printed memorial volume on Fanny, probably 1865.

CHAPTER TWO (pp. 26–37)

1. HL. FB to DAB, 20 April 1789.

2. East India Company Records, L/MAR/C/506, log of the chief mate.

3. Sir E. Cotton and Sir C. Fawcett, *East Indiamen,* 1949, pp. 109–10.

4. HL. Alicia's résumé of her girlhood (undated); W. M. Beaufort.

5. RAS. FB obituary (based on material supplied by Captain W. H. Smyth), *Proceedings,* 1858.

6. For a full discussion of the designation, see Michael Lewis, *A Social History of the Navy,* 1960.

7. John Masefield, *Sea Life in Nelson's Time,* 1905 (3rd edition 1971), p. 34; Henry Baynham, *From the Lower Deck,* 1969, p. 248.

8. *The Mariner's Mirror, 46,* pp. 286–95; *47,* pp. 61–3 and 309.

9. East India Company Records, log of the *Vansittart,* 46AA.

10. Rear-Admiral G. S. Ritchie, *The Admiralty Chart,* 1967, p. 96.

11. The account of the shipwreck and of subsequent events is from the East India Company Records, captain's and chief mate's logs, L/MAR/B 46H.

12. Trinity College, Dublin, MS Department, DAB's diaries.

CHAPTER THREE (pp. 38–46)

1. HL. 23–24 October 1790.

2. Lewis, p. 394.

3. Lewis, p. 24.

4. Commander Randolph Pears, *Young Sea Dogs,* 1969, p. 11.

5. Masefield (p. 33) says £20 to £100; Lewis (p. 38) says £30 to £50.

6. Masefield, p. 38.

7. Commander Geoffrey Penn, *Snotty,* 1957, p. 8.

8. Asa Briggs, *The Age of Improvement*, 1959, p. 125.
9. Leslie Gardiner, *The British Admiralty*, 1968, p. 188.
10. *Notes and Queries*, 2nd S. VI, 144, 2 October 1858.

CHAPTER FOUR (pp. 47–56)

1. HL. 26 August 1792.
2. Excerpts from the letter were reprinted in several of FB's obituary notices in 1857–8, and in William Monk, *Euthanasia or Medical Treatment in Aids of Easy Dying*, 1887.
3. ADM 51/7/54/1144.
4. H. T. Fry, 'Lord St Vincent's Discipline', *The Mariner's Mirror*, 1953, pp. 306–7.

CHAPTER FIVE (pp. 57–67)

1. HL. 3 June 1794.
2. G. J. Marcus, *A Naval History of Great Britain* 2, *The Age of Nelson*, 1971, pp. 16–17.
3. Quoted by Marcus, p. 12.
4. S. Ayling, *George the Third*, 1972, pp. 370–3.
5. NMM. STO 1–4.
6. Captain William James, *The Naval History of Great Britain* (1837 edition) *1*, pp. 60–2.
7. See, among others: Oliver Warner, *The Glorious First of June*, 1961; James, *1*, pp. 125–82; Edward Pelham Branton, *Naval History of Great Britain* (1837 edition), pp. 122–61; Captain A. T. Mahan, *The Influence of Sea Power upon the French Revolution and Empire*, 1892, *1*, pp. 123–61.
8. Brenton, pp. 149–50.
9. This and all subsequent accounts by FB of the engagement are from his private journal (HL) 19 May–1 June 1794.
10. Warner, p. 140.
11. ADM 51/54.

CHAPTER SIX (pp. 68–82)

1. HL. 8 September 1848.
2. ADM 51/1147.
3. James, *1*, p. 237.
4. William Morris Beaufort, p. 19.
5. The action is described by James, *1*, pp. 238–43.
6. William R. O'Byrne, *Naval Biographical Dictionary*, 1849, p.1127; ADM 51, logs of *Phaeton*, *passim*.
7. Marcus, p. 144.

CHAPTER SEVEN (pp. 83–92)

1. HL. FB to DAB, 16 December 1798.
2. RAS. Beaufort obituary notice, 1858.
3. The *ex post facto* diagnosis is that of Dr Naomi M. Kanof of Washington, DC, Clinical Professor of Medicine, Georgetown University, and former editor of the *Journal of Investigative Dermatology*.

CHAPTER EIGHT (pp. 93–101)

1. HL. Copy of a letter from Nelson to (Richard) Bulkeley, 8 Nov. 1799.
2. William St Clair, *Lord Elgin and The Marbles*, 1967, Chapter 1.
3. HL. 1 November 1799.
4. NLI. Edgeworth papers, MS 13176.
5. Francis Beaufort Edgeworth, *A Memoir of Maria Edgeworth*, 1807, p. 102.
6. ADM 51/1320, *Phaeton* log.
7. ADM 1/2138.
8. MO. FB's journal.
9. Navy Records Society, Keith papers, II, 92–3.
10. James, *3*, p. 9.
11. HO. Letters In, B–1411, 11 April 1852.
12. Noted by St Clair, Chapter 3.
13. Marcus, p. 199.
14. ADM 51/1369, *Phaeton* log.
15. Given by Brenton, *1*, pp. 502–3.
16. Brenton, *1*, p. 502; James *3*, p. 27.
17. MO.

CHAPTER NINE (pp. 102–8)

1. HL. 12 December 1800.
2. The account of the capture of the *San Josef* and FB's injuries is taken from his letters (HL) of October-November 1800; his journal (MO); the log of the *Phaeton* (ADM 51/1369), and the report of Captain Morris to Admiral Lord Keith (ADM 1/403).
3. James, *3*, pp. 55–6.
4. NLI. Edgeworth papers, MS 13176 (2), FB to Sneyd Edgeworth, 16 May 1804.

CHAPTER TEN (pp. 109–22)

1. HL. FB to Wm, 8 April 1805.
2. Gardiner, p. 193.
3. *Ibid.*
4. ADM 1/1528.

5. Respectively: *Memoirs of Richard Lovell Edgeworth*, concluded by Maria Edgeworth, 1844; Desmond Clarke, *The Ingenious Mr Edgeworth*, 1965; Marilyn Butler, *Maria Edgeworth*, 1972. I have drawn principally on these works for the material on RLE.

6. *Memoirs of Richard Lovell Edgeworth*, pp. 20–91.

7. NLI. Edgeworth papers, MS 12176.

8. Butler, p. 203.

9. Commander H. P. Mead, 'The Story of the Telegraph', *The Mariner's Mirror*, *19*, 1933.

10. NLI. Edgeworth papers, MS 7393, 21 November 1803.

11. NLI. Draft report by RLE, undated (late 1803?).

12. NLI. MS 81820/o. FB to RLE, 23 July 1804.

13. Arthur Bryant, *Years of Victory*, 1944, p. 114.

CHAPTER ELEVEN (pp. 123–8)

1. IIL. FB to Wm, 4 January 1804.

2. Isabel C. Clarke, *Maria Edgeworth, Her Family and Friends*, 1950, p. 189; Butler, p. 186.

3. Beaufort–Edgeworth papers, in private possession of Butler family, 31 May 1803.

4. *Ibid.*

5. *Ibid.*

6. NLI. Edgeworth papers, 17 March and 1 May 1804.

7. Beaufort–Edgeworth papers, 8 April 1807.

CHAPTER TWELVE (pp. 129–41)

1. HL. FB journal, 5 June 1806 (*sic.* 1805 is intended).

CHAPTER THIRTEEN (pp. 142–7)

1. HL. FB to RLE, 9 December 1809.

2. MO. FB's private log.

3. Those surviving are in the MO archives.

4. Sources for the history and use of the Beaufort Scale are his private log; Commander L. G. Garbett, 'Admiral Sir Francis Beaufort and the Beaufort Scales of Wind and Weather', *Quarterly Journal of the Royal Meteorological Society*, April 1926; Sir Napier Shaw, *Manual of Meteorology*, 1926; H. T. Fry, 'The Emergence of the Beaufort Scale', *The Mariner's Mirror*, *53*, no. 4, 1967, pp. 311–13; *54*, no. 4, 1968, p. 412.

5. Fry.

6. Robert Fitzroy, *Narrative of the Surveying Voyages of His Majesty's Ships Adventure and Beagle between the years 1826 and 1836*, 1839, 2, p. 37.

7. ADM 51/3054.

8. Commander L. S. Dawson, *Memoirs of Hydrography*, 1855, 2, p. 48.

9. HO. Letters In, C 720.
10. Ritchie, p. 192.

CHAPTER FOURTEEN (pp. 148–61)

1. HL. FB journal, 1 March 1806.
2. ADM 1/1538.
3. See Owen Rutter, *Turbulent Journey: A Life of William Bligh*, 1936, pp. 216ff.
4. ADM 51/1632.
5. Masefield, p. 75.
6. It is exhaustively dealt with by C. Northcote Parkinson, *Edward Pellew, Viscount Exmouth, Admiral of the Red*, 1934.
7. ADM 1/1540.
8. ADM 1/1649; Full details are in Colonial Office Papers, Maitland to Minto, CO 54/22.
9. ADM 1/1540.

CHAPTER FIFTEEN (pp. 162–8)

1. HL. FB to Wm, 29 February 1808.
2. ADM 1/1543; W. W. Pole to FB, 16 March 1808.
3. Howard T. Fry, *Alexander Dalrymple and the Expansion of British Trade*, 1970; ADM 1/13523.

CHAPTER SIXTEEN (pp. 169–76)

1. HL. 19 April 1809.
2. H. L. Fry, 'The Emergence of the Beaufort Scale', *The Mariner's Mirror*, 58, no. 4, 1967, p. 312.
3. Document in private possession of Angela, Lady Walker.
4. Edward Taggart, *A Memoir of the Late Captain Peter Heywood, RN*, 1832.

CHAPTER SEVENTEEN (pp. 177–81)

1. HL. FB to RLE and Fanny, 17 June 1810.
2. Private possession, Butler family.

CHAPTER EIGHTEEN (pp. 182–92)

1. HL. 28 July 1811.
2. See Briggs, p. 161.
3. See G. M. Trevelyan, *Illustrated English Social History*, 1952, 4, p. 4.
4. *Society of the Dilettanti*, 'Ionian Antiquities', 1769–97.
5. For a complete list, see W. M. Leake, preface to *Journal of a Tour in Asia Minor*, 1824.
6. Marie-Gabriel-Florent-August Choiseul-Gouffier, *Voyage Pittoresque en*

Grèce, Paris, 1782; Claude Etienne Savary, *Letters on Greece*, 1782; Edward Daniel Clarke, *Travels in Various Countries of Europe, Asia and Africa*, 1810–23.

7. See Bernard Lewis, *The Emergence of Modern Turkey*, 1961.

8. This and all subsequent accounts in the text of the *Frederickssteen*'s cruises of 1811–12 are taken from FB's journal (HL), his book, *Karamania*, 1817, his charts (HO) and his *Memoir*, 1820 (HO).

9. Sybille Haynes, *The Land of the Chimaera*, 1974.

10. Letter to author from Professor George E. Bean.

11. W. M. Calder and G. E. Bean, 'A Classical Map of Asia Minor', 1958.

CHAPTER TWENTY (pp. 202–17)

1. HL. Journal, 18 June 1812.

2. Charles Robert Cockerell, Travel Journal, 1811–12, in the Greek and Roman Department of the British Museum.

3. Arif Müfid Mansel, *Die Ruinen von Side*, Berlin, 1963, p. 133.

4. Robin Fedden and John Thomson, *Crusader Castles*, 1967.

5. ADM 1/423.

6. ADM 1/424.

7. *Ibid.*

CHAPTER TWENTY-ONE (pp. 218–24)

1. HL. Undated, probably summer 1817.

2. ADM 1/1553.

3. John Marshall, *Royal Navy Biography*, 1853, 4, part 2.

4. Dawson, *1*, p. 47; Ritchie, p. 102.

5. *The Times*, 3 September 1817.

6. The *British Critic*, 8, November 1817.

7. Sir John Barrow, *Auto-Biographical Memoir*, 1847, p. 395.

CHAPTER TWENTY-TWO (pp. 225–33)

1. HL. 1816.

2. William Morris Beaufort, pp. 24–5.

3. Dawson, *1*, p. 101.

4. HO. Letters Out, 5 May 1853.

5. e.g. HO. Letters In M. 164, from Captain Marshall, 28 July 1844.

6. O'Byrne, entry for Francis Beaufort Quin.

CHAPTER TWENTY-THREE (pp. 234–44)

1. HL. FB to Harriet Beaufort, 4 November 1825.

2. *Edinburgh Journal of Science*, 1826.

3. DNB, James South.

4. For a more extensive account of the affair, see J. L. E. Dreyer and H. H. Turner, *History of the Royal Astronomical Society*, 1923, pp. 52 ff.

5. Dawson, *1*, p. 122.

6. Dreyer and Turner, p. 68; Dawson, *1*, p. 122.

7. For a summary of its activity and publications see J. G. Crowther, *Statesmen of Science*, 1965, and the entry on itself in its own *Penny Cyclopaedia*, 1841.

8. Briggs, pp. 223–4.

9. William Morris Beaufort, p. 130.

10. Sir Henry Lyons, *The Royal Society 1660–1940*, pp. 212, 238.

11. Dawson, *1*, pp. 99–101.

CHAPTER TWENTY-FOUR (pp. 245–54)

1. Rear-Admiral George H. Richards, *Memoir of Hydrography*, 1868, p. 9.

2. Day, p. 23.

3. *Ibid.*, p. 32.

4. HO. Letters In, from Captain W. F. W. Owen, 26 September 1829.

5. Richards, pp. 9–10.

6. Mary Blewitt, *Surveys of the Seas*, 1967.

7. A. G. N. Wyatt, *Charting the Seas in Peace and War*, 1947.

8. HO. Misc. files, no. 4.

9. See, e.g., HO Minute book, 26 March 1831.

10. In the Huntington Library.

11. Richards, pp. 11–12.

12. Dawson, *2*, p. 3.

13. HO. Misc. files, no. 5, 9 December 1837.

14. Quoted by Blewitt, p. 35.

15. HO. Letters Out, to Captain H. J. Austin, 20 April 1852.

16. Parliamentary Papers: 'Arctic Blue Books', *passim*; James Clark Ross, *Voyage of Discovery and Research in the Southern and Antarctic Regions*, 1847, *1*, p. 217; HO files, *passim*.

17. HO. Misc. files, no. 81.

18. Day, p. 26, quoting Captain John Washington.

19. Ritchie, p. 190.

20. Day, p. 16.

21. HO. Misc. files, no. 5, Parry papers.

22. Dawson, *2*, p. 8.

23. *Ibid.*, *2*, p.10.

24. Day, p. 63.

25. Dawson, *2*, pp. 13–14.

CHAPTER TWENTY-FIVE (pp. 255–66)

1. HO. Letters Out, 1844.

2. Dawson, *2*, pp. 14–15.

3. HO. Letters Out.

4. More numerous and extended summaries are to be found in Dawson, Day, Ritchie and K. St B. Collins, *Institute of Navigation Journal*, 11, no. 3, July 1958.

5. Beaufort obituary notice, *Royal Astronomical Society Proceedings*, 1858.

6. Sir Charles Fellows, *Travels and Researches in Asia Minor*, 1852, pp. 422–56.

7. HO. Letters In, F–144.

8. Letter to author from Rear-Admiral Ritchie.

9. Collins, p. 273.

10. Quoted by Dawson, 2, p. 13.

11. HO. Letters In, B–1318.

12. Dreyer and Turner, p. 60, footnote.

CHAPTER TWENTY-SIX (pp. 267–75)

1. HL. 18 October 1842.

2. *Naval and Military Gazette*, 1 March 1862.

3. *London Daily News*, 15 January 1858.

4. Quoted by Isabel Clarke, p. 168.

5. *London Daily News*, 15 January 1858.

6. Reproduced in Christina Colvin, *Maria Edgeworth, Letters from England*, 1971.

7. Colvin, p. 454.

8. Beaufort–Edgeworth letters, private possession, Butler family.

9. Colvin, p. xxxiv.

10. Beaufort–Edgeworth letters.

CHAPTER TWENTY-SEVEN (pp. 276–84)

1. HL. 16 October 1844.

2. *London Daily News*, 15 January 1858.

3. HO. Minute book, 19 April 1843.

4. HO. Letters Out, 21 June 1837.

5. HO. Letters In D–289, 30 June 1948, from Lieutenant Algernon de Horsey.

6. Day, p. 47.

7. *London Daily News*, 15 January 1858.

8. Day, p. 58.

9. HO. Letters Out, 30 March 1830.

10. HO. Letter book no. 7.

11. Day, p. 59.

12. Collins, p. 276.

13. HO. Letters Out, 11 May, 1853.

14. HO. Letters In, B, 194.

15. HO. Minute book 2, 31 December 1833.

16. HO. Letters Out, 18 November 1854.

17. HO. Letters Out, K–145–173.

18. HO. Letters Out, S–141.

19. HL. FB 78, 82, 84.

20. HO. Misc. files, no. 22, item 2.
21. HO. Letters Out, F–117.
22. HO. Letters Out, 24 May 52.
23. HO. Letters Out, 25 May 52.
24. HO. Letters In, C–98.
25. HO. Letters Out, 1 November 1836.
26. HO. Letters Out, 26 September 1845.
27. HO. Letters In, B–1038.
28. HO. Letters In, H–319.
29. HO. Letters In, F–117.
30. HO. Letters In, D–173.
31. HO. Letters In, B–868.
32. HO. Letters In, K–15, 16.
33. HO. Letters In, H–828–30.
34. HO. Letters In, A–537.
35. HO. Letters In, B–320.
36. Letters In, L–46.
37. HO. Letters In, R–723.
38. HO. Letters In, H–219.
39. HO. Letters Out, 6, 11 June, 30 August 1851.
40. HO. Letters In, F–192.
41. HO. Letters Out, 14 December 1842.
42. HO. Letters In, L–244.
43. HO. Letters In, F–259.
44. HO. Letters In, H–650.
45. HO Letters In, H–742.
46. See David Duff, *Victoria Travels*, 1970, pp. 59–67, for an account of the trip.
47. HO. Letters Out, 9 May 1845.

CHAPTER TWENTY-EIGHT (pp. 285–300)

1. RS. Herschel papers, 25 September 1833.
2. Lyons, pp. 245–8.
3. Private possession of Angela, Lady Walker.
4. HO. Misc. files, no. 14, item 1.
5. L. Pearce Williams, 'The Royal Society and the Founding of the British Association for the Advancement of Science', *Notes and Records of the Royal Society of London*, *16*, no 2, 1961, p. 226.
6. Walter F. Cannon, 'Scientists and Broad Churchmen: An Early Victorian Intellectual Network', *Journal of British Studies*, *4*, no. 1, November 1964, p. 74.
7. Lyons, pp. 258–63.
8. Hugh Robert Mill, *The Records of the Royal Geographical Society 1880–1930*, p. 5. The summary of the founding of the RGS is drawn principally from this source.
9. Christopher Lloyd, *Mr Barrow of the Admiralty*, 1970, p. 1581.
10. HO. FB letter to Herschel, 14 April 1851.
11. RS. Sabine papers, letter from FB, 23 July 1853.

12. See Cannon.

13. James Clark Ross, p. xviii.

14. Ernest S. Dodge, *The Polar Rosses*, 1973, pp. 217–18.

15. For a full discussion of their work see Margaret Deacon, *Scientists and the Sea 1650–1900*, 1971, especially Chapter 11, on which I have largely drawn for this section.

16. *Ibid.*, p. 255.

17. RS. Lubbock papers, 158–97.

18. Deacon, p. 257.

19. *Ibid.*, p. 260, summarizing Whewell in RS *Philosophical Transactions*, 1835.

20. Most of them, from 1832 to 1854, are listed in the HO summary index volume of Letters Out, by subject, under the headings of 'Tidal Observations' and 'Tide Tables'.

21. Day, p. 58.

22. 9 April 1857, private possession of Rear-Admiral M. J. Ross, RN (Ret.).

23. A. J. Meadows, *Greenwich Observatory*, 2, 1975.

24. The episode is related most fully by H. E. L. Mellersh, *Fitzroy of the Beagle*, 1968.

25. HO. Letter book no. 3.

CHAPTER TWENTY-NINE (pp. 301–22)

1. HO. Letter book 4 October 1851.

2. SPRI.

3. Leslie H. Neatby, *The Search for Franklin*, 1970, p. 92.

4. ABB.

5. Neatby, p. 76.

6. SPRI. Lady Franklin's diary, 1 February 1848.

7. ABB. I, Ross Memorandum, February 1848.

8. ABB. I, 45223, 6 February 1850.

9. Neatby, p. 100.

10. ABB. I, 45216, 5 May 1847.

11. HO. Letters Out.

12. HO. Minute book, 11 February 1847.

13. ABB. I, 45216, 9 February 1847.

14. *Ibid.* 5 March 1847.

15. *Ibid.* 2 December 1847.

16. *Ibid.* 25 February 1847; 5 May 1847.

17. HO. Letters Out.

18. HO. Letters Out, 16 March 1848.

19. HO. Letters Out to Admiral Sir William Parker, 7 November 1849.

20. HO. Letters Out, 16 November 1849.

21. HO. Letters Out to Kellett, 16 March 1850.

22. HO. Minute book, 15 December 1849.

23. HO. Minute book, 24 November 1848

24. HO. Letters Out, to Dr Robert McCormick, 17 January 1850.

M*

25. HO. Letters Out, to Kellett, 15 December 1849.
26. ABB. I, 45223, 30 November 1849; 1 December 1849.
27. See, *inter alia*, BM, Barrow Papers, MSS 35 308, Letters from Captain R. Maguire to John Barrow, Jr. 14 October 1854.
28. HO. Minute book, 25 January 1850.
29. HO. Letters Out, to Collinson, 6 March 1850.
30. HO. Letters Out, to Colonel Colquhoun, 16 March 1852.
31. HO. Minute book, 10 November 1849.
32. ABB. I, 45223, 24 November 1949; 29 January 1850.
33. SPRI. Memorandum to Admiralty, (undated) 1849.
34. SPRI. Memorandum to Admiralty, 28 January 1850.
35. See Lloyd, *Mr Barrow of the Admiralty*, p. 194.
36. HO. Letters Out, to Kellett, 15 December 1849.
37. HO. Letters Out, to Belcher, 3 December 1849.
38. HO. Letters In, B 320, 18 July 1845.
39. HO. Letters In, C 147, 20 October 1834.
40. HO. Letters Out, 25 February 1853.
41. SPRI. Letters from Rae to FB, 20 July 1852; 26 October 1854.
42. HO. Letters Out, to Captain Trolloppe, 16 December 1853.
43. HO. Letters Out, April 1854.
44. HO. 8 December 1849.

CHAPTER THIRTY (pp. 323–34)

1. RGS. Back papers. Undated but presumably written by Back in December 1857 for his own files.
2. Dawson, 2, p. 3.
3. RAS. Beaufort obituary, 1858.

Bibliography

PRINCIPAL MANUSCRIPT SOURCES

British Library, London. Sir John Barrow papers, MSS 35–308.

British Museum, London. Journal of Charles Robert Cockerell, 1812, in the Greek and Roman Department.

Huntington Library, San Marino, California. Francis Beaufort Collection: about 2000 items of letters, journals, diaries, miscellaneous papers and memorabilia of Francis Beaufort, members of his family and correspondents, c. 1764–1858.

Hydrographic Department, Taunton, Somerset. Archives: in-coming and out-going letters and minute books, 1829–55.

India Office Library, London. East India Company papers: L/MAR/C 506; L/MAR/B 46H; Log of *Vansittart*, 46AA.

Meteorological Office, Bracknell, Berkshire. Archives: Beaufort's weather logs, 1790–1800, 1805–12, 1820–5, 1841–57; journals, 4 vols, 1790–1800, 1806.

National Library of Ireland, Dublin. Beaufort–Edgeworth letters, c. 1801–5, MSS. 7393, 8122, 8785, 13176.

National Maritime Museum, Greenwich. Admiral Sir Robert Stopford papers, STO 1–4. Letters of Beaufort to Rear-Admiral Sir Richard Collinson.

Public Record Office, London. Admiralty records: ADM 1, 2, 24, 51, 107. Material bearing on Beaufort's Naval service, including ships' logs, orders and instructions, accounts, captains' and admirals' letters.

Public Record Office, Belfast. Massareene papers: D 207/36. Correspondence of Sir John Foster relating to Beaufort, 1807–10.

Royal Geographical Society, London. Archives: Admiral Sir George Back papers, correspondence from Beaufort and miscellaneous letters.

Royal Society, London. Archives: Correspondence of Beaufort with Sir John Herschel, 1828–40; General Sir Edward Sabine, 1848–53; and Sir John William Lubbock, 1830–45.

Scott Polar Research Institute, Cambridge. Archives: Letters and memoranda from Beaufort; Lady Franklin's diaries; letter to Beaufort from Captain Sir John Ross, 1829–33.

Private possession. (Edgeworth) Butler family, Oxford: Edgeworth family
    and Beaufort-Edgeworth letters, *c.* 1805–9
    Rear-Admiral M. J. Ross, Leaveland, Kent: letters from Francis
       Beaufort to Rear-Admiral Sir James Clark Ross, 1849–57.
    Angela, Lady Walker, Jersey C.I, miscellaneous Beaufort papers.

PUBLISHED WORKS

Ireland: family, friends and the 'tellograph'

BARROW, Sir John, 'Telegraph', *Encyclopaedia Britannica*, Supplement,
    1824 edition.
BEAUFORT, Daniel Augustus, *Memoir of a Map of Ireland*, 1792.
BEAUFORT, Emily, *Egyptian Sculptures and Syrian Shrines*, 1861.
(BEAUFORT, Harriet), *A Dialogue on Botany*, 1819.
    Bertha's Journal, 1836.
BEAUFORT, William Morris, *The Family of de Beaufort in France, Holland,
    Germany and England*, 1886.
BUTLER, Marilyn, *Maria Edgeworth, A Literary Biography*, 1972.
CLARKE, Desmond, *The Ingenious Mr Edgeworth*, 1965.
COLVIN, Christina (Ed.), *Maria Edgeworth, Letters from England*, 1971.
EDGEWORTH, Frances Anne Beaufort, *A Memoir of Maria Edgeworth*, 1807.
EDGEWORTH, Richard Lovell, *Memoirs*, concluded by Maria Edgeworth
    (3rd edition), 1844.
    Communication, *Nicholson's Journal*, *26*, 1810.
    'An Essay on the Art of Conveying Secret and Swift Intelligence',
    Transactions of the Royal Irish Academy, June 1795.
ELLISON, Canon C. C., 'Remembering Dr Edgeworth', *Quarterly of the
    Irish Georgian Society*, 1975.
INGLIS-JONES, Elizabeth, *The Great Maria*, 1969.
MEAD, H. P., 'The Story of the Semaphore', *Mariner's Mirror*, *19*, 1933.
Notes and Queries, 'Mayfair Marriages', 27 January 1800.

The years afloat

ALLAN, Joseph, *Battles of the British Navy*, 1852.
BARROW, Sir John, *Life of Richard Earl Howe, KG*, 1838.
BAYNHAM, Henry, *From the Lower Deck*, 1969.
    Before the Mast, 1971.
BRENTON, Edward Pelham, *The Naval History of Great Britain*, 1837
    edition.

COTTON, Sir E. and FAWCETT, Sir C., *East Indiamen*, 1949.

DE MORGAN, Augustus, 'Midshipman's Three Dinners', *Notes and Queries*, 2 October 1858.

EVATT, H. V., *Rum Rebellion*, (Sydney) 1938.

FRY, H. T., 'The Emergence of the Beaufort Scale', *Mariner's Mirror*, 53, no. 4, 1967; 54, no. 4, 1968.

GARBETT, L. G., 'Admiral Sir Francis Beaufort and the Beaufort Scales of Wind and Weather', *Quarterly Journal of the Royal Meteorological Society*, April 1926.

GARDINER, Leslie, *The British Admiralty*, 1968.

GILL, Conrad, *The Naval Mutinies of 1797*, 1913.

HENDERSON, James, *The Frigate*, 1970.

HOUGH, Richard, *Captain Bligh and Mr Christian*, 1972.

JACKSON, T. Sturges, *Great Sea Fights*, 1889.

JAMES, William, *The Naval History of Great Britain*, 1837 edition.

LEWIS, Michael, *A Social History of the Navy*, 1960.

LLOYD, Christopher, *The British Seaman*, 1968.

   Mr Barrow of the Admiralty, 1970.

MACKANESS, George, *The Life of Sir William Bligh*, 1931.

MAHAN, A. T., *The Influence of Seapower upon the French Revolution and Empire*, 1892.

MARCUS, G. J., *A Naval History of England, 2: The Age of Nelson*, 1971.

   Heart of Oak, 1975.

MASEFIELD, John, *Sea Life in Nelson's Time*, 1905 (3rd edition, 1971).

Naval Records Society, *Keith Papers*, 1950.

PARKINSON, C. Northcote, *Edward Pellew, Viscount Exmouth, Admiral of the Red*, 1934.

PEARS, Randolph, *Young Sea Dogs*, 1960.

PENN, Geoffrey, *Snotty: The Story of the Midshipman*, 1957.

RATHBONE, Charles, *Famous Frigate Actions*, 1900.

RUTTER, Owen, *Turbulent Journey: A Life of William Bligh*, 1936.

ST CLAIR, William, *Lord Elgin and the Marbles*, 1967.

SHAW, Sir Napier, *Manual of Meteorology*, 1926.

TUNSTALL, Brian, *The Anatomy of Neptune*, 1936.

WALKER, C. F., *Young Gentlemen*, 1938.

WARNER, Oliver, *The Glorious First of June*, 1961.

Karamania

BEAN, George E., *Turkey's Southern Shore*, 1968.

   'A Classical Map of Asia Minor' (with CALDER, W. M.), 1958.

BEAUFORT, Francis, *Karamania*, 1817.
  Memoir of a Survey of the Coast of Karamania, 1820.
  'Account of an Earthquake at Sea,' *Edinburgh Journal of Science*, 1826.
BROWNE, William George, *Travels in Africa, Egypt and Syria from the Years 1792–1798*, 1799.
CHANDLER, Richard, *Travels in Asia Minor, 1764–65*, 1825 (1971 edition).
CHOISEUL-GOUFFIER, M. G. F. A., *Voyage Pittoresque en Grèce*, (Paris) 1762.
CLARKE, Edward Daniel, *Travels*, part 2, 4, 1817.
FEDDEN, Robin and Thomson, John, *Crusader Castles*, 1967.
FELLOWS, Sir Charles, *The Xanthian Marbles*, 1842.
  Travels and Researches in Asia Minor, 1852.
HAYNES, Sybille, *Land of the Chimaera*, 1974.
LEAKE, William Martin, *Journal of a Tour in Asia Minor*, 1824.
LEWIS, Bernard, *The Emergence of Modern Turkey*, 1961.
MANSEL, Arif Müfid, *Die Ruinen von Side*, (Berlin) 1965.
SAVARY, Claude Etienne, *Letters on Greece*, 1788.
SOCIETY OF THE DILETTANTI, *Ionian Antiquities*, 1769–97.

Hydrographer and scientist

BABBAGE, Charles, *Reflexions on the Decline of Science in England*, 1830.
BARLOW, Nora (Ed.), *Charles Darwin and the Voyage of the* Beagle, 1945.
BARROW, Sir John, *An Auto-Biographical Memoir*, 1847.
(BECHER, A. B.), 'Sir Francis Beaufort's Plan for Secret Correspondence', *Nautical Magazine*, August 1855.
  'The Log-Board', *Nautical Magazine*, March 1832.
BEAGLEHOLE, J. C., *The Life of Captain James Cook*, (Stanford) 1974.
BLEWITT, Mary, *Surveys of the Seas*, 1957.
CANNON, Walter F., 'Scientists and Broad Churchmen: An Early Victorian Network', *Journal of British Studies*, (Hartford, Conn.) 4, no. 1, November 1964.
  'History in Depth: The Early Victorian Period', *History of Science, 3*, 1964.
COLLINS, K. St B., 'Admiral Sir Francis Beaufort', *Journal of the Institute of Navigation, 2*, 1958.
DARWIN, Charles, *Autobiography, 1809–1882* (Ed. Nora Barlow), 1958.
DAWSON, L. S., *Memoirs of Hydrography*, 1885 (1969 edition).
DAY, Sir Archibald, *The Admiralty Hydrographic Service, 1795–1919*, 1967.
DEACON, Margaret, *Scientists and the Sea, 1650–1900*, 1971.
DREYER, J. L. E. and TURNER, H. H., *History of the Royal Astronomical Society*, 1923.

DUFF, David, *Victoria Travels*, 1970.

FITZROY, Robert, *Narrative of the Surveying Voyages of His Majesty's Ships* Adventure *and* Beagle *between the years 1826 and 1836*, 1839.

FORBES, Eric G., *Greenwich Observatory, 1*, 1975.

FRY, Howard T., *Alexander Dalrymple and the Expansion of British Trade*, 1970.

HALL, Basil, *Extracts from a Journal Written on the Coasts of Chile, Peru and Mexico in the years 1820, 1821, 1822, 1824.*

HAMPSHIRE, A. Cecil, '"Father" of Naval Hydrography', *The Nautical Magazine, 214*, no. 4, October 1975.

KAHN, David, *The Codebreakers*, (New York) 1967.

LUBBOCK, Adelaide, *Owen Stanley, RN*, 1968.

LYONS, Sir Henry, *The Royal Society 1660–1940*, 1944.

MEADOWS, A. J., *Greenwich Observatory, 2*, 1975.

MELLERSH, H. E. L., *Fitzroy of the* Beagle, 1968.

MERZ, John Theodore, *A History of European Thought in the Nineteenth Century*, 1904.

MILL, Hugh Robert, *The Record of the Royal Geographical Society, 1830–1930*, 1930.

MOORHEAD, Alan, *Darwin and the* Beagle, 1969.

MORRISON, Philip and Emily, 'The Strange Life of Charles Babbage', *Scientific American*, (New York) April 1952.

RICHARDS, George H., *Memoir on the Hydrographic Office*, 1868.

RITCHIE, G. S., *The Admiralty Chart*, 1967.
'Great Britain's Contribution to Hydrography During the Nineteenth Century', *Institute of Navigation Journal*, 20, no. 1, January 1967.

ROSS, Sir James Clark, *Voyage of Discovery and Research in the Southern and Antarctic Regions*, 1847.

ROYAL GEOGRAPHICAL SOCIETY, *Journals*, 1831–50.

WILLIAMS, L. Pearce, 'The Royal Society and the Founding of the British Association for the Advancement of Science', *Records of the Royal Society of London, 16*, no. 2, 1961.

WOODWARD, Horace B., *The History of the Geological Society of London*, 1907.

WYATT, A. G. N., *Charting the Seas in Peace and War*, 1947.

The search for Franklin

CYRIAX, Richard J., *Sir John Franklin's Last Arctic Expedition*, 1939.
'Recently Discovered Traces of the Franklin Expedition', *Geographical Journal*, June 1951.

CYRIAX, Richard J., 'The Two Franklin Expedition Books Found on King William Island', *Mariner's Mirror*, *44*, 1958.

'The Unsolved Problem of the Franklin Expedition Records', *Mariner's Mirror*, *55*, 1969.

DODGE, Ernest S., *The Polar Rosses*, 1973.

GOULD, Rupert T., *Oddities*, 1928 ('The Two Ships Seen on the Ice').

JONES, A. G. E., 'Sir James Clark Ross and the Voyage of the *Enterprise* and *Investigator*, 1848–49', *Geographical Journal*, *137*, part 2, 1971.

NEATBY, Leslie H., *The Search for Franklin*, 1970.

Parliamentary Papers: Arctic Blue Books.

PARRY, Ann, *Parry of the Arctic*, 1963.

THOMSON, George Malcolm, *The North-West Passage*, 1975.

WRIGHT, Noel, *Quest for Franklin*, 1959.

General

AYLING, S., *George the Third*, 1972.

BRIGGS, Asa, *The Age of Improvement*, 1959.

BRYANT, *Years of Victory, 1802–1812*, 1944.

The Age of Elegance, 1950.

CROWTHER, J. G., *Statesmen of Science*, 1965.

JAEGER, Muriel, *Before Victoria*, 1956.

MARSHALL, John, *Royal Naval Biography, 1823–35*.

O'BYRNE, William R., *A Naval Biographical Dictionary*, 1849.

Penny Cyclopaedia, *21*, 1841, 'The Society for the Diffusion of Useful Knowledge'.

SMYTH, W. H., *The Sailor's Word-Book*, 1867.

TAGGART, Edward, *A Memoir of the Late Captain Peter Heywood, RN*, 1832.

Obituary notices

(MARTINEAU, Harriet), *London Daily News*, 15 January 1858.

Proceedings of the Royal Society, *9*, 1858.

(SMYTH, W. H.), *Journal of the Royal Astronomical Society*, 1858.

Index

Abercromby, Gen. Sir Ralph, 99
Aberdeen, Lord, 204
Adalia, Pasha of, 197–200, 206
Adana, Pasha of, 216
Addington, *see* Sidmouth
Addison, Joseph, 84, 87
Adventure, 255
Airy, Sir G. B., 234–5, 266, 287,
  297–8
Albert, Prince, 281
Alexander VI, Pope, 279
Alexander the Great, 205, 212n, 213
Allen, Capt. William, 280
American Independence, War of,
  43, 53, 62, 68
Amiens, Peace of, 110, 111, 112,
  123–4
Anson, 107
Antoine, 58
Anville, Jean-Baptiste d', 184
Aquilon, 46–7, 51–4, 58–9, 60–8, 77,
  84
Arago, Dominique, 239
Arctic Council, 307–9, 319
Armstrong, mariner, 155
Arnold, Thomas, 279
Arrian, 183, 205, 212n
Arthur, President Chester A., 320n
Assistance, 316n
Auckland, Adm. Lord, 328
Augustus Frederick, Prince, 61, 61n,
  62, 287, 287n
Austin, Capt. Horatio, 301, 313,
  316n, 318

Babbage, Charles, 235–6, 241, 280,
  293–4, 286–7
Back, Adm. Sir George, 303,
  308–9, 315, 323, 328, 330
Baden-Powell, Prof., 330

Baily, Francis, 235, 241, 288
Baird, Gov. David, 156–7, 159
Baldock, Cdr Thomas, 147
Bangka Strait, 27, 33–5
Banks, Sir Joseph, 173, 219, 265, 285
Barham, Lord (Sir Charles
  Middleton), 43–4, 122, 129, 148
Barlow, Peter, 242
Barnett, Lt Edward, 250
Barrow, John (Jr), 331
Barrow, Sir John, 48, 63n, 95n, 224,
  244, 277, 288, 291, 302–3, 306–7
Batavia (Jakarta) Observatory, 31, 32
Bayfield, H. W., 258
Beacon, 258–9
Beagle, 14, 144, 146, 255, 257n
Beaufort, Alfred, 226, 325
Beaufort (*née* Wilson), Alicia
  Magdalena, 27, 178–80, 217–19,
  225–6, 228–31, 268–71, 273, 327,
  333
Beaufort, Revd Dr Daniel Augustus
  18–25, 27, 37, 39, 44, 51, 60, 75,
  85, 112–14, 115n, 123, 126, 134,
  167, 180, 225–7
Beaufort, Daniel Augustus (Jr),
  225, 267, 274, 326, 332
Beaufort, Daniel Cornelis de, 18
Beaufort (later Strangford), Emily
  Anne, 226, 325, 328–9, 330
Beaufort (later Edgeworth),
  Frances (Fanny) Anne, 21, 88,
  96n, 102, 114, 123–4, 127, 165,
  171, 177, 180, 225–6, 230, 232,
  271–2
Beaufort, Adm. Sir Francis: early
  life, 13–14, 23; education, 14–15,
  24–5; family background, 17–23;
  idolatry of father, 22–3; physical
  appearance, 23; health, 23, 25–6,

Beaufort, Adm. Sir Francis – *cont.*
  38, 38n, 50, 75, 90–2, 102–3, 324;
  early interest in astronomy, 24;
  early obsession with the sea, 26;
  personal charm, 28–9, 39–41;
  temperament, 32, 41–2, 45–6, 56,
  65, 75, 94, 135–6, 327; accidents
  and wounds, 48–50, 62, 104–7,
  215–16; use of cipher, 50–2, 55,
  75, 86, 124; voracious reading,
  83–4, 87–8; religious convictions,
  84–7, 137–8, 270, 274; career
  disappointments, 127–9, 162–3,
  166–8, 172, 178, scale of wind
  force, 143–7; first marriage,
  218–19; appointed Hydrographer,
  243; honours received, 15, 262,
  262n, 329; incestuous relationship
  with Harriet Beaufort, 270; second
  marriage, 271–5; children, 326–7
Beaufort, Francis Lestock, 226, 267,
  326
Beaufort, François de, 117–18
Beaufort, Henrietta (Harriet), 22,
  154–5, 156, 164, 234, 269–70, 329
Beaufort (*née* Edgeworth), Honora,
  270–3, 324, 333
Beaufort, Louisa Catherine, 22, 97,
  122, 127, 230, 269, 316
Beaufort (*née* Waller), Mary, 23, 112
Beaufort, Rosalind Elizabeth, 226,
  325, 333–4
Beaufort, William Lewis, 21–2,
  50–1, 86, 95, 107, 124–5, 167,
  223, 227, 230–1, 240, 243, 245,
  269, 273
Beaufort, William Morris, 226,
  282–3, 327–8
Beaufort Islands, 252
Beaufort Sea, 237, 303
Becher, Lt (later Rear-Adm.) A. B.,
  146, 247–8, 282–3, 295, 296
Beechey, Capt. (later Rear-Adm.)
  F. W., 147, 237–8, 246, 253, 295,
  303, 309, 314–15
Belcher, Sir Edward, 255, 257, 257n,
  258, 260, 319–20
Bellamy, Thomas, 242
Bellot, Lt Joseph-René, 321
Benbow, Adm. John, 136

Bennett, Revd W. J. E., 87, 274,
  326
Berthon, Revd E. Lyon, 296
Bertie, Capt. Albemarle, 39, 44, 46,
  78
Bertie, Lord, Robert, 39
Bessel, F. W., 235n
Bethune, Capt. Charles, 280
Bethune, Capt. Robert, 319–20
Bickerton, Adm. Sir Richard, 99
Bird Allen, Cdr, 259
Blenheim, 164
Blewitt, Mary, 247, 263
Bligh, Capt. William, 36, 137, 139,
  148, 150, 151, 156–7
Blossom, 169–71, 176, 180–1,
  232–3, 237, 303, 309
Boileau (later Wilson), Bonne, 27
Boone, T., 257n
Boone, W., 257n
Booth, Felix, 302
Boteler, Cdr T., 259
Boulton, Matthew, 114
Bounty, 36, 137, 176
Bouverie, Capt. D. P., 173
Bouverie, E. P., 100
Brest, 64, 69, 72, 76, 80–1, 148
Brewster, Sir David, 234–5
Bridport, Adm. Lord (Alexander
  Hood), 80, 81
Briggs, Asa, 240
Briggs, Vice-Adm. Sir Thomas, 98
Brinkley, John, 224, 235
British Museum, 95n, 205n, 259
Brooke, Sir James, 257, 280
Brougham, Henry (later Lord),
  240, 267
Browne, Lt Willy, 318
Bruix, Adm., 81, 82
Brunel, I. K., 274–5
Bulkeley, Richard, 96n
Bunsen, R. W. von, 262
Byng, Hon. George, 55
Byng, Vice-Adm. John, 55
Byron, Lord, 204n, 279

Caesar, 65
Caesar, Julius, 279
Caledon, Lord, 165
Calpe, 106

Canada, 73

Canning, Stratford, 185, 199, 205, 216

Cape of Good Hope, 28, 30, 127, 137–9, 151, 156–9, 163–5, 289, 297

Cape Town Observatory, 14, 289, 292, 297–8

Cardigan, Earl of, 39

Carlyle, Prof. J. D., 95

Carruthers, Mr, 30

Carysfort, 45

Cavendish, Henry, 175

Cellarius, 184

Chanticleer, 239, 260, 289

Chappe, Claude, 115, 115n, 116

Charles IV of Spain, 38, 43

Charlotte, Queen, 67

Churchill, Sir Winston, 55

Cicero, 183

Clarence, Duke of, 43, 43n, 247

Clark, Sir James, 324

Clarke, E. D., 223

Clarke, Mrs M. A., 168, 168n

Cochrane, Capt. (later Adm.) Alexander, 100

Cockerell, C. R., 205, 205n, 206–10, 212–13, 215–16, 218, 223, 242

Colchester, Lord, 286

Collinson, Richard, 315–16, 317, 318, 322

Collon (Ireland), 19, 21, 23, 36, 42, 51, 89, 111–13, 115n, 167, 219, 270

Colossus, 40, 78

Colpoys, Rear-Adm. 81

Colvin, Christina, 272

Conybeare, Bishop John, 84

Cook, Capt. James, 237, 246, 253, 258, 298, 301, 302

Copernicus, 255

Cork and Ross, Bishop of, 21

Cornwallis, Gen. Lord Charles, 68

Cornwallis, Vice-Adm. Sir William, 68–72

Cortes, Hernando, 184

Courtown, Lady, 39, 46

Courtown, Lord, 39, 46, 162, 168–9

Crimean War, 321–3

Croker, J. W., 221–2, 224, 228–9, 243–4, 247–8, 279

Crozier, Capt. F. R. M., 291, 307

Curtius, Ernst, 262

D'Alembert, 87

Dalrymple, Alexander, 142, 143n, 147, 154n, 166, 173, 175, 180, 217, 223, 246, 253, 260

Daniell, Edward, 242

Daphne, 73

Darius III of Persia, 213

Darwin, Charles, 14, 112, 146, 242, 255, 266, 274 5, 281, 299, 299n, 300

Darwin, Dr Erasmus, 112, 114

Darwin, Sir George, 266

Darwin, Dr R. W., 112

Davy, Edward, 275n

Davy, Sir Humphry, 241–2, 285–6

Dawson, Cdr L. S., 15–16, 228–9, 253n, 261n, 328

Dayman, Lt, 280

Deagon, gunner, 105

Dease, P. W., 303

Defoe, Daniel, 87

De La Beche, Sir Henry, 266

Delaval, Sir Francis, 115

De Morgan, Augustus, 45, 236

Denham, Henry, 257–8

Dessiou, Joseph, 293–4

De Witt, Gov. Clinton, 238

Dickens, Charles, 333, 334

Diderot, 87

D'Ott, Baron, 98

Drummond, Thomas, 267–8, 292–3

Drury, Byron, 258

Dryden, John, 87

Duncan, 159

Dundas, Hon. G. H. L., 106n

Dundas, Henry (Viscount Melville), 106n, 121–2, 243, 244

Dunmore, Earl of, 61

Dunsink Observatory (Dublin), 24, 234

Dutch East India Company, 32

East India Company, 25–9, 34–6, 158, 160, 162, 179, 261n, 268, 326

Edgeworth, Charlotte, 123–8, 130, 153, 160

Edgeworth (*née* Beaufort), Frances (Fanny) Anne, 88, 96n, 102, 123–4, 127, 165, 171, 177, 180, 225–6, 230, 232, 271–2
Edgeworth, Henry, 119, 120
Edgeworth (later Beaufort), Honora 131, 270–3, 324, 333
Edgeworth, Maria, 19, 21, 96n, 113–14, 123–4, 126–7, 180, 226, 230, 232, 271–2
Edgeworth, Richard Lovell, 88, 88n, 96n, 113–15, 115n, 116–20, 123–4, 126, 134, 142–3, 162, 165, 173–5, 177, 203, 219, 221, 223, 227–8, 232, 272, 284, 286
Edgeworth, Sneyd, 232
Edgeworth, William, 232
Edgeworthstown (Ireland), 114, 119, 123–4, 219, 232, 270–1,
Elgin (*née* Nisbett), Lady, 94–6
Elgin, Lord, 83, 94–8, 182, 190, 190n, 288
Elijah, 301
Ellison, Canon C. C., 19
Endymion, 113
Enterprise, 311, 315–19
Erebus, 254, 291, 306, 308–9, 334
Ericsson, John, 274, 296
Ernest, Prince, 67
Everest, George, 242
Excellent, 93, 94
Exeter, 179
Experiment, 76

Fairy, 260, 295–6
Faraday, Michael, 275, 281
Favourite, 151
Felix, 313
Fellows, Sir Charles, 259
Ferns (Wexford), Bishop of, 39
Ferret, 106
Finlay, George, 279
Fitton, W. H., 242, 287
Fitzherbert, Mrs Maria, 86, 86n
Fitzroy, Cdr Robert, 14, 144, 146, 255–6, 257n, 280, 289, 298–300, 332
Fitzwilliam Museum (Cambridge), 224
Flinders, Matthew, 246

Forbes, Edward, 259
Fortune, John, 164–6
Foster, Cdr Henry, 239–40, 242, 260, 289
Foster, John, 18, 19, 162
Foucault, Jean, 275
Fox, C. J., 88
Fox, R. W., 296
Franklin, Lady, 308, 312–13, 319, 321–2, 332, 334
Franklin, Sir John, 237–9, 241, 277, 286, 301–3, 306–12, 314–22
Frederick, Duke of York, 115n, 168n
Frederick III, Emperor, 262
Fredericksteen, 178, 180, 182, 184, 186–7, 193–5, 198–9, 202, 204–6, 210, 215, 217–18
French Revolution, 53, 57, 88
Frobisher, Sir Martin, 301
Fury, 237

Gammon, Lt W. S., 118, 217
Gardiner, Leslie, 111
Garrow, Mr, 121, 121n
Gaspar Strait, 27, 32–3, 35
Gauss, J. K. F., 290
Gell, Sir Richard, 204
General Elliott, 36
Geological Society, 203
George III, 20, 43, 61, 61n, 67–8, 92n, 136n, 179, 287n
Gibraltar, 53–5, 58–9, 69, 96, 99–100, 104, 106–7, 148, 150, 167, 208
Gilbert, Davies, 241–3, 286–7, 293
Gilpin, William, 84
Gisbourne, Thomas, 84, 87
'Glorious First of June', battle, 63–9
Godwin, William, 88
Goldsmid, Sir Isaac, 330
Goodall, Rear-Adm., 58, 60
Gordon, Lt David, 259
Gould, R. T., 248
Grafton, Duke of, 299
Graham, Adm. Sir James, 267, 323, 328, 331
Graves, Thomas, 258–60, 279
Grenville, Lord William, 158

Grinnell, Henry, 313, 321, 331
Griper, 237
Grotius, Hugo, 84

Hadley, John, 264
Hall, Capt. Basil, 242, 288
Halley, Edmond, 280
Hamilton, C. A., 103–5
Hamilton, Adm. C. P., 163, 169, 176
Hamilton, Edward, 242
Hamilton, Lady Emma, 96
Hamilton, W. J., 266
Hamilton, Sir W. R., 235
Hamilton, W. R., 95, 95n, 182, 204–5, 288
Hammer-Purgstall, Joseph, 212n
Hardwicke, Lord, 121
Hardy, Andrew, 29, 29n
Hardy, Lt (later Cdr) Edward, 331
Harrington, Lord, 18
Hay, Sir J. D., 42n
Hecla, 236, 309
Henderson, Thomas, 280
Henslow, J. S., 299
Herald, 311–13
Herodotus, 183
Herschel, Sir John, 266, 285–7, 290–2, 294
Herschel, Sir William, 235, 239, 241
Hervey, Lord, 332
Hewett, Capt. William, 260, 295
Heywood, Capt. Peter, 176, 242, 244, 253
Heywood, Mrs, 244
Hillyar, Lt (later Capt.) James 74, 76–7, 93–4
Hofland, Thomas, 242
Homer, 263
Hood, Alexander (Adm. Lord Bridport), 80, 81
Hood, Adm. Lord Samuel, 58–60
Hooker, J. D., 291
Hooker, Sir Joseph, 281
Hooker, Sir William, 275
Hope, Comm. Henry, 202, 216
Howe, Adm. Lord Richard, 39, 62–8, 80
Howe, Gen. William, 62n

Huguenots 17–18, 27, 29n
Huish, Lt, 104–5
Humboldt, Baron von, 234
Hunt, Revd P., 95
Hunter, publisher, 226
Huntingdon Library (California), 21, 236, 241
Hurd, Capt. Thomas, 180, 217, 228–9, 244, 246–7, 260, 263
Huxley, T. H., 258, 281, 300
Hydrographic Office, 14–15, 146, 218–19, 231, 246–8, 251, 254, 257, 260, 262, 264–5, 279, 289, 293, 295–6, 319

Investigator, 311, 315–19
Irish Rebellion (1798), 88, 88n, 116
Iskenderun, Pasha of, 216

Jacob, W. S., 241
Jakarta (Batavia) Observatory, 31–2
James, Capt. William, 63, 66, 100, 106
Jervis, Sir John (Lord St Vincent), 109–13, 121, 136
Johnson, Dr Samuel, 89, 231
Joseph I, Emperor, 17

Kahn, David, 283
Kane, Dr Elisha, 321
Kater, Henry, 242
Keir, James, 114
Keith, Vice-Adm. Lord, 98–9, 102, 105–6
Kellett, Capt. Henry, 258, 311–13, 317, 319
Kelly, Mrs, 152
Kelvin, Lord W. T., 175n
Kennedy, President, J. F., 320n
Keykubad I, Sultan, 208
King, Dr Richard, 308–9, 314
Knox, Robert, 242
Krusenstern, Adm. A. J., 279

La Bonne Citoyenne, 73
La Charente, 73
L'Actif, 73
La Découverte, 73
Lady Sinclair, 137, 151

La Flore, 73–4
Laird, Macgregor, 280
La Légère, 73
Lamarck, 210n
La Petite Chérie, 73
Laplace, 210n, 234, 243
La Résolue, 73
La Ressource, 73
Lascelles, 37, 42
Latona, 38–9, 39n, 42, 44–6
L'Aventure, 73
Lavoisier, 210n
Lawrence, Lt G. B., 259
Leake, W. M., 184, 184n, 192n
Le Chasseur, 73
L'Echoue, 73
Leghorn, 51, 53, 59, 61–2, 99, 287n
Le Lévrier, 73
Le Mercure, 73
Lennon, A. M., 233
Lennon, Mrs Maria, 232–3
Lewis, Prof., 55, 111n
L'Hasard, 73
L'Hermite, Comm. Jean-Marthe-
    Adrien, 151–2
L'Hirondelle, 73
Liddell Hart, Sir B. H., 57
L'Indien, 73
Livingstone, David, 330
Livy, 183, 193
Long, George, 279
Longford, Lord, 112, 162, 168
Louis-Philippe, King, 281
Lubbock, J. W., 14, 293–5
Lyell, Sir Charles, 281
Lyon, Cdr G. F., 237, 241, 302
Lyttleton, Lord George, 87

Macaulay, Lord, 333
Mackenzie, Murdoch (Jr), 246
McLean, Hector, 95
M'Clintock, Leopold, 322
M'Clure, Robert, 316–17, 317n,
    318–19
Macredie, John, 132
Mahan, Capt. A. T., 63, 63n, 66
Mahmud II, Sultan, 199
Maitland, Lt-Gen. Sir Thomas,
    159–60
Malcolm, David, 176

Manhattan, 313n
Mansel, Prof. A. M., 207
March, Lord, 115
Marcus, G. J., 63, 63n, 66, 81–2
Maritime Congress (1874), 147
Marlborough, 67
Marryat, Capt. Frederick, 172
Mars, 70–1
Marsden, William, 160
Martin, Sir T. B., 68, 242
Martineau, Harriet, 271
Masefield, John, 29, 41
Master David Bates' Military and
    Marine Academy (Dublin), 24
Mastiff, 251, 279
Maury, Lt M. F., 13, 147, 279, 330
May, Sir T. E., 332
Meath, Bishop of, 19
Melas, Gen., 98
Melbourne, Lord, 290–1
Melville, Viscount, 106n, 121–2,
    243–4
Melville, 2nd Viscount, 222–3
Meryon, C. L., 202
Meteor, 279
Meteorological Office, 78, 250n
Middleton, Sir Charles (later, Lord
    Barham), 43–4, 122, 129, 148
Miletus, 184
Miller, W. H., 296
Minto, Adm. Lord, 328
Mohammed Ali, Pasha of Egypt, 52
Mohr, J. M., 31, 31n, 32
Monck, Lord, 332
Montagne (later *Peuple*), 69
Montagu, Capt. 57
Montagu, Vice-Adm. Sir George,
    138–40
Montefiore, Sir Moses, 330
Montesquieu, 87
More, Hannah, 204
Morla, Don Thomas, de, 99–100
Morrier, J. P., 95
Morris, Capt. (later Vice-Adm.)
    J. N., 94, 96–8, 100, 102–3,
    105–6, 226, 242
Morse, Samuel, 116
Moses, 263
Mulgrave, Lord, 162, 166, 168–9,
    173, 177

Murchison, Sir R. I., 321
Murray, Lady Augusta, 61, 61n
Muscat, Sultan and Imam of, 262

Napoleon I, 15, 97–8, 108, 120,
    135, 146n, 156, 242, 301
Napoleonic Wars, 32, 71, 240, 258
Nassau, 29n
National Library of Ireland, 120
National Maritime Museum, 263
Nautical Almanac Office, 264
Navan (Ireland), 18–19, 23, 114
Navy Society, 274
Neatby, L. H., 318
Neilly, Rear-Adm., 64
Nelson, Adm. Lord Horatio, 51,
    53, 74, 82, 93, 96, 110, 134–5,
    177, 333
Nepean, Sir Evan, 158
Nereus, 176
Newport, Thomas, 5th Earl of
    Bradford, 20, 25
Ney, Marshal, 170
Nisbett, Mary (later Lady Elgin),
    94–6
Nonsuch, 36
Noyes, Dr Russell, 49n

Oliver, Lt R. D., 48n, 51
Olphert, midshipman, 216
Osborn, Lt Sherard, 308, 314
Owen, Capt. W. F. W., 246, 253,
    257n

Paley, William, 84, 87
Pallas, 76
Palmer (*née* Beaufort), Lady Sophia,
    325
Palmer, Revd (later Lord) William,
    325
Palmer, Wilson & Co. 179
Palmerston, Lord Henry, 162–3,
    280
Pandora, 258
Parker King, Capt. Philip, 255
Parry, Capt. W. E., 229, 236–7,
    243–4, 247, 253, 260–1, 261n,
    263–4, 302–3, 306–7, 309, 313,
    317, 319, 321
Patriot, 65

Pausanias, 204
Peace of Amiens, 110, 111, 112,
    123–4
Peacock, George, 287, 290, 294,
    298–9, 299n
Peacock, T. L., 240
Pearce, Stephen, 331
Pechell, Sir John, 292
Peel, Sir Robert, 291n
Pelham, Thomas, 2nd Earl of
    Chichester, 163
Pellew, Rear-Adm. Sir Edward,
    80–1, 158–60, 164, 164n, 166, 176
Peninsular War, 170–1
Penn, Cdr Geoffrey, 42n
Penny, Capt. William, 313–14, 318
Pentland, J. B., 332
Pepys, Samuel, 122
Peuple (formerly *Montagne*), 69
Phaeton, 52, 66n, 68, 69, 70–5,
    76–81, 83, 87, 90, 92–100, 102–5,
    226, 287n, 288
Phipps, Henry (Lord Mulgrave),
    162, 166, 168–9, 173, 177
Pictet, Marc-Auguste, 123
Pitt, William (the Elder), 88
Pitt, William (the Younger), 57,
    62, 121, 122, 158
Pliny, 183, 193–6
Plover, 311
Plymouth, 63, 72, 89, 127, 136, 146,
    154, 160, 162–3
Pole, W. W., 163–4
Pompey, 209
Pope, Alexander, 87
Popham, Sir Home, 163
Porpoise, 132, 140, 151
Porter, G. R., 230
Portsmouth, 65–7, 80, 95, 132,
    134, 139, 143, 180
Prescott, Henry, 242
Pringle Stokes, Cdr, 255
Pritchard, J. C., 266
Protector, 296
Putland, Lt Charles, 151

Queen Charlotte, 65
Quin, W. H., 232

Rae, Dr John, 311, 315, 319, 321–2

Rattlesnake, 257n, 258, 281
Rennell, Maj. James, 223, 229, 239,
    241, 287–8, 290, 293, 302
Renouard, G. C., 192, 223, 288
Resolute, 319–20
Ricardo, David, 242
Richardson, Dr John, 303, 306,
    310–12, 315, 321
Ritchie, Adm. G. S., 16
Robespierre, 64
Robinson, H. B., 257n
Roget, P. M., 241–2,
'Rondy', the, 45
Rosetta Stone, 95n
Ross, J. Clarke, 14, 241, 254,
    290–2, 295–7, 303, 306, 308–10,
    311, 312–17, 321
Ross, Sir John, 302, 306–7, 307n,
    308–10, 312–13, 315, 318
Rossell, Paul-Edouard, 302
Roussin, Baron, 256
Rowley, Adm. B. S., 132
Royal Astronomical Society, 235,
    274, 288, 279–8
Royal Geographical Society, 95n,
    224, 287–8, 290, 303
Royal George, 113
Royal Institute, 275
Royal Irish Academy, 22, 116, 116n,
    118, 262n
Royal Observatory (Greenwich),
    14, 235, 264, 267, 274, 289,
    296–8, 331
Royal Society, 219, 234–6, 239,
    242–3, 260, 274, 285–9, 297, 303,
    306
Royal Sovereign, 69, 71
Rupell, W. 87
Russell, Lord John, 280
Ruxton, Mrs Margaret, 114

Sabine, Col. Sir Edward, 229, 266,
    290–2, 296, 306, 309–10
St Roch, 313n
St Vincent, Lord, 109–13, 121, 136
Salsette, 181, 202, 216, 234
Sampson, 159–60
Sandon, Capt. Huxley, 168, 168n
San Josef alias *L'Aglia*, 102, 104–6,
    109, 163, 172, 231

S. Nicolo, 185, 187
Schilling, Baron, 116
Scott, Capt. R. Falcon, 291
Scylax, 194
SDUK (Society for the Diffusion
    of Useful Knowledge), 240–1,
    267, 274, 289, 293
Selim III, Sultan, 95
Sestri, Giovanni, 283
Seven Years War, 55n, 62
Shaftesbury, Lord, 332
Shomberg, Comm., 256
Short, Comm. Joseph, 132, 137,
    139–40, 148, 150–1, 156
Siddons, Mrs, 179
Sidmouth, Viscount Henry
    Addington, 109, 158
Simpson, Dr George, 303
Skyring, W. G., 260
Small, Dr William, 114
Smeaton, John, 143n
Smith, Adam, 87
Smith, Christopher, 165
Smollett, T. G., 87
Smyth, C. Piazzi, 297
Smyth, Capt. W. H., 246–7, 264n,
    287–8, 297–8
Sneyd, Charlotte, 124, 130, 180
Sneyd, Elizabeth, 124, 130, 180
Society for the Diffusion of Useful
    Knowledge (SDUK), 240–1,
    267, 274, 289, 293
Society of the Dilettanti, 182, 204
Sonnini, 184, 184n
Sotheby, William, 288
South, Capt. Sir James, 236, 241,
    264n, 285–6, 332
Spencer, Adm. Lord, 102, 168
Spencer, Lady Lavinia, 102, 160,
    168
Spratt, Lt Thomas, 259, 279
Staël, Mme de, 87
Stanhope, Lady Hester, 202
Stanley, Owen, 258–9
Stanton, midshipman, 105
Starling, 253
Sterne, Laurence, 113n
Stirling, Rear-Adm. Charles,
    164–5
Stokes, J. L., 258

Stopford, James, 2nd Earl of Courtown, 39, 46, 168–9
Stopford, Capt. (later Adm.) the Hon. Robert, 46, 51–3, 58–61, 67–8, 70–2, 74, 76–8, 93–4, 103, 166, 169, 176–7, 221, 302
Strabo, 183–4, 192–4
Strachan, Rear-Adm. Sir Richard, 148–50
Strangford (née Beaufort), Viscountess Emily Anne, 325, 329–30
Strangford, Viscount, 325
Street, Sir G. E., 334
Sulphur, 253. 257n

Terror, 254, 291, 306–9, 334
Thucydides, 279
Thunder, 250
Thunderer, 65
Tiber, 65
Torrington, Lord, 55
Toulon, 53, 58, 98, 181
Tractarians, 87, 274, 325
Trinity College (Dublin), 18, 20, 24
Trinity House, 248, 274, 277
Trio, 151
Trotter, Thomas, 90, 90n
Troubridge, E. T., 164
Troubridge, Rear-Adm. Sir Thomas, 82, 158, 164, 164n
Troughton, Edward, 172–3, 220, 236
Tryphon the Voluptuary, 208
Tussaud, Mme, 273

Ushant, 39, 68–9, 80–1
Ussher, Dr Henry, 24–5, 28, 30–1, 37
Ussher, Thomas, 242

Valiant, 43, 43n, 75
Vancouver, George, 253
Vansittart, 25–31, 33–4, 36–7, 40–2, 83, 178–9
Van Stabel, Rear-Adm., 64, 66
Vence, Rear-Adm. Jean-Gaspar, 69–70
Victoria, Queen, 136n, 281, 291n, 314, 324

Victoria and Albert, 281
Victory, 58
Vidal, A. T. E., 257
Vigenère, Blaise de, 283, 283n, 284
Villaret-Joyeuse, Rear-Adm. Louis-Thomas, 64–6, 69–71
Ville de Paris, 181
Voltaire, 55n, 86, 87

Wales, Prince of (later George IV), 39, 86, 86n
Walker, John, 247, 248
Wallace, A. Russell, 300
Waller (later Beaufort), Mary, 21, 23
Walpole, Robert, 223
Warren, Adm. Sir J. Borlase, 136, 139–40, 148, 150–2, 156
Washington, Capt. John, 261, 331
Watt, James, 114
Wedgwood, Josiah, 114
Wellesley, Sir Arthur, see Wellington
Wellington, Lord (Sir Arthur Wellesley), 170, 172, 274, 295, 312n
Wheatstone, Sir Charles, 275n, 284
Whewell, William, 14, 290, 294–5
Whitshed, Adm. J. Hawkins, 121
Wickham, Cdr J. Clements, 277
Wilberforce, William, 84, 87, 204, 300
William IV, 43n
William Henry, Duke of Clarence, 43, 43n, 247
Willoughby, Nesbit, 242
Wilson (later Beaufort), Alicia Magadalena, 23–4, 27, 178–80, 217–19, 225–6, 228–31, 268–71, 273, 327, 333
Wilson (née Boileau), Bonne, 27
Wilson, Mrs Lestock, 127–8, 177–8
Wilson, Capt. Lestock, 27–34, 36–8, 177–9, 217, 219, 225, 227, 230
Wilson, Bishop Thomas, 85
Wollaston, W. Hyde, 47–8, 234, 241

Wood, Cdr James, 259
Woolwich, 127, 129–34, 139–40, 143,
  148–52, 154, 157–60, 162, 164,
  166–7, 170, 173, 232, 253, 271

Wright, Mr, 130
Wyatt, Rear-Adm. A. G. N., 248

Yorke, C. P., 177–8, 183, 224, 244